E 14 95

Financing Education in a Climate of Change

second edition

Percy E. Burrup
Brigham Young University

Allyn and Bacon, Inc.
Boston   London   Sydney

Library of Congress Cataloging in Publication Data

Burrup, Percy E   1910–
    Financing education in a climate of change.
    Bibliography: p.
    Includes index.
    1. Education—Finance. I. Title.
LB2825.B86 1977   379′.121′0973   76-54267
ISBN 0-205-05696-2

Contents

Contents

Preface

This volume is a revision of one of the first books to appear after the historic decision of the California Supreme Court in the *Serrano* v. *Priest* case in 1971 but before the effects of the court cases related to school finance could be appraised or even anticipated. It is intended as a broad and elementary treatment of school finance theory and practice for administrators, teachers, graduate students, and lay citizens.

As was true with the first edition, education is portrayed as an investment in human capital. Emphasis is placed on the school finance reform movement that is now being given so much attention in this country. It points to the need for and the problems that accompany greater state participation in financing education—whether it be in the form of full state funding or district power equalization, or some combination of these or other plans. It raises the question and discusses the problems attending a possible expansion of federal aid to education. It also relates the field of school finance to that of economics.

The development of school finance theory and practice is traced from the period of complete local school funding through various other plans —such as flat grants and foundation programs, to the emerging post-*Serrano* alternatives involving greater equality of educational opportunity for students and greater equity for taxpayers. The concept of providing equal funds per student to be educated is condemned in favor of providing equal funds per weighted student, thus taking into consideration the relative costs of individual students and programs.

The book notes some of the inexplicable and unique problems encountered in financing education that remain unsolved—adequate financing of large city school disrticts, finding defensible and legal ways to keep nonpublic schools operative in the face of accelerating costs, and reversing the practice in many of our schools that charge excessive fees for some aspects of their instructional program. The failure of the planning-programming-budgeting system to be adopted in school systems or to measure up to its anticipated potential is noted. The criticism and indictment of the property tax is discussed in the light of its condemnation by many people but its fundamental need as a source of local school funds.

Since the volume is intended as a text for a beginning course in school finance, some elementary concepts in school business management and the administration of student activity finances have been included. Problems involving state and local financing programs and an annotated bibliography are included in the appendix.

A new and promising era of reform has emerged from the *Serrano* v. *Priest* case. It would be impossible to measure the positive effect that landmark decision has had, and will yet have, upon much needed school finance improvement in the several states of this nation. Despite the reversal by the United States Supreme Court in 1973 of the comparable *Rodriquez* case in Texas, during the 1970s most states have moved forward with zeal and with foresight to improve their school finance programs.

Many people have made recommendations for the second edition. The opinions of numerous graduate students and practitioners have been considered; some of these suggestions have been included in the manuscript. Sincere thanks is herewith expressed to all who have made such suggestions and to all those who have given permission for the use of some of their materials and ideas.

P.E.B.

Financing Education in a Climate of Change

Unit 1

EDUCATION: NECESSARY COST OR WISE INVESTMENT?

No one denies that good schools are essential to the national welfare; the most important resource of the United States is its citizens—not its soil, minerals, climate, or extent of territory, important as these resources are. Every American child has a right to an adequate educational opportunity.

Commission on
Intergovernmental
Relations, 1955

1

Economics and School Finance

Annual expenditures for public elementary and secondary education have increased dramatically since the end of World War II. Unfortunately, however, objective information showing commensurate increases in educational output or improvement in the products of the schools is not available. This lack of supportive evidence of positive results of increases in educational input has caused many American citizens to look askance at public education. They often view it as an unnecessarily large industry whose high costs result in excessive tax burdens on many people and an overextended drain on the public treasury. Many of them have forgotten that education has had much to do with the great progress and remarkable economic development of this country over the two centuries of its existence. Some, too, have not yet discovered that education is not really a cost but is, more accurately, an investment in human capital.

Recognition of the close relationship between economics and education becomes more and more crucial as spiraling expenditures for education continue. That being true, educational leaders at all levels of government cannot continue to give mere fleeting glances and incidental references to economic theories and principles if they are to help solve, or reduce, the complex and persistent problems involved in financing education adequately and equitably. Some knowledge of economics and its partnership role with education is therefore deemed to be important for school finance students and practitioners. For that reason, a brief discussion of some of the fundamental principles and concepts of economics that have application to the field of school finance is presented here. Excellent references are cited at the end of the chapter for those who may desire to go beyond the discussion here.

ECONOMICS: A STUDY OF GOODS
AND SERVICES

In simple terms, economics is the study of the production, allocation, and consumption of goods and services for the satisfaction of human wants. It is concerned with economic goods: material as well as non-material (service) goods, consumer as well as producer goods, durable and nondurable goods, and single-use as well as multiple-use goods. Economics involves and relates the often unlimited desires of man to obtaining and using the limited goods and resources available to him. Rogers and Ruchlin describe the issues involved in economics in the following:

> Economics is concerned with two primary phenomena, desires and re-sources. Because desires are psychological and physical, economics deals with man; because resources are constructed from matter, economics deals with nature. Economic issues involve a basic confrontation between opposing forces: desires and resources, or man and environment. The confrontation is brought into being primarily because desires are infinite, whereas resources are finite. The history of civilization is a continuous illustration of man's wants exceeding his means; and it appears safe to predict that as affluent as our society may yet become there will always be unfulfilled wants.[1]

Some aspects of the relation of education to economics are shown in Figure 1.1. Education can be seen to be an economic (not free), nonmaterial good (service), durable (if in regular use), multiple-use, and a producer as well as a consumer good (service).

Since primary interest here is with financing public education, concern with economics will deal largely with its relation to the allocation of scarce resources to competitive consumers in the public sector. What will be the effect on the economy if the rapidly increasing demands for greater spending in the public sector are met? Is education to be considered an expensive luxury that has reached such proportions that it threatens the foundation of our economic structure? Or is it, as most educators declare, an investment in human capital that stimulates rather than retards economic growth? These and many other questions relating education and economics must be answered if education is to continue to serve its purpose. Some of the "answers" of past years that pointed the finger of blame at education for stifling the economy and overburdening the tax-paying public will need to be reanswered in terms of the needs of the future. Recent years have seen an accumulation of new evidence of the value of education to social and economic growth and development.

1. Daniel C. Rogers and Hirsch S. Ruchlin, *Economics and Education* (New York: The Free Press, 1971), p. 5.

4

FIGURE 1.1.   Education as an Economic Good

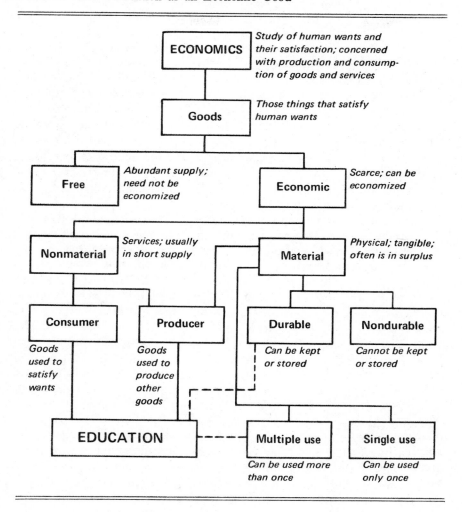

The major concern of economics is related to the proper and satisfactory allocation of scarce resources—goods and services—to the individuals, households, and institutions that desire and need them. Since
there is no infallible law or formula for this distribution, the economist
must become concerned with the anticipated results of resource allocation with the many alternative choices for such distribution. Goods or
services allocated to one segment of the economy are, of course, being
denied to another. The economist must determine the proper mix of
such distribution that will bring maximum satisfaction to the various
segments of society.

ECONOMICS AND SOCIAL PROGRESS

There are many diverse ways of measuring or rating the degree of advancement, or upward progress, of a society. One way is to apply the economic dimension that attempts to determine the degree or percentage of total human effort that is being diverted to production and allocation of the material goods required for survival, such as food, clothing, and shelter. This measure of human effort is then compared with that devoted to producing nonmaterial goods that make life more comfortable but are not required for survival. Societies at the low end of the social progress continuum devote all or nearly all their efforts to producing essential material goods. As societies move up the scale of civilization, the percentage of human effort expended to produce services and goods not required for subsistence increases.

There is no valid reason or rationale that defends unlimited or surplus production and consumption of primary material goods beyond those required for survival or subsistence in any society. Most culturally advancing societies soon reach the limit in the production of material goods that are required for the absolute necessities for existence. Surpluses of durable goods for emergency purposes are often necessary, and production of these is defended before the forces of production are directed to those goods and services that are classified as luxuries. At this point, further human effort in producing necessities becomes indefensible. Consequently, human effort is directed toward the production of educational, cultural, and other socially acceptable goods and services.

Thus it appears that the greater the degree of advancement of a society, the greater its potential for producing luxury goods and services, including education. Those countries that by their lack of resources or lack of people with technical ability must spend most of their time and effort in producing goods for subsistence and survival will have commensurately little time and ability to produce a good educational system. A country that cannot divert a great effort to producing educational services is constantly increasing the range of economic productivity and affluence between itself and countries that need spend only minor effort to produce the material goods necessary for subsistence. The educational system thus becomes a very important result, as well as a determinant, of the social and economic progress of a nation.

EDUCATION: AN IMPORTANT
INDUSTRY

A common and certainly defensible description of education is that it is an industry in the sense that it utilizes money and other valuable resources to produce its product. Although it is this country's largest industry, it produces only intangibles in the form of valuable, but immeasurable, amounts of nonmaterial goods or services. It is an industry where objective data are readily available to easily and accurately determine its financial input but where no research or empirical study has yet found a satisfactory way to measure, or even to approximate, its total output with accuracy, validity, or reliability. It is devoid of a profit motive and is usually operative by government but dependent on private enterprise for its financial support. It uses over 7 percent of our gross national product and directly involves about 20 percent of our population in one way or another.

Produces Nonfree Services

Any college student will attest the undeniable fact that education is not a free good in the economic sense. When he (or she) considers the indirect costs—the income he is losing while attending school, and also the direct costs—living expenses and tuition, he needs no additional reminder that education is far from being free.

As a purchaser of educational services, he recognizes education as a consumer good; he pays his money for the avowed purpose of consuming as much education as he can in the circumstances under which he finds himself. On the other hand, his instructor, whose salary has been augmented owing to the accumulation of some amount of education, confirms the fact that education is simultaneously a producer good —for it provides the economic ability (money) to satisfy his wants for other goods and services.

As the college graduate receives an academic degree and moves into the world of work, he takes with him no stock of accumulated material goods as evidence of his educational experiences. His investment has been made in nontangible goods (services) that he hopes to be able to pass on to others in the necessary process of earning a living. These services may be used and reused almost without limit and are therefore described as multiple-use goods or services. In contrast with machines, equipment, and other physical goods that depreciate with use, the durability or utility of educational services normally increases with use.

While some learning is sought and obtained for its intrinsic and cultural value, much of the purpose of education is to increase the ability of the recipient to engage in some useful occupation or profession and thus to produce other goods and services. This process is an economic one since it provides the means for him to satisfy his wants as a consumer as well as to produce goods and services for other consumers. An education adds to the richness of life for its recipients and widens their scope in choices of consumer goods such as books, magazines, works of art, and musical compositions. Thus, education is literally a consumer's good as well as a producer's good.

Aids Economic Growth

Although interest in the economics of education is said to date back to the time of Plato, its close relation to the financing of education went almost unnoticed in this country until about the middle of the twentieth century. Since that time numerous economists and educators have given in-depth consideration to this relationship. They have established and documented the fact that increases in education bring increases in productivity and gains in social, political, and economic life. They have come to support the idea that the costs of education are in reality necessary and real investments in human capital.

Since educational institutions collectively are one of this country's biggest disbursers of public money, and since education is the greatest contributor to the production and consumption of many kinds of essential services, the positive relation of education to economic growth is very real and obvious. This close and interdependent relationship has been understood by educators and economists for some time now, but its inferential meaning has been ignored or misunderstood by American citizens generally. The extent to which education contributes to the total economy of this country was noted by The Phi Delta Kappa Commission on Alternative Designs for Funding Education in the following:

> Education's contribution to economic development of both the individual and the general public is well documented. An education vests the person not only with independent thought but also with private economic power. Education, though, cannot be justified solely on the grounds that it equalizes economic power; on the contrary, it may even create greater disparities among persons than existed before education. It does give to every person the opportunity to increase his economic status and it does undoubtedly raise the minimum level of overall economic attainment. Therefore, it cannot be realistically assumed that education will negate the inherent individual differences and capacities which may ultimately play such a significant role in personal economic gain. The state, through education, can only guarantee each person the opportunity to develop his economic potential to its fullest extent. Economic development of the individual is, of course, reflected as a portion of the aggregate economic accomplishment of the entire state or nation. While there is argument over the degree to which education contributes to the total economy, there is little doubt that it does play a significant role.[2]

2. *Financing the Public Schools* (Bloomington, Ind.: Phi Delta Kappa Commission on Alternative Designs for Funding Education, 1973), pp. 6–7.

The American Association of School Administrators noted long ago that educational expenditures contribute greatly to our economic growth and development:

> Finally, there must be no misunderstanding on the point that expenditures for education are economically productive. The schools are not economic parasites, draining off national income into some nonproductive enterprise. On the contrary, education (a) provides the intelligence and skill essential to modern industry; (b) contributes to health and safety; (c) results in better conservation of natural resources; (d) leads to personal thrift and the development of capital resources; (e) is the basis of efficiency in business management; (f) increases the volume and lifts the level of consumer demands; (g) improves the earning power and spending power of the people; and (h) thru the purchase of buildings, equipment, materials, and thru the salaries of its employees, turns its expenditures quite directly back into the economic life-stream of the nation.[3]

One of the first professional education groups to emphasize the positive relationship between education and economics was the influential Educational Policies Commission in one of its major publications in 1940.[4] Organized by the National Education Association and the American Association of School Administrators, this Commission did a number of studies and issued reports that pushed forward the frontier of educational thinking, particularly during the 1930s and 1940s. "In its consideration of the highly important relationships between education and economic well-being, the . . . Commission . . . sought the counsel of economists, educators, and other competent scholars in this field," in making its study of education and economics. The following statement is indicative of the Commission's thinking concerning that relationship:

> The problem of financing the kind and amount of education which will maintain a high technology in a democratic, industrial society demands fundamental examination of the inter-relations of education and economics. It calls for thoughtful appraisal of the contribution which education makes to productivity and general economic well-being, and judicial consideration of the economic limitations of the amount which may be spent for education.[5]

The first modern-day school finance writer to give emphasis to the economics of education was Charles S. Benson. His book[6] received pop-

---

3. *The Expanding Role of Education* (Washington, D.C.: American Assn. of School Administrators, 1948), pp. 281–282.
4. *Education and Economic Well-Being in American Democracy* (Washington, D.C.: Educational Policies Commission, 1940).
5. Ibid., p. 5.
6. Charles S. Benson, *The Economics of Public Education* (Boston: Houghton Mifflin Co., 1961).

ular acceptance and established a relation between education and economics that has been recognized by most school finance writers since that time. His point of view is summarized in the following statement:

> Throughout the world, both philosophers and men of affairs appear to have reached consensus on this point: education is a major force for human betterment. Quality of education is intimately related to its financing. How much resources are made available, and how effectively these resources are used stand as crucial questions in determining the degree to which education meets the aspirations that people hold for it. . . .[7]

That expending adequate funds for education will provide economic dividends to society is now established as a fact that is seldom disputed by students of economics. Quality education is expensive but it brings commensurate benefits to individuals, to families, to business and professional people, and to social agencies and institutions. Although direct and objective facts are difficult, if not impossible to obtain, economists are generally agreed that adequate expenditures for education lead to increases in markets for goods and services, increases in business and industrial sales, and increases in the buying power of individuals and households. Such expenditures also tend to reduce the production costs of goods and services, to increase and hasten the adoption of technological changes, and to improve the performance skills and efficiency of the working force.

The debate concerning the degree of economic growth that comes as a result of national investment in education is summarized in the following statement:

> On the first subject (the relation between our national investment in education and the resultant payoff in economic growth and its impact on inequality and poverty), I find certain truths in education to be self-evident. Number one: In spite of Coleman, Jencks, and Averch and their challenging and challengeable studies, I subscribe to the economic articles of faith that ploughing more money and more resources into education raises its quality and that higher educational quality produces higher educational achievement and higher economic productivity. And much empirical economic research supports my belief.[8]

A Public Sector Responsibility

Education can be produced in the private sector of the economy as well as in the public. While the educational system is largely pro-

7. Ibid., p. vii.
8. Walter W. Heller, "The National Economic Setting for Education," *Today's Education* (Washington, D.C.: National Education Assn., November–December 1973), p. 66.

duced by government at public expense, many kinds and numbers of schools are sponsored by private individuals, companies, or churches. In certain other countries, education is largely a product of the private sector.

Schools in the private sector operate under a different set of theories and rules than those in the public sector follow. The organizations and institutions in the private sector, by the nature of their relations to their clientele, are controlled and changed more readily than those in the public sector. Consumer requirements, and the ability of the private school to meet them, largely determine how much financial support is available for future operation. The desires, or even the whims, of potential purchasers are soon met in the private sector, for to ignore such would mean a curtailment of sales and a loss of profits. Inefficiency, incompetence, or other internal ineptness soon make themselves known, and usually bring changes in schools in the competitive marketplace. No such rules apply to public schools. Government institutions, including public schools, do not and are not required to react as quickly or as patronizingly in the face of external pressure and public criticism as their counterpart in the competitive world. Compulsory school attendance laws, taxation laws, and social pressures combine to erode the effect of dissatisfaction and clamor for improvement of government-sponsored schools. Right or wrong, public institutions usually move more slowly to reduce the criticisms or implement the recommendations for improvement that their patrons make. Unfortunately, this fact has too often resulted in a high degree of resistance or practical indifference to change and innovation in public education.

RESOURCE ALLOCATION TO EDUCATION

Although the affluence of the people and the abundance of resources of the United States are well beyond the wealth of most if not all other countries, they have limits. The spiraling costs of the constantly increasing services of government and its institutions have made competition for the tax dollar more accentuated now than ever before. As an important economic service with steadily increasing responsibility to the people of the nation, education would seem to have established itself as a strong and deserving competitor for the economic resources of each state responsible for its support. However, McLure has pointed out that education suffers in decision making that allocates resources in comparison with highways, conservation of natural resources, and health services that are particularly in the public domain.[9] He noted that "education is so complex that its total scope is extremely difficult for individuals in society to comprehend. Hence there is no aggregate demand schedule of a comprehensive nature."[10]

Since the nonprofit public sector has no way to obtain funds directly for establishing and operating the social, cultural, and governmental institutions (including schools) that it sponsors, money must be diverted from the private sector to the public sector by some process of taxation. The academic disciplines of education, economics, and political science are all vitally concerned with the process and the results of such diversion.

One of the chief problems of government is to determine how much of private sector income can and should be diverted to the public sector. As Burkhead indicates, "Ours is an economic system that is predominantly private in character, but with a large public sector. One of the most challenging of economic problems is the task of devising guidelines, principles, and procedures that will assist in the decisions concerning the relative size of the two sectors and the allocation of resources within each."[11]

What degree of choice should the individual have in purchasing governmental services as contrasted with his almost unlimited freedom of choice in purchasing goods and services in the private sector? Burkhead affirms that we have understood the theory of economic choice that describes and explains the making of decisions in private markets but that we are just beginning to understand theory of choice in the public sector.[12]

A Political Responsibility

Allocating economic resources to education is one of the primary responsibilities of local, state, and federal lawmaking bodies. According to Garvue, the procedures and guidelines they have used to determine such allocations in the past have been ambiguous and nonscientific.[13] In the

9. William P. McLure, "Allocation of Resources," in Warren E. Gauerke and Jack R. Childress, eds., *The Theory and Practice of School Finance* (Chicago: Rand McNally & Co., 1967), p. 65.

10. Ibid.

11. Jesse Burkhead, *State and Local Taxes for Public Education* (Syracuse, N.Y.: Syracuse University Press, 1963), p. 1.

12. Ibid., pp. 1–2.

13. Robert J. Garvue, *Modern Public School Finance* (London: The Macmillan Co., 1969), p. 67.

absence of objective guidelines for determining the proper balance of resource needs of public sector institutions and agencies, governmental agencies usually base allocation decisions on factors such as organizational objectives and needs, potential contribution and overall influence of each institution, and ordinary political expediency. Education tends to suffer comparatively in such allocations because it is unable to show in objective terms the measured and increased output provided with additional units of input.

Of the several methods of allocating funds to education, perhaps the most common is trying to maintain an average practice model—a leveling up to provide all weaker units with the same proportionate resources as the average unit. Occasionally, the antithesis is practiced to a limited extent, with more affluent units being leveled down or required to "mark time" until the weaker ones reach a comparable plateau.

Resource-allocating bodies may also use some presumed measurement of educational outcomes as the determinant for education's share of limited resources. Such measurements are often more imaginary than real, for many of the results of a good educational program cannot be measured objectively. One of the basic problems education faces in its highly competitive request for greater resource input is caused by the common belief that it is so complex that members of lawmaking organizations cannot understand its purposes, needs, and contributions to society. Then, too, economy-minded legislators often are quick to minimize or eliminate allocations of scarce resources to high-cost programs, for they do not understand their contribution to the overall educational program.

The reluctance of educators to communicate with the politicians in lawmaking bodies and tell them their problems has added to the allocation puzzle. Fortunately, the educational establishment now recognizes that decisions concerning resource allocation are made in the political arena.

Political leaders in the various legislatures often find themselves under pressure from economic and educational advocates as they attempt to make decisions and enact laws to establish and support public educational institutions. They understand only too well that education as an industry does not and cannot operate in a vacuum without reference or relation to economics, politics, or related disciplines. Educational leaders, too, now seem to recognize the long dormant understanding that all major social forces must not only recognize each others objectives and alternatives but they must work cooperatively to solve the problems of each other.

Until recent years, educators and political leaders were largely indifferent to the needs and problems of each other. Bailey noted the negative effect of this mutual indifference and lack of concern in the following:

However understandable the reluctance of political scientists and educators to articulate the politics of education it is probable that many educators and the lay public have paid something of a price for this lack of illumination. In some states and regions the failure to understand political realities has resulted in a general inability of those interested in education to cope with problems of adequate public support. In other cases, because of the low visibility of educational politics, astute manipulators and single-track reformers have been able to achieve for segments of education advantages which should have been achieved only for education as whole. . . .[14]

Bailey also indicated the need for cooperation between educators and politicians in meeting the future needs of education:

The future of public education will not be determined by public need alone. It will be determined by those who can translate public need into public policy—by schoolmen in politics. Since the quality of our society rests in large measure upon the quality of our public education, a widespread recognition that schoolmen must be not only aware of politics, but influential in politics, may be the key to our survival as a free and civilized nation.[15]

Determining the Extent of Educational Services

Generally, in the competitive market consumers of economic goods and services determine by their ability and willingness to purchase just what a particular industry will make available for sale—within the limits of the supply of resources. Demands for goods and services are determined by those who consume such products directly. The public and individual demands for education, however, are unlike the demands for most other goods and services. In education, these must originate from those who pay for its services, but who do not usually receive its benefits directly. In education, the quality and quantity of its services are determined in large measure by the pleasant or unpleasant experiences adults have had with education in their own lives as well as by how such demands will affect their share of the tax cost. The degree of satisfaction of the direct recipients of education is too often secondary to the degree of tax burden sustained by those who determine the extent of such services available. Thus, educational expenditures are often determined in a right-to-left direction—much the same as an unaffluent, or a prospective

14. Stephen K. Bailey et al., *Schoolmen and Politics* (Syracuse, N.Y.: Syracuse University Press, 1962), pp. ix, x.
15. Ibid., p. 108.

customer who is short of available cash, may approach the menu in a luxurious restaurant.

Often, the individuals who determine the supply of education to be made available may have no family or other direct relationship with any of the individuals who are its potential consumers. For that reason board members and others responsible for educational supply may approach school finance with a neutral or even a negative attitude, for their decisions may be made in terms of their own real, or even imaginary, financial tax burden to the exclusion of more relevant and necessary educational needs. This fact often results in exaggerated criticism of increases in educational expenditures, especially in areas where there is little objective evidence of commensurate results. Regular and substantial increases in input are necessary, however, for teachers and others who spend their time in educational activities must be protected against the ravages of inflation and increasing living costs even though only small increases in their productivity are possible.

The Marginal Dollar Principle

How does a free society determine the amount of resources it will spend for such an important service of government as education? Theoretically, it would be done in the same way an individual decides how much money he will spend for a particular good or service in a free market—by considering the marginal utility of that good or service. The utility is determined in large measure by the value the prospective consumer places on the good or service to be purchased and by the number of such goods or services already in his possession or available to him.

The usefulness and utility of additional units of a particular item usually decrease as they are added; a third car usually has less real value to a purchaser than a second one and the second car has less value than the first. Similarly, the public may place high value on the purchase of elementary education for all its children at public expense and give high priority to this undertaking; but it would put less stress and effort on education for four years of high school and still less emphasis on providing necessary funds for higher education. The public may feel, too, that an expenditure of $800 per pupil per year is highly desirable, that an additional $200 would be nice but less desirable, and that a still further addition of $100 would be undesirable or unwise—for it might require taking funds away from some other seemingly more important goods or services.

Marginal utility thus becomes a measure of desire for additional units of a good or service. The marginal dollar is the the dollar that would be better spent for some other good or service. Thus, allocating funds for education becomes a problem of determining at what point an additional amount proposed as an expenditure for education would bring greater satisfaction or worth if it were to be spent for other goods or services.

Allocating resources by this method is difficult, as McLure noted:

> The theory of marginal utility cannot be applied as clearly in education as in some other operations. It is difficult, for example, to determine when the addition of one more staff member may or may not produce results which would be equal to or less than the value of the money paid the person. In industry, however, the addition of one worker would be at the margin if the increased income would be equal to the cost of the worker.[16]

The Point of Diminishing Returns

Undoubtedly there is a point of diminishing returns in the expenditure of funds for education. This, by definition, refers to a point beyond which additional expenditures will yield very little or no additional educational returns. Where this point is—in terms of expenditures per pupil —has not yet been determined. Most of the schools of this country have been forced to operate on a financial level far below such a theoretical point.

Determining the relation of the per pupil expenditures for education to the quality of the product has proved to be a somewhat popular, but elusive, research subject for many years. Cubberley was concerned with it in the early years of this century. It has been an important topic of study for many school finance scholars since that time.

It is normal for people, especially overburdened taxpayers, to compare the costs and apparent productivity of various public institutions or industries—particularly those in direct competition with each other for scarce tax dollars. Such comparisons may react unfavorably upon education for reasons not under the control of those involved. Advocates of the sciences, agriculture, medicine, and industry point with understandable pride to the fact that increased expenditures for upgrading their operations and increasing their research effort over a period of time have greatly increased their annual production of goods and services. This has been particularly noticeable in agriculture and in medicine. Such results are, of course, applauded by people everywhere.

The problem of producing spectacular improvements in education with the allocation of additional funds is another matter. Greatly increased expenditures for education have not, can not, and will not pro-

16. McLure, "Allocation of Resources," p. 78.

duce such large or fantastic increases or improvements in its products. The nature of the learning process being what it is, increases in learning effectiveness must be anticipated only in small percentages regardless of the magnitude of the financial increments applied to the improvement process. It is unlikely that the field of education, even with the application of almost limitless resources, will ever have available ways and means to multiply the quantity or the quality of learning that can take place in human beings in a predetermined amount of time. Such a fact may cause some to believe that public education has already reached the marginal dollar and a point of diminishing returns and that available funds should be diverted from it to other industries with the potential for higher percentage increases in their productivity. This would be folly of the highest order, for whatever improvements can be made to make education more effective, more extensive, and more applicable to the lives of American citizens should be made regardless of what spectacular results could be produced elsewhere with similar dollars.

EDUCATION AS HUMAN CAPITAL

The importance of education to the growth of the national economy has long been recognized and is no longer challenged. Education is the largest public function and our biggest business when viewed in terms of the numbers of people and dollars of income and expenditure involved in its operation. The expansion of educational services and the greatly increasing costs of education year after year have had a tremendous beneficial effect on the nation's economy. It is not likely that this condition and this relation will change.

Economists are belatedly recognizing the importance of investment in education for developing our large reservoir of human capital. The economists of an earlier era emphasized the roles of land, labor, and capital in achieving economic growth, and they gave only passing or minimum attention to the economic importance of education.

The economist paid little attention to this point of view until after World War II. Since that time, most economists have emphasized the value of education as a factor in stimulating economic growth. Education is now popularly referred to as investment in human capital. Such leaders in the field as John Kenneth Galbraith, Harold Groves, Milton Friedman, Theodore Schultz, and Charles Benson have documented the relation between education and economic growth. They have deplored the waste of manpower and human resources that automatically accompanies inadequate education, regardless of its causes.

The apparent paradox that some economists have attached to the concept that human beings are a form of capital goods is pointed out by Schultz in the following:

> The mere thought of investment in human beings is offensive to some among us. Our values and beliefs inhibit us from looking upon human beings as capital goods, except in slavery, and this we abhor. We are not unaffected by the long struggle to rid society of indentured service and to evolve political and legal institutions to keep men free from bondage. These are achievements that we prize highly. Hence, to treat human beings as wealth that can be augmented by investment runs counter to deeply held values. . . . No less a person than J. S. Mill at one time insisted that the people of a country should not be looked upon as wealth because wealth existed only for the sake of people. But surely Mill was wrong; there is nothing in the concept of human wealth contrary to his idea that it existed only for the advantage of people. By investing in themselves, people can enlarge the range of choice available to them. It is one way free men can enhance their welfare.[17]

Human capital has the fundamental characteristics of any form of economic capital. It is a source of future satisfaction or of future earnings, or both. It is human capital because it is a part of the person possessing it. Such capital deteriorates with inactivity, but it does not disappear completely until the death or complete incapacity of the person possessing it. It often needs to be reactivated and up-dated to lessen its degree of obsoleteness or the extent of its inadequateness.

Economic Benefits of Education to Individuals

Right or wrong, the main thrust of expenditures for public education is toward transmitting known information to individual consumers. Since generally accepted philosophy of education requires that all citizens have a high-quality education through most of their preadult life, the costs of a formal education program must of necessity be proportionately higher for the United States than for countries that are disposed to release their youth at an earlier age. But what of the benefits of education to individuals under a system that requires participation for such an extended period?

Many studies have been conducted and estimates made to determine the economic benefits that accrue to the average person with varying amounts of formal education (see Table 1.1). Universally, these reports indicate the high pecuniary benefits of education. The figures

17. Theodore W. Schultz, "Investment in Human Capital," in Charles S. Benson, ed., *Perspectives on the Economics of Education* (Boston: Houghton Mifflin Co., 1963), pp. 13–14.

TABLE 1.1 Mean Income of Men 25 Years Old and Over, by Years of School Completed, 1961–1972, (in 1972 Dollars)

Years of School Completed	1961	1964	1967	1970	1972
Elementary					
Less than 8 years	4,193	4,451	4,436	4,778	5,235
8 years	5,883	6,100	6,268	6,503	6,756
High School					
4 years	8,316	9,093	9,417	9,898	10,433
College					
4 years	13,066	13,167	13,812	14,409	15,256
5 years or more	13,968	14,850	15,835	16,953	17,346

SOURCE: "Annual Mean Income, Lifetime Income, and Educational Attainment of Men in the United States, for Selected Years, 1956 to 1972," as cited by Stephen B. Thomas, "Investment in Education: General/Specific," *Journal in Education Finance* vol. 1, no. 2 (Fall 1975), p. 229. Reprinted with permission.

reported are usually adjusted to consider the indirect costs that each person incurs; these include loss of salary and of other economic benefits during the time he is obtaining his formal education.

The educated person enjoys a broader range of job opportunities than his less well-educated counterpart. Since unemployment is usually closely related to lack of education and adequate work skills, education provides some security against loss of jobs in periods of change or a slackening of business and industrial activity. However, no figures can be quoted to indicate the economic benefits of education to individuals in such matters as increases in vocational alternatives, increases in vocational and avocational interests, and greater appreciation for cultural and intellectual pursuits.

INCREASING EXPENDITURES AND THE ECONOMY

It has already been established that a close and positive relationship exists between investment in education and the productivity of a nation. Educational development is more important than the extent of natural resources in determining the productivity and individual income level of nations. Fortunate indeed is that nation that has extensive natural resources and also highly developed human resources. A nation with high educational development may overcome to a great degree any lack of natural resources, but no nation having a poor educational system, even with tremendous stores of natural wealth, has been able to approach high individual economic productivity. A deficiency in both these areas or assets automatically relegates a nation to low productivity and inferior economic status.

Expenditures Return Quickly to Private Sector

Expenditures for school purposes, particularly those for salaries (75–80 percent of the total for current expenditures), quickly find their way back into the private economy through normal flow in the economic system. Thus their withdrawal from the private sector in the form of of taxes paid, their passage into and through the public sector via the payroll, and their return to the sector of their beginning usually form a cycle that is operative in such a short period of time that the original withdrawal effect on the economy is minimal. Their use is somewhat analogous to the "pump-priming" expenditures of New Deal agencies in the Depression of the 1930s. Carpenter's point concerning funds and resources expended for education is noteworthy:

> The resources flow subsystem consists of funds and material resources that flow into and through the institution. . . . The resources stream does not end in schools, colleges, and universities, for the *invested resources* are modified and in many ways increased. . . . Both the invested funds and their increases are returned to the supporting society. *In a sense, education merely borrows funds for use until the resources flow system returns them with interest to the people.*[18]

Burton Weisbrod listed seven broad economic benefits that are attributed to education:

1. Direct financial returns. Although partly due to ability, ambition, and a host of socioeconomic variables, no researcher has denied the positive role played by education.
2. Financial options. Each level of education prior to the highest achievable level provides the opportunity (option) of acquiring yet additional education and reaping the extra benefits of that education.
3. Hedging options. Increasing the probability that an individual will be able to adapt to the effects of technological change.
4. Non-market returns. Result from all the do-it-yourself types of work that a person can perform as a result of his education, such as filing one's own income tax.

18. C. R. Carpenter, "Society, Education and Technology," in Edgar L. Morphet and David L. Jesser, eds., *Planning for Effective Utilization of Technology in Education* (Denver: Designing Education for the Future, August 1968), p. 25.

5. Residence-related benefits (external to the individual). Those bene-
    fits accruable to the family of the individual, his neighbors, and tax-
    payers at large.
6. Employment-related benefits. The effects of the educated individual
    on the overall productivity of his colleagues.
7. Societal benefits. Literacy is a requisite for an intelligent citizenry,
    for economic activity, and for economic growth; education minimizes
    welfare services.[19]

Thus, the economic benefits of education to those obtaining it are
many. "People who have a good education produce more goods, earn
more money, buy and consume more goods, read more magazines and
newspapers, are more active in civic and national affairs, enjoy a higher
standard of living, and in general, contribute more to the economy than
those who are not as well educated."[20]

NONECONOMIC BENEFITS OF EDUCATION

The positive economic effects of good education are extremely important. Much is said and written about "education as an investment in
people." Sometimes, however, in an effort to show its economic investment characteristics people may inadvertently overlook one of its social
benefits that may outweigh all the others. As Lee DuBridge has expressed it, education does much to preserve a free, highly productive,
and democratic society:

> A technologically advanced nation requires an educated body of citizens.
> When every man on the street is concerned about nuclear war or fallout,
> about automation, or space; when every family has possession of dozens
> of the products of modern technology, ranging from an automobile to a
> television set, automatic toaster, and electric clock; when every citizen
> must vote for candidates for public office, who in turn must make deci-
> sions on matters of national defense, atomic power, space exploration,
> the regulation of industry, communication, and transport, it is clear that
> an educated citizenry is an essential national requirement.[21]

19. As quoted by Rogers and Ruchlin, *Economics and Education*, pp.
3–4.
20. *Education: An Investment in People* (Washington, D.C.: Chamber of
Commerce of the United States, Education Dept., 1955), Introduction.
21. *Education Is Good Business* (Washington, D.C.: American Assn. of
School Administrators, 1966), p. 12.

Norton argues that when education is thought of for other reasons than its economic benefits, it loses the necessary amount of financial support to keep it in operation:

> Education for intellectual development and for informed and perceptive minds was never needed more than it is today. The danger is that when education is thought of solely in these lofty and noble terms it is likely to suffer financial limitations which will prevent full achievement of both its intellectual and its economic goals. The latter cannot be ignored in a nation such as the United States, in which world leadership and even survival depends upon economic power.[22]

Some of the benefits of education that come to an individual also come to society. Perhaps this point is obvious, but Marshall's statement in this regard is significant:

> We may then conclude that the wisdom of expending public and private funds on education is not to be measured by its direct fruits alone. It will be profitable as a mere investment, to give the masses of the people much greater opportunities than they can generally avail thmselves of. . . . And the economic value of one great industrial genius is sufficient to cover the expenses of the education of a whole town; for one new idea, such as Bessemer's chief invention, adds as much to England's productive power as the labour of a hundred thousand men. Less direct, but not less in importance, is the aid given to production by medical discoveries such as those of Jenner or Pasteur, which increase our health and working power; and again by scientific work such as that of mathematics or biology, even though many generations may pass away before it bears visible fruit in greater material well-being. All that is spent during many years in opening the means of higher education to the masses would be well paid for if it called out one more Newton or Darwin, Shakespeare or Beethoven.[23]

EDUCATION PRODUCES EXTERNAL BENEFITS

Education, just as other public services, produces and extends benefits beyond the internal values obtained by its recipients. It is therefore said to possess externalities—values and benefits for people outside or beyond those who are its direct consumers. This fact is used to justify its being paid for by a process of taxation rather than by fee collecting,

22. John K. Norton, Education and Economic Well-Being in American Democracy (Washington, D.C.: Educational Policies Commission, 1940), p. 2.

23. Alfred Marshall, "Education and Invention," in Benson, *Perspectives on the Economics of Education*, p. 83.

rate bills, or tuition charges. Education's externalities are such that society does not permit individuals to purchase it, or even determine the minimum amount of it to be purchased, on the basis of desire or felt need alone, for some would purchase little or none of it if allowed to exercise their individual option. As a result, society has deemed it advisable to require the consumption of a minimum amount of education by all its citizens with such services being supported financially by some form and amount of tax support based on some measure of ability to pay. This system presumes no direct relation between the amount of taxes paid and the amount of direct or internal value received by the taxpayer. To a great degree it denies the individual the right of choice of the kind or amount of educational services he is required to assume. Goffman referred to the significance of educational externalities in the following:

> The significance of the presence of externalities is that a private solution will not be economically efficient in that external benefits (or spillovers) will not be included in the student's decision equation and, therefore, there will be under-provision of resources to education. In other words, the student (or his family) may be willing to spend just enough to cover all the benefits he himself expects to receive. But what about secondary benefits received by others? To the extent that there is no adequate mechanism for charging for these benefits, they are simply disregarded. This results in under-allocation and, therefore, misallocation of resources.[24]

It is evident that individuals are not only aware of, and concerned with, the amount of education they consume, but they are concerned with the extent of education others consume. Standards of living are raised and economic growth is enhanced by the externalities that are generated by the education of the members of a social group. It appears that individuals tend to gain more personally with the education of the many in a society than they will gain if only a few purchase education's services.

Externalities and the Benefit Principle

The private sector is much better qualified than the public sector to produce and distribute goods and services that can be purchased at the option of individuals and households. Such purchases of most goods and services ordinarily bring no automatic or residual benefit to society, but bring such benefits only to the purchaser. This is commonly referred

24. *Productivity in Education* (Washington, D.C.: Committee on Educational Finance of the National Education Association, 1972), pp. 43–44.

to as the "exclusion" principle. As an example, the private sector can provide gasoline and other service-station products to any and all individuals and organizations that need and can pay for such goods and services. The purchaser receives personal benefits directly related to the quantity of such products he buys, but others derive no particular or direct benefit. It is thereby possible to assess costs in terms of potential benefits to purchasers and at the same time exclude nonpurchasers from these same or similar benefits or satisfactions.

To tax an individual in direct relation to the benefits he receives from the service or commodity that is provided by that tax would seem to be defensible provided that the benefit is observable and to a high degree measurable, and provided further that he alone benefits from the tax he pays.

A weakness of the benefit principle of taxation is included in the following statement by Salisbury: "If everyone paid only for benefits received, there could be no surplus to support other functions. Modern governmental services must go far beyond such a limited view and extend to many functions which simply cannot be measured by so restricted a base."[25] On the other hand, the argument is made that since purchases in the private sector are paid for in terms of the amount of the products received, they should be paid for the same way in the public sector.

Externalities Justify the Ability Principle

The problem of financing education is different from that of marketing most other goods and services. The existence of externalities and the nonexistence of the exclusion principle changed old methods of financing education by the benefit principle to that of the ability principle. The lessons learned in the prepublic school era in this matter should not be forgotten. Unfortunately, some individuals in every society would not be partakers of education if it were purchasable only on a voluntary basis. Not only do they not demand the service, but they must be required by government to obtain it in some minimum quantity by compulsory school attendance laws. A second important factor is that education not only benefits individuals in proportion to their purchase or consumption of it but it pervades society and indirectly affects all citizens. These effects lead to higher standards of living and allow greater consumption of cultural goods and services.

It is impossible to measure the benefits that come to the individual

25. C. Jackson Salisbury, "The Theory of Taxation as Related to School Finance," in Gauerke and Childress, *Theory and Practice of School Finance*, p. 46.

or to society from individual purchases of educational services. That being true, the most defensible approach is to assume that all individuals in society benefit to about the same degree or extent. On that basis, the costs of education should be paid by all members of society in terms of their economic ability to pay. Under this "ability" principle, the wealthy pay more for the services of government, but their comparative burden is no greater than that borne by the less affluent.

Proponents of the benefit system of taxation argue that taxation by the ability principle penalizes the affluent and financially successful person. Such a process, they contend, stifles and curtails further activities of an economic nature and tends to create an indolent society. They point to the extremely high rate of the upper level of income tax of a few years ago and its negative effect on business and industrial expansion.

Education and certain other services of government do not lend themselves to the benefit principle of taxation. Every state has had or now has a compulsory school attendance law requiring all children and youth of certain ages to spend a predetermined amount of time in formal education. And what about those required to attend who do not have the financial ability to pay for such required services of government? Are the parents of six children to pay six times as much as the parents of one child? Is the adult without children to be exempt from school taxation altogether? These are questions that have faced the states through the years. Even today the relative importance of this form of taxation varies considerably among the states.

NONPUBLIC SCHOOLS AND THE ABILITY PRINCIPLE

Reversion to a nonpublic school system to answer the problems of financing education (a solution recommended by some citizens) would create more difficulties than it would solve. The ability principle of paying for education would no longer be valid and would give way to the benefit principle—incompatible with sound educational finance theory. It would again be impossible for large families with low incomes to purchase even the minimum quantity of educational services needed or required in such households.

Other problems would undoubtedly arise if the private economy were to provide education. The state would face the dilemma of requiring attendance at privately operated schools not directly under the state's authority; at best solving attendance problems would be in the periphery of state responsibility. The problems of handling pupil attendance, pupil and teacher militancy, and other similar matters with such a division of authority would be greatly increased.

Swearingen and others acknowledge that in the nation's economic system the public sector must continue to support and operate educational systems:

> As long as there is free choice of employment, investments in humans must be a function largely supported by the public sector of the economy. Individuals and parents might not be able to finance such developments, and private enterprise would hesitate to do so for fear of loss to a competitor.[26]

Some economists have proposed that education be altered to provide a minimum of schooling at public expense, with the parents of school-age children paying the additional cost for a better program. Friedman has advocated publicly financed but privately operated schools. According to him, "Government could require a minimum level of education which they could finance by giving parents vouchers redeemable for a specified maximum sum per child per year if spent on 'approved educational services.'"[27] Under this proposed arrangement, the parent or guardian would be able to use the vouchers at whatever school he chose to send his children. Costs above the amount of the vouchers would be paid by the parents.

At least two conditions must be met if education is to operate as a service performed in the private sector:

> (1) that there [be] an individual demand for the service and (2) that the "exclusion principle" can be applied. [The exclusion principle refers to the power of a buyer to "exclude" nonbuyers from consumption of the particular goods or services he himself has purchased.] Yet education also yields "social benefits," i.e., services which are consumed in approximately equal amounts by all. For example . . . education contributes to the economic strength of the country, which is to say that it contributes to the survival of our democratic institutions; this is a benefit that is shared in approximately equal measure by all citizens. Education, thus, has elements of both a private want and a public want. . . .[28]

COST-QUALITY RELATIONSHIP IN EDUCATION

Most economic, political, and educational leaders in this country are vitally concerned with the timeworn question of how the amount of

26. E. L. Swearingen et al., "Relation of Economic Theory to Educational Finance," in Gauerke and Childress, *Theory and Practice of School Finance*, pp. 31–32.

27. Milton Friedman, "The Role of Government in Education," in Robert A. Solo, ed., *Economics and the Public Interest* (New Brunswick, N.J.: Rutgers University Press, 1955), pp. 127–128.

28. Benson, *Perspectives on the Economics of Education*, p. 93.

money spent for education relates to the quality of the educational product. This poses the difficulty of obtaining data and other available evidence of such cost-quality relations.

The difficulty of solving the cost-quality problem in education is increased by the fact that the term *high quality* has not been defined in terms that are measurable and acceptable to all concerned. Is high-quality education something that can be measured by scores on achievement and other tests? What relation does it have to vocational training or to the kinds of attitudes and habits developed by students? Is a student's score of 95 on an examination compared with a score of 80 by another student a measure of a difference in quality or in quantity of education? Does extending the school year provide for potentially greater quality of education, or is quantity the variable? These and many other similar questions make the resolution of this important problem difficult, if not impossible.

The goals of education have been under almost continuous critical evaluation with resultant frequent restatements. The quality of education should be a measurement of the extent to which the recipients of the educational offering of the schools have attained the established goals. But therein lies the difficulty—the "goals" of education vary from place to place and from time to time, and even if they are agreed on, there is no way to measure all of the changes in human behavior that are the products of formal education. While advances in scholarship and academic achievement can be measured objectively, there have always been other goals of varying importance for which there are, at best, only the crudest methods of determining their degree of inculcation in the lives of the school's clientele.

The cost-quality relation, in reality a matter of the efficiency with which the schools reach their objectives with the smallest outlay of money, is not unique to education. All institutions that are financed with public funds are, to some degree at least, concerned with maintaining maximum efficiency—if such can be attained. This must always be true with the institutions and agencies of government that are responsible for wise and defensible expenditures of the necessary, but limited, tax dollar. To be less than that tends to destroy public confidence in social and governmental institutions.

Research Studies

Research studies of cost-quality relations in education have been numerous but their results have not been conclusive. They have been centered around the measurement of *input* (time, money, and human capital that has been used to create a product or provide a service) and *output* (quality of the product that has been produced). Input measurement offers no particular problems, but measurement of the output of educational institutions is at best a highly subjective procedure.

Cost-quality research studies had their real emphasis under the late Paul Mort. He summarized his studies with the statement: "Every empirical study of the relationship between expenditure level and quality of education adds its bit to the presumption that the relationship is strong."[29] This relation, he reported, appears to hold through all levels of expenditures experienced up to the date of his studies.

Mort and Reusser summarized the results of numerous studies of cost-quality relations in education as follows:

> Expenditure level is one of the highly important factors in achieving good education. Communities spending more for education get more in the way of results generally desired by people.
>
> The early studies showed that those communities which spend more get more in the way of services: longer terms, better trained teachers, more special services, etc.
>
> Later studies show that communities which spend more tend to be more adaptable, tend to utilize improved methods more quickly. In addition, higher expenditure schools get a different behavior pattern in the schools; the skills and knowledges are taught more in line with the best understanding of how human beings learn; more attention is given to the discovery and development of special aptitudes; more attention is given to the positive unfolding in individual boys and girls of stronger patterns of behavior—citizenship, personality, character.[30]

The relation of cost and quality in education has been questioned more critically in the years since 1966 as a result of studies related to the question, particularly those of Coleman[31] and Jencks.[32] The results of these studies seem to indicate that costs (as evidenced in such things as salaries and facilities) have only a minor effect upon achievement of students when compared with the much larger effect of their intelligence and family background. The net effect of these studies has been to raise doubts and controversy concerning in-put—out-put relations in education. Perhaps the debate was best summarized by Coons, Clune, and Sugarman in the following:

> There are similar studies suggesting stronger positive consequences from dollar increments, and there are others suggesting only trivial conse-

29. *Problems and Issues in Public School Finance* (Washington, D.C.: National Conference of Professors of Educational Administration, 1952), p. 9.

30. Paul R. Mort and Walter C. Reusser, *Public School Finance*, 2nd ed. (New York: McGraw-Hill, 1951), pp. 140–141.

31. James S. Coleman et al., *Equality of Educational Opportunity* (Washington, D.C.: U.S. Government Printing Office, 1966).

32. Christopher Jencks et al., *Inequality: A Reassessment of the Effect of Family and Schooling in America* (New York: Basic Books, Inc., 1972).

quences, but the basic lesson to be drawn from the experts at this point is the current inadequacy of social science to delineate with any clarity the relation between cost and quality. We are unwilling to postpone reform while we await the hoped-for refinements in methodology which will settle the issue. We regard the fierce resistance by rich districts to reform as adequate testimonial to the relevance of money. Whatever it is that money may be thought to contribute to the education of children, that commodity is something highly prized by those who enjoy the greatest measure of it. If money is inadequate to improve education, the residents of poor districts should at least have an equal opportunity to be disappointed by its failure.[33]

Salary Policies Create Problems

The organization and operation of schools create some difficult problems that tend to prevent realistic studies of cost-quality relations. Teacher organizations have consistently resisted the use of devices and mechanisms to determine the degree of success or failure of individual teachers. Salary schedules with automatic increments are almost universally accepted to the almost complete exclusion of merit or achievement provisions. Some of the rather severe indictments made against education in this regard are pointed at rather strongly by Levin:

> Finally, incentives for maximizing educational outcomes for a given budget do not seem to be important characteristics of schools as organizations. Financial rewards and promotion for school personnel are handed out in a mindless fashion according to the years of service and accumulation of college credits. Individual schools, teachers, or administrators who are successful in achieving important educational goals are treated similarly to those who are unsuccessful, mediocre, or downright incompetent. In lockstep fashion the schools reward all equally. It is no wonder, then, that schools can fail persistently to teach children to read, or to foster the formation of healthy attitudes, for there are no direct incentives to change the situation. That is, success is not compensated, or formally recognized, and the reward structure is systematically divorced from educational effectiveness. In contrast, commercial enterprises tend to compensate their personnel on the basis of their contributions to the effectiveness of the organization. Commissions for sales personnel, bonuses, promotions, profits, and salary increases all represent rewards for individual or organizational proficiencies.[34]

33. John E. Coons et al., *Private Wealth and Public Education* (Cambridge, Mass.: Belknap Press of Harvard University Press, 1970), p. 36.
34. Henry M. Levin, "The Effect of Different Levels of Expenditure on Educational Output," in Roe L. Johns et al., *Economic Factors Affecting the Financing of Education* (Gainesville, Fla.: National Educational Finance Project, 1970), p. 181.

While the critics of the single-salary schedule are legion, the suggestions for its replacement have been conspicuous by their absence. Although few people seriously defend a system where the mere passage of time and/or accumulation of college credits automatically bring equal salary increases to the competent and the incompetent alike, a system or systems guaranteed to solve the problem of determining teacher salaries on the basis of success or merit has not yet been supported by the teaching profession. This, of course, is unfortunate and indicates that for the time being little can be done to make effective comparisons of cost-quality relations until some process is found to determine the degree of success of individual teachers.

Economists refer to education as a labor-intensive activity. Since approximately three-fourths of the costs of education are required to pay the salaries of personnel, and since these salaries are not related to the degree of success achieved by the individuals receiving them, additional funds for education may be merely increases in salaries. This is particularly true in areas where teacher organizations have become powerful and effective in their bargaining with local boards of education.

Some of the operations of the schools seem to recognize the strong persuasion that there is a positive relationship between cost and quality in education. Coons, Clune, and Sugarman state a practical and reasonable rationale concerning that point of view:

> The statutes creating district authority to tax and spend are the legal embodiment of the principle that money is quality in education. The power to raise dollars by taxation is the very source of education as far as the state is concerned. By regulating the rates of taxation, typically from a minimum to a maximum, the state is in effect stating that dollars count (at least within this range) and that the district has some freedom to choose better or worse education. If dollars are not assumed to buy education, whence the justification for the tax?[35]

Selected Readings

Benson, Charles S. *The Economics of Public Education*, 2nd ed. Boston: Houghton Mifflin Co., 1968.

―――, ed. *Perspectives on the Economics of Education*. Boston: Houghton Mifflin Co., 1963.

Cohn, Elchanan. *Economics of State Aid to Education*. Lexington, Mass.: Lexington Books, D.C. Heath and Co., 1974.

Education, An Investment in People. Washington, D.C.: Chamber of Commerce of the United States, 1955.

35. Coons et al., *Private Wealth and Public Education*, p. 26.

Education and Economic Well-Being in American Democracy. Washington, D.C.: Educational Policies Commission of the National Education Assn., 1940.

Johns, Roe L.; Goffman, Irving J.; Alexander, Kern; and Stollar, Dewey H. *Economic Factors Affecting the Financing of Education.* Gainesville, Fla.: National Educational Finance Project, 1970.

————, and Morphet, Edgar L. *The Economics and Financing of Education,* 3rd ed. Englewood Cliffs, N.J.: Prentice-Hall, Inc., 1975.

O'Connor, James. *The Fiscal Crisis of the State.* New York: St. Martin's Press, 1973.

Rogers, Daniel C., and Ruchlin, Hirsch S. *Economics and Education.* New York: The Free Press, 1971.

2

Education: An Investment in People

Constantly increasing school expenditures, inequities in the amounts of revenue available per person to be educated, and heavy property tax burdens on individual citizens were the principal reasons for the numerous court decisions in the early 1970s that have provided motivation for school finance reform in this country. The reasons for increases in expenditures have been related to three main forces: (1) increasing and changing enrollments, (2) accelerating inflation, and (3) inequality and discrimination in the quantity and quality of services provided for students in different school districts. Although some degree of stabilization in enrollments has occurred, little has been done as effective measures to curb inflation, and the several states are still struggling to solve the problem of providing equitable funds to all the children and youth in their respective states and school districts.

DIMENSIONS OF EDUCATION

In the United States in 1974, 60.1 million pupils were enrolled in regular schools, public and private, at all grade levels. (See Table 2.1) The number of full- and part-time workers in the schools was estimated at 6.9 million. The total expenditures for the 1974–75 school year were estimated at $107.2 billion.[1] Since the figures cited here are principally those in regular school programs, they "understate the involvement of the total population in education and work-related training and retrain-

1. *Financial Status of the Public Schools* (Washington, D.C.: National Education Assn., 1975), p. 5.

TABLE 2.1   School Enrollment, 1964 and 1974, Projections and Percents of Increase

Level	Fall Enrollment (in millions)			Percent Change	
	1964	1974	Projec-tions, 1979	1964 to 1974	1974 to 1979
1	2	3	4	5	6
Public elementary and secondary	41.4	45.1ª	41.9	8.9	−7.1
Private elementary and secondary	6.3	4.8	4.3	−23.8	−10.4
Public higher education	3.5	7.9	8.4ª	125.7	6.3
Private higher education	1.8	2.3	2.3	27.8	0.0
TOTAL	53.0	60.1	56.9	13.4	−5.3

SOURCES: U.S. Department of Health, Education, and Welfare, Office of Education. *Projections of Educational Statistics to 1982-83.* 1973 edition. Washington, D.C.: Government Printing Office, 1974.
U.S. Office of Education, National Center for Educational Statistics, Prepublication Release, preliminary data, November 1974.
ªNEA Research estimate.

ing. These include nursery school and some Head Start programs, adult education programs, post-high school subcollegiate vocational training, Job Corps training, apprentice programs, and inservice training programs for employees. Other types of enrollment not included are those in residential schools for exceptional children, elementary and secondary schools associated with institutions of higher education, and some federally operated schools on reservations and installations. Enrollments in special schools, such as trade schools and business colleges, which are not reported as enrollments in regular schools, totaled 1.2 million according to the Fall 1973 enrollment survey of the U.S. Bureau of the Census.[2]

Although few people realize the size of the seemingly prodigious amount of money spent annually for public education, fewer still would agree that it is enough to accomplish its comprehensive purposes. The attitude of the knowledgeable American in this regard was expressed at a meeting of the Education Commission of the States in July 1969: "The time has come to give education the same top national priority that was given to the moonshot. . . . U.S. Commissioner of Education James E. Allen reflected the mood of the meeting when he called for an immediate overhaul of educational operations, particularly in the area of school finance. 'The time is now . . . and if we persist in delaying, we shall have at best chaos, at worst disaster.' "[3]

2. Ibid.
3. *Education U.S.A.* (Washington, D.C.: National School Public Relations Assn., Aug. 1, 1969), p. 231.

Few, if any, adequate substitutes have been coined and used to replace the well-worn cliché, "education in the United States is big business," or alternatively, "education is a major user of our economic resources." Although the meaning of the statement is obvious, it still fails to communicate its real significance and relatively few people realize the enormity of educational operations in this country. Tables and comparative figures concerning involvement of people and money in this, the largest and one of the most complex activities of government, may help the reader to visualize the magnitude of the structure and activity we casually refer to as "education."

EDUCATIONAL GOALS AND SCHOOL EXPENDITURES

Education is most meaningful when it is fashioned in terms of goals or objectives, whether they are implied or formally stated in the literature. Education without purpose or philosophical commitment would have little value and would stimulate little, if any, support or dedication.

The purposes of education have much to do with the cost of the program that is established and operated to achieve those objectives. To compare the problems of financing a three Rs curriculum with those of financing a program constructed to achieve the far-reaching and comprehensive goals of present-day education is a futile exercise guaranteed to result in frustration. As the schools reach out to supply new curricula and provide new media and methods of attaining increasingly complex and comprehensive goals for their clientele, the costs multiply, and taxpayers are forced to reach deeper and deeper into depleted treasuries for their support. And the end is not near, for the public adds additional goals and responsibilities to the school program year after year and seldom, if ever, relieves it of any purposes or programs that might be offered at lower cost or with greater effectiveness elsewhere.

In determining how much should be spent for education, it is necessary to determine and agree on what the schools are expected to do. As the goals and objectives of education become more inclusive and more difficult to achieve, the taxpayer must face the stark fact that the costs will likewise increase.

Goals Have Increased

Perhaps one of the best indicators of the persistent, but irregular, march of change and innovation in the public schools is shown by the many unofficial adoptions of goals and objectives of education in the last half-century. Such redefinitions have usually come after serious study based on changing needs. Not all resultant statements have made an indelible imprint on American education, but a few have.

Early statements of the objectives of education were very limited, relatively easy to achieve in a limited way, and correspondingly inexpensive. But the goals of the school became more comprehensive and costly as the schools improved and as public confidence in them increased. The Seven Cardinal Principles of Secondary Education, the Four Objectives of the Educational Policies Commission, and the Ten Imperative Needs of Youth are examples of some of the important statements of what Americans have at different times viewed as the important goals of education.

In 1966 there appeared another important study devoted to a statement of the current needs and problems of American education. This statement, published by the American Association of School Administrators,[4] expressed the thinking of a commission on the goals or "imperatives" of education in the years ahead. The commission had been appointed by the AASA and was charged "with responsibility for identifying and stating in clear and concise fashion major educational imperatives that must be at the forefront as curriculums are modified, instructional methods revised, and organizational patterns reshaped to meet the educational needs of this country in one of its dynamic periods."

The nine imperatives of education formulated by the commission are ample evidence of the changing and increasing needs of education in this country. The general theme of development of the individual and need for social betterment pervades the statement. The nine imperatives are:

1. To make urban life rewarding and satisfying.
2. To prepare people for the world of work.
3. To discover and nurture creative talent.
4. To strengthen the moral fabric of society.
5. To deal constructively with psychological tensions.
6. To keep democracy working.
7. To make intelligent use of natural resources.
8. To make the best use of leisure time.
9. To work with other peoples of the world for human betterment.

Although these imperatives were not intended to be "educational goals" nor to encompass the entire educational program, "they are points at which the educational program must be revised and reshaped to meet the needs of the times." In whatever way the association may have

4. *Imperatives in Education* (Washington, D.C.: American Assn. of School Administrators, 1966).

viewed its contribution, the imperatives strike tellingly at some of the main problems of education today. They indicate the areas of greatest concern, the areas of greatest failure toward the needs of the day, and the areas where improvements must be made if education is ever to be efficacious for all. In that sense they are the goals, the objectives, the "cardinal principles" of today and of the immediate future.

As one views the inclusiveness of this set of imperatives for education, their pervasiveness and inclusiveness seem to signal a degree of financial trouble for the already overburdened taxpayers who must assume the garantuan costs of such an ambitious but necessary program. That these high costs, if properly and efficiently applied to meet these imperatives, will actually become large investments that will bring great economic benefits to all our citizens cannot be denied. That supposition, however, does not help too much in determining how to provide such necessary and large sums of money from the private sector of the economy to give public education its chance to provide the quality and quantity of education necessary to meet these challenges.

Just as the costs of education have increased almost geometrically, so have the demands placed upon schools. Each level of government, each important social organization, and almost every individual increases the expectations with which the school is confronted and upon which its achievements are evaluated. To complicate the problem, the emphasis placed upon educational demands also changes often, as indicated by Grubb and Mickelson:

> But the demands placed on education change rapidly. The launching of Sputnik in 1957 resulted in a determination to "catch up" through science education. In the mid-1960s, with the civil rights movement, we "discovered" the second-class status of blacks, prompting an evaluation of the role of education in alleviating both poverty and discrimination. The emphasis shifted from development of a technological elite to Great Society programs for the economically and educationally poor. By the end of the sixties, evaluations of large-scale programs raised doubts that compensatory education was compensating; and soon a controversy arose over the possible efficacy of such programs, a controversy still very much alive in the early 1970s. At present, numerous proposals for reorganizing public schooling compete for attention, including community control of schools, "free" or alternative schools, voucher plans, greater control by higher levels of government, and no schools at all. What unites these proposals is only that they are all, in one dimension or another, radical—they either promise or threaten to thoroughly transform public schooling. In less than two decades, we have moved from specific goal-oriented elitist demands on education through compensatory education to the present stage of sweeping proposals for structural change.[5]

5. W. Norton Grubb and Stephen Michelson, *States and Schools* (Lexington, Mass.: Lexington Books, D.C. Heath and Co., 1974), p. 1.

People Want Better Education

American citizens continue year after year to make large investments in the educational enterprise in spite of its alleged inadequacy in many states and school districts. The reasons for these perennial increases are often beyond the power of school boards or administrators to change. But justified as these increasing costs become when viewed in proper perspective and in comparison with the alternatives, they tend to irritate the overburdened taxpayer whose resistance tends to become a cumulative matter and often one of deep personal concern.

For what reason, or reasons, do people continually approve high taxation rates to provide revenue for financing education? According to the Phi Delta Kappa Commission on Alternative Designs for Funding Education, there are at least three major bases for such expenditures:

> This vast commitment of funds by the government can realistically be justified on grounds that the people want it. After all, the expenditure of government funds should reflect the needs, wants, and demands of the people. But the justification for expenditure of public funds for education goes much deeper than a mere common desire to possess knowledge. Mass public education can be justified on the more basic grounds that it creates and perpetuates the culture, promotes social equality, and enhances economic development.
>
> Each of these alone may be ample reason for government to finance education, but to view them in combination leaves little doubt as to the importance of education. Of the three, the most significant is undoubtedly to gain and advance the accumulated culture and knowledge of man, create a respect for humanity, promote the attributes of citizenship, and inculcate ethical and moral character. Education not only preserves the cultural heritage but also exalts the status of man and provides at least a minimum level of citizenship. In this regard the advantages of education cannot be quantified. The benefits of reading a book, appreciating a painting, playing a violin, speaking a foreign language, and understanding a theorem are priceless, even though they may not be of any substantial economic importance.[6]

THE RATIONALE FOR INCREASING COSTS

Expenditures for elementary and secondary education increased from $18.5 billion in 1964–65 to $51.8 billion in 1974–75—an increase of 179 percent. There are, of course, many reasons for this tremendous increase

6. *Financing the Public Schools* (Bloomington, Ind.: Phi Delta Kappa Commission on Alternative Designs for Funding Education, 1973), p. 6.

in one decade—not all of which are directly related to enrollment increases and inflation.

Enrollment Increases

In the past, increasing enrollments, especially at the secondary and higher education levels, have been a primary cause of the increasing cost of education. Recent decreases in elementary school enrollments were offset by higher percentages of increase at the secondary and college levels, where annual per pupil costs are usually higher. It is apparent now that public elementary and secondary school enrollments have leveled off and will actually decrease slowly in the next few years. It is estimated that they will decrease by 3.2 million, or 7.1 percent, by 1979 with a loss of 1.7 million forecast for elementary grades and 1.5 million for secondary grades.[7]

Extension of the Years of Schooling

Exemplifying how the age scope of children who may attend public schools has widened is the provision of state money for kindergartens by about two-thirds of the states. One state anticipates providing free public education by the middle of the 1970s to all three- and four-year-old children who want to attend school. This plan, beginning with disadvantaged children, would provide for the physical, social, intellectual, and emotional development of all children of those ages.

The need for, and implementation of, programs for early childhood education have received considerable attention by educators since the 1960s. The effect of this can be seen by the increasing number of these children receiving some amount of formal education (See Table 2.2). A side effect of this interest in the education of early childhood children was noted by McLure:

> Programs of parent education are formally organized activities of instruction and counseling in the home, and occasional meetings with groups. These programs are aimed at instructing the parents how to direct and guide some special activities of children in their personal development. There are activities for parents of children not in school, and others for those with children in a school program.
>
> This study proposes a minimum development of these programs by the public schools in 1980 to reach the parents of 3 million children under 3 years of age. This estimate is for somewhere between one-fourth and one-third of the parents who would not be involved in parent

7. *Financial Status of the Public Schools*, p. 5.

TABLE 2.2   Percent of School-Age Population Enrolled in Regular Schools

Year	Age Group						
	3-4	5-6	7-13	14-17	18-19	20-21	22-24
1960[a]	—	80.7	99.5	90.3	38.4	(—13.1—)	
1966	12.5	85.8	99.3	93.7	47.2	29.9	13.2
1970	20.5	89.5	99.2	94.1	47.7	31.9	14.9
1974	28.8	94.2	99.3	92.9	43.1	30.2	15.1

SOURCES: U.S. Department of Commerce, Bureau of the Census. *School Enrollment: October 1966, 1967, 1968, 1969, and 1970.* Current Population Reports, Series P-20, Nos. 167, 190, 206, and 222. Washington, D.C.: Government Printing Office.
U.S. Department of Commerce, Bureau of the Census. *School Enrollment in the United States: 1971, 1972, 1973, and 1974.* (Advance Report). Current Population Reports, Series P-20, Nos. 234, 247, 261, and 278. Washington, D.C.: Government Printing Office.
[a]Figures for 1960 did not include pupils enrolled in nursery school.

programs in connection with other children in the family who might be enrolled in school. The target population would include parents on welfare, low income, low educational level of attainment, and other indicators of environmental disadvantages for children.[8]

At the other end of the age scale the popularization of educational programs for adults has become evident in many areas of the country. The community school is becoming a reality. More and more, adults who entered the mainstream of American life without a high school education, and also many who want to extend and expand their post-high school training, are taking advantage of opportunities to attend classes and activities for economic as well as cultural reasons. As a result, night schools have flourished with parallel increases in school costs.

Percent of Population Attending is Increasing

The various states and school districts have always had a relatively high percent of their eligible school population in attendance in regular schools. That percent has increased at the same time that the age limits at both extremes have increased. The percentage of our high school-age population attending school in this country is considerably higher than in most others. Thus, the business of education in the United States is much more a function and problem of government than is generally true elsewhere. The educational program at the high school level is

8. William P. McLure, as quoted by Roe L. Johns et al., eds., *Planning to Finance Education* (Gainesville, Fla.: National Educational Finance Project, 1971), p. 5.

geared to the masses. Most other countries, however, still consider education to be for the relatively small numbers who can qualify academically, sociologically, and economically, and they so adjust their programs. On that basis, the "business" of education in this country exceeds its counterpart in other nations.

Lengthened School Day and Year

Extension of the number of school days in an academic year and extension of the length of the school day have both helped to increase significantly the total cost of public education in recent years. It is likely that such a trend will continue. Summer school programs, extended time contracts for administrators, teachers, and other school employees, and a gradual increase in the total number of days of school required by states have added their proportionate weight to the cost factor. Such legitimate extensions seem likely to be accelerated in the future if we are going to make acceptable progress in promoting efficiency of learning, at the same time repudiating the fallacious tradition that all students and teachers need three or more months of summer vacation to make the nine months of academic learning effective.

Some other countries already maintain school years much beyond the typical nine months utilized in the public schools of this country. Whether the school year extension comes in the form of summer schools, divisions of the year into quarters, simple extension of the number of school days in an academic year, or some other form is not important at this point. What is important is that any such arrangement will require the allocation of additional large sums of money to the school budget. The urgent need for extension of the school year is implied in the following:

> The average school year in the U.S. is 179 days, with state averages ranging from Arizona's 168 days to South Dakota's 184. Of forty-seven countries recently surveyed by UNESCO, only seven had secondary school years of less than 180 days. Nineteen had school years of from 180 to 209 days, eighteen had 210 to 239 days, and three claimed 240 or more school days. In ten countries the school year is shorter for secondary schools than for elementary, while in six countries the secondary school year is longer. The length of the college year ranged from 150 days in Ecuador to 246 in the R.S.F.S.R. (U.S.S.R.).[9]

As indicated by the New York State Education Department, "There is no logical reason for closing schools in July and August."[10] The

9. *Phi Delta Kappan,* September 1964, p. 36.
10. *Education U.S.A.* (Washington, D.C.: National School Public Relations Assn., Apr. 1, 1968), p. 170.

department, as a result of its study of the problem, recommended an 11-month school year to improve education, especially for disadvantaged children. Its study showed that 22 New York school districts and about 60 systems in other states were seriously considering a longer school year.

As school attendance areas become larger and as more pupils must be transported to the school complex, the inequality and injustice created among students becomes more evident when important school activities are sponsored at night. Many schools are finding a partial answer to this problem by a simple lengthening of the regular school day (at additional cost) with only a minimum number of night activities. Such a procedure not only releases teachers from school night responsibilities but also makes the school buildings more accessible to the public for community school activities and services.

Decreasing Pupil-Teacher Ratio

Since the salaries of teachers represent the greatest cost in the school's budget, the pupil-teacher ratio is an important determinant of the total cost of education. That ratio for secondary schools decreased from 21.5 in 1963–64 to 19.2 in 1973–74. The National Education Association projects a further decrease to 18.0 by the year 1980. At the elementary school level the decrease was from 28.4 in 1963–64 to 23.3 in 1973–74, with a projection figure of 21.3 by 1980.[11]

Increases in Programs and Services

The programs and services of today's schools show a substantial increase over the offerings of previous years. Comprehensive junior college programs, prekindergarten and kindergarten curricula, adult education, expanded summer schools, more emphasis on compensatory education for disadvantaged children and adults, new interest and thrust in research and innovation, increased emphasis on counseling and guidance, expanded health services, and extension of the entire curriculum, especially in vocational education—all represent important additions to the school program in recent years. The implications of these additional and increased services to already tight budgets are obvious.

The failure of American schools to teach effective reading skills to all their clientele is recognized by friends as well as critics of the educational establishment. Whatever progress the schools may have attained toward this extremely important objective, the results are not

11. *Standard Education Almanac, 1975–76,* p. 174.

satisfactory and must be improved. In trying to meet one of the many needs for improved services in this area, the late James E. Allen, while serving as U.S. commissioner of education, proposed a program to eliminate the reading deficiencies and semi-illiteracy of many of our citizens. The objective is a worthy one; such a project would require a large investment of time and money to carry out. The number of other equally worthy projects that are needed to augment today's educational program is almost endless.

School Building Requirements

Various estimates have been made from time to time of the deficit in classrooms needed to house present and future school programs. A deficit developed during the first half of this century largely as a result of a number of national and international emergencies, during which school building programs were seriously curtailed. World War I, the Great Depression of the 1930s, World War II, the Korean conflict, the Vietnam War, and other costly though less spectacular events assumed priority over most of the school building needs of the public schools. The exact size of that classroom need is subject to dispute largely because of disagreement over how old and obsolete a school building or a classroom should be before it is abandoned. Capital outlays for buildings have had to be increased in the last few years, thus increasing the normal costs of education. Such costs will likely continue to increase in the immediate years ahead if our innovative programs continue to gather support.

Increasing Teacher Salaries

In past years, teachers' salaries have been low compared with those of many other professional and occupational groups. One of the many reasons for this injustice has been that most teachers were women and salary schedules were constructed principally for single male individuals who did not have families to support or for married women earning a second income for a family. Until recently, comparatively little pressure was applied to remedy the injustice. Some progress has been made, but much more needs to be done to make education more attractive to men with families. The influx of higher proportions of men into teaching in the last few years has forced schools to increase their salaries for instruction. Note the following:

> Recently teacher organizations have demonstrated increased militancy in their salary demands—a situation that can be traced in part to a large

influx of men into the teaching profession. In 1949–50, only one in every five teachers was male; in 1963–64, male teachers constituted slightly more than one-third of the teacher population.

Recent teacher strikes may manifest a natural desire by male teachers for wages commensurate with the costs of raising a family. Twenty years ago the average annual salary of the instructional staff in public schools just about matched average earnings of full-time employees in all industries. In the course of two decades, however, average annual earnings of public school instructional personnel have forged ahead of other employees.[12]

In the years since 1967, an apparent change in the general attitude of large numbers of teachers combined with the firm, and sometimes militant, stand taken by some of their professional organizations resulted in greatly increased incidence of teacher strikes across the country. According to the National Education Association,[13] there were 154 strikes in 1973–74 in 20 states, involving 74,873 teachers with an estimated loss of 718,518 teacher-days of work. The effect of such strikes, in addition to the countless sessions of school board-teacher negotiation sessions in thousands of school districts has been to increase teacher salaries to where they are generally competitive with those of most other groups of employees with similar qualifications.

The degree to which teacher salaries are now competitive is disputed by the National Education Association. Note the following:

> Average starting salaries of classroom teachers compare poorly with starting salaries of bachelor's degree graduates who are employed in industry. In 1974–75, starting salaries for men in industry, which averaged $10,691, were 33.6 percent higher than beginning teachers' salaries at $8,000. Salaries paid new women graduates in all occupational classes reported were higher than salaries in teaching. The starting salaries shown . . . give considerable evidence of economic discrimination against teachers as an occupational class of workers.[14]

Much of the problem in comparing the salaries of teachers with those of most other groups arises from the fact that the most occupational groups work for a longer work-year than do teachers. In the light of the summer school attendance requirements of many teachers and the second-job needs of others, a completely satisfactory resolution of the teacher salary fairness controversy has not yet been formulated.

---

12. *State Aid to Local Government* (Washington, D.C.: Advisory Commission on Intergovernmental Relations, U.S. Government Printing Office, April 1969), pp. 31, 33.

13. *Financial Status of the Public Schools*, p. 19.

14. Ibid.

Inflation

The erosive effect of continuous inflation of the dollar on school budgets needs few illustrations and little documentation, for it is a phenomenon that affects every citizen. The purchasing power of the dollar depreciated by some 40 percent in the ten-year period from 1954 to 1964. This steady 4 or 5 percent inflationary rate more than doubled itself in the years of the controversial Viet Nam conflict during the late 1960s and early 1970s.

Some of the inflationary effect on instructional staff salaries is shown in the following:

> Between 1963 and 1967 the Consumer Price Index rose moderately at an average annual rate of 2.0 percent. From 1968 to 1972 the Index increased an average of 4.6 percent per year; in 1973, 6.2 percent; and in 1974, 11.0 percent. Through March 1975 the CPI was increasing at an annual rate of 6.0 percent. Average instructional staff salaries increased by $1,737 from $10,213 in 1971–72 to $11,950 in 1974–75. However, in constant 1967–68 dollars, the purchasing power of instructional staff salaries actually decreased by nearly $546, from $8,455 in 1971–72 to $7,909 in 1974–75.[15]

Beginning in 1965 the federal government's attempts at expansion and increased support of the Viet Nam war effort generated a general rise in prices that resulted in a two-digit rate of annual inflation. Fortunately for the country, government and economic officials have been able to slow down the annual rate of inflation, but high inflation continues to plague the economy.

Inflation not only reduces the real income of individuals but it also increases their tax obligations under a progressive income tax system. For example, doubling one's income because of inflation—even though the real value may not have changed—will automatically put an individual in a higher income tax bracket and thereby more than double his tax obligation. As the negative effects of inflation become operative, households tend to cut back on the purchase of goods and services in an attempt to maintain their economic position. The result is disastrous for schools, for at the same time that taxpayers reduce their tax effort the necessary costs of operating an educational program continue to increase. One of the results of this dilemma has been an unofficial "taxpayers' revolt" with obvious retarding influences on public education.

School Social Problems Are Increasing

Vandalism and school violence have become major problems for many public schools. The cost of combating such antisocial behavior is begin-

15. Ibid., p. 18.

ning to be noticed in the budgets of school districts, especially in large urban centers—as indicated in the following report:

> The single most all-pervading problem in the nation's schools today is probably violence and vandalism, "and so far, it is a problem that defies solution," according to a new EDUCATION U.S.A. Special Report. After surveying 340 school districts, the report, *Violence and Vandalism*, says these twin problems now cost the average district between $1 and $13.50 a student and can jump to $24 a pupil when arson, the most costly type of vandalism, is involved. Quoting the Senate Subcommittee To Investigate Juvenile Delinquency, the report says that school crime, which affects virtually every district, now costs at least $600 million annually and there is no ceiling in sight.[16]

In an attempt to implement the desegregation requirement of the U.S. Supreme Court decision in the *Brown* case of 1954 and other decisions since that time, many school districts of this country are spending large sums of money annually, although no accurate figures of cost are available. It is impossible now to forecast the effect these court decisions will have on future school costs.

While each of these incidental problems taken alone will probably not cost school districts much in comparison with the enormous total cost of education, collectively they represent a burden that the districts can ill afford. Unfortunately, present socioeconomic conditions appear to be an ominous threat to the social welfare as well as to the already tight budgets of many urban school districts.

Mobility of Population

The steady trend toward urbania and the increasingly high mobility of our people result in increased school costs, particularly for new school buildings and facilities. As people move with their families from rural to urban areas, they leave behind partially occupied school buildings and classrooms and reduced pupil-teacher ratios. They frequently find that the cities or the suburbs to which they move have overcrowded buildings and classrooms and high pupil-teacher ratios. Such imbalances naturally increase the total cost of education and change the responsibility of the various states and the nation for financing education. The effects of this mobility are noted in the following:

> Because of the growing mobility of the population and the steady rise in educational costs, upper governmental levels have come to play increasingly important roles in financing elementary and secondary educa-

16. *Education U.S.A.* (Washington, D.C.: National School Public Relations Assn., Dec. 15, 1975), p. 91.

TABLE 2.3   Migration of Population Between March 1970 and March 1974, for Selected Age Groups (Movers as percent of population)

Age Group (years)	Total Movers	Within Same SMSA[a]	Between SMSA's	From Outside SMSA's to SMSA's	From SMSA's to Outside SMSA's	Outside SMSA's at Both Dates
1	2	3	4	5	6	7
4-14	40.7	18.7	5.9	2.2	3.1	10.6
15-19	31.4	14.7	3.7	1.8	3.4	8.7
20-24	61.1	28.3	9.1	5.3	2.5	14.4
Total, 4 years and over	36.9	17.4	5.5	2.1	3.1	8.8

SOURCE: U.S. Department of Commerce, Bureau of the Census. *Mobility of the United States: March 1970 to March 1974.* Current Population Reports. Series P-20, No. 273. Washington, D.C.: Government Printing Office, December 1974, p. 12.
[a]Standard Metropolitan Statistical Area.

tion. State governments in particular have a long and well-established responsibility. More recently, the Federal Government—through the Elementary and Secondary Education Act of 1965—assumed part of the financial responsibility for provision of elementary and secondary education albeit on a compensatory basis. Thus, while local initiative and support remain paramount, the financing of public education has become—and will undoubtedly continue to be—intergovernmental in scope.[17]

Greater Concern for Educational Research

Educational research does not have a particularly pleasant history, for American public education has been notoriously indifferent to its existence. Funds for this potentially important aspect of education have been lacking, and public school personnel, for the most part, have been ill-equipped by training and experience to initiate and conduct research on a satisfactory level. Traditionally, the research function has been reserved for higher education, and little has been done, until recently, to alter the pattern. But we have turned the corner, and future expenditures for education will be increased by more adequate allotments for educational research. The colleges, universities, private institutions, and state departments of education (each with federal funds) have shown the way. Thus, some progress is under way, and public school teachers, especially those who have revolted against past routines, are becoming research oriented.

School budgets of the future must therefore anticipate increased allowances for educational research. Predictions of future expenditures

17. *State Aid to Local Government,* p. 37.

suggest large increases. Harris has noted the insignificant outlay up to now of funds for educational research; he implies more general acceptance, however, of such costs in the future:

> Research expenditures equal to ¼ to ½ of 1 percent of educational expenditures are a dismal accomplishment as compared with 30 times as large outlays in the medical field, in which the expenditures are roughly equal to educational outlays. Failures to spend on research are especially costly since up to now the production of technological equipment is much ahead of the research which is necessary to implement machine technology with idea technology, and to integrate the work of industry with that of the educational establishment. Opposition of teachers and other members of the educational establishment—in part the result of callous disregard of the interests of teachers and students—contributes to the serious lag of the learning process in relation to the advances in instructional technology which, it is hoped, will ultimately provide for individualized instruction.[18]

Implementing Change and Innovation

Changes and innovations now becoming an important part of the educational scene are represented by many technological advances—from closed-circuit television, teaching machines, and the like, to computers and retrieval systems. Their effect on the future costs of education will be considerable. Certainly, it is impossible to determine how much the technological advances of the years ahead are going to cost.

NONPUBLIC SCHOOL FINANCIAL PROBLEMS

The increasing costs of education have affected nonpublic schools even more than public schools. While the public schools can tap the public treasury for needed additional funds, nonpublic schools have no such recourse. As a consequence, some of the nonpublic schools are finding it necessary to close their doors to students. This adds to the costs of education for the public schools, which are forced to provide educational opportunities for many students who are not now a part of their responsibility.

Nonpublic school closings have been occurring at the rate of more

18. Seymour E. Harris, "The Economics of Technological Advances in Education," in Edgar L. Morphet and David J. Lesser, eds., *Planning for Effective Utilization of Technology in Education* (Denver: Designing Education for the Future, August 1968), p. 366.

than one a day, thereby creating a serious impact on many public schools. Although direct financial aid by the states to nonpublic schools is a violation of the First Amendment, which declares that "Congress shall make no law respecting an establishment of religion, or prohibiting the free exercise thereof . . . ," several states have tried to provide funds to private and parochial schools. Such state efforts have been frustrated, however, by refusal of the courts to accept this as a constitutional function of state government. For example, the U.S. Supreme Court in June of 1971 declared that Pennsylvania and Rhode Island laws that subsidized nonpublic school teacher salaries were unconstitutional. "While the acts in question required an enforcement scheme by the state to ensure that none of the services or materials bought with state funds would ever be used to teach religion, the Court held that this kind of surveillance would involve the state in 'excessive and enduring entanglement' with churches, thus violating the Constitution's requirement that church and state be kept separate."[19]

The Supreme Court rendered a similar unfavorable decision against the Connecticut law soon after the Pennsylvania and Rhode Island rulings. Numerous other comparable cases are in the courts with little likelihood that they will be upheld. It appears that the future of the nonpublic schools of this country is uncertain for the immediate years ahead. That future will be determined largely by the success or lack of success of state programs to provide them with some financial assistance. Some aid has already been approved by the courts—providing funds for transportation of children to parochial schools, provision for lending state-owned textbooks to nonpublic school students, and provision for school-lunch programs in all schools, for example. "Meanwhile, the plight of private and parochial schools is growing. The NCEA reports enrollments in Catholic elementary and secondary schools down by almost 500,000 students in the past two years. . . . Catholic leaders are urging even broader aid proposals, pointing out that the public school system will bear the brunt of the enrollments from parochial school shutdowns."[20]

THE HIGH COST OF NOT EDUCATING PEOPLE

Perhaps all people think of the high cost of educating our citizens, but comparatively few give much thought to the higher cost of *not* educating

19. *Hot Line 4,* no. 7 (Washington, D.C.: American Assn. of School Administrators, July 1971), p. 1.
20. *Education U.S.A.* (Washington, D.C.: National School Public Relations Assn., Sept. 1, 1969), p. 3.

them. Many prominent Americans, however, have said much about this latter cost. The following statement is typical of many others:

> Another method of studying the social benefits of education is to consider the *cost of not educating people.* The crime rates and the rates of dependency on public welfare or private charity are many times greater among those without sufficient education to enable them to succeed in present-day society than among those who have an adequate education. The direct cost to the taxpayer of keeping a man in prison may range from $3,000 to $4,000 per year in terms of 1967 prices. This does not include the cost to other individuals of the crime committed or the social cost which may be incurred by the prisoner's family being forced on relief. . . . As one views the future, it is reasonable to predict that the economic cost of failing to educate the population will be far greater than would be the cost of the additional financial inputs necessary to provide the quality and the quantity of education necessary for all of the people.[21]

Many Americans express shock and disbelief when they belatedly discover that some schools cannot afford a satisfactory or high-quality school program and consequently do not provide one. The idea of free public education through grade twelve for all, with each person having the same opportunity to obtain the best education of which he is capable, is remarkably sound in theory but it does not always exist in practice. Failure to apply the theory of equality of educational opportunity results in some penalties to the students involved and is a costly injustice to society in general. Interestingly enough, this view concerning inadequate education is rather widespread, as indicated in the following statement:

> Our nation's private businesses are also beginning to voice major concerns over our inadequate financial support for education. As far back as 1959, the Committee for Economic Development, an organization of 200 of our nation's top businessmen and university presidents, issued a policy statement entitled "Paying for Better Public Schools" which called for substantially increased governmental support for elementary and secondary education. . . . Private business is sensitive to the direct relation between improved education, higher incomes, and increased economic growth. Moreover, the private sector recognizes the extreme economic costs that accompany our failure to educate our children. A magazine advertisement sponsored by the Addressograph Multigraph Corporation states: "The trouble with a cheap education is that we never stop paying for it."[22]

21. Roe L. Johns, "The Economics and Financing of Education," in Edgar L. Morphet and David L. Jesser, eds., *Emerging Designs for Education* (Denver: Designing Education for the Future, May 1968), p. 207.
22. Francis D. Murnaghan, Jr. and Richard Mandel, "Trends and Musts in Federal Education Legislation," *Phi Delta Kappan,* June 1969, p. 559.

Illiteracy

Notwithstanding compulsory school attendance laws, illiteracy is more common in this country than is generally believed. Note the following in this regard:

> Much of our adult illiteracy exists in states that find difficulty in supporting an adequate program of education for children and youth. In fact, states with the lowest level of support for general education tend markedly to show the largest number of educationally deprived adults. However, illiteracy is found throughout the nation, which means that in some states it is imported while in others it is homegrown. . . . It becomes, therefore, a national problem.[23]

Whatever the causes, the socioeconomic results of illiteracy represent a financial and social loss that this country cannot afford. Certainly, this condition of inadequate or no schooling, with attendant unemployment and the problems that accompany low incomes, has contributed significantly to the extensive race and riot conditions that have become so devastating and threatening in the last few years.

Unemployment

Unemployment is closely related to lack of adequate education. Figures show that it is much more of a problem to school dropouts and to those with a minimum education than to those who have attended schools and succeeded academically. Unemployment is further complicated by the need to retrain and reequip countless workers in the maelstrom of American business and industry every few years. Those with adequate education are usually able to adjust to new jobs and new occupations more easily and with less frustration than those with limited schooling.

According to the National Committee for Support of the Public Schools, the financial and social losses from unemployment are great and can never be recovered:

> Economic losses from unemployment are never regained. The social costs of unemployment are even greater than the economic losses. The discouragement and frustration of able-bodied men and women, eager to work but unable to find employment, cannot be measured in dollars any more than can the distress of their families. Prolonged unemployment contributes to further unemployment, since human capital deteriorates when

---

23. Sterling M. McMurrin, *Adult Basic Education Act of 1962* (Washington, D.C.: U.S. Government Printing Office, 1962), p. 17.

it is idle. Unemployment impairs the skills that workers have acquired. It also contributes to family disintegration, crime, and other social ills.[24]

Military Service Incapability

Those who think that investment in education is adequate and that schools are satisfactory should look at the disgraceful record of educational preparation of youth that was brought to light by World War II. It was a record that shocked the nation—a nation that had believed with firm conviction that our educational system was adequate if not superior. The rejection of large numbers of young men from induction into military service was a severe indictment against the effectiveness of pre-war education in this country.

"In World War II, some 400,000 illiterates were accepted for military service. The Armed Forces provided these men with the educational fundamentals necessary for useful service. Another 300,000 illiterates— equal to 20 army divisions—were rejected completely."[25] (See Table 2.4.)

> Despite the pressing demand for military manpower, nearly thirty percent of all men examined by Selective Service in World War II were rejected as mentally, physically, or morally unfit to serve their country. This is all the more shocking in view of the fact that the incidence of unfitness could have been greatly reduced. Rejection rates cannot be attributed to lack of schooling alone, but they correlate highly with lack of education and with low expenditures. . . . Rejection rates ranged from fifty to fifty-five percent for the entire period. More recent statistics show that this tragic inadequacy has continued to plague the states where education is poorly financed and where large numbers attend school for only a few years. In short, under-education saps the nation's defense potential and places a disproportionate share of Selective Service demands on the states which provide better education.[26]

Inadequate Occupational Preparation

Although accurate figures are not available, the mass rejections of unqualified applicants seeking occupational positions in business and industry indicate a high percentage of people with inadequate educa-

24. *Changing Demands on Education and Their Fiscal Implications* (Washington, D.C.: National Committee for Support of the Public Schools), p. 11.

25. Wilbur J. Cohen, *Adult Basic Education Act of 1962* (Washington, D.C.: U.S. Government Printing Office, 1962), p. 12.

26. *National Policy and the Financing of the Public Schools* (Washington, D.C.: Educational Policies Commission, 1969), pp. 10–11.

TABLE 2.4 Percentage of Selective Service Draftees Failing Preinduction and Induction Mental Tests, 1968 (Ten Highest and Ten Lowest States)

Rank	State	Percentage Rejected
1	Minnesota	1.6
2	Rhode Island	1.7
3	Iowa	1.9
4	Nebraska	2.2
	North Dakota	2.2
6	Washington	2.6
7	Wisconsin	2.8
8	Utah	2.9
9	Idaho	3.3
10	South Dakota	3.4
	United States	11.8
41	Florida	16.2
42	Virginia	16.5
43	Arkansas	17.0
44	Tennessee	17.9
45	Louisiana	20.4
46	North Carolina	22.4
47	Alabama	23.0
48	Georgia	24.6
49	South Carolina	27.2
50	Mississippi	33.3

SOURCE: U.S. Army, Office of the Surgeon General, "Results of the Examination of Youths for Military Service, 1967," as reported in *Rankings of the States, 1970* (Washington, D.C.: Research Division of the National Education Association, 1970), p. 29. Reprinted by permission.

tional qualifications. This condition results in an obvious waste of much of the time and cost of maintaining employment offices. Unrewarded job-hunting represents a big loss to employers as well as to those applying for positions. The problem becomes more acute as technology replaces common labor and the qualifications and skills required in most occupations continue to increase.

Dependence on Public Relief

There appears to be a high positive relation between inadequate education and an individual's need for financial assistance. A number of recent studies have shown that recipients of public assistance are likely to be individuals of low educational attainment. A study conducted in New York in 1957, for example, indicated that almost one-fifth of the mothers on the aid to dependent children rolls had not gone beyond the fifth grade. The study also showed that among families receiving general assistance, about one-half of the family heads had completed no more than six years of schooling.[27]

A Chicago study of relief recipients showed that 50.7 percent of the sample studied could not pass reading and vocabularly tests at the fifth grade achievement level. "The conclusion was that the problems of public welfare stem from unemployment and economic and technological displacement and, most important, from relief recipients' lack of basic educational skills which are essential to compete in our modern society."[28]

Society Suffers the Effects of Poor Education

The individual who suffers the consequences of poor or inadequate education does not confine himself to a particular ghetto area, town, city, or state. The frustrations that unemployment, inadequate income, and substandard living conditions bring and that often accompany limited education or result from it often produce high mobility rates among those who suffer them. The problems related to poor education in one locality then become the welfare or reeducation problems of another community. High mobility rates of people may quickly move the problems of the disadvantaged—higher welfare and law-enforcement costs, for example—from the source of their creation to a state or locality whose educational system is adequate or even superior. Thus, the effects of poor education cannot be localized. That being true, the problems of providing adequate and high-quality education are not only local but also statewide and national in scope. No longer can states and districts have concern for their own citizens only.

EDUCATION AND ACCOUNTABILITY

The spiraling costs of education and the changing social climate of the country have combined to raise serious questions concerning public education. Have the increased costs resulted in proportionately increased productivity? Has education, with an increase of 1000 percent in expenditures while the gross national product was increasing 400 percent (1947 to 1969), really justified such vast expenditures? Why has the public lost confidence in the schools? Why does the public not accept

27. *Changing Demands on Education and Their Fiscal Implications,* pp. 49–50.
28. Ibid.

the arguments for increased costs of education as explained by the professionals? These are a few of the unanswered questions that have resulted in taxpayer revolts, student militancy, racial unrest in the schools, and a general deterioration in the traditional confidence that citizens have usually shown in their schools.

The Public Demands Improvement

The public demands improvement and increased efficiency in the operation of public schools. Their cry is couched under the broad umbrella of *accountability*. The accountability syndrome has gathered momentum, and critics and also friends of public education hold the schools firmly accountable for making output commensurate with input. Public sentiment is virtually demanding that the educational establishment produce objective information and proof that the schools are achieving what they are designed for and that in the process they are using tax revenues efficiently.

Although actions toward accountability are desirable and should be encouraged, some potential dangers are inherent in rushing too quickly into the process. One danger is that taxpayers may expect the schools to be accountable, at the same time ignoring their own responsibility for providing adequate funds for achieving the comprehensive goals of education. Closely related is the possibility that some lawmaking bodies may, without fully understanding the ramifications, legislate school accountability laws; these could involve such questionable notions as requiring all pupils to take certain academic examinations to determine the degree of success or failure of the schools to achieve their purposes.

Equality Not Yet Attained

Equality of educational opportunity is no longer simply a matter of philosophy or of ethics or of the moral rights of individuals. It is now popularly referred to as a constitutional right. Threatened lawsuits in some states and also actual litigation in others point to the changing attitude of people. Not only are they agreeing that equality of educational opportunity should be provided; they are beginning to demand that it be mandated, even if it requires unequal inputs in the educational program for those whose needs require large expenditures.

One of the primary problems in this regard—dealing fairly and objectively with social and racial injustices—must base its chances for solution on education. The hordes of disadvantaged Americans that congest urbania must be given the educational opportunity and the motivation to bring them into the mainstream of society and social progress. No other agency or institution has greater hope and greater responsibility than education for eradicating the hazards that prevent such a cultural and economic improvement. Just as the schools have justified national faith in them in their responsibility for dissolving the great problems created by differences in national origin of students, so they are now challenged with the tremendous problem of obliterating the imagined differences of race. The price of such a worthy goal will be high in money and human effort, but it is a price that all thinking Americans will be willing to pay. If education fails in this, its most challenging charge, future generations may never receive the same chance or responsibility.

EDUCATIONAL INVESTMENT
SHOULD BE INCREASED

The question whether or not we are investing enough money in education is always relevant. What are some evidences that our investment may need to be increased so that maximum development of our human capital and greater protection to the already large sums invested in buildings and equipment can be completely assured? A persistent and continuing shortage of qualified teachers in a few areas of instruction (although an oversupply exists in most areas), an abundance of substandard classrooms still being used despite their obsoleteness and defects, inadequate laboratories and libraries, and vitiated curricula are examples of underinvestment in education that are much too common and too readily accepted in many of our school districts.

To Protect Our Current Investment

No prudent person would invest large sums of money in an enterprise and then forget it or refuse to use all possible means of protecting that investment. Sometimes adequate protection may involve spending additional funds. Such is the case with investment in education, for inadequate future expenditures may result in loss of all or a major part of the original investment. John Ruskin expressed the point involved here when he said, "It is not wise to pay too much, but worse to pay too little. When you pay too little, you sometimes lose all—because the thing you bought is not capable of doing that which you bought it to do."

Every economist and most intelligent citizens readily recognize the fallacy of assuming that economy requires spending the smallest amount of money possible in purchasing a good or service. Certainly, examples of underspending that have resulted in lack of protection of original investment are easy to discern in any area of business, industry, or education. For example, the school board that employs an unqualified or an incompetent teacher at low salary, or refuses to keep its buildings and equipment in good repair with the excuse of saving money, will sooner or later recognize such actions as poor business and a violation of true economy. The educational system that provides only a small part of an optimum program for its students will at some time come to realize that the taxpayers' investment in human capital has not been protected adequately. The following statement illustrates this point:

> Boards of education have failed miserably . . . and too often the only criterion of success was that they kept the tax bill for education low. In this respect, and this goes for the state legislatures as well, there has never been a greater form of economic idiocy than that which has resulted in our saving millions of dollars in educational expenditures in the schools, and then spending hundreds of millions of dollars to mop up the failures of the school system.[29]

This country must protect the value of its investment in the education of its citizens although this cannot be fully measured in standard dollars and cents. It must also protect the individual's indirect and intangible benefits that are a part of the educational process. This is indicated by the American Association of School Administrators:

> Extra earnings are only a part of the benefits the student receives from education. With few exceptions, the higher the level of education, the broader the range of job opportunities one has to select from. This is a good thing in itself; most people like to choose their jobs from among a variety. However, this broader range of job choice is especially important today, because the job market is changing so rapidly.[30]

A Question of Priorities

In the past, educators and economists have done remarkably well in convincing large numbers of taxpayers that education is an investment in people. But we have done far less well in showing the investor how much he has earned on his added investments that education has required each year. In our current frenzy to try to produce a dollar value on the student who submits to the educational process, it must be understood

29. Philip Hauser, as quoted by Ralph W. Yarborough, "Making Your Own Circumstances," in *Interdependence in School Finance: The City, the State, the Nation* (Washington, D.C.: National Education Assn., 1968), p. 19.
30. *Education Is Good Business* (Washington, D.C.: American Assn. of School Administrators, 1966), p. 3.

that benefit-cost studies have not been producing conclusive results concerning this complex problem and cannot be expected to do so.

All groups of people that are concerned with education appear to be demanding their own version of accountability—often with little regard for their own responsibility. But the principle of accountability applies to all segments of the school complex—administrators, students, teachers, boards of education, parents, and the legislative bodies. The public schools cannot prosper or achieve their intended destiny in the lives of their students if any one of these groups is not held accountable to play its part in the educational process. However, the important point as far as school finance is concerned is that the educational fraternity—administrators, teachers, and other staff members—should note that the taxpaying community needs and is demanding more comprehensive and objective ways to measure output of education compared with input. Without such accountability, it appears that the theories and principles of economics that are generally followed in financing education may be counterbalanced by the actions of skeptical taxpayers. Education will suffer irreparable damage if the public decreases its support because of insufficient evidence that schools are doing what they purport to do.

Many Americans believe that education is receiving its equitable share of the wealth of this country and that even in our state of affluence additional funds are not available. Others insist that our priorities are inconsistent with our values and that there is little if any defense for the fact that cosmetics, liquor, and tobacco cost more than education. A study reported in 1969 shows a great discrepancy between what Americans are saying and what they are doing in this regard.[31] It reports that no single front has been elevated to higher importance (in words) than education, but nowhere more than on the educational front has loud assertion of the problem been thwarted by deficient efforts.[32]

Education's Share of the Gross National Product

Of all the available measures of the nation's productivity and the state of its economy, gross national product is the most meaningful, the best understood, and the most often used. It refers to the market value of all final goods and services produced within a specified period—in practice, one year. The GNP, as it is commonly called, has been increasing yearly at a substantial rate (until the early 1970s), as the following extract shows:

31. *Education U.S.A.* (Washington, D.C.: National School Public Relations Assn., Jan. 29, 1968), p. 115.
32. Ibid.

FIGURE 2.1. Total Expenditures for Education as a Percentage of the Gross National Product: United States, 1929–30 to 1971–72

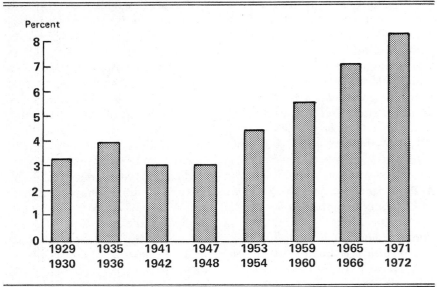

SOURCE: *Digest of Educational Statistics, 1974.* Washington, D.C.: National Center for Education Statistics, 1975.

During the first two-thirds of the twentieth century, the gross national product (GNP) multiplied 34 times, but the revenue of all government (federal, state, and local) multiplied 133 times. Expressed in dollars of constant value, the GNP multiplied 8 times and governmental revenue 31 times. Such productivity of the fiscal machinery enabled the nation to build a huge defense establishment, to aid foreign lands, and to expand the range and intensity of the domestic public service.[33]

The gross national product is often used to determine potential expenditure levels for education as well as for other public services. What percentage of the GNP should be invested in education? Garvue estimated that it would require about 8 percent to achieve the educational goals listed in 1960 by the President's Commission on National Goals.[34] According to Johns, "present trends indicate that it is not unreasonable to estimate that at least 12 percent of the gross national product will be allocated to all education by 1980."[35] (See Figure 2.1.)

33. Robert J. Garvue, *Modern Public School Finance* (London: The Macmillan Co., 1969), p. 12.
34. Ibid., p. 314.
35. Johns, "The Economics and Financing of Education," p. 198.

According to the Standard Education Almanac, "The percentage of the GNP that went for education has varied widely over the past 40 years. Educational expenditures were relatively high in the mid-1930s, exceeding 4 percent of the GNP in 1933–34. They later declined to a low point of 1.8 percent during the war year of 1943–44. Except for a brief period during the Korean conflict, when the annual investment in education tended to stabilize, there has been a steady increase in the proportion of the GNP spent for education since the end of World War II. Expenditures in 1971–72 were higher than ever before, both in terms of actual dollars and as a percentage of the GNP (8.0 percent).[36]

Selected Readings

A Time for Priorities: Financing the Schools for the 70's. Washington, D.C.: National Education Assn., Committee on Educational Finance, 1970.

Coons, John E.; Clune, Wm. H., III; and Sugarman, Stephen D. *Private Wealth and Public Education.* Cambridge, Mass.: Belknap Press of Harvard University Press, 1970.

Education Is Good Business. Washington, D.C.: American Assn. of School Administrators, 1966.

Financial Status of the Public Schools, 1975. Washington, D.C.: National Education Assn., 1975.

Financing Education: Who Benefits? Who Pays? Washington, D.C.: National Education Assn., Committee on Educational Finance, 1972.

Johns, Roe L.; Alexander, Kern; and Jordan, Forbis. *Financing Education.* Columbus, Ohio: Charles E. Merrill Publishing Co., 1972.

Schools, People, and Money. Washington, D.C.: President's Commission on School Finance, U.S. Government Printing Office, 1972.

Wise, Arthur A. *Rich Schools, Poor Schools: The Promise of Equal Educational Opportunity.* Chicago: University of Chicago Press, 1968.

36. *Standard Education Almanac* (Chicago: Marquis Academic Media, 1975–76), p. 109.

3

The Theory and
Practice of Taxation

Although change and innovation continue to accelerate in matters relating to almost all aspects of education—including its financing—general dislike for the taxes that make such education possible changes little. "Nothing is so sure as death and taxes" and "the power to tax is the power to destroy" are two common statements that illustrate the general public's attitude toward paying high taxes. As indicated by O'Connor,

> Every economic and social class and group wants government to spend more and more money on more and more things. But no one wants to pay new taxes or higher rates on old taxes. Indeed, nearly everyone wants lower taxes, and many groups have agitated successfully for tax relief. Society's demands on local and state budgets seemingly are unlimited, but people's willingness and capacity to pay for these demands appear to be narrowly limited. And at the federal level expenditures have increased significantly faster than the growth of total production. [1]

Dislike for paying taxes that increase year after year is a normal reaction for people for many reasons: (1) If the tax rate is high, paying taxes may seriously curtail other activities and reduce the quantity and quality of other economic goods and services then available to the taxpayer. (2) The complex society of interrelated institutions makes it increasingly more difficult for a taxpayer to see and understand the personal benefits resulting from his tax dollars. (3) The increased services that are required as the population increases and social institutions become more complex are not understood or favored by many people. (4) When increased taxes are being considered, much mislead-

1. James O'Connor, *The Fiscal Crisis of the State* (New York: St. Martin's Press, 1973), p. 1.

ing information, or even propaganda, concerning taxation is often issued by those who favor increased taxes as well as by those who oppose them. (5) The average taxpayer still thinks of the "cost" of education rather than the "investment" in human capital that results from taxation for that purpose. (Unfortunately, there is little opportunity to provide the information necessary to develop this important concept for a majority of the adults in society.)

In spite of popular opposition to tax increases, it should not be assumed that the several states have reached an absolute upper limit in the amount of tax revenue that can be raised for useful purposes, if and when the need arises. This is indicated in the following:

> Recent studies by the Advisory Commission on Intergovernmental Relations and the National Educational Finance Project indicate that substantial tax potential exists for most states. The ACIR estimated that in 1970–71 an additional $34.7 billion could have been raised by all states if each had put forth the same effort as the state with highest effort. Using a less stringent capacity test of a midpoint between the highest for a region and the highest for the nation, the ACIR found an untapped capacity of $25.6 billion.[2]

THE RATIONALE FOR TAXATION

The term *tax* serves as a firm reminder to a person that he has been given a personal and mandatory responsibility to divert a certain amount of his income—past, present, or future—to become part of the revenue required by some institution or unit of government performing a public service. A direct relation may or may not exist between the amount of tax paid and observable benefits to the individual taxpayer.

Taxes are a function of three variables: (1) the tax base (value of the objects or items to be taxed); (2) the assessment practices being followed (the percentage of market value applied to the object being taxed); and (3) the tax levy (the rate applied to the assessed value of an object or item to determine amount of tax obligation). Tax rates mean little until they are related to assessment practices and values or compared with them. When comparing taxes and tax effort where there are differing assessment practices, one must convert assessed value into market or sale value of the property in question.

Since profits are a product realized only in the private sector, and since the public sector requires funds to perform its manifold functions

2. *Financing the Public Schools* (Bloomington, Ind.: Phi Delta Kappa Commission on Alternative Designs for Funding Education, 1973), p. 39.

and provide its services, the taxing system is a justifiable and adept process for transfering resources from where they are produced to where they are needed. No country has devised a better system for the necessary transfer of resources. As indicated by Due, this is the only possible way to finance public activities:

> Most government activities, by virtue of their community benefits, must be financed by taxation rather than by sale to the users. Since these governmental services convey their benefits to the community as a whole, there is no possible way in which they can be divided into segments and sold. It is this characteristic of certain activities which initially led governments to undertake them.[3]

In the words of John Kenneth Galbraith, "Our private economy is affluent but our public economy is poverty stricken." With limited funds, schools are able to guarantee their clientele only a poor quality and a limited quantity of education, for good schools are expensive. The problem thus becomes one of diverting adequate funds from the private sector to the public sector to provide the quality of education needed and desired without undue jeopardy or burden on individuals in the private sector.

The tax system, even though it has been established and has operated for a long time in each state, does not provide an easy answer to the question of how much or what percentage of government revenue should be alloted to each of the institutions or agencies it sponsors. What formula or what device should be used to allocate private funds to the publicly sponsored organizations in order to bring maximum benefits to society? Unfortunately, no one claims to have found the answer to this perennial question.

Although the public sector obtains most of the revenue it uses by taxation, several other minor sources are used to supplement tax funds. The sale of government services or products, the sale of government-owned property—including land and such other assets as war-surplus equipment—licenses, fines, forfeitures, incomes from investment, special fees, gifts, and transfer funds from other levels and agencies of government are all examples of other sources of such funds.

Education is a beneficial service (nonmaterial good) that should be made available to all the eligible citizens of a country regardless of their degree of affluency. Under such a system it is necessary for education to be financed by government with its capability of collecting resources from the private sector and distributing them equitably

3. John F. Due, "The Principles of Taxation," as quoted by Charles S. Benson, ed., in *Perspectives on the Economics of Education* (Boston: Houghton Mifflin Co., 1963), p. 163.

among institutions in the public sector. In spite of the fact that education produces externalities and large-scale spillovers that benefit the larger society, it has been financed largely at the local school district level. In the opinion of many, this fact creates one of the most difficult problems with which educators must concern themselves—providing equitable school programs and creating equitable tax burdens with the almost exclusive use of a regressive and inadequate property tax system.

Early in its history, this country proved to the satisfaction of its citizens that rate bills, tuition charges, fees, and the like would not provide universal and equal education for its children and youth. Discrimination against the poor and against large families destroyed the supporting philosophy for this method of financing education. The only defensible alternative was the development of a taxing system with a supporting rationale. While it was slow in its implementation, states gradually adopted their own unique systems of taxation. Although these were satisfactory for a long period of time, local dependence on property taxes to the almost complete omission of other forms of taxation has become a source of major criticism of this apparently necessary form of local support of education.

GENERAL CLASSIFICATION OF TAXES

Taxes may be classified as proportional, progressive, or regressive. The proportional tax requires the same percentage of each person's total taxable income, regardless of income size, to be paid in taxes. A tax is progressive if the percentage of the total taxable income required for taxes increases as the taxable income becomes higher. A regressive tax finds higher incomes paying lower percentages of the total taxable incomes for taxes than do lower incomes. For example, three households with incomes of $5,000, $10,000, and $20,000 that pay taxes of $500, $1,000, and $2,000 are paying a proportional tax, for each is paying 10 percent of income for taxes. If the three households pay $500, $1,500, and $5,000 in taxes, the tax is said to be progressive, for the household with the smallest incomes pays 10 percent in taxes, the next larger one pays 15 percent, and the largest pays 25 percent. On the other hand, if the same three households pay $500, $750, (or anything less than $1,000), and $1,000 (or anything less than $2,000), the tax is regressive. In the last instance, the lowest income was taxed at 10 percent, the middle income at 7.5 percent, and the highest income at 5 percent.

The economist uses somewhat more sophisticated terms to describe these three general classes of taxes. In his view, taxes are said to be

TABLE 3.1   Percentage of Type of Tax Collected By the Three Levels of Government, 1971

Type of Tax	Federal	State	Local
Property	—	3.0	97.0
Individual Income	87.9	10.3	1.8
Corporation Income	88.7	11.3	—
Sales and Gross Receipts Taxes	36.9	56.1	7.0
Motor Vehicle and Operators Licenses	—	94.0	6.0
Death and Gift	77.2	22.8	—
Other	20.3	59.2	20.5

SOURCE: Roe L. Johns and Edgar L. Morphet, *The Economics & Financing of Education*, 3rd ed. Englewood Cliffs, New Jersey: Prentice-Hall, 1975, p. 148. Reprinted by permission of Prentice-Hall, Inc., Englewood Cliffs, New Jersey.

elastic if tax revenue increases proportionately more than the tax base (the federal personal income tax, for example); they are classed as having *unitary elasticity* if tax revenue increases proportionately with the tax base (a general tax on all sales, for example); and they are described as *inelastic* if tax revenue increases less than proportionately with the tax base (sales taxes based on staples, for example). The comparison is further explained in the following: "Although there is no theoretical correspondence between this trichotomy (progressive, proportional, and regressive taxes) and the elasticity schema, in the United States economy progressive taxes are usually revenue elastic, proportional taxes usually display unitary revenue elasticity, and regressive taxes are usually revenue inelastic."[4]

Some of the principal taxes used to transfer funds to the public sector include property, personal income, corporation income, sales, and sumptuary taxes. Most of these are used to some degree in financing education in all of the fifty states. Others that are being considered, but which have not yet received general acceptance, include site-value and value-added taxes. Many of the states still emphasize the property tax as their most reliable and lucrative source of revenue with only minor reliance on other forms of taxation.

THE PROPERTY TAX

A property (*ad valorem*) tax is a tax levied against the owner of real or personal property. Real property is not readily movable; it includes land,

4. Daniel C. Rogers and Hirsch S. Ruchlin, *Economics and Education* (New York: The Free Press, 1971), p. 302.

buildings, and improvements. It is usually classified as residential, industrial, agricultural, commercial, or unused (vacant). Personal property is movable; it consists of tangibles, such as machinery, livestock, automobiles, and crops, or intangibles, such as money, stocks, and bonds.

Property taxes were the first kinds of school taxes, and they still constitute almost the complete local tax revenue for schools. Property tax rates are usually expressed in mills per dollar of assessed valuation or dollars per hundred dollars of assessed valuation. Facility in changing or interpreting different ways of stating tax rates has some value for those who are interested in comparing district budgets and taxing procedures in different states.

Historical Use

The several states have based their local school revenue systems on a property tax. This policy seems to have been justified in its early history, for property ownership was considered to be a good measure of the wealth of people—especially before the advent of industrialization. For a long time the property tax seemed to be reasonably satisfactory, and severe critics of it were relatively few.

Over the years of the nineteenth century and much of the twentieth, the property tax at the local level has proved to be a good and reliable source of revenue for operating schools and providing many other services of government. It has demonstrated many of the characteristics generally accepted as desirable in a tax. Until recently, it produced adequate revenue for most school districts. It has operated as a direct tax with most people understanding its purposes and knowing the amount of their obligation before the tax payment period. The property tax is easily collected by the regular machinery of state and county governments, and it can be regulated and controlled by local boards of education within the provisions of state laws. Certainly, one of the advantages of the real property tax is that avoidance of payment is almost impossible; this is not equally true with personal property taxes. Two of the traditional virtues claimed for the property tax are noted in the following statement: "Virtues in the property tax are claimed by many. First it is a highly productive tax and has been a mainstay of local government revenue for generations. Second, it is a highly visible tax and provides a direct linkage for many citizens between services provided by local government on the one hand and the cost of services on the other."[5]

5. *Aid to Local Government* (Washington, D.C.: Advisory Commission on Intergovernmental Relations, April 1969), p. 35.

Assessment Practices

Widespread unfairness exists in the assessment practices and in the degree of adequacy of property tax administration in the various states. Unequal assessment practices are often found among the parcels of property within any one school district. While it may be argued that such a condition simply means that a higher tax rate must be used to get the desired amount of revenue, such an argument is of little value because the general public resists increased tax levy rates and state laws often prohibit them. Thus, a school board often finds itself powerless to overcome the revenue problems caused by underassessment.

The application of the foundation program concept of allocating state funds to local districts has created another problem concerned with underassessment. Fractional assessment was originally only a problem involving inadequate revenue to the district concerned. Now, however, in financing the foundation program, underassessment becomes an advantage to that district by the fact that its decreased revenue from its own property taxation will be offset by the addition of an equal increase in state funds. This, in reality, places a premium on underassessment and certainly is not fair to the other districts that are fully assessed.

Fractional assessment of property for taxation purposes often violates the law, as indicated in the following:

> If we measure administrative effectiveness in terms of compliance with the law, it must be conceded that the property tax stands out as a classical case of maladministration. The laws of most states clearly direct assessment officials to assess all taxable property at estimated market value. These constitutional and statutory full value mandates have been flagrantly violated by the perennial and pervasive practice of fractional valuation.[6]

While assessment practices of the several states vary widely, few states actually assess at more than 60 percent of the market value of property. Many of them assess at less than 20 percent. Market value, as used here, refers to the price that would be paid in a free market by a willing buyer to a willing seller. Some states assess real property according to its classification or type, and some assess personal property at a different rate from that applied to real property.

Tax authorities argue for assessment of property at 100 percent of its market value. While such a practice would be desirable, its im-

6. John Shannon, "Property Taxation: Toward a More Equitable, Productive Revenue Source," in *Trends in Financing Public Education* (Washington, D.C.: Committee on Educational Finance of the National Education Assn., 1965), p. 138.

practicality under present taxing systems makes the argument meaningless. The main reason for fractional rather than full assessment of property has been that assessors have been unwilling and unable to keep assessment increases in line with market value increases, particularly since World War II. Present problems of property assessment are largely the result of the predominantly political system under which taxation laws have been made and are being administered. Elected county, town, or township assessors, often not particularly well qualified for their responsibilities, face the difficult problems of raising assessments because of inflation or actual improvements in the property, keeping assessments fair and equitable among all property owners, deciding on the relative worth of different kinds of property, and many other similar and equally difficult problems. Assessors, under this obsolete system of tax administration, have to weigh the value of fairness and equity against their desire to be reelected to their positions.

The problems concerned with fractional assessment of property were summarized by the officials of the Kentucky Department of Welfare:

1. The practice of fractional valuation stands in flat contradiction to the constitutional intent that property is to be assessed at market value.
2. Low assessments are undermining the financial integrity of local government and school districts.
3. Fractional value places assessment officials in a position to assume the tax and budget responsibilities of local legislative bodies.
4. Nonuniform fractonal value confuses taxpayers and severely aggravates the problem of intra- and intercounty equalization of assessments.
5. Competitive undervaluation has hindered efforts to distribute state equalization grants equitably to needy school districts.[7]

In addition to the problem of fractional assessment, determining whether or not to use classified property assessments still remains in question. Should property used for one purpose be assessed differently from property used for another purpose? If so, how should relative rates be determined? What should be the relative assessment value placed on residential property as compared with income property? What is the proper relation of assessment to be applied to a corner business lot as compared with that for a similar lot in the middle of the block? These and many other unresolved assessment problems make the property tax system less equitable and less defensible than would be expected.

7. *Know Your Schools Fact Sheet* (Washington, D.C.: National Committee for Support of the Public Schools, August 1969), p. 3.

Defects of the Property Tax

Even though the property tax has served the schools well, it has always been under some criticism. Its abuses and disadvantages have become more apparent year after year. Some of the generally accepted advantages early in its existence now seem to have changed to disadvantages. It is not now the fair or equitable measure of taxpaying ability that it was years ago. People are now inclined to invest their surplus earnings in property, much of which can escape taxation. The owner of land and buildings fares less well than his counterpart who puts his wealth into more intangible assets that are less likely to be included in the normal taxation process. This makes the property tax regressive and a violation of the ability-to-pay principle on which sound tax systems for financing education are based. A few states are making some progress in reducing regressivity by using tax credit plans that provide property tax relief to low-income families, particularly to elderly people.

A few states have experimented successfully with taxing plans that adjust an individual's property tax load to his ability to pay. There is need for other states to make similar changes in their tax structure, for as property taxes increase, the need for some type of tax relief for low-income households becomes more evident, and the social pressure to provide such relief likewise increases.

Another serious defect of the property tax system arises from the limitations that states sometimes place on it. This has been achieved by state-imposed tax rate restrictions—legislated during depression years to protect beleaguered taxpayers. Although such restrictions have been liberalized to some degree since World War II, many school districts are still struggling to find how to raise adequate local revenues with state limitations on tax levies. In some states (Utah, for example), the state legislature has imposed a mill-levy tax rate limit, which can be increased to a higher limit only by a favorable vote of the people in the district. The practical effect is that few school districts are able to exceed the limit under which the school board is required to operate.

Jaffe referred to some of the most obvious defects of the property tax in the following:

> The property tax hits poor communities as well as poor people. Not only is it a local tax, it is a highly localized tax, for its base is confined to the boundaries of political jurisdictions. Thus, the central city of a metropolitan area has no way of tapping the wealth of its affluent neighbors. Property values in many of these central cities are growing slowly, if not declining, while industry, shopping centers, and new residential developments enrich their neighbors' tax bases. Meanwhile, their expenditure demands grow as they are left with more high-cost citizens to educate, to maintain on the welfare rolls, and to protect against a

rising crime rate. Some have been able to levy local sales and income taxes, but their main revenue source remains an increasingly burdensome property tax.[8]

Administration

Since all taxes are paid from income, past, present, or future, the critics of the property tax and other taxes wonder why there should be any other form than one on income. The local school board, however, is virtually powerless to control an income tax, but a property tax is comparatively easy for it to administer. Its use as a source of local revenue for schools has been alternately praised and condemned. The following statements are brief samples of such opinions of the property tax of a few years ago:

> Twenty years ago the experts in public finance were virtually in unanimous agreement on three propositions: (a) From a revenue standpoint, the property tax was a sluggish performer, highly unresponsive to economic change. (b) The property tax did not lend itself to equitable and efficient administration. (c) This tax was highly regressive at the lowest income levels because there was no necessary relationship between property ownership and the ability to pay taxes.[9]

> The property tax is and will continue to be an important source of local tax support for schools in spite of certain weaknesses in the tax due to inefficient administration, erosion of the base by exemptions, fractional assessments, and questionable equity. The most important reason for this prediction is that the amount of yield from this tax is so great and so constant that a better substitute is probably not obtainable.[10]

Recently, condemnation of the property tax has reached new heights as a result of court decisions in many states and adverse opinions of the tax by governmental leaders. The much discussed revolt is largely directed at the property tax. It is described by numerous governmental officials in high positions as the most oppressive and unfair tax of all, and much of its traditional "popularity" as a source of revenue for schools has disappeared. Many of the segments of society—taxpayers, educators, government officials, and economists—have added their voices in protest to its use, and particularly to its extension. While the courts have not said that it is an unconstitutional tax, they have said the disparities and inequalities generated in its application to finance public education are

8. *Productivity in Education: Measuring and Financing* (Washington, D.C.: National Educational Assn. Committee on Educational Finance, 1972), p. 145.

9. Shannon, "Property Taxation," p. 136.

10. C. Jackson Salisbury, "The Theory of Taxation as Related to School Finance," in Warren E. Gauerke and Jack R. Childress, eds., *Theory and Practice of School Finance* (Chicago: Rand McNally & Co., 1967), p. 58.

discriminatory and that therefore state finance laws must be changed. The structure of school finance is threatened, and the years ahead may see vast changes in administration of the property tax.

Circuit Breakers

A plan used to protect certain classes of individuals from excessive property tax burdens is that of the "circuit breaker." It was introduced in Wisconsin in 1964 and had been adopted in some form in twenty-four other states by 1975. It is designed to provide that people with low incomes will pay property taxes not to exceed a stated portion or percent of their annual income, regardless of the value of their property or the tax rate in effect in their taxing unit.

As an illustration of the circuit breaker principle, a person with an annual taxable income of $6,000 who owns property assessed at $17,500 with a tax rate of 20 mills would ordinarily pay a property tax of $350. Under a circuit breaker provision requiring that not more than 4 percent of income be paid in property taxes, the calculated amount of taxes due ($350) would be reduced to $240. Although the person would be required to pay the $350 of property taxes (ostensibly to avoid erosion of the funds necessary to provide public services—including education) he would receive a tax refund from the state for $110. Under this arrangement, local property tax increases would not affect low-income taxpayers for all such tax increases would be paid by the state in the process outlined above.

More complicated circuit breaker plans than the one described here are used by the states using such a device. Progressive percentage limits of income to be paid in property taxes with increases in annual income may be used, or the state might be required to pay a certain percent of a person's property taxes. The main point, of course, is that the lower the income the greater the percent of property tax relief.

The circuit breaker system, in spite of its accelerating popularity, as indicated by the number of states that have adopted it in some form since 1964, has some inherent problems. Determination of "income," and how to apply the circuit breaker principle to welfare recipients and renters are some of the most difficult problems facing states that use this method of providing property tax relief.

Expansion of Tax Relief Programs

Expansion and extension of various property tax relief programs for certain classes of individuals and households continues to be advocated by numerous citizens—including the governors of a number of states. All the states and the District of Columbia now provide such programs for the elderly; several include the nonelderly. More than half of the states enacted property tax relief legislation in 1974. Most of the programs now in existence extend tax relief to renters as well as to the owners of real property.

During 1975, the governors of Colorado, Idaho, Indiana, Iowa, Kansas, Nevada, New Jersey, and Wisconsin advocated expansion of circuit-breakers and property tax relief measures for the elderly. New tax relief programs for the elderly were also proposed in Montana and North Dakota. The governors of Georgia, Minnesota, South Dakota, New Mexico, Mississippi, Nevada, Kansas, and South Carolina also advanced different forms of property tax relief.[11] Thus, it is apparent that the several states are actively adopting programs to reduce the gross unfairness that exists in property taxation.

Personal Property Taxes

While the real property tax with all its objectionable features remains the backbone of the local school finance structure, the personal property tax is an enigma in local tax theory and practice. On the surface the personal property tax has many defensible characteristics and it is used quite successfully in some states. Benson reported in 1968 that ". . . the most common practice is to include commercial inventories, industrial inventories, agricultural implements, and livestock, but to exclude personal property not used in business pursuits."[12]

Today, much of the wealth of people is invested in personal property holdings such as stocks, bonds, mutual funds, and savings accounts. This vast pool of wealth is a potentially lucrative source of revenue to help defray the costs of government, but the problem of getting such property assessed and on the proper tax rolls has not been solved. Lack of information or evidence of ownership and almost complete reliance on owners to report the extent of their personal property assets have served to defeat this form of taxation. Unfortunately, this defensible measure of the wealth and taxpaying ability of people is therefore minimized as a source of public school or other government revenue. Hence, local taxes continue to be almost exclusively taxes on real property.

11. *Financial Status of the Public Schools* (Washington, D.C.: National Education Assn., 1975), pp. 40, 44.

12. Charles S. Benson, *The Economics of Public Education,* 2nd ed. (Boston: Houghton Mifflin Co., 1968), p. 108.

INCOME TAXES

The personal income tax is usually a progressive tax levied on the income of a person received during the period of one year. It is the basis of the federal financial structure, but it is also used to a much lesser degree by nearly all of the states. In principle, it is probably the fairest of all taxes, and it has the advantage of producing large amounts of revenue at proportionately low collection costs. In practice, archaic laws and unfair provisions make it less than its potential ideal as a revenue-collecting measure.

A complete revamping and overhaul of the federal income tax laws —as well as those of many of the states—is long overdue. As these states and the federal government plan income tax increases to produce more revenue, they should first eliminate much of the special treatment given to certain categories of income under present laws. For example, income tax laws need to be amended so that the source of an individual's income does not determine the amount of tax to be paid. The tax should be a function of the amount of taxable income and not the source of the income. Taxpayers receiving equal amounts of taxable income—one taxpayer from working, the other taxpayer from social security or unemployment compensation payments or both—should be treated equally for tax purposes. Such items as expense account deductions, reciprocal state and federal tax deductions, tax writeoffs, the preferential treatment given to the homeowner over the renter in determining income taxes, and the special treatment of capital gains are some of the areas of unfairness that need to be corrected to improve the income tax— particularly at the federal level.

The relationship of income taxation and the ability-to-pay principle was pointed out by the National Education Association in the following:

> Long after Adam Smith's time, there developed in economics the principle that as more and more of any good is purchased, its utility to the consumer becomes less and less. The first pair of shoes, for example, is a necessity, the second very important, the third important, the fourth useful perhaps, and the fifth, sixth, and the like, successively less desirable. Application of this theory proved useful in explaining the fact that as the supply of a commodity increases, the price at which it is sold decreases. Then, as often happens, this principle, formulated for use in one area of human thought, was extended to others. It came to be believed that the law of declining utility also applied to money. Once that was accepted, the extension to taxation was thought to be clear. The rate, it was said, should increase in some ratio to the declining utility of the dollars of increased income. Thus the theory of ability to pay was born.[13]

13. *Taxes Contribute to Progress* (Washington, D.C.: National Education Assn. Committee on Educational Finance, 1960), p. 18.

Income taxes should include taxes on personal and on corporation incomes. The rationale justifying taxes on corporations is that without it individuals and organizations would incorporate to avoid taxation. "Corporation income taxation has been justified on the ability to pay, privilege or benefit, cost of service, state partnership, and control theories."[14] It is used in nearly all the states. It is responsive to economic and income changes, but it is sometimes complex in form and difficult to administer.

The real value of the personal income tax (and by implication the corporate tax as well) was emphasized by Jaffe:

> A personal income tax is the essential added ingredient to erase the regressive effects of property and sales taxes. Moreover, the income tax is far more sensitive to economic growth than are property or sales taxes and therefore can help solve the state-local fiscal crisis. Once the initial political hurdle of enacting an income tax is overcome . . . future rate increases can be few and far between—economic growth takes over.[15]

SALES TAXES

A sales tax is a levy imposed on the sale value of certain goods and services. It is generally imposed at the retail operation, rather than the wholesale. Sales tax rates are usually at the same level for all transactions; but if food and other necessities are subject to a sales tax, the tax becomes regressive. The sales tax is used most often at the state level of government, although it is sometimes used at the county and city . levels. It produces large amounts of revenue, but its use without exclusion of necessary goods and services tends to overburden poor families.

The sales tax could become a fairer and more effective tax with certain improvements, including (1) an adequate and well-trained group of auditors (auditors have much to do with the honesty and the efficiency of administration of the tax); (2) strict enforcement by the states of tax collections and reportings; (3) restriction of exemptions to items of food and medicine; (4) inclusion of a service or use tax; (5) elimination of loopholes in taxes on goods purchased in other states, on casual sales between individuals (such as on used cars), and simplification of tax collection in those states that provide for more than one agency of government to collect tax revenues.

The value of the sales tax as a source of state revenue is indicated in the following:

14. Ibid., p. 19.
15. *Productivity in Education: Measuring and Financing,* p. 146.

The general sales tax is the largest single state tax source, accounting for almost one-third of all state tax revenue. It is a broad-based tax and fairly sensitive to economic growth. But in one respect it is too broad based, for in most states it taxes food. Since low-income families spend a larger proportion of their budget on food than do high-income families, the tax on food introduces a strong element of regressivity.[16]

SUMPTUARY TAXES

A sumptuary tax is sometimes imposed by government with the primary purpose of helping to regulate or control a certain activity or practice not deemed in the public interest. In this kind of tax, the collection of revenue is secondary to the purpose of the tax. For that reason, this revenue is usually comparatively small, and there is little room for expansion or extension of the tax. Such taxes provide a division of interest, as indicated by Corbally:

> In general, sumptuary taxation receives little support from tax theorists. The fact that sumptuary taxes do, in fact, produce revenue often leads to a situation in which a governmental unit in need of funds is tacitly encouraging an activity which tax legislation sought to discourage. Liquor taxes, for example, have the intent of "punishing" the user of an "immoral" commodity and yet the revenue from these taxes often becomes such an important source of funds that a government unit establishes attractive establishments for the retail sale of the heavily taxed product.[17]

Taxing goods and services that are generally held to be against the public interest is usually a defensible practice, but it can be overdone. Such sumptuary taxes should be used with caution and wisdom to minimize the negative effects of taxing any particular segment of society for the benefit of another. Such controversial forms of taxation become highly discriminatory if used too extensively. Governmental control of socially unacceptable practices usually requires more than excessively high taxation to curb the activities of the sponsoring organizations.

POTENTIAL NEW TAXES

It seems likely that the great pressure that courts are now applying on the states to achieve equity in financing education will be followed by

16. Ibid., pp. 145–6.
17. John E. Corbally, Jr., *School Finance* (Boston: Allyn and Bacon, 1962), p. 14.

similar legal pressure to provide equity in other functions of government. With the accompanying acceleration of criticism of the property tax will come increased emphasis on attempts to discover and use other kinds of taxes. This will require revision and upgrading of the taxing pattern of the states and local school districts. With the state assuming more of the responsibility of financing education, the principal base for the taxing structure increases, and the property tax will undoubtedly assume proportionately greater importance in financing education.

Site-Value Tax

Recommendations for improving or replacing the present property tax system have taken many different forms. Some economists advocate a site-value, or land, tax. This is a tax on the actual value of the land, whether improved or not. As the land appreciates in value from investments or changes of any nature, the value of the tax revenue produced increases proportionately. Some other countries are using such a tax, and the plan has gained some support in this country, where the idea of property tax reform is old but untried.

Value-Added Tax

Another tax proposal that has received some support is a national value-added tax—popularly referred to as VAT. In simplest form and terms, it is a tax on the value of goods at each transaction level from production to consumption. Its proponents point to its wide acceptance in the industrialized nations of Europe and the fact that it would be a single-rate tax with few exemptions. Opponents of the tax point to its regressivity and its potential for extreme unfairness to low-income families. To offset this characteristic, proposals have been made to make tax rebates to the poor who are most adversely affected by the tax. The value-added tax would probably result in higher wages in the labor market. The opponents of the tax urge that its use would result in serious inflationary trends.

CHARACTERISTICS OF A GOOD TAX SYSTEM

School finance and tax authorities agree on many of the important guidelines that should be followed in establishing or evaluating a tax system. It is extremely difficult to achieve complete or even satisfactory implementation of these general principles, however. Consequently, no taxing unit—local, state, or federal—has yet produced a taxation program that engenders universal acceptance by all its taxpaying clientele. Nonetheless, certain principles and theories of taxation are generally accepted as defensible characteristics of a viable tax system at any level of government.

Tax Systems Should Be Coordinated

Even though there is usually little if any planned coordination in the tax programs of the three levels of government, none of the three can be evaluated realistically without simultaneous consideration of the other two. An individual tends to measure his tax "burden" by the total taxes he is required to pay rather than those he is required to pay to any one level of government. It is important, then, that the total number of tax systems operable in any community or geographic unit should be coordinated and interrelated in a defensible and balanced program. Any duplication of taxation structure should be minimal. Equity and balance should exist among the various forms of taxes that are an integral part of the total system.

All Citizens Should Be Taxed

The benefits of government services are shared by all our citizens in varying degrees. Protection from fire and from acts of violence, and also many other aspects of the police power exercised by government, are the inherent right of all individuals, businesses, and other organizations. Financial support for these services is therefore required from all who receive the benefits. It must be remembered, however, that payment for such services cannot be assessed in exact relation to the number or amount of such services available to each person or organization.

A good tax system provides that every person and every profit-making business be required to pay some tax to government. The services of government are for all its citizens according to their needs; these services should be paid for by all according to their ability to pay. It is a distinct violation of good taxing theory to use tax laws that have gaping loopholes whereby wealthy citizens can escape paying their commensurate share of the tax burden. Such unlawful and prejudiced exclusions result in requiring those with average incomes to pay much more than their fair share of the costs of government services.

Justice and Economic Neutrality

As a matter of simple fairness and justice, a good tax system distributes the burden it creates among all its citizens in an equitable manner. Admittedly, determining what is "equitable" is often related to the frame of reference of the person or organization making such determination. Generally, however, it can be shown that a progressive income tax on businesses as well as on individuals is the most equitable single tax. Income is the best of all the measures of taxpaying ability; progressive tax rates make the tax fair, for even though higher incomes require much higher taxes, the burden to the taxpayer is not greater. In spite of the advantages of the income tax, no economist or tax authority would favor using it to the exclusion of all others. A single tax, regardless of its basic or apparent fairness, can never be fair for all citizens of a taxing unit. Taxation theory requires diversification as a base so that an individual's "escape" from a particular kind of tax does not automatically mean complete exemption from paying a tax of any kind.

While diversification of taxes is important, simplicity is equally necessary in any good tax system. Taxpayers cannot be expected to support intricate and complicated taxing laws they cannot understand. In theory, every taxpayer should be able to calculate his own tax with minimum help or instruction.

The maintenance of economic neutrality among taxpayers must not be disturbed by any patterns of taxation. Citizens and business should be left in the same relative position to one another after paying taxes as they were before. The person with greater income before taxes are paid should still have greater unspent income after taxes are deducted from his lower-income friend. It is important that special taxes that affect certain individuals or businesses be minimized in comparison with broadly based taxes.

Adequacy of Yield

Maintenance of the extensive services of government requires large sums of tax revenue. It is therefore important that taxes be applied to productive sources. There is no point in complicating the system by the addition and use of taxes that have little individual potential for yielding revenue in substantial amounts. Nuisance taxes that provide only minimum revenue should be avoided as much as possible in the taxing system of any level of government.

Progressive Versus Regressive Taxes

The proportional, progressive, and regressive features of taxes should be considered in devising or improving a tax system. Taxes should involve at best the defensible characteristic of being progressive; at worst, they should be proportional. Ideally, they should never be regressive; practically, they often contain regressive features. All taxing devices should be constructed to reduce their regressive features as much as possible. High incomes should never pay lower rates than lower incomes, if we assume that the taxing system should be based on the ability-to-pay principle.

Tax Erosion Should Be Minimized

Tax erosion possibilities and provisions should be minimized or eliminated for every tax. For example, the deserving veteran and the worthy widow or homesteader may well deserve pecuniary benefits from government, but they should be provided by government in some other form than exclusion from property-tax-paying obligations. Erosion of the tax base, regardless of the worthiness of the cause, entails more problems than it solves. Special pleadings and other avenues of escape from tax paying should be reduced to a more defensible base by tighter laws and better enforcement practices. Estimates by some tax authorities of the amount of such tax base erosion have amounted to as high as one-fourth of the total real property value in the United States. The effect of such tax losses on schools and other government agencies and institutions that depend on tax revenues for their operation is obviously great.

A tax system should avoid or minimize preferential tax treatment sometimes offered to attract individuals or businesses to a state or community. Experience indicates that the differences in initial tax burden are usually relatively minor factors in influencing the locating of businesses and industries. More important, perhaps, is the quality and the quantity of public services—especially education—that are available for the employees of those companies seeking a new location. On the other hand, it is obvious that the tax system should not be oppressive to the point where it discourages new industry.

Taxpayer Convenience Is Important

It is generally believed that taxes should be direct rather than indirect. The taxpayer should know when he is paying a tax, and he should be able to do so as conveniently as possible. Paying hidden or indirect taxes, standing in long lines to pay taxes, and being aware of those who have escaped similar tax payments are examples of practices that demoralize many otherwise conscientious taxpayers. Fairness and courtesy in collecting taxes and in dealing with tax problems must characterize any successful taxation structure.

Collection Costs Should Be Low

To the extent possible, taxes that are used should have a relatively low collection and administrative cost. Governmental institutions are interested in amount of net revenue available to them rather than gross amount of dollars collected. This point is adequately illustrated in the fact that the high cost of locating, assessing, and eventually collecting— especially when delinquent—personal property taxes has been such that most of the states and other governmental taxing units have either minimized or eliminated this potentially excellent source of tax revenue.

Taxes and Services Should Be Visible

One of the common comments of taxpayers is that they cannot see what value they are receiving for the taxes they pay. Too often, they appear to take the services of government for granted. It is a proper function of government and its institutions to make taxpayers aware that their payments are contributing to the necessary and important services of government that they have demanded. Theoretically, this makes them much less demanding of such services and increases their demand for operational efficiency.

Tax Shifting Should Be Minimized

The tax system of any unit of government should be such that tax shifting possibilities are minimized. To the casual observer it would seem that taxes are paid by the person on whom they are imposed and that it would be an easy matter to add taxes on any group in society or drop them therefrom. This would mean that if property owners or wage earners were not being taxed to their fair share of bearing the burdens of governmental services, the correction could be made by additional taxes on property in the first case or by increased income taxes for the wage earners. The impact of the tax would appear to be at the intended point. But this reasoning ignores the complex and popular device of tax shifting—passing the tax burden to someone else. In the first example, the property owner shifts the increased tax to the renter in the form of increased rent; the second example often finds the wage earner demanding highes wages, with the result that the increased tax is paid by the employer. In neither of these examples does the tax shifting stop at the point intended.

Shifting taxes to the point that the impact of a tax (point of tax imposition) is different from the incidence of that tax (person who finally pays the tax) makes taxation extremely delicate and difficult to regulate. In far too many instances, it may result in overtaxation of some groups and undertaxation of those groups or persons who can successfully shift some or all of their tax burdens to others.

Earmarked Taxes Should Be Minimized

Earmarking or dedicating tax revenues to a particular purpose should be avoided as much as possible. Such earmarking provides for too much rigidity in the budget practices of the receiving institution. Under such regulations, the minimum expenditure tends to become the maximum, thus depriving administrative boards of the flexibility of movement so necessary in publicly controlled organizations. On the other hand, designating the use of some taxes based on the benefit principle is justifiable, as when a gasoline or motor fuels tax is earmarked for the maintenance of streets and highways.

Tax Structure Should Avoid Restrictions

Taxes sometimes generate effects that may seriously change the economic practices of the individuals who pay them. The intent of taxation is to divert private funds into the public sector to produce necessary goods and services; it is not its purpose to alter the behavioral patterns of taxpayers.

Superhigh taxes on certain commodities or services may destroy their competitive potential in the market or reduce their economic productivity. This violates a fundamental concept of taxation, for the tax on a desirable economic good should never be such that its more favored competitor has free and easy access to a noncompetitive market.

Neither should the taxing pattern unduly restrict an individual in determining his economic behavior in earning a living or in choosing the goods or services he desires to obtain to satisfy his needs or wants. Nor should the taxing system be such that it stifles or creates a desire to restrict production of economic goods and services by individuals or organizations. In short, the taxing pattern should be such that its impact has the least possible negative effect on the living style of its contributors and the greatest possible positive effect in developing and achieving the goals of the agencies and institutions it is constructed to serve.

CRITERIA FOR EVALUATING TAX STRUCTURE

McCann and Delon emphasized certain criteria for evaluating a tax system and the governmental structure necessary to administer it.[18] The characteristics that they rated important in any tax system include efficiency, equity, adequacy, and adaptability. By *efficiency,* they referred to the structure for fiscal administration, which is best when operated with the least economic and social costs and which provides the highest order of services for the money spent. They used the term *equity* to mean that the best structure is one that supplies the highest degree of fairness in the treatment of the individual citizen. The criterion of *adequacy* indicates that the system ought to provide enough funds to support the level of public service that is adopted for the particular governmental agency in question. By *adaptability,* they meant that any system that provides for the administration of a program of school finance ought to be adaptable to (1) changing economic conditions, (2) modified social demands for education, and (3) significant changes in education.

Taxpayers themselves are constantly evaluating the tax system to which they are responsible. While they usually do not formally rate all the individual segments of the structure, they have a practical way of making their opinions known concerning the total tax pattern. School administrators know all too well what will happen to their appeals for increased taxes when the public view is that they are already high enough. Citizen evaluation of the taxes required for governmental services often results in lost elections for bond and even current expenditure levy questions. Taxation cannot be pushed to a point beyond the limit

---

18. Lloyd E. McCann and Floyd G. Delon, "Governmental Structure for School Finance," in Gauerke and Childress, *Theory and Practice of School Finance,* pp. 90–93.

of taxpayer acceptance. Benson refers to the "normal" as well as the "absolute" limits of taxation in the following:

> During any period of relative stability in a society, certain "normal" levels of taxation are extremely difficult to breach. Such conventional levels of taxation should never be confused with absolute limits. For any major tax instrument an absolute limit to yield does not in the practical sense exist. In a major social upheaval, such as a war, the conventional limits of taxation are likely to be discarded. After the period of upheaval has passed, the volume of nonemergency public services is more likely to expand and absorb the revenue than are tax rates to fall to their former levels.[19]

FUTURE TAX PATTERNS

Certain trends in taxation have come to the front in the 1970s. In view of the current school financial crisis and the uncertainty of future court rulings on such problems, the duration of many of these trends cannot be predicted for more than the immediate future, however. In the light of the present tax structure and economic conditions, it seems likely that the following will be some of the chief characteristics of future taxation patterns to provide revenue for public education.

1. Although real property taxes will continue to be the main source of local revenue for schools, the future of this important local tax is in doubt. Recent court decisions and those yet to come, accompanied by the thrust in some states toward full state funding of education, make it impossible to predict the future role of property taxation.

2. The administration of property taxation will continue to improve and will receive increased emphasis so long as this form of taxation has an important role in financing education. Some areas of potential property tax improvement are suggested in the following:

> Practices and proposals for partial exemption of property from taxation should be critically scrutinized. . . . On the other hand, it may be desirable to remove broad classes of property (personal tangible and intangible property) from this tax base for taxation under a new tax designed as a fairer measure of tax-paying ability. . . . Many states place unduly restrictive limits on local property-taxing powers. The state should not arbitrarily limit the rates which a board of education and the people of a community may levy on taxable property for the financing of current

19. Benson, *Perspectives on the Economics of Education,* p. 160.

expenses for schools. . . . Some states are taking steps to correct these conditions by increasing the tax limits or by basing limits on full value of property.[20]

3. Earmarked (dedicated) taxes will probably continue to decline in importance, but not to the point of complete elimination.
4. Greater stress will likely be placed on the discovery and utilization of new sources of tax revenue. Although much greater revenue is a necessity for financing public education, many of the main sources of tax revenue have already reached a point of saturation and normal limits.
5. Sales (including use) and income taxes will become a more important part of tax structure in most states. In a few states, only the most meager beginning has been made in the defensible use of these two excellent sources of revenue.
6. The investment and economic benefits derived from spending tax revenues for education will be emphasized and their "cost" will receive some deemphasis in the years ahead. Taxing systems will receive less opposition after they have better built-in equity and as the public better understands the investment features of education.
7. The role of the federal government in financing public education will continue to be debated and probably will be stabilized at a higher level than at present. The partnership relationship of the local, state, and federal units of government will be emphasized, with an expected increase in the role of the latter and a decided decrease in the role of local government.
8. The financial relation between the states and nonpublic schools will continue to offer opportunity for debate and honest difference of opinion concerning this highly controversial matter. Without financial assistance for the public treasury, the nonpublic schools will likely decline in number and importance nationally. Whatever decline ensues will represent additional educational expenditures and corresponding pressures on the tax structure organized to operate the public schools.
9. The taxing system and state financial programs will have to be altered to help solve the overburden crisis that now almost overwhelms our big cities and metropolitan areas. Overdue relief measures will be discovered and practiced to extend the benefits of equal educational opportunity to more of our citizens dwelling in urban areas.
10. Taxation will be pushed to the point where it will seem to be

20. *What Everyone Should Know About Financing Our Schools* (Washington, D.C.: National Education Assn., 1966), p. 39.

either unwise or impossible to go further. This may result in raising the so-called normal limit of taxation until it approaches an absolute limit.

Selected Readings

Benson, Charles S. *The Economics of Public Education,* 2nd ed. Boston: Houghton Mifflin Co., 1968.

Cohn, Elchanan. *Economics of State Aid to Education.* Lexington, Mass.: Lexington Books, D. C. Heath and Co., 1974.

Coons, John E.; Clune, William H. III; and Sugarman, Stephen D. *Private Wealth and Public Education.* Cambridge, Mass.: Belknap Press of Harvard University Press, 1970.

Financing Education: Who Benefits? Who Pays? Washington, D.C.: National Education Association Committee on Educational Finances, 1972.

Grubb, W. Norton, and Michelson, Stephan. *States and Schools.* Lexington, Mass.; Lexington Books, D. C. Heath and Co., 1974.

Johns, Roe L., and Morphet, Edgar L. *The Economics & Financing of Education.* 3rd ed. Englewood Cliffs, N. J.: Prentice-Hall, 1975.

O'Connor, James. *The Fiscal Crisis of the State.* New York: St. Martin's Press, 1973.

Pincus, John, ed. *School Finance in Transition.* Cambridge, Mass.: Ballinger Publishing Co., J. B. Lippincott Co., 1974.

Reischauer, Robert D., and Hartman, Robert W. *Reforming School Finance.* Washington, D.C.: The Brookings Institution, 1973.

Unit 2

EDUCATION: A THREE-LEVEL GOVERNMENT ENTERPRISE

The American public school system is a complex partnership with responsibilities distributed among the three levels of government. . . . The effectiveness of this partnership depends upon the wise assignment of educational responsibilities so that the special strength of each level of government is fully utilized and its inherent weaknesses compensated for. Moreover, each partner must perform his duties without interfering unnecessarily with the essential contribution of the other two partners.

American Association of
School Administrators,
1965

4

Education: A Decreasing
Local Responsibility

The long-standing tradition of local control of education remains a strong and virile force in American life. Many citizens view their closeness to and power over the educational scene as a last frontier of local influence in a world where trends toward centralization and standardization are in evidence everywhere. In the face of such changes, the average citizen clings proudly and tenaciously to localism in our public schools. He values his importance as a citizen in the selection of board members, in the voting for or against levies and bond issues, and in his right for personal evaluation of the achievements of his schools.

At the same time, he feels a degree of helplessness and inability to influence state legislatures; the federal government he envisions as being far beyond his horizon of influence. Thus, he protects and holds firmly to his individual commitment to local control of education. He accepts with pride its accomplishments when it excels and faults himself and his community when it falls short, or fails to compare favorably with similar schools elsewhere. In his pride for his school he often loses sight of the high price that must usually be paid for maintaining small districts and small attendance areas. He tends to evaluate the school in terms of what they were when he was in school and often turns a doubting ear or a closed mind to the potential virtues of school reorganization and consolidation.

LOCAL CONTROL: CHALLENGES
AND CHANGES

The increasing financial support of local school districts by the various states in recent years, with attendant increases in state controls and standards, has brought an accelerating challenge to our traditional concept of local control of education.

Nyquist noted the trend toward less local and more state use of power in decision making in public education:

> Many factors . . . have a central thrust that is forcing a redistribution of decision-making power in American education and reshaping educational leadership. This decision-making power is: (1) rising vertically to higher levels of government (regional, state, and federal) and is therefore becoming more centralized, and (2) paradoxically, is being dispersed laterally, voluntarily or involuntarily, to other groups, lay, professional, and civil. In short, the forces behind these trends and concepts strongly suggest that: (1) the traditional concept of local control in education is becoming increasingly mythical, and (2) either the local school superintendency and the . . . state department of education and state superintendency as traditionally perceived are obsolete, or that many school and state superintendents are obsolete, and what we are witnessing is a redefinition of professionalism at these levels.[1]

Decreasing Rural Influence on Education

Throughout the history of American legislative action, legislators representing rural areas have often dominated or controlled the lawmaking bodies of the states. Disproportionate representation in at least one branch of the legislature was usually given to small towns, counties, and sparsely populated areas, as compared with the representation given to large towns, cities, and metropolitan areas. With property taxes bearing a major portion of school costs, rural legislators and rural school board members tended to be conservative and reluctant to provide the funds necessary for satisfactory or optimum school programs. The reapportionment of the membership of state legislatures in the 1960s to meet court demands of "one-man—one-vote" reduced the relative legislative power of rural areas and increased that of cities.

Although cities have gained in their representation in legislative bodies, they have lost their economic advantage in the operation of schools. When property taxes were the main source of school revenue and when state allocations were minimal, city school districts usually enjoyed certain revenue advantages. City school boards were usually less vocal in their opposition to property tax increases for education than their rural counterparts. As a consequence, city schools generally

1. Ewald B. Nyquist, "State Organization and Responsibilities for Education, in *Emerging Designs for Education* (Denver: Designing Education for the Future, May 1969), p. 135.

outdemonstrated their rural neighbors in providing good education. City schools became the leaders in administrative efficiency and in achievement in the public schools.

In recent years, however, the pattern has changed. Gradual changes in the socioeconomic makeup of our larger cities, with consistent emigration of the more affluent to suburbia, have resulted in cities losing much of their previous financial advantage. Legislative bodies that once faced the formidable problem of financing small rural schools equitably now face a larger problem in providing adequate and equitable revenue for large city districts with their constantly increasing tax problems caused by what has become known as municipal overburden.

School District Size: A Modern Dilemma

The number of school districts in this country reached the staggering total of 127,649 in 1932. Fortunately, much progress has been made in reducing the number since that time. As might be expected, reorganization of school districts proceeded at a snail's pace in its early history. However, improvements in the laws providing for such mergers did much to accelerate the process, especially during the 1940s and 1950s. Nebraska, Illinois, Texas, and California continue to have more than 1,000 independent school districts. Michigan, New York, Missouri, Oklahoma, New Jersey, Pennsylvania, Ohio, and Montana have more than 500. (See Figure 4.1)

In the past, most of the problems of school district reorganization were concerned with combining small districts into larger ones to improve the educational opportunities for children and at the same time provide a broad tax base, reduce variations in the tax-paying ability of districts, and provide some degree of stabilization, equity, and satisfactory management of funds. Recently, however, the problem of decreasing the size of some large metropolitan school districts has received much attention, especially in such cities as New York and Chicago.

The traditional argument that large school districts allow greater economy in the operation of schools may easily be overemphasized. Quite often the funds saved in some aspects of the programs are spent to enrich or extend educational services—one of the main reasons for combining the districts in the first place. The argument that reorganization will save educational dollars, which may appeal to some taxpayers as a possibility for tax relief or reduction, often falls of its own weight. Instead of saving school tax money, reorganization usually results in a better school program, with little if any reduction in cost. However, reduction in the number of school districts will usually result in some

FIGURE 4.1. Number of Basic Administrative Units (Operating School Districts), 1972–1973.

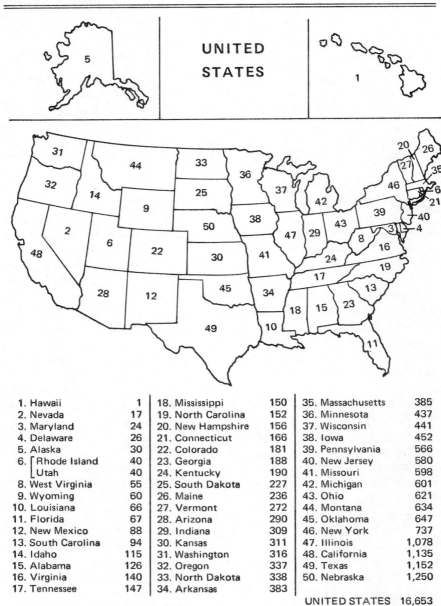

1. Hawaii	1	18. Mississippi	150	35. Massachusetts	385
2. Nevada	17	19. North Carolina	152	36. Minnesota	437
3. Maryland	24	20. New Hampshire	156	37. Wisconsin	441
4. Delaware	26	21. Connecticut	166	38. Iowa	452
5. Alaska	30	22. Colorado	181	39. Pennsylvania	566
6. ⎡ Rhode Island	40	23. Georgia	188	40. New Jersey	580
⎣ Utah	40	24. Kentucky	190	41. Missouri	598
8. West Virginia	55	25. South Dakota	227	42. Michigan	601
9. Wyoming	60	26. Maine	236	43. Ohio	621
10. Louisiana	66	27. Vermont	272	44. Montana	634
11. Florida	67	28. Arizona	290	45. Oklahoma	647
12. New Mexico	88	29. Indiana	309	46. New York	737
13. South Carolina	94	30. Kansas	311	47. Illinois	1,078
14. Idaho	115	31. Washington	316	48. California	1,135
15. Alabama	126	32. Oregon	337	49. Texas	1,152
16. Virginia	140	33. North Dakota	338	50. Nebraska	1,250
17. Tennessee	147	34. Arkansas	383		

UNITED STATES 16,653

Note: Basic administrative unit: the local school district, the unit for the operation of elementary and secondary schools or for contracting for school services.

Source: National Education Association, *Rankings of the States, 1973*, Research Report 1973 R-1 (Washington, D.C.: The Association, 1973), p. 15. Reprinted by permission of NEA. Data from NEA, *Estimates of School Statistics, 1972–73*, p. 24.

subtle, but important and relevant, improvements in financing education, such as:

1. The range in local ability to pay for education in the wealthiest as compared with the poorest district (as measured by the assessed value of taxable property per pupil to be educated) will be reduced.
2. State support formulas can be simplified and greater equality of educational opportunity for all school pupils can result as the number and kinds of administrative units are reduced.
3. Larger school districts make possible greater efficiency in the expenditure of funds (but do not guarantee it) in nearly all categories of the maintenance and operation of schools, but particularly in administration, instruction of pupils, and purchasing of supplies and equipment.

Merrill noted that the most important reason for school district reorganization—as far as school finance is concerned—is that it creates an improved and more equitable tax base:

> In view of the cost of education, the financial bases for school support become a cause for reorganization. Reorganization *per se* may result in noticeable, but seldom extensive, economies; it will usually, however, provide an improved tax base and a much better use of tax money for the support of schools. Of all the reasons for reorganization, this is the easiest one for the public to appreciate.[2]

"Unless we are willing to make dramatic changes in school system organization—both in the largest and the smallest districts—the chances of moving the educational programs of these districts effectively into the mainstream of the changes demanded by the society of the 1980s remain extremely small—no matter how careful the planning for change or how innovative the changes themselves."[3] In recent years, spiraling costs and the constantly increasing inadequacy and weakness of property taxation practices have forced many states to take a more realistic view of their financial obligation to public education. Whenever this is done, the idea of reducing the number of school districts to a more nearly optimum number is revived and debated.

Each state has hitherto been free to determine the kind and number of local school units or districts that can be operated within its own boundaries. Through the years, the number of such districts within a state has varied from approximately 12,000, in Illinois a quarter of a century ago, to one, as now functioning in Hawaii.

2. E. C. Merrill, "School District Reorganization: Implications for Financial Support," in *Trends in Financing Public Education* (Washington, D.C.: National Education Assn., Committee on Educational Finance, 1965), p. 113.
3. Kenneth H. Hansen, "Planning and Change," in *Cooperative Planning for Education in 1980* (Denver: Designing Education for the Future, January 1968), p. 75.

The arguments concerning relative costs and quality of education in large, medium, and small school districts are still being debated in some parts of this country. Most informed students of educational administration recognize some relation between the costs of education and the organizational pattern of schools and school districts the state operates. There are some principles concerning small and large schools that have become accepted as a result of the experience of the several states over the years.

1. Maintaining a small school district with only one or two small attendance areas is indefensible in terms of aims and objectives of present-day education. This does not rule out the obvious fact that some small schools and districts will always be needed in some sparsely populated areas of this country.
2. Small school districts and small attendance areas are comparatively inefficient and often represent an unnecssary waste of tax funds.
3. Small schools suffer from curriculum limitations, even if the wealth of the district makes it financially possible to employ proportionately more and better-trained school staff members.
4. Small schools are often unable to attract the best teachers, regardless of the wealth or the available revenues in those districts.
5. Small schools suffer from lack of special services, such as health, psychological and counseling programs. No amount of revenue can provide these services if there are not enough pupils to warrant them.
6. While largeness of school districts and attendance areas operating with adequate revenue provides the potential for an efficient and effective school system with a high quality educational product, it does not and cannot guarantee it.
7. Although the admitted advantages of large school districts over smaller ones are important and can usually be documented, decisions over such matters are nearly always made on the basis of the emotions of the people involved rather than the educational benefits that the school pupils will derive.
8. Even though we have too many small school districts, we likewise have some city districts and attendance areas that are too large and unmanageable. The problem of decentralization must be faced in some city districts at the same time that centralization is being emphasized in many other areas.

The Changing Role of Local School Boards

Although few people question that the role and importance of local school boards in controlling the operation and financing of schools have changed in the last few years, complete agreement does not exist about the causes of this change. As the federal government has extended its financial assistance to schools, its influence over local districts has increased. As the several states have increased state monies to school districts and as they have increased curriculum requirements, certification requirements, levy limitations, and other related requirements, the powers and duties of local school boards have been correspondingly eroded and usurped. Thus, in the opinion of many, the traditional philosophy and practice of localism has become suspect and is in need of change.

The problems of education can no longer be considered as only local. Improved transportation and increased mobility of people have changed the status of local responsibility for education, as indicated by James.

> Presumably many of the demands for financial support formulated by city school boards will be appropriately directed to the Congress, on grounds that urban populations are mobile, and the national interest dictates large expenditures for improving pools of potential manpower which may not benefit the local economy in the short run, but will benefit the nation in the long run.[4]

Some of the typical problems faced by local boards of education—including problems related to separation of church and state, providing equal educational opportunities for all students, including minority groups, and control of dissidents and incorrigibles—have been accentuated by a society that is constantly demanding additional services by government. On the other hand, boards of education find themselves subservient to new directives and the new rationale of the state and federal governments that attend their extended programs to alleviate poverty, extend educational opportunity, and push forward the frontier of new knowledge. All these conditions, plus the embryo proposal that seems to be gaining momentum that the states administer the collection and allocation of all funds for education, may seriously curtail the importance of local boards of education and need for them.

Local Control Not Guaranteed

State responsibility for education is guaranteed by the Tenth Amendment to the United States Constitution. Local control of schools has long

---

4. H. Thomas James, "Interdependence in School Finance" in *Interdependence in School Finance: The City, the State, and the Nation* (Washington, D.C.: National Education Assn. Committee on Educational Finance, 1968), p. 16.

been taken for granted, but there is no guarantee of the extent or the duration of such authority. Since power comes to local districts by delegation from the several states, it can be withdrawn at any time at the option of the delegating unit. Consequently, local school districts in each state have always operated somewhat tenuously at the pleasure of the state's legislature operating within the limits established by the state constitution. With the states gradually assuming more and more responsibility for financing education, the role of the local school district in its own governance has decreased commensurately. There is no indication that this trend is about to be reversed.

THE PROS AND CONS OF LOCAL FISCAL CONTROL

The question of the degree or extent of power local districts should have in the control of their own fiscal operations is a controversial and unsettled one. If the state provides most of the local school revenue, should it exercise more authority over local school districts than when it provides less? Do the advantages of local district control over their own fiscal operations counterbalance the disadvantages? These and other similar questions need to be answered in the several states as they continue to increase their proportionate share of public school revenues.

Excessive Reliance on Property Taxes

The property tax has not always been local; it has been used by some state governments and is still in use. It originated during America's colonial period as a selective tax on particular kinds and classes of wealth. Although for a century or more its base was increased until it included both real and personal property, the past one hundred years has seen a narrowing of that base with gradual elimination of personal property from tax rolls. Most of the states have discontinued or minimized the property tax at the state level, in favor of income and sales taxes. But local units of government, including schools, have found no substitute for this means of transferring funds from the private to the public sector of the economy.

With all its weaknesses and limitations, the real property tax has been the basic form of taxation for education at the local level of government, and it appears that it will continue to be. Even though taxes on tangible and intangible personal property have been used with varying degrees of success in some states, the real property tax continues to provide more than 95 percent of locally raised school revenue. However, as states—and more recently the federal government—have recognized and implemented their financial responsibility for education, the percentage of total school revenue (but not the amount) derived from local property taxation has decreased.

A quarter of a century ago, the school districts of this country claimed and received annually about one-third of the local property taxes collected. Even though this tax has been condemned by many tax and educational authorities, and even though the various states have to some degree restricted and denied its unlimited use, school districts now use approximately half of the local property tax revenues collected. They have displaced other units of government—cities and counties—as the principal recipient of such revenues. One of the results of this has been a popular opinion that the property tax is virtually a school tax. Higher property taxes—whatever the purpose or reason for their having been levied—often are considered to be solely attributable to public education.

Local control of education—even though strongly embedded in the American mind—has many limiting factors that thwart its purposes and mitigate its effectiveness. Limitations in providing equality of educational opportunity for all from local tax sources alone are evident in every state. Obtaining adequate local funds for education is complicated by at least two facts: (1) Local revenue is obtained almost completely from taxes on property—which is not a fair measure of the ability of people to pay; and (2) competition for the local tax dollar is becoming increasingly more severe. Most citizens are familiar with the arguments for improvement of local tax administration.

All local institutions and agencies have felt the increasing costs of government. Just as teachers need higher salaries, so do policemen, firemen, and other local governmental employees. Since local government can seldom go very far afield from a system of local property taxation, competition for these tax dollars has increased and probably will continue to increase. In the light of existing tax conditions, it is understandable that the local institutions and agencies, as well as the taxpayers, face almost overwhelming financial problems. Thus, complete local responsibility for financing education is unfair and impracticable and makes the American dream of equality of educational opportunity for all little more than a mockery.

States Limit Local Taxing Authority

The question whether or not a state may limit the power of voters at the local level to increase their taxes for public education has not yet been answered. About 70 percent of the states now operate their school finance programs with such a restriction. As a result of this limitation, wealthy districts can usually provide as good a program as they desire to pay for and still operate within the law. On the other hand, poorer districts are severely handicapped if they attempt to provide additional tax revenues with limited tax levies. Within recent years, a number of cases contesting state limitations on local tax rates have been before the courts.

At the local level, school district administration of the financial and instructional aspects of the educational program is largely legalistic. Actions of school boards and their employees must be within applicable statutory or other legal authority. Thus, no board of education may act to establish and finance any school program except as constitutional mandate, statute, or court decision provides the specifics or implied legal authority. The boards themselves, acting within this framework, may establish their own rules and regulations that have the force and power of law to govern the schools.

Inadequate and Unequal Resources

One of the most obvious weaknesses of local control of fiscal operations is that in nearly all states local school districts vary greatly in their access to taxable resources. They must, of course, depend almost completely on property tax revenues for financing education. In poorer districts—those with a low assessed valuation per pupil to be educated—local tax requirements place heavy budens on some property taxpayers with the result that citizen pressure to hold down tax rates may result in inadequate revenue for a good school program. Local school systems tend to become conservative and often refuse to inaugurate or operate higher cost programs regardless of their potential value or the unmet needs of students.

A big problem each state faces in providing equal educational opportunity for all of its citizens involves the extreme differences among its districts in ability to pay for education as measured by the assessed valuation of taxable property per student to be educated. One of the strong arguments favoring elimination of many small school districts in most states is that this range of differences in local ability would be sharply reduced by such a process—thereby simplifying the equalization formula to be used. When it is realized that the typical community in the United States derives more than half of its total school revenue for public education from local sources—particularly the property tax—the significance of wide ranges in local ability to support education becomes evident.

The wide disparities in the amounts of money available for the education of children and youth that continue to exist in the various states are a firm reminder of the unfairness of local financing of education with little or no state support. While it is true that the extremes in such inequities have been reduced in most of the states, the problem is still far from being solved. For example, in 1971–72, California's wealthiest district had fifty times as much local wealth per pupil as its poorest.[5] While intolerable this inequity was an improvement over the 10,000 to 1 ratio that existed in the same state in 1945,[6] or the 129 to 1 ratio that existed in an Iowa county in 1956.[7] Such imbalances in fiscal ability among the school districts within a state have been the cause of numerous court cases in most, if not all, of the states.

The negative effects of inadequate support for schools are most noticed by families of low income. Although affluent families may provide alternatives to a poorly supported school—such as sending their children to more adequately financed public schools, sending them to private schools, employing tutors, or purchasing additional supplies and equipment, no such alternatives are available to low-income families. As pointed out by Benson:

> Lower-income families are trapped in the public education system. Already saddled with heavy tax burdens to support public education, they cannot possibly afford leaving the public sector to find alternatives in private education. To be sure, private education can be an expensive alternative even for wealthier families, but at least it remains an option for them. For poorer families, there is no choice at all. . . . Wealthier families possess the economic and political power to assure them that their desires for educational services will be met. They may form exclusive residential communities providing the kind of public schools they want. They may dominate school boards and, therefore, affect the formulation of educational policy. They can afford private schools that provide the type of special attention they seek for their children.[8]

Keppel pointed to other differences between wealthy and poor districts. "The wealthier, better-staffed school districts are the ones with the language laboratories, science equipment, planetariums, mathematics laboratories, greenhouses, integrated textbooks . . . testing services, public address systems, and the like. It is not only that educational leaders with more original ideas serve in the wealthier districts, or that the less imaginative serve in poor districts, but rather the ability or lack of

5. *Financing the Public Schools* (Bloomington, Ind.: Phi Delta Kappa Commission on Alternative Designs for Funding Education, 1973), p. 18.
6. *School District Organization* (Washington, D.C.: American Assn. of School Administrators, 1958), p. 84.
7. Ibid.
8. Charles S. Benson et al., *Planning for Educational Reform* (New York: Dodd, Mead and Co., 1974), p. 96.

ability to buy is also a factor—for even salesmen and distributors steer clear of those districts with which they cannot 'do business.' "[9]

Erosion of Local Taxing Power

The local unit of government has lost much of its proportionate taxing power when compared with the other two levels of government, particularly the federal. In the late 1920s the federal government collected approximately one-third of the total of all taxes collected in the United States. By 1947, it collected three-fourths of the total. Since that time, the fractional part it collects has stabilized at about two-thirds, leaving the state and local units together to collect the other third. The state has increased its relative importance as a tax collector by enacting sales and income taxes, while the local unit has been able to add very little to the property tax—its only real source of tax revenue. This reversal of taxing power among the three levels of government represents a tremendous exclusion of funds not now subject to allocation for public education except as the federal government or the appropriate state government or both are influenced to make such provision.

Municipal Overburden

Most of the large city school systems in this country are now facing some degree of financial distress. Their tax bases are either declining or they are growing too slowly to meet the rapidly increasing costs of education. The financial plight of city school districts is much like that of rural districts a few years ago—unusual conditions that raise the costs of education beyond their ability to pay without additional state revenue. In most areas the rural problem has been "solved" by the use of sparsity factors in state finance formulas, but solutions have not yet been implemented for most large city school systems. Since the unfortunate plight of big city districts is a relatively new phenomenon, very little has been done to solve the problem.

Municipal overburden results from the fact that public schools and city governments must use the same property tax base to obtain the relatively large revenues required for their operation. The budgets of cities include large sums for noneducational public services such as police and fire protection and health services. The high percent of total city property taxes required to finance these services (as compared to the percent required in small city and rural areas) limits the property taxing power of city school districts for education.

9. Francis Keppel, *The Necessary Revolution in American Education* (New York: Harper & Row, 1966), p. 77.

Most large city school districts must provide education for large groups of high-cost students—minority groups, disadvantaged pupils, and handicapped pupils, many of whose parents migrated there in the hope of finding more satisfactory social and educational programs. The situation became more complicated and the tax burdens more accentuated as affluent inner-core city residents moved to the suburbs and were replaced with less affluent citizens who moved there in search of employment. Erosion of the tax base thus accompanied the increase in the need for governmental services including education. The high cost of these additional city social and educational services resulted in a higher burden on property taxpayers.

Cities, of course, have made attempts to overcome their problems of overburden. Some have overassessed certain types of property; some have adopted income taxes in order to involve suburban residents in paying part of city government costs; some have appealed to the state and federal governments for financial assistance. A few states have attempted to alleviate this condition by giving large city school districts additional student weightings or a density factor in their school finance formulas.

Until after World War II, the large city school districts maintained a well-earned position of leadership in education. They had more available resources, expended more money per pupil for education, and generally reacted more favorably to innovation and improvement. But the wheel has turned and we now face an appalling situation in most of our city schools. According to Knezevich:

> The plight of public education in large cities began to be dramatized in the years following World War II. The wealth of the big cities and the quality of their educational programs were the envy of rural and suburban schools during the last half of the nineteenth and the first half of the twentieth centuries. Then certain shifts occurred. The more affluent of the population moved to the suburbs, and in their place, the deprived and disadvantaged came to live in the core cities. Municipal services were added and expanded to help the immigrants to the city adjust to urban values and work their way out of conditions that approached poverty. The schools were faced with students of significantly different characteristics from those who previously had been served well. The many individualized and special services required increased greatly the costs of operation. Expenditures began to rise faster than enrollment increased. Development of superhighways and urban renewal projects moved property from the tax rolls to intensify problems of school finance.[10]

Thus, the financial advantages that most city school districts, if

10. Stephen J. Knezevich, *Administration of Public Education*, 2nd ed. (New York: Harper & Row, 1969), p. 426.

not all, enjoyed over their rural counterparts no longer exist. The favorable position of city districts that led to the formation of foundation programs to give greater financial strength to small districts has disappeared. This reversal has come as a result of the ever changing character of our cities, with their increasing needs and requirements to provide high-quality education for all their citizens regardless of race or color or any other contributing factors that might add to the cost of education.

A number of contributing factors relate directly to the overwhelming financial problems now in evidence in large city school districts in all parts of this country. Some of these include:

1. Conditions related to student militancy, student mobility, and integration problems have reversed the traditional trend for candidates for teaching positions to go to the cities where salaries were more favorable, where working conditions were better, and where individual initiative could more easily be directed to innovation and experimentation.

2. Problems dealing with the education of the socially and culturally deprived and also problems dealing with the physically and mentally handicapped are accentuated in city districts. Cities must deal with many of these problems, while rural school districts, because of lack of numbers, very often ignore or minimize them. The inequality engendered by this problem is accentuated by the great expense of these programs.

3. Increases in city property values have not kept pace with the rapidly accelerating increases in school expenditures. The movement of large numbers of middle- and higher-income people from the city core area to the suburbs has curtailed building needs, and hence property valuations have not risen in cities to the same extent that they have elsewhere.

4. The relative tax-paying potential of city school districts has been reduced by the migration of large numbers of low-income, deprived families to the cities. Large demand for compensatory education programs, great need for welfare programs, and the high cost of educating underprivileged and deprived citizens—now in a majority in many of our cities—have combined to downgrade the educational program and threaten the once favorable financial structure of our metropolitan area. The problem is relatively new, but one that has crept up on the American scene before its effect and its solution have been anticipated or resolved. According to Kelly, forecasting how cities will meet these challenges cannot be done with any accuracy:

> How well city school districts will meet the challenges they face cannot be forecast accurately, but without fundamental reform of state and local

fiscal structures, their future is less than bright. What is certain is that those responsible for financing city school districts are in the very center of the fray as this nation, magnificent in abundance and *munificent* in *ideology*, struggles in its city slums to save its own soul.[11]

The American Association of School Administrators noted the problems of our big cities in the following:

> The big city has been overtaken by new realities. The basic facts that pertain to the growth and changing character of the big city are well known. But the meaning of these facts is not always clear. The history of this country is being shaped in no small degree by what is taking place in the big cities. And evidence strongly suggests that education is a prime factor in determining whether the big city will satisfy the deep-seated desires of people; develop further as a cultural center; continue as a focal point of economic enterprise with full employment opportunities, rising levels of living, strong institutions, and a better life for the people or whether it will deteriorate; lose its attraction for people, business, and industry; and lead the way into cultural decline.[12]

Urban schools have sometimes suffered financially because of our state school finance formulas.

> Urban school systems have for years been handicapped by state finance programs based on unrealistic measures of educational need and of local effort. It should be recognized that many present programs have done much to raise the level of expenditure and quality of education in rural and suburban areas. But it is increasingly apparent that the provisions were incomplete; that they failed to recognize important factors which invalidate the idea that rough measures of school tax equality produce equality of educational opportunity. Especially harmful to cities (and to some other areas) was the failure of these formulas to recognize the heavy property tax load in these areas for purposes other than schools; the costs of compensatory education; concentration of special education services required, especially in cities; the lower income of city residents than of suburban residents (who often benefit greatly from equalization formulas); the tendency of assessors to undervalue rural property; and the failure to recognize the substantial funds received in lieu of taxes by some other units of government.[13]

School financing programs have long recognized the fact that small schools are generally more expensive per pupil than larger ones. To

11. *Financial Status of the Public Schools, 1968* (Washington, D.C.: National Education Assn. Committee on Educational Finance, 1968), p. 53.

12. *Imperatives in Education* (Washington, D.C.: American Assn. of School Administrators, 1966), p. 1.

13. Melvin W. Barnes, "Planning and Effecting Needed Changes in Urban and Metropolitan Areas," in Edgar L. Morphet and David L. Jesser, eds., *Planning and Effecting Needed Changes in Education* (Denver: Designing Education for the Future, June 1967), p. 215.

compensate for this, school finance formulas have usually included provisions for sparsity factors, which have been accepted as a necessary and fair requirement. Only recently, however, has serious consideration been given to the higher costs of education per pupil in large cities. The density factor in determining costs has not yet been accepted to the same degree as its older counterpart, the sparsity factor. The need for a solution to this financial inconsistency is immediate.

Local Nonproperty Taxes Are Ineffective

Accompanying the growing criticism and disillusionment of people with the property tax has been an increasing attempt by government to provide additional revenue for public schools from local nonproperty taxes. For a number of reasons, this effort has been to a great extent unsuccessful, except in a few large school districts: (1) School districts are not organized to lay and collect taxes; they rely on other units of government for this purpose. (2) Although school districts have fared better than other local institutions in receiving state financial aid in various forms, city and county governments enjoy a much more favorable position in obtaining the receipts from such nonproperty taxes as sales taxes, payroll taxes, and gross receipts taxes. (3) School districts are generally organized in units too small to make certain nonproperty taxes (such as a sales tax) effective; except in large districts, such taxes can be avoided by purchasing goods and services in neighboring communities that do not have such a tax. (4) The net effect of using nonproperty taxes is as disequalizing as the property tax; there is therefore little incentive for extension of such taxes at the local level. (5) The states, having left the property tax almost exclusively to local units of government, are forced to procure their revenues largely from nonproperty tax sources; this, to a great degree, excludes such tax revenue from local school districts.

Some tax and finance authorities have looked with much hope and expectancy at local nonproperty taxes, viewing them as a strong potential supplement to property taxes. Local sales taxes, income or earnings taxes, and others have been suggested and used in some communities for school purposes. Unfortunately, the revenues obtained and the inconvenience of collection, plus taxpayer resistance, have made these taxes of doubtful value in many school districts, especially in small cities or communities. Some larger city school districts have, however, used local nonproperty taxes satisfactorily.

Local nonproperty taxes became somewhat popular after World War II, especially in urban centers where the total populations were large enough to make such taxation practicable. Tax authorities who had expected good results from such taxes were disappointed in their application and in their ineffectiveness in smaller districts. Fiscally independent districts have benefited little from such taxes. Some districts, however, have received substantial amounts of money from tax sharing with the state or county in the application of some forms of nonproperty taxation—the sales tax, for example. Up to this time, nonproperty taxes have been so small in comparison with the total costs of education that they can be considered to be of little significance in the school finance structure of most school districts.

For those who may believe that nonproperty taxes may be an effective supplement to property taxes at the local level, the following statement is significant:

> There is no evidence whatever that the property tax will be supplanted by local nonproperty levies for the support of public education or for the support of other local government functions. Local nonproperty taxes have stabilized out at about 12 to 13 percent of all local government tax collections in recent years. Although additional levies will, of course, be enacted in specific jurisdictions from time to time and rates of existing levies increased, the relative contribution of these nonproperty revenues will surely continue to be modest.[14]

Altogether, the effect of nonproperty taxes on local school revenues has been minimal in most states. The value of this source of local school funds has never reached the potential envisioned for it by economists and school finance leaders in recent years. Although Pennsylvania realized almost a fifth of its school revenues from local nonproperty taxes in 1969, most other states have received much less from this source.

With the condemnation by the courts of many state school financing programs and the attendant thrust toward greater, or even full, state support for local public school expenditures, it appears that local nonproperty taxes will be reserved largely as sources of state revenue. At present, nonproperty taxes do not seem to have an encouraging future as a source of local school revenues.

Mobility and Local School Finance

> Crises of industry for skilled workers and the plaintive call of educators for additional support remain unheeded. The reasons for nonrecognition of legitimate needs of the whole nation are largely due to the antiquated machinery of school finance—centered on the local property tax—which for many reasons has proven its inability to meet the need and demand

14. H. Thomas James, in *Long-Range Planning in School Finance* (Washington, D.C.: National Education Assn. Comittee on Educational Finance, 1963), p. 95.

for educational opportunity by the people. It is time to decide that schools are not a purely state matter. The mobility of population demands state and federal concern for the lack of equality in educational opportunity. Measures must come from these levels to eliminate inadequacies resulting from local problems.[15]

The great mobility of our people has had much to do with our "unsolvable" problems of financing education. As the little red schoolhouse has faded out of the American picture, so has the extreme pride of citizens for a particular school decreased. The average citizen wants good schools wherever he goes—to a different district or to a different state. The effects of good and of poor education diffuse among the towns and cities of the land. It thus becomes evident that good education is a state responsibility and cannot safely be left to local communities working alone.

EFFECTS OF LOCAL DISTRICT INADEQUACY

The failure of numerous school districts to maintain full-year school programs in the years of the Depression is a matter of American historical fact. One can understand such failures in terms of the impotent economy of that time. On the other hand, it is a source of some embarrassment in this day of unprecedented affluence and economic aplomb to note that school districts still face the same problem—some of them without power to resolve it in the midst of America's much publicized economic virility. When some local districts are required to take unneeded "vacations" until local funds can be accumulated in large enough amounts to reopen their doors of learning, and when patriotic and loyal citizens voluntarily pay their taxes before they are due in order to keep their schools open, it is apparent that our local and state partnership plan in financing education in some of the states needs to be shored up and given greater strength and viability.

Some of the undesirable conditions which come as a result of inadequate resources are noted in the following statement:

> The horrendous conditions which can prevail in schools with inadequate resources have been thoroughly documented. It seems unjust indeed to provide some children with swimming pools and the range of activities of the wealthier suburban schools while other children receive inadequate

15. C. Jackson Salisbury, "The Theory of Taxation as Related to School Finance," in Warren E. Gauerke and Jack R. Childress, eds., *Theory and Practice of School Finance* (Chicago: Rand McNally & Co., 1967), p. 58.

shelter and lighting. Perhaps the productive value of schooling is not the sole criterion by which it should be judged.[16]

The difference between discrimination in education caused by unequal resources among districts and the discrimination caused by poverty and other social ills is noted by Coons:

> There is, however, an important difference between discrimination in public education and most of those other social ills we tend to associate with poverty. Crime, slum housing, illness, and bad nutrition are not the anticipated consequence of government planning. Discrimination in education, on the other hand, is precisely the anticipated consequence of the legislated structure of public education. Far from striving to overcome poverty's effects upon education, the state in structuring the system, has taken that poverty itself as the measure of quality in education. Such a system bears the appearance of calculated unfairness.[17]

ADVANTAGES OF LOCAL CONTROL

The local community and the local school district in the United States are far more influential in their relations to their own educational programs than their counterparts in other countries are. Our educational philosophy generally supports the belief that a large degree of local control not only stimulates local interest and support but also more easily permits innovations and improvements. The idea of strong national administrative control of education is repugnant to most of our citizens.

In certain ways the local districts have an advantage over the states and the federal government in obtaining additional funds for education. Those who have observed the long history of federal aid attempts point to the many years of indecision and frustration caused by the bitter debates involving problems of racial discrimination, separation of church and state, political jealousies, and the ever present fear of federal control. Immediate action at the federal level to shore up the finances of school districts appears to be a practical impossibility. Securing substantially increased funds at the state level meets the same situation as at the federal level. Political overtones and acute competition for state revenues often delay or even defeat proposals for providing additional school funds. Only recently have some states provided as much as 10 percent of the operating costs of public education.

16. W. Norton Grubb and Stephan Michelson, *States and Schools* (Lexington, Mass.: Lexington Books, D.C. Heath and Co., 1974), p. 10.
17. John E. Coons et al., *Private Wealth and Public Education* (Cambridge, Mass.: Belknap Press of Harvard University Press, 1970), p. 7.

Although the local level of government usually is least able to increase its tax effort, it is the only unit that has existing machinery to provide such an increase in a short time—with voter approval. Submission of tax increase proposals to voters for their approval or disapproval can be made and decisions reached in a relatively short period. Legislative action requires much more time and is unpredictable at best. The following, while not typical, is an example of how citizens at the local level can "solve" a problem of immediate concern while waiting for a more permanent and more satisfactory solution through the slow process of legislative action:

> Citizens and businesses in Fremont, Ohio, have paid their real estate taxes early this year in a unique move to keep the schools open. The Fremont school board had voted to close the schools from November 17 to January 2 because of a lack of funds. Voters turned down two proposed levies this year and although they finally approved one this month, the funds could not legally be collected until next year. A citizens' group, led by a local radio station owner, started the pay-your-taxes-early campaign which brought in more than $600,000. . . . Although Fremont's 7,200 students will not get the extended vacation they expected, 10 more school districts in Ohio have closed or will close soon and others are saying they will have to do the same thing next year if they don't get more money.[18]

The local district cannot afford to forego its natural money-raising advantage altogether in expectation of state and federal allocations and legislative solutions to financial problems. To let property tax levies rest comfortably at low levels with the hope of immediate tax relief from state and federal sources may very well be accompanied by disastrous results.

FISCAL INDEPENDENCE OF SCHOOL DISTRICTS

> School districts in most States are independent units of government—Maryland, North Carolina, Virginia, and Hawaii represent organizational exceptions. In these States, school systems are dependencies of general governments. In Hawaii, the general government is the State itself; in Maryland, the counties of Baltimore City; in Virginia and North Carolina, county and city governments. In all, about half the States have one or more school systems dependent upon units of general government but

18. *Education U.S.A.* (Washington, D.C.: National School Public Relations Assn., Nov. 24, 1969), p. 14.

these dependent school systems number only 1,608, almost half of which are in the New England States.[19]

The question whether or not the local school board should have autonomy within the law in the use of local tax sources and revenues is relevant in a discussion of local responsibility for education. As a group, educators almost universally favor fiscal independence of school boards. However, many in the fields of economics and political science argue in favor of the fiscally dependent district—one which places the local district board of education under some degree of jurisdiction by the city or county government. Usually this involves city or county approval of the school district's annual budget. Under this arrangement, city or county officials make final decisions for school budgetary requests, which are based upon deliberations of the board of education without the understanding or active participation of the municipal authorities involved.

According to Firman, the question of fiscal independence of school systems may be stated as follows: "Is it possible for a school board, especially in a municipality where expenditure pressure is severe, to have a viable fiscal responsibility without fiscal independence?"[20] He states further:

> Conventional budget theory holds that the ideal resolution of competing claims on revenue resources is best found when all claims on tax resources for any related group of functions are considered at one level of responsibility. The assumption here is that claims on tax resources have quantitative differences rather than qualitative differences.
>
> Such is not the case in education, however; and it is at this point that the professional educator has to part philosophical company with the political scientist and business administrator. The claims of education are clearly qualitative as well as quantitative. The schools cannot apply uniform specifications to their inputs, nor to their processes, nor to their products. They deal with human beings who are as variable in characteristics as they are numerous; and there is no place for more rejects in the human scrap pile.[21]

The relative numbers of school districts that are fiscally independent as compared with those that are dependent are indicated in the following:

> By far the majority of the school systems in the United States are fiscally independent, with powers of taxation and expenditure separate from

---

19. *State Aid to Local Government* (Washington, D.C.: Advisory Commission on Intergovernmental Relations, April 1969), p. 34.

20. *Trends in Financing Public Education* (Washington, D.C.: National Education Assn. Committee on Educational Finance, 1965), p. 117.

21. Ibid.

other local government. Only 2,347 of the 37,025 school systems in 1961–62 were classified as "dependent," i.e., fiscally dependent upon another government such as a city, county, town, or township. Yet, in 1960 the school systems of five of the biggest cities (500,000 and over) and 32 in the 100,000–499,999 range were "dependent."[22]

The proponents of fiscal independence for school districts and the proponents of fiscal dependence usually offer the following separate arguments as the main reasons for supporting their positions:

For Fiscal Independence
1. Assures fiscal responsibility.
   (Those who determine budget needs also determine budget revenue sources.)
2. Tends to keep schools from partisan politics.
   (School boards are not usually involved in party politics; city and county governmental officials are.)
3. Retains education as a state function.
   (The school board is responsible to the state—not to the city or county unit of government.)
4. Lessens competition among governmental agencies for the tax dollar.
   (The school board can determine its tax levy without competing with other agencies.)
5. Assures more money for education.
   (On the average, these districts spend more money per pupil than fiscally dependent ones. Reviewing agencies often reduce school levies but seldom increase them.)

For Fiscal Dependence
1. Have greater access to nonproperty tax revenue.
   (Cities have had more power to use nonproperty taxes than schools have had.)
2. Tends to coordinate the services of all government agencies that depend on property-tax revenues.
   (Reviewing agencies tend to look for, and correct, duplications of effort among all governmental services.)
3. Tends to emphasize the school's responsibility to local rather than state government.
   (Such a practice seems to reinforce our philosophy, which supports local control of education.)
4. A single board or branch of government controlling all tax-supported agencies or institutions encourages the weighing of the relative value or merit of each component part.

22. Robert E. Mason, "Decline and Crisis in Big-City Education," *Phi Delta Kappan* 48 (March 1967), p. 309.

(Education cannot be affluent at the same time that county or city government is poverty-stricken, and vice versa.)

Fiscal independence of school districts is not always complete; some districts have only relative degrees of freedom and autonomy. Firman listed eight practical tests to determine the degree of independence of a school system:

- *Budget.* The board of education has the power to establish a budget for the ensuing school year.
- *Taxing power.* The board of education has the power to levy taxes needed to meet the budget.
- *Adequacy.* The board of education has an adequate tax base within the school district for providing the local share of education cost.
- *Limits.* If legal requirements set limits for a tax rate and/or indebtedness of the school district, the maximum limit is sufficient to permit raising the amount required for the support of schools.
- *Leeway.* If constitutional limits are placed upon tax leeway and/or indebtedness for schools, the limits are sufficiently high to permit the board of education to engage in realistic, long-term planning, at least for five years ahead.
- *Accounting.* The board of education has the right to spend funds within the total amount of the budget, to keep its own books of account, and to provide for adequate auditing and reporting of revenue and expenditures.
- *Responsibility.* Citizens and staff deal with only one local body, the board of education, in every appeal related to education and its support and control; in presenting ideas, making requests, asking for information, and questioning policies and decisions.
- *Response to educational needs.* The fiscal powers of the board of education are sufficiently adaptable and flexible to permit the adjustment of educational plans to changing situations and emerging needs.[23]

McCann made a study of the broad ranges of intergovernmental control of public education. He noted that "the usual consideration of fiscal autonomy is too narrow since other agencies do in fact control the financial actions (especially expenditures) of school authorities in specific ways."[24] His study produced data to show that court decisions, competing laws, and the mores connected with governmental operation had tended to neutralize any ill effects of fiscal independence of schools.

---

23. *Trends in Financing Education*, pp. 117–18.
24. Lloyd E. McCann, *Legal Problems in the Administration of Education by Educational and Non-Educational Government Agencies.*

TRENDS IN LOCAL TAXATION PRACTICES

While many hope for relief for local property-tax-payers with an increase in the state and federal revenues for education, present practices and trends indicate that:

1. Property tax administration will be improved, and even though tax-payer resistance against such taxes increases, the property tax will continue to be an important source of funds for operation of our public schools. Professionally trained career assessors, more realistic laws concerning property tax administration, the establishment of larger taxing districts to encourage specialization in tax administration, more adequate and efficient state supervision of the program, and more effective communication between those who administer the tax program and those who pay the taxes—all are reasonable improvements that logically can be expected in the near future.
2. Competition among local agencies for the tax dollar will continue to increase; schools will succeed in this competitive arena only as they are able to prove the quality and importance of the educational product that they produce.
3. The urban communities will continue to suffer most from revenue needs unless given preferential treatment in local, state, and federal allocation of funds.
4. Efforts will be made to make the property tax less regressive and to relieve those who suffer economically from too much emphasis on this kind of taxation. In states that leave the financial responsibility of education almost completely up to the individual local districts, some property-tax-payers often have justifiable cause for complaint.
5. Property tax rates will generally be kept at near maximum or normal limits because of certain political factors that indicate less taxpayer reaction to increases in this form of taxation than to increases in most other kinds. This was indicated by Shannon in the following:

> When it comes to raising tax rates, local property tax policy-makers do not appear to be hedged in by as many political barriers as in the case for their counterparts at the state level. There are several factors responsible for this situation.
>
> First, because of the widespread diffusion of responsibility for the setting of local property tax rates, it is usually difficult for property owners to single out the person or persons directly responsible for the decision to increase the property tax. . . .
>
> Second, the system of political sanctions appears to operate more rigorously at the state level. . . .
>
> Third, due largely to the absence of an alternative method for raising revenue, a decision to raise a local property tax does not precipi-

tate a bitter partisan debate between the spokesmen for labor and the spokesmen for management. . . .

Fourth, in sharp contrast to the relatively slow and steady rise in property tax rates, increases in state sales and income taxes are usually abrupt and dramatic. . . .

Fifth, property tax increases are more directly related to visible local public expenditure needs. . . .[25]

MEASURES OF LOCAL TAX-PAYING ABILITY

The ability of a local school district to pay the costs of education without state or federal support is a function of two variables—the value of taxable property and the number of pupils to be educated. This is usually expressed as the assessed valuation of taxable property per person in average daily attendance or in average daily membership in school.

For nearly a century, scholars and practitioners in school finance have been studying how to measure comparative abilities of local units of government to finance education and to provide other services. State equalization programs—particularly those involving power equalization—must be vitally concerned with some valid and reliable measure of local fiscal ability if state and federal allocations of funds to local districts are to be defensible.

Scholars have conducted extensive research in an attempt to refine the measures of local fiscal ability. Some of these studies, such as the Cornell study, combined a series of complicated and statistically treated procedures to determine local fiscal ability.[26] Other researchers, such as Mort and Burke, rejected the idea in favor of using only those resources and procedures that local districts have legal authority to use. There seems to be little justification for using a theoretically computed index of ability, but there is a strong rationale for using the ability as measured by the tax structure and system currently being used. Little is to be gained in comparing the abilities of school districts in terms of potential taxes and revenue that are not available to those districts. These are measures that may have real value in determining a state's ability to support education, since the state legislative body can make them

25. John Shannon, "Property Taxation: Toward a More Equitable, Productive Revenue Source," in *Trends in Financing Public Education*, pp. 137–38.
26. Francis G. Cornell, *A Measure of Taxpaying Ability of Local School Administrative Units* (New York: AMS Press, reproduction of 1936 edition).

available by statute; but their value in comparing local districts is limited and questionable.

LOCAL, STATE, AND FEDERAL TAX RESPONSIBILITY

A difficult problem arises in coordinating the taxing system of the three levels of government—federal, state, and local. The ideal, or even the most practical, combination of taxing powers and authority of these levels of government that will produce maximum social and cultural benefits with maximum taxpayer equity and minimum taxpayer burden and inconvenience has never been determined. To a very great extent these three units of government operate their tax patterns in isolation from each other. Ideally, their taxing systems should be coordinated. The elements of taxation that are usurped to some degree by any one unit of government would seemingly be sources beyond the powers of the other two units to use. But adequate funds must be provided regardless of source if good education is to be provided for all our citizens.

Traditionally, in most states the local school districts have had to raise the major part of the tax revenues required to finance their public schools. Reluctantly, the several states have assumed important but varying degrees of responsibility for financing education; but the federal government has fluctuated in its participation. For the most part, the latter has remained aloof from the problem, until recently. As the states and local districts approach the limits of their taxing power for education, they expect financial assistance from the federal government, with its broader tax base and superiority as a tax-collecting agency.

For a long time, the educational establishment has emphasized the potential role of the federal government in collection and distribution of tax revenue to states and local school districts. Federal support for a number of important public functions, such as agriculture, highways, housing, hospitals, and welfare, is taken for granted by the general public. However, the role of the federal government in financing education has not yet been determined. It is noteworthy that its taxing power has been strong enough so that it has been able to avoid high tax increases in recent years in spite of increased federal services to many agencies and institutions.

With the advantages the federal government has in collection of taxes, it is small wonder that educational and governmental leaders look to this unit of government as best equipped to come to the rescue of the public school systems of the several states with their inadequate financial bases and their accompanying tax overburdens. However, until a significant change occurs in the generally accepted philosophy of financing education, the principal responsibility for that activity will probably continue to rest with the states and their local units.

Selected Readings

Financing the Public Schools—A Search of Equality. Bloomington, Ind.: Phi Delta Kappa, 1973.

Hirsch, W. Z. *Financing Public First-Level and Second-Level Education in the U.S.A.* Unesco: International Institute for Educational Planning, 1973.

Hooker, Clifford P., and Mueller, Van D. *The Relationship of School District Organization to State Aid Distribution Systems.* Minneapolis: Educational Research and Development Council of the Twin Cities Metropolitan Area, 1970.

Interdependence in School Finance: The City, the State, and the Nation. Washington, D.C.: National Education Assn. Committee on Educational Finance, 1968.

Johns, Roe L., and Morphet, Edgar L. *The Economics and Financing of Education,* 3rd ed. Englewood Cliffs, N.J.: Prentice-Hall, 1975.

Knezevich, Stephen J. *Administration of Public Education.* New York: Harper & Row, 1969.

Levin, Betsy; Muller, Thomas; and Sandoval, Corazon. *The High Cost of Education in Cities.* Washington, D.C.: The Urban Institute, 1973.

Pincus, John A., ed. *School Finance in Transition.* Cambridge, Mass.: Ballinger Publishing Co., 1974.

State Aid to Local Government. Washington, D.C.: Advisory Commission on Intergovernmental Relations, April 1969.

5

Education: A Primary
Function of State Government

Education appears to have been considered important in early America largely because of its presumed preventive effect in fortifying its consumers to resist evil. Important as that purpose may have been, the rationale for the establishment and operation of schools has changed in the two hundred years of our existence as a nation. Education is now provided on the basis that it not only makes a contribution to the economy and growth of the country, but, more fundamentally, it is a constitutional right of all citizens. It is provided and required now because statutes and court decisions in the intervening years have placed a more humanistic interpretation on the meaning of equal protection as guaranteed and implied in the United States Constitution.

The individuals and events that have brought this country from a rather doubtful interpretation of governmental intent to provide education for its citizens to its present stress upon individual rights and government-guaranteed equal protection under the law are numerous indeed. They are the heroes, the heroines, and the heroic events that shaped the colorful history of this great country. But such progress and achievement came at a price. The popular figures of the history of American education often were not popular in their own time. Their contributions, so highly regarded today, often came at personal sacrifice, for the reforms they championed were often opposed by uncompromising and sometimes militant majorities.

CHANGING STATE RESPONSIBILITY

Establishing and operating a system of public schools has been recognized as a function of government rather than of private enterprise since the formation of the United States of America. Early Americans recognized the importance of education in building and maintaining a democratic government and in properly developing the individuals and organizations serving that government. The general tone of the early American leader toward schools and education was succinctly expressed in the now famous statement the Continental Congress proposed and included in the Northwest Ordinance of 1787: "Schools and the means of education shall forever be encouraged." The spirit of that declaration continues to be a part of the American ideal.

The present relation of government to education has evolved over two centuries. For the most part, the practical "partnership" of federal, state, and local levels of government has worked well, at least until recent years. Each state has been responsible for its own system of education, with power to delegate whatever degree of control it chose to local districts of the kind and number it desired. As a result, we have had fifty versions or interpretations of that relation in as many states. On the other hand, the federal government has been relegated to an advisory capacity with very little real authority over education.

The gradual development of local and state incapability of adequately supporting an ever expanding educational program, as well as the rather recent and dramatic cases of court condemnation of various state school finance systems, have brought about the current need for reconsideration and a new look at governmental responsibility for education. As pointed out by the American Association of School Administrators, "The partnership that has served America so well must now be reexamined in the light of changing conditions."[1]

Changes and innovations are part and parcel of the maturing education scene. The need for improvement of education is becoming more observable day after day and year after year. But how shall the course of the three-level governmental relation to education be determined? Is the stage being set for more state and less local responsibility for financing education? Have the traditional arguments favoring local control become obsolete? Should the federal government be pressed back into its shell of indifference and lack of serious responsibility for education, or should it be directed to become a full-fledged partner in the business of public education? These and many other problems suggest serious

1. *The Federal Government and Public Schools* (Washington, D.C.: American Assn. of School Administrators, 1967), p. 1.

consideration of the status quo as this nation moves forward to meet the imposing challenges which face it in the years ahead.

EARLY DEVELOPMENT OF STATE RESPONSIBILITY

Education is conspicuous by the lack of reference to it in the United States Constitution. The writers of that important document avoided specific prescription and designation of responsibility for the structure and pattern that formal education should take in this country. The reasons for such an obvious and important omission are presumed to have been: (1) Certain other needs of the newly formed states were more urgent at that time. (2) Many of the leaders of government presumed that a discussion of controversial educational responsibility might lead to an impasse, or at least add greatly to the already overwhelming problems about which there was great dissension. (3) The original thirteen colonies had already established their own patterns of school organization and had recognized and accepted their individual obligations for education, at least to some degree, by previous action and legislation during their colonial periods.

The Constitution should be interpreted and evaluated in terms of the unique conditions under which it was formed and adopted rather than in terms of its presumed deficiencies or its areas of emphasis or deemphasis. The United States of America was born as a legal entity after a period of stress and strain that resulted in the American Revolution. The colonies won that bitter conflict after almost superhuman effort and sacrifice on the part of many, but not all of their citizens. The founding fathers, recognizing and abetting their break with the philosophy of government of that day, were vitally concerned with how to establish perpetuity of government. They felt a need to avoid endowing the federal government with powers that might at some time overwhelm or overbalance the powers of the several state governments. This they hoped to achieve by delegation of certain powers to the federal government while strengthening the structure and framework of the individual states. Such an arrangement appears to have been wise and necessary to assure formal adoption of the Constitution by the thirteen individualistically oriented and mutually suspicious colonies destined to form the foundation of the new country.

It should not be assumed that all of the colonies were indifferent to education or had little interest in it. The establishment of Harvard in 1636, the Laws of 1642 and 1647, and the Ordinances of 1785 and 1787 are examples of their actions to provide for some important aspects of an educational program. Education had been at low ebb during the dark days of the Revolution with most of its control having been exerted by private schools, with only local community support and with little or no cooperative experiences among schools. The real battle for free public schools under colonial or state supervision had not yet even begun.

Undoubtedly, the framers of the Constitution believed that the governmental framework they were creating implied provision for education. James Madison proposed the establishment of a university. Thomas Jefferson advocated appropriations of public lands for education. George Washington pressed hard for a national university. With such support for specific aspects of education by these and other leaders of that time, few historians accept the opinion that education was not considered by the founding fathers.

Some of the deficiencies of the Constitution were evident as soon as it was adopted. It was apparent immediately that it did not protect individual rights to the extent expected or desired. Consequently, the first ten amendments were adopted in 1791 as the Bill of Rights. These, especially the Tenth Amendment, form much of the legal basis for our present system of education. The Tenth Amendment provides that "the powers not delegated to the United States by the Constitution, nor prohibited by it to the States, are reserved to the States respectively, or to the people." Thus, education has been and continues to be a function of state government. This responsibility is further documented by state constitutional provisions acknowledging and accepting this power, plus numerous court decisions supporting it.

State Interpretation of Educational Responsibility

The fifty states have not all accepted their educational challenge and obligation to sponsor education with the same degree of enthusiasm. Some have created large numbers of local districts and left most of the problems of education in the hands of local boards of education. Some have exerted very little administrative control or leadership over local units; others have developed an almost complete state school system. Although some of the states have accepted a large degree of financial responsibility for education, a few have almost completely ignored the problem at the state level.

The state school systems developed from local units. State responsibility for education was accepted in theory but little leadership at this level was in evidence until the forepart of the nineteenth century, when a few educational leaders, particularly Horace Mann and Henry Barnard, began their historic efforts to develop state leadership for education.

Local units of diverse sizes and philosophy dominated the American scene, as indicated in the following:

> It was not unnatural, during the days of the frontier, that education, though plainly enough a legal function of the state, should have been carried on with a very large measure of local operational discretion. The frontiersman disliked governmental restraint and found it especially odious when it touched a matter so personal and domestic as the rearing of his children. So long as these frontiersmen sent their children to school and did not press for financial assistance the most exacting state government was willing to let them alone.[2]

Thus, the story of the development of the fifty state school systems is a story of diversity, struggle, and dedication to an idea, the idea of a decentralized system of education without a national system or minister of education or any national control. Thurston and Roe described the situation well in the following:

> In tracing these developmental influences one is struck by the awareness that events and situations surely and inevitably seemed to be drawing this new country toward state-established universal free public education as the only logical solution which would correlate with a system of government based on the freedom and dignity of man. The struggle within the colonial government over the perplexing problem of localism and state rights versus national power shaped eventually our curious trilogy of educational control and cast the mold of our legal structure of education. The solution today seems natural—with the state maintaining legal supremacy and acting as the fulcrum to provide proper balance for the local community on the one side, where schools can be kept close to the people, and the national government on the other, where the general welfare of the nation can be safeguarded.[3]

The actions of many state legislatures in recent years point to the fact that they are taking a more serious attitude toward state school finance problems and their solutions. The Education Commission of the States reported that more than half of the states made changes and improvements in 1969 in their methods of allocating school funds. Increases in many kinds of taxes, establishment of minimum teacher salary schedules, passage of sales and income taxes, and increases in such taxes as the cigarette tax are examples of efforts made in some states to increase state financial responsibility for education. Much of the avowed purpose for such changes appears to have been efforts to relieve the inequities and overburden of property taxation at the local level.

The typical American citizen tends to think of our state school sys-

2. Lee M. Thurston and William H. Roe, *State School Administration* (New York: Harper & Row, 1957), pp. 137–38.
3. Ibid., p. 11.

tems as having existed as they now are from our beginning as a nation. They fail to recognize that our patterns of education, including our financial formulas and schemes, are the products of more than two centuries of development under a grass-roots process of building—a process that was often erratic and irregular. However, appreciation for these systems, with all their limitations, comes quickly to the conscientious student of educational history. Those who understand the contributions of such men as Washington, Jefferson, Franklin, Paine, Barnard, and Mann must share some degree of pride in our systems of education, which have made such rich contributions to this country during its 200-year existence.

Thus it seems that the omission of specific educational provisions from the Constitution has proved to have been wisdom on the part of those who were responsible for such an "oversight." Sound philosophy espousing decentralization, a willingness to involve people at the local level, and national patience have proved to be better developers of our state school systems than what could possibly have been planned by the foresight of earnest but unsophisticated and inexperienced educational and governmental leaders two centuries ago. From this process there emerged the best organizational pattern of education the world has yet produced.

DEVELOPMENT OF SCHOOL FINANCE POLICIES

The history of financing public school education in the United States is an interesting one. Actually, it is fifty separate stories of controversy, of fumbling, of false starts, of long periods of inaction, and of application of various forms and degrees of informal local and state action. In the early part of our history, most of the costs of school operation were defrayed with nonmonetary services provided by school patrons to the school itself or to the teacher. Provision for fuel, custodial services, board and room for the teacher, and other similar services were made in lieu of salaries, insurance, and fringe benefits.

As the schools grew in size and complexity, so did the problems and methods of financing them. These finance systems, and even the processes used to develop them, represent diversity and lack of standardization in the fullest meaning of those terms. Too often, the states profited little by the experiences of other states. Much too often, the states seem to have recognized variety as virtue and following the leader as vice. The lessons learned in one state seldom reduced the learning period required by taxpayers and professional leaders in another.

Land Grants and Other Nontax Funds

It is difficult to determine the exact beginning of state support for public education. Paul Mort reported that by 1890 the existing states provided about thirty-four million dollars—almost 24 percent of that year's total school revenue. Since some of that state revenue was obtained from land given to the states by the federal government in the famous Northwest Ordinance of 1787, Mort classified the state funds as state and federal funds.

Although the various states accepted responsibility for education rather readily, their acceptance of financial responsibility was slow in its development. Although the states generally provided means of legalizing local school taxes in their early statehood years, equalization and sound theories and practices of state-local partnership in financing education were developments of the twentieth century for the most part.

In the early history of the American colonies, land grants for the establishment and support of schools were somewhat common, especially in Massachusetts. As an example, out of the early pioneer work in the field of land grants by Massachusetts was to emerge the state of Maine. Other more or less popular sources of the limited funds used to establish and maintain schools in the colonies included gifts, rate bills, and lotteries. Before taxation became the accepted method of financing schools, most of the known and practical ways of collecting money were used in one or more of the thirteen colonies to obtain school funds. The early settlers of this country brought with them the traditions of their European homelands. Although these traditions embodied a close relation between church and state, they had little relation to practical and proven methods of financing decentralized schools as they began to emerge in America. Thus there followed a long period of conflict over how to solve this difficult and important problem.

In early America with its seemingly unlimited expanses of land and other valuable resources, it was natural that the granting of lands should become a significant reality in financing education. This policy reached a climax in the passage by the Continental Congress of the Northwest Ordinance of 1787. Primarily to stimulate migration to the West and secondarily to foster education, this law provided for the survey of the western lands and the reservation of section 16 of every township for education. Few would deny the efficacy of its purpose in its now famous statement, "Religion, morality, and knowledge being necessary to good government and the happiness of mankind, schools and the means of education shall be forever encouraged."

The land grants of 1787 became effective with the admission of Ohio to the Union in 1802. When California became a state in 1850, the grant included two sections per township. Arizona, New Mexico, and Utah received four sections per township on becoming states in the latter part of the nineteenth and early part of the twentieth centuries.

The effect of the land grants on education was monumental. However, the lands were mismanaged in some of the states; the funds obtained from the rent or sale of the land were sometimes squandered. As a consequence of gross mismanagement and inefficiency in many of the states, the potentially large revenues from this source were never fully realized. The same carelessness that characterized the use of our natural resources in much of the western migration of our people seemed to pervade the operation of the school land program.

The land-grant states relied to a great extent on the land grants to supply school funds until the end of the nineteenth century. Even though some people of that day considered these funds a way for financing education, that dream never materialized. The size of the grant was great, even in terms of the enormous expanses of unsettled territory of that day. Twelve states received one section per township; fourteen states received two sections; and three states received four sections per township. The thirteen original states received no federal lands, nor did Kentucky, Maine, Texas, Vermont, or West Virginia.[4]

Since the original granting of land, the federal government has granted additional lands to some of the states, including salt lands, swamp lands, and internal improvement lands. Altogether, the land grants have been estimated to be more than 154 million acres, with a value of about $1 billion—not including statehood grants to Alaska and Hawaii. In spite of the inefficiency of management of some of these lands, the funds derived therefrom provided many of the states with the means required to establish and operate schools while their state and local tax structures were being developed. They antedated state property taxes and thus became the revenue source for state improvement programs in extending the quantity and improving the quality of school services during the early development of state school systems, especially in the midwestern and western states.

Early Taxation Patterns

The early taxation patterns for education in the newly formed United States were largely permissive, creating a situation that generally favored the city school districts, which were progressive, and penalized the rural areas of the country, which were more tax-resistant. The taxing

4. For further information see Fletcher H. Swift, *Federal and State Policies in Public School Finance in the United States* (Boston: Ginn and Co., 1931).

policies of the several states emerged gradually from the patterns that had been used in the New England states. By 1890, all the states then in the Union had tax-supported public educational systems, with about one-fourth of them providing more than half of their public school costs from state funds, and with only eleven states providing less than 15 percent of their public school costs. The states not only felt certain responsibilities to help build sound educational programs but were concerned with the settlement of western America. Hence, the first quarter of the nineteenth century saw the real beginning of a taxing pattern for the support of public education. By then most of the nontax sources—the gifts, the lotteries, the bequests, and the rate bills—were beginning to vanish from the scene. Their complete abandonment, however, required a time element of several decades, and a few of these practices are still evident even today.

THE DEVELOPMENTAL STAGES OF SCHOOL FINANCE THEORY

The development of public school finance theory and practice can be divided into five somewhat arbitrary stages or periods. Admittedly, the periods overlap and no specific dates divide them. Although the theories have developed logically, their acceptance and use by the states has often been sporadic or even almost nonexistent. Examples may be found of states that even now are in each one of the five stages of development. Of course, the size of a state, its educational finance needs and traditions, and its educational leadership may have equipped it for easier and freer transition and movement, compared with other states, into a modern and realistic stage of school finance theory and practice. Although a few states have continually pushed forward the frontier of educational finance theory, some are still trying to operate twentieth-century school programs with nineteenth-century financing practices.

The five stages of development of state-local relations (avoiding the federal level for the moment) are (1) the period of local district financial responsibility, with little or no assistance from the state; (2) the period of emerging state responsibility, with the use of flat grants, subventions, and other nonequalizing state allocations to local districts; (3) the period of emergence of the Strayer-Haig concept of a foundation program; (4) the period of refinement of the foundation program concept; and (5) the presently emerging period of "power" or "open-end" (shared costs) equalization practices and stress on high-quality education.

Period One: Emphasis on Local Responsibility

Since schools were first established in America on a local basis, it was natural for school finance to be a local community or church problem. Although the original colonies used rate bills or tuition charges, a procedure that they brought from their European homelands, some of the New England towns began very early in their history to use property taxes to help finance education. Massachusetts and Connecticut were the leaders in this field, and each used this practice somewhat during the latter half of the seventeenth century. Tax support was used to a limited extent in the original southern states and in some Middle Atlantic states for the support of pauper schools.

The permissive property tax laws that existed when the colonies became states gradually became mandatory in the latter part of the eighteenth century and the early part of the nineteenth. As the westward movement of settlers accelerated and the number of local school districts began to multiply, the "popularity" and acceptability of the local property tax as the mainstay of the school financing program increased. By 1890, with the closing of the frontier, all of the states were using property taxes supplemented in many instances with revenue from the land grants and from other sources.

Even though most of the states were supporting local tax effort in school districts with the allocation of some state funds as early as 1890, some of them have continued to ignore this important financial responsibility even up to the present. As an example of this, as late as the 1965–66 school year, ten of the fifty states provided less than one-fourth of the total revenue required for operating their public schools, with four of them providing even less than 15 percent. By 1969–70, however, only two states (South Dakota and New Hampshire) provided less than 20 percent.

The lack of state assumption of the major portion of the responsibility for financing public education was noted by Johns and Morphet:

> It is evident that the citizens of many states have not yet clearly recognized their responsibility or, at any rate, have not taken steps to utilize it effectively. . . . Most people in this country subscribe in theory to the idea that the schools cannot be financed satisfactorily on the basis of local funds alone. However, the situation with reference to state funds in certain states is somewhat like the status of local taxation for school support more than a century ago.[5]

5. Roe L. Johns and Edgar L. Morphet, *The Economics and Financing of Education*, 2nd ed. (Englewood Cliffs, N.J.: Prentice-Hall, 1969), p. 238.

The gross weaknesses and limitations of financing education at the local level are all too evident. Extremely wide differences in local tax-paying ability to meet the costs of education in the hundreds of school districts (and in a few instances more than a thousand) in a state make a mockery of our theory of equality of educational opportunity for all school pupils, unless the state does something to help financially weak districts. Since each district is almost completely on its own as far as finances are concerned, the place of each pupil's residence becomes the all-important determinant of the quantity and quality of education available to him. Local initiative and local ability, important as they are in our philosophy of decentralization in education, should never be allowed or required to become the sole determinants of the calibre of education that the citizens in any community or school district receive.

The Advisory Commission on Intergovernmental Relations pointed to one reason why this method of financing schools was once acceptable, even though it is entirely unsatisfactory today: "The burden of supporting public schools was bearable even in the poorer communities because local schools did not initially have to compete for funds with a wide array of other local services and school costs were relatively low."[6] This type of situation, however, has long since disappeared. There is now intense competition for the tax dollar among many agencies and institutions of government and the costs of education are comparatively high.

The weakness of complete local financing of education becomes more evident as the property tax becomes less and less based on the ability-to-pay principle of taxation. Since it is evident that the greater the number of school districts in a state, the greater the likelihood of wide disparities in wealth, the states with hundreds of school districts can least well afford to confine themselves to this obsolescent approach to the school finance problem.

As rural communities and neighborhoods in early twentieth-century America grew into larger ones, without accompanying expansion of tax-able wealth, the need for state support of education became more evident. States were slow to move in this direction, however, until the Depression of the 1930s showed the helplessness of financing education by complete reliance on local property taxes.

Some forms of state support had existed for some time before the Depression. The early work of Cubberley in 1905 was the beginning of an era of study and experimentation in devising and using state plans that might assure equality of educational opportunity for all and at the same time improve school programs and equalize the tax burden.

6. *State Aid to Local Government* (Washington, D.C.: Advisory Commission on Intergovernmental Relations, April 1969), p. 39.

Period Two: Early Grants and Allocations

About the turn of the century public schools in most population centers acquired their present structure—12 grades and a nine-month school term —and came to represent a greater cost to local taxpayers. As States legislated local programs of this scope, the issue of inequality in local wealth surfaced. Rural communities in particular found it increasingly difficult to impose tax rates stiff enough to meet the State mandated programs. Cities with their concentration of valuable properties could and did provide high level educational programs with moderate tax effort.[7]

From the very beginning of public financing of schools, a few states began to recognize and implement their responsibilities in the matter. A number of reasons may be given for this early development: (1) The extreme inequalities that local property taxation generated among local school districts were soon obvious. (2) The funds that the sale and rental of the public lands provided were intended to find their way into the treasuries of local districts where control of education existed. (3) Many leaders in the educational movement recognized that the responsibility for education that the Tenth Amendment thrust on the states encompassed financial responsibility as much as any other kind.

Ellwood P. Cubberley, in the early part of the twentieth century, was the pioneer and foremost figure in the early and serious consideration of state apportionments of funds to local school districts. Some of the principal tenets of his philosophy of school finance are expressed in the following:

> Theoretically all the children of the state are equally important and are entitled to have the same advantages; practically this can never be quite true. The duty of the state is to secure for all as high a minimum of good instruction as is possible, but not to reduce all to this minimum; to equalize the advantages to all as nearly as can be done with the resources at hand; to place premium on those local efforts which will enable communities to rise above the legal minimum as far as possible; and to encourage communities to extend their educational energies to new and desirable undertakings.[8]

Cubberley's study in the early part of this century of state allocations of funds to local districts, including flat grants, percentage grants, and others, showed that such allocations did not reduce inequalities and may even under certain circumstances have increased them. He saw little

7. Ibid., p. 40.
8. Ellwood P. Cubberley, *School Funds and Their Apportionment* (New York: Teachers College, Columbia University, 1906), p. 17.

evidence that state fund allocations had reduced the wide range in the quality of education produced in school districts or the great disparity in ability to finance their programs. He made the first scientific study of the problem.

Cubberley was dedicated to the principle of equality of educational opportunity for all. Most of his ideas of how to provide such equality were far ahead of the practices of his time, even though most of them have been revised and improved in recent years. Noteworthy among the ideas and principles that Cubberley espoused were:

1. The belief that education was indeed a state financial responsibility, which it could not and should not ignore.
2. The firm conviction that state financial support was in addition to local effort and not intended as justifiable tax relief to local districts.
3. The awareness that existing methods of allocating state monies not only did not equalize the financial ability among local districts but may actually have increased financial inequalities among districts.
4. The need to increase the number of educational programs offered in the schools with attendant increases in state money for those districts with such extensions. This was his widely known version of reward for effort.
5. The wisdom of using aggregate days attendance over census, enrollment, average daily attendance, or any other measure used in determining the amount of state funds to local districts. This would encourage the extension of the school year and would penalize those districts that shortened the total length of their school year.
6. Distribution of some part of the state funds on the basis of the number of teachers employed in a district. He felt that this provision would aid the rural districts, which usually had a low pupil-teacher ratio.

Most of the Cubberley-inspired theories of school finance have become discredited and outmoded. It is easy to show that he was right in condemning flat grants, percentage grants, and subventions as nonequalizing. It is likewise easy, however, to show that his reward-for-effort principle was also nonequalizing. The wealthy districts already were employing more teachers, conducting more and better school programs, and holding more days of school per year than the poorer ones were. Thus, his reward for effort was applicable in the wealthier districts and much less applicable in the less wealthy ones.

Some of the states still use a few of the features of Cubberley's finance proposals. Fortunately, some of these practices are in combination with other more equalizing methods of allocating state funds. Although some nonequalizing grants may have justification in school finance formulas, they are not justified if used alone. While they represent progress beyond local effort alone, they are glaring examples of some of the inconsistencies so readily discernible in the Cubberley concept.

It must be emphasized that there are some potential dangers involved in allocating state funds to local districts regardless of how this is accomplished. Two principal dangers are (1) the possibility that the state could increase its control over local districts as it increases its financial support and (2) the possibility that state monies may be used to replace rather than supplement local monies for education.

The first of these two considerations requires little discussion, for the state already exercises plenary power over its school districts. The degree of state authority and power over education is entirely a legislative matter that the will of each successive session of each state's legislative assembly controls and regulates. The extent of such control need not be in direct relation to the fiscal policies of the state as far as education is concerned, and it has not been so.

The purpose of state financial support of education is not to replace or reduce local effort unless that effort has been considered to be unduly burdensome to local taxpayers. Its purpose has been to supplement local tax revenues in order to provide an acceptable school program. The obvious answer to this problem is to require minimum school district levies before state funds are forthcoming. The following is an example of many statements recommending such a procedure:

> A second way that states can interfere in the balance of demand for educational services versus tax relief is by mandating minimum levies on local districts, thus reducing the freedom of local boards to substitute state funds for local levies. We concluded from our recent study of state finance systems that this is an effective way to assure that state funds are used for educational purposes rather than for local tax relief. For instance, we ascribed much of the markedly higher expenditures for education in New York State, as compared to California, to the fact that New York's mandated levies are about three times as high as California's.[9]

Period Three: Emergence of the Foundation Program Concept

Modern school finance theory had its origin in the monumental work of George D. Strayer and Robert M. Haig. The real theory of equalization with its foundation program concept began with the findings of the Educational Finance Inquiry Commission of the schools of New York

9. H. Thomas James, "Modernizing State and Local Financing of Education," in *A Financial Program for Today's Schools* (Washington, D.C.: National Education Assn. Committee on Educational Finance, 1964), p. 52.

in 1923. The equalization of educational opportunity through the inception of a foundation or of a minimum program came as a direct result of the Strayer-Haig intensive studies of school finance programs built around the Cubberley philosophy and practiced in several states in the United States, particularly New York.

The Strayer-Haig studies discovered that in the school finance program of the state of New York, built as it was primarily around the distribution of state funds on a "per teacher quota basis," favored "the very rich and the very poor localities at the expense of those which are moderately well off." From this, and other discoveries of deficiencies in the state finance plans of that era, Strayer and Haig advocated their foundation, or minimum program, concept. Their plan centered around several fundamental factors or standards:

1. A foundation program should be devised around the rich district idea—each local district would levy the amount of local tax that was required in the richest district of the state to provide a foundation, or minimum, program. The rich district would receive no state funds; the other districts would receive state funds necessary to provide the foundation program.

2. All foundation programs should guarantee equality of educational opportunity up to a specified point, but all local districts should have the discretionary right to go beyond that point and provide a better program through tax-levy increases.

3. The program should be organized and administered to encourage local initiative and efficiency.

4. The features of the program should be defined in the law and should be objective and apply to all school districts of the state.

5. Foundation programs should be constructed, after thorough study and careful planning, around the needs and resources of each individual state.

6. The cost of the foundation program should include a major part of the total cost of public education in that state.

7. The program should be organized so that no district receives additional funds because it is underassessed for property taxation purposes at the local level; uniform property assessment is essential in all foundation programs.

8. While the plan should encourage the reorganization of school districts into a reasonable number and the consolidation of attendance areas wherever practicable, provision must be made to avoid penalizing necessary small schools.

9. The foundation program should be a minimum and not a maximum program; local initiative and increased expenditures above the foundation program must be practicable in all the districts of a state.

The Strayer-Haig concept of equalization is summarized in the following brief statement:

> The Strayer-Haig approach became the model for numerous State adaptations. Compromises with the strict application of the equalization objective were made in most States to accommodate: (a) the long-standing tradition of flat grants; (b) the reluctance of State officials to increase State taxes to fully finance an equalization plan; and (c) the desire of some localities to finance truly superior public schools. In most States the foundation plan ended up providing the poorest district with a basic educational program at a level well below that which many school districts willingly supported. Wealthy districts were left ample local tax leeway to exceed the minimum foundation plan level without unduly straining local resources. Retention of flat grants as part of most State school financing plans left the wealthiest communities free to forge ahead.[10]

Period Four: Refinement of the Foundation Program Concept

The foundation program concept opened the gates for widespread experimentation and refinement of this method of approaching equal educational opportunity. In New York State, Paul Mort, working with Strayer and Haig, developed a program providing a degree of equalization plus the use of flat grants. The question whether to take "surplus" monies from wealthy districts to help the states obtain equalization revenue was often debated and "settled" in the various states. The question of the reasonableness of continuing the Cubberley concept of payment for effort was likewise debated by the individuals and commissions that were facing the problem of improving state finance programs. Wide differences in interpretation of the foundation program concept were developed and experimented with during this period.

Some important improvements have followed experimentation with the Strayer-Haig concept of equalization in the last half-century:

1. There began an early movement away from the levy of a statewide property tax, the proceeds of which were to be distributed to schools on a school population or average daily attendance basis.
2. Fiscal independence of school districts was attained in most sections of the country.
3. The change from state property taxation to local property taxation brought intricate problems of obtaining fair and equitable property assessments.

10. *State Aid to Local Government*, p. 40.

4. The Depression years saw the establishment of laws in most states limiting the taxing power of school districts. (These restrictions have been eased to some extent since the end of World War II.)
5. Beginning efforts have been made in the use of local nonproperty taxes. These, however, have been insignificant except in a few large local districts.
6. The Cubberley emphasis on improvements and reward for effort with state funds was deemphasized by the Mort emphasis on equalization.

Mort found that this concept of equalization was incompatible with Cubberley's emphasis on reward for effort:

> The conclusion follows that these two purposes (equalization and reward for effort) that have controlled attempts to build state aid systems since the work of Cubberley two decades ago are found to be incompatible. We are, therefore, faced with the necessity of choosing one or the other. It is a choice between meeting the demands of a principle that cannot be met without state aid—the equalization of educational opportunity—and the use of one of many methods for meeting another principle.[11]

Modern school finance theories were spawned and developed by relatively few great and well-known leaders in the field, such as Cubberley, Strayer, and Mort. Their contributions are known to all who read the literature of school finance. But historians generally seem to have forgotten or at least minimized the importance of some others whose contributions to the field were also important. This apparent oversight may have been due to the unpopularity or lack of acceptance of their ideas at the time of their introduction.

Two school finance pioneers of the early part of this century whose contributions to the field were important but who have not always occupied their rightful positions in school finance history were Henry C. Morrison and Harlan Updegraff. Their theories, while not particularly popular in their own time, are relevant in today's school finance reform movement with its emphasis on increased state support for education and district power equalization.

Henry C. Morrison emphasized the fact that the methods of financing education in the early 1900s were unsatisfactory. Local school districts, by their organizational structure, were perpetuating unequal educational opportunities for the school children of each state. The allotment of state funds or grants to districts for special purposes was not bringing the kind or amount of equalization its advocates expected. Morrison

---

11. Paul R. Mort, as quoted by Erick L. Lindman in *Long-Range Planning in School Finance* (Washington, D.C.: National Education Assn. Committee on Educational Finance, 1963), pp. 38–39.

favored a new and different approach to the problem. He theorized that if the state were one large district it could not only equalize the tax burden but it could distribute the funds derived without complicated formulas such as were being used. Some of his main ideas—use of the income tax, full state funding, and considering the state as one large district—are much more acceptable today than they were in Morrison's own time. For example, several states now use the income tax to relieve the unfair and regressive property tax from some of its traditional burden, and Hawaii has become a one-district state under much the same conditions as Morrison advocated.

The unpopularity of Morrison's view resulted from his lack of support of a philosophy of local control of education and his willingness to replace "popular" property taxes with "unpopular" income taxes. Two conditions have changed which have brought a degree of popularity to Morrison's ideas: (1) local control has lost some of its traditional glamor; and (2) the property tax—even though still necessary at the local level—has sunk to the bottom of desirability as a major source of school revenue.

Harlan Updegraff in 1922 developed a formula that would combine equalization and reward for effort without the objectionable features of the Cubberley plan. This was simply allowing the state to provide funds for program improvement (as well as for equalization), with each local district free to determine what the improvement program should be (Updegraff's work in New York preceded the work of Strayer-Haig, but his contribution to the philosophy of school finance is more related to this period than to that of Cubberley).

As indicated elsewhere in this text, the states have moved somewhat blindly from one form of state and local financing of education to another. The foundation program was accepted as the best method of leveling the inequalities that seemed to exist and persist among the districts within every state. But even the foundation program has not proved to be a panacea. The high costs of compensatory education, the financial problems that result from municipal overburden, the unfairness among districts that varying policies and degrees of property underassessment create, and the inability of poor districts to go very much beyond the minimum program are evidence of the need for improving the minimum, or foundation, program concept in its current form.

The Advisory Commission on Intergovernmental Relations noted some of the ways in which the Mort program improved on the Strayer-Haig theories:

Perfecting amendments to the basic Strayer-Haig equalization thesis were developed as States enacted their foundation plans. For example, Paul Mort and other practitioners showed that educational costs differ for elementary and secondary pupils and that the unit of need in the foundation plan should be appropriately weighted to reflect these differences. . . . The physically and mentally handicapped children became the subject of special solicitude.[12]

Period Five: Emerging Power (Open-End) Equalization

The foundation program concept was an improvement over the older methods of distributing state funds to local school districts. In spite of that, however, school districts of differing financial capacities continue to have unequal abilities to exceed the foundation program. Thus, in the less wealthy districts the foundation program has been not only a "minimum" but also a near "maximum" program, for tax levies above the foundation, or base, without state help remit such small amounts of revenue that they discourage local effort to exceed the base program.

The predominant theme in school finance practice for the first half of this century has been "equalization of educational opportunity." The wealth of the state was to be taxed to educate all the children of the state regardless of where they lived or the tax-paying ability of their parents or their school district. Various devices and formulas have been tried and notable improvements made. Equalization meant that the state and local districts were exercising a degree of partnership in establishing and paying for a basic program of education for every school-age child in the state.

But the point of emphasis in this regard has been changing, as indicated in the following statement by Hutchins:

> Currently, less is being said about the equalization of educational opportunity. More concern is now expressed for higher quality of educational services. Educational standards must be raised. This places less emphasis on raising the low expenditure levels in the financially less able school districts and more emphasis on improving programs in all parts of the state, particularly in those districts that might be ready and able to provide superior programs. Higher quality programs are needed to reduce loss in human resources.[13]

In the midpart of this century, Paul Mort and others experimented with and advocated a new concept of equalization—a "new look" in incentive financing. Their proposal guarantees a foundation program at state and local expense for all districts, and also encourages local initiative for a better educational program by continuing to maintain a high degree of state-local partnership for whatever distance above the

12. *State Aid to Local Government*, p. 40.
13. Clayton D. Hutchins, "New Developments in State School Finance Systems," in *Financing Education for Our Changing Population* (Washington, D.C.: National Education Assn. Committee on Educational Finance, 1961), p. 79.

foundation program the local district cares to go. Wisconsin used a variation of this concept between 1949 and 1969. Rhode Island, Alaska, New York, Maryland, and a few other states have initiated similar plans in the past decade, largely under the leadership of Mort. The need for this type of change was indicated by James:

> I suspect we are nearing the end of half a century of emphasis on equalization, and that a trend has begun and will be extended toward state encouragement to local communities which put forth additional effort to provide good educational programs. The states will guarantee minimum programs through machinery comparable to the foundation program as we know it, but will begin to devise partnership arrangements for sharing the costs with those districts which choose to go beyond the mandated program in the pursuit of excellence.[14]

This open-end (shared cost or power) equalization plan for state and local financing of education is not really a new idea; only the practice is new. In the early 1920s, Updegraff proposed such a plan, but it was too far ahead of the financial practices of the time. Its increasing favor and limited adoption has resulted from wider acceptance of state financial responsibility for education. It tends to be more acceptable in states that supply a high percentage of the total public education at state expense. In those states that exert only a minimum of effort to finance education, the plan is far ahead of the financial philosophy of that state and therefore out of the question for immediate acceptance.

In its simplest terms, the open-end, or shared-cost, equalization plan proposes that a foundation program be established, with determination of the percentage of this program to be paid by each individual district and by the state. This percentage of state funds will be high for poor districts and low for wealthier ones. Once that determination has been made for each district, the same partnership ratio would be maintained to pay the total cost of the school program in each district. Each local board of education would still determine the levy to be made—thus preserving the concept of local control of education. There would be many variations and applications of this basic principle, but the fundamental premise of the program remains the same—state partnership throughout the complete finance program and thus a guarantee of a sound educational program for every district within the borders of every state.

Running through the educational finance philosophy of the last half-century, but almost submerged and forgotten until recently, is this far-reaching policy, first enunciated by Harlan Updegraff, of an equalized matching formula that would combine equalization and reward for effort. In contrast to Cubberley's idea, Updegraff would have the state

14. H. Thomas James, "New Developments in State School Finance," in *Financing the Changing School Program* (Washington, D.C.: National Education Assn., 1962), p. 89.

help to provide the finances for improved programs but leave the expenditure decisions to the local school boards. Under the guidance and initiative of Paul Mort, this principle has been activated in a few of the states, but its use is not yet widespread.

DISTRICT POWER EQUALIZATION

In the development of school finance theory, various terms have been used to describe what has become known as district power equalization. Equalized percentage matching (EPM) and open-end equalization are being used in this text synonymously with district power equalization in referring to this form of reward for effort incentive for school districts. Perhaps the term "power" is more appropriate than any of the others because the principle literally provides ability or power to a poor school district to obtain as much revenue per student as more wealthy districts making the same local tax effort.

Burke summarizes the current thinking concerning extension and improvement of the foundation program concept in the following:

> Some new possibilities have been seen by some in the reward-for-effort theory as first developed by Harlan Updegraff in 1919 and as applied in Wisconsin in 1949 and Rhode Island since 1960, and as proposed in a number of other states such as New York. Under these plans, a given unit of tax effort in a locality with low fiscal ability is made to produce the same number of dollars of revenue per pupil as would result from the same effort in a district with average or above-average fiscal capacity. Thus, the level of the state-supported equalization program rises with local tax effort in the ready and willing local units and with the success of state and/or local leadership in overcoming nonfiscal limitations in others.[15]

Rhode Island and Wisconsin (and to a lesser degree, some other states) require state equalization at the same rate for the entire educational program as is determined in the foundation program. The local district determines the limits of the local effort, and the state maintains financial responsibility for the entire program. This open-end equalization program is often referred to as equalization percentage matching (EPM). It is sometimes viewed as a means of opening a state's financial coffers to every local district. However, it is extremely effective in its obliteration of financial advantages for one district over another in pro-

---

15. Arvid J. Burke, "Financing of Elementary and Secondary Schools," in Warren E. Gauerke and Jack A. Childress, eds., *Theory and Practice of School Finance* (Chicago: Rand McNally & Co., 1967), p. 127.

TABLE 5.1   An Example of Equalized Percentage Matching (Power Equalization)

Dist.	Assessed Value/ Student	Tax Levy	Guar- anteed Amount/ WPU	Local Rev.	State Rev.	Local- State Ratio
			Foundation Program			
A	$50,000	0.010	$ 600[a]	$500	$100	5:1
B	40,000	.010	600[a]	400	200	2:1
C	10,000	.010	600[a]	100	500	1:5
D	5,000	.010	600[a]	50	550	1:11
			Optimum Program			
A	$50,000	0.018	$1,080[b]	$900	$180	5:1
B	40,000	.018	1,080[b]	720	360	2:1
C	10,000	.018	1,080[b]	180	900	1:5
D	5,000	.018	1,080[b]	90	990	1:11

[a]Equivalent to approximately $900 per student.
[b]Equivalent to approximately $1,620 per student.

viding for good-quality education rather than simply a minimum, or foundation, program.

Table 5.1 is a simplified example of how an equalized percentage matching program might work. In this example, four mythical districts of widely varying assessments of property per pupil to be educated are compared in the calculation of a foundation program with an expenditure of $600 per weighted pupil unit (equivalent to approximately $900 per student) and a required local levy of 10 mills. The local and state revenues are then determined, and the ratio of local revenue to state revenue is calculated for each district. In District A (the wealthiest one) the local revenue is five times as great as the state revenue; in District D (the poorest one) the required state revenue is eleven times as high as the local amount.

If the Strayer-Haig concept of equalization were to be followed, each district would then be on its own to go above the foundation program. Herein lies an obvious weakness, for District A is able to raise $50/WPU for each mill of tax while District D would raise only $5/ WPU. In the equalized percentage matching program, the state is required to continue its degree of partnership for the full program. Thus, if a $1,080/WPU expenditure is considered an arbitrarily established optimum, the state would contribute $180/WPU to District A and $990/ WPU to District D. By this process, financially weak districts are able to offer as good a program as wealthier ones. This is the essence of the American philosophy of equality of educational opportunity.

At first glance it may seem that this creates a standard program for every district within a state. Such is not the case, however, for each local district would have the right and the responsibility to determine what the local tax rate would be over and above the mandated foundation program levy. In this way local control is assured and state partnership responsibility is mandated.

The equalization percentage matching (EPM) concept was given strong support by the decisions in the recent court cases, beginning with *Serrano* v. *Priest*. It received some objection, however, in the Supreme Court's reversal of Rodriguez (March 1973). Opponents of this principle of power equalization fear that it will deplete already overburdened state treasuries. While this reasoning remains as the chief deterrent to adoption of this principle in state school financing, studies and experiences noted in some states that have used it indicate that the process does not bankrupt state treasuries. Note the following:

> The state share for any district thus varies according to the need and ability of the school district. Therefore, on superficial theoretical analysis, people have concluded that completely open-end EPM grant without a ceiling on per pupil expenditures would lead to a raid on the state treasury. Better theoretical formulations and the experience of the past decades have proved this conclusion to be faulty.[16]
>
> Studies by Benson and Kelly in Rhode Island and by Daniere in Massachusetts as well as theoretical analysis by Daniere and by Pauly showed that an EPM grant would not increase educational funds much beyond that experienced in other states during the same period. In Rhode Island, state funds did increase faster than in other states; that is, state funds substituted for local funds without great increases in total funds for schools. Thus, one might claim or not claim that there was a raid on the state treasury.[17]

The merits of the EPM philosophy are readily apparent. Local control of the educational program rests with each individual school board, but the state cannot escape its proportionate financial responsibility. Districts are encouraged to make adequate tax effort, for if they spend less they lose more. Complete equalization is achieved in spending as well as in tax effort. Since there is no ceiling in tax effort, the inequalities encountered between wealthy and poor districts, which are so obvious in a typical foundation program, disappear. The only restriction to an adequately financed program thus becomes the willingness or unwillingness of the people at the local level to tax themselves within reasonable

16. Eugene P. McLoone, "Modernizing State School Finance Programs: Six Selected Areas," in *Interdependence in School Finance: The City, the State the Nation* (Washington, D.C.: National Education Assn. Committee on Educational Finance, 1968), p. 23.

17. Ibid., p. 24.

tax limits. With the state matching the local district on a predetermined basis in terms of local ability, the previously unrealistic tax requirements for a high-quality education program in a poor district are reduced greatly or even eliminated.

It would be difficult to conceive of many valid arguments against the shared-cost philosophy. The principal deterrents to early acceptance of some form of this simple financial plan are apathy, traditional acceptance of archaic plans of school finance, lack of state leadership in the much needed improvement of property tax administration, especially in assessment practices, too many kinds and numbers of school districts with differences in taxing and spending powers, and widespread realization that such a program may liberalize the financing program in a great many of our school districts in this country. However, a significant step forward is long overdue in most states, and progress appears to be imminent.

THE STATE ROLE: A FUNCTION OF VARYING CONDITIONS

Cubberley's emphasis on incentive grants for special purposes, with less stress on equalization, was a reasonably satisfactory approach to state school finance policy during the early part of this century. The states were using state property taxes to obtain revenue to be distributed to local school districts. Cubberley advocated state incentive grants to promote specific improvements with less emphasis on equalization needs.

During the 1920s, the states generally gave up their state property taxes and placed almost complete responsibility on the local districts and the counties for administering the property tax. Equalization became a necessity to get state funds for financially weak school districts. Strayer, Haig, Mort, and their colleagues began to emphasize the foundation program and to minimize incentive grants.

During this period of change, the states found it imperative to modify somewhat their finance laws and practices to help solve the problems created by leaving all property tax responsibility with the local districts. Some of the main problems were (1) the need to provide the best possible equalization program to make equal educational opportunity available to all—even in the financially weak school districts created by this change in taxing procedure; (2) the need to provide fiscal independence for all school districts in an effort to give school boards budgetary power and authority commensurate with their educational responsibility; (3) the need to provide assistance to local districts in their administration of local property tax—in which they sought equality in assessing practices, efficiency in tax collection procedures, and other improvements; (4) the need to expand the tax base and provide some property tax relief by using nonproperty taxes, where practicable; and (5) the need to give local districts greater autonomy in administering the property tax by reducing or eliminating state-imposed restrictions on levies—a carryover from the Depression years.

Much progress has been made in the last half-century in solving the above-mentioned problems. But the finance laws and the state-local partnership are far less acceptable than they might be. Sound financial theories are much ahead of practices in most states, including those that have led in experimenting with new programs. Present conditions in many of our beleaguered school districts—such as inadequate local revenues and municipal overburden—dictate the need for increasing and improving the role of the state in financing education. The state must increase its partnership responsibility, preferably by continuing its support through the full educational program in every district on an equalization basis. Although many people think of this as a new and perhaps radical idea, the experience of the last fifty years validates it as a sound approach to the perennial and almost insurmountable financial problems now facing the public schools of this country.

GREATER STATE RESPONSIBILITY FOR EDUCATION

The clamor for greater state involvement in financing education continues to increase. The critics of the property tax point to the much greater equity and fairness in a school finance plan centered around a sales tax, an income tax, and a limited property tax all administered entirely by the state. Such a proposal has been made by many who have despaired of producing equality of educational opportunity under our present state-local relation pattern. The governors of two of our more populous states have recommended such a plan. The effect of this point of view has been felt in many of the legislative bodies of the several states:

> In 1969, State legislatures continued the trend of shifting financial burdens to the state level to relieve the overburdened property taxpayer. Vermont passed its first sales tax. . . . New income taxes were approved in Washington (pending voter approval), Illinois, and Maine. Income taxes were raised in 11 other states and sales tax went up in 13 states. North Carolina became the 50th state to levy a cigarette tax and 10 other states hiked existing cigarette taxes.[18]

18. *Education U.S.A.* (Washington, D.C.: National School Public Relations Assn., Sept. 22, 1969), p. 21.

138

The slow and uncertain development of state support for education has not necessarily been a result of continuous lack of interest on the part of the people involved. Much of our indecision has come from lack of know-how or prescription in the solution of school finance problems. Passage of time has increased the acuteness and difficulty of these problems, but it has also provided some answers. The rationale that suited the inaction of the past is no longer valid. The principles and the theories to mold a justifiable state-local relation in financing education have been developed and proved. Further inaction and indecision in this matter cannot be condoned if viable programs are to be sponsored and financed with their accelerating costs year after year.

PURPOSES OF STATE FINANCIAL SUPPORT

While people in general favor additional state financial support for education, few would like to see greater state control, with attendant elimination of local responsibility in the matter. What then are the main purposes of state support? Several have been emphasized and have had their advocates; few are controversial. The following are some of the most important of these:

1. Providing state support to promote local school improvements was championed by Cubberley. It is particularly important to have state support for local educational programs that are too expensive for the weaker school districts to finance.
2. State funds are needed to equalize educational opportunity for all children of the state. Strayer, Haig, and Mort stressed the need for state-supported foundation programs for this purpose.
3. State support is required to provide incentives for greater local tax effort. Mort's work in Rhode Island and New York, conceived around the Updegraff equalized matching formula concept combining equalization and reward for effort, illustrates the practical result of this form of state financial support.
4. State support broadens the tax base of school support. To the local property tax revenues, the state adds funds that have been collected from many kinds of nonproperty taxes. Thus, the burden to property-tax-payers for educational services is made lighter, and more elements of the private sector are involved in financing education.

FEDERAL FUNDS AND STATE SUPPORT OF EDUCATION

We have pointed out that state funds should not be used to reduce local tax effort except in instances of obvious overburden. Likewise, federal funds should not be used to replace state funds for education. The costs and the administrative responsibility for education should rest as close as possible to the people receiving educational services. State support is provided when reasonable local taxes produce inadequate revenue, and federal support is defensible only when local and state revenues resulting from reasonable effort are insufficient for an excellent school program throughout the state.

In the past, there have been some violations of the above principle, particularly with funds that local districts obtained from the federal government under PL 874 (federal aid for federally impacted areas). Most of the states, especially those that have provided only small general-purpose grants to local districts and those that provided only a small percentage of education costs from state sources, ignored PL 874 in determining fund allocations to public schools. That is as it should be, for federal funds should not decrease state funds. However, some other states—particularly those that have provided a high percentage of the total amounts that their local districts used—have reduced their allocations of state monies to those local districts receiving PL 874 funds. Various processes have been used to make such an adjustment, but it has usually been by some percentage of the amount of federal funds that local districts received under this program. This was a source of great controversy until a "solution" to the problem was obtained when the federal government made it illegal for a state to receive credit for federal funds under this program by any reduction in the amount of state funds to be allocated to any district.

STATE ABILITY TO SUPPORT EDUCATION

Measurement of a state's ability to support education is difficult. While local districts must confine their main tax effort to the property tax, the states have no such limitations. Sales taxes, income taxes, and many others are available for state use, thereby complicating the problem of measuring and comparing total tax effort and ability.

The ability of the states to support education varies greatly regardless of the criteria or devices used in its measurement. Here again, as with measurement of local ability, the question arises as to whether taxpaying ability should be measured in terms of potential revenues from all sources, many of which are not legally authorized, or whether it should be measured in terms of the tax system that is authorized and operable. Does a state have the ability to produce any given amount of school revenue from a state sales tax if such a tax is not being used? Another unanswered question is related to the relative economic effects of varying forms and kinds of taxation; for example, what property tax rate is equivalent to a 4 percent sales and use tax?

Some old practices of measuring state taxing ability have outworn their usefulness. An example is the use of per capita wealth as measured by the assessed or the real value of taxable property within the state. The deemphasis or complete elimination of the use of the state property tax and the introduction of sales and state income taxes have resulted in the demise of this method of comparing the abilities of states to finance education.

The most common method now used to compare the financial ability of states to support education seems to require the inclusion of income. The close relation between some state income tax systems and the federal income tax program makes determination of total income relatively easy. Relating the total personal income to the total population does not consider the disparity among the states in the ratio of school-age children to total population. Using the average daily membership or average daily attendance of pupils in public schools does not consider the wide ranges among the states in the numbers of pupils attending private or parochial schools. Some authorities in the field support the seemingly defensible method of using total personal income minus total federal income taxes paid by the people of a state divided by the total number of children of school age as the best method of measuring state ability to pay for education. Still others advocate complex combinations of data and mathematical formulas, which are difficult to determine but which if obtained lend some validity to such methods of comparing the ability of states to finance education.

The various measures of ability to finance education have always shown considerable disparity among the states regardless of the method or measure used. The 6 to 1 ratio discovered half a century ago of the ability of the wealthiest state compared with the poorest had been reduced to a little less than 4 to 1 by the time of the White House Conference on Education of 1955. Undoubtedly, the current comparisons all would agree that the ratio has been further reduced, for prosperity, highly progressive income taxes, and inflation tend to reduce the range. The important point, however, is not what the ratio may be at any particular time or with any particular measuring device; it is, rather, that real differences continue to exist among the states in their ability to finance education.

The National Committee for Support of the Public Schools supports the use of per capita personal income as a valid measure of a state's capacity to support education, as indicated in the following:

> Among various measures which have been developed to gauge the fiscal capacity of the states, per capita personal income is the one most generally accepted, and one which has a high correlation to per pupil expenditure. . . . From 1957 to 1967 the average per capita personal income increased 54%. In 1957, the highest ranked state had 2.6 times as much personal income as the lowest; in 1967, the highest had 2.1 times as much.[19]

STATE EFFORT TO SUPPORT EDUCATION

> The willingness of a state to provide educational services can be measured by the amount of local and state revenue for public schools as a percentage of total personal income. Tax effort has increased from an average of 3.4% in 1957–58 to 4.6% in 1967–68. Only 8 states now allocate less than 4% of personal income to public schools. Four of these states have over 20% of their total elementary and secondary school enrollment in non-public schools—a factor which may affect tax effort.[20]

Since the ability of the fifty states to support education varies, and since each spends a different amount per child being educated, it follows that their taxing efforts also vary. Those less wealthy states (measured in terms of wealth per child to be educated) whose citizens choose to have good educational programs will necessarily make a greater effort than their more fortunate counterparts in more wealthy states. Effort, too, is an elusive term and one that lends itself to complicated means of measurement.

Selected Readings

Bailey, Stephen K.; Frost, Richard T.; Marsh, Paul Ed.; and Wood, Robert C. *Schoolmen and Politics*. Syracuse, N.Y.: Syracuse University Press, 1962.

Cohn, Elchanan, and Millman, Stephen D. *Economics of State Aid to Education*. Lexington, Mass.: Lexington Books, D. C. Heath and Co., 1974.

19. *Know Your Schools Fact Sheet*, no. 11 (Washington, D.C.: National Committee for Support of the Public Schools, March 1969), p. 1.
20. Ibid.

Coons, John E.; Clune, William H. III; and Sugarman, Stephen D. *Private Wealth and Public Education*. Cambridge, Mass.: Belknap Press of Harvard University Press, 1970.

Grubb, W. Norton, and Michelson, Stephan. *States and Schools*. Lexington, Mass.: Lexington Books, D. C. Heath and Co., 1974.

Johns, Roe L., and Morphet, Edgar L. *The Economics and Financing of Education*, 3rd ed. Englewood Cliffs, N.J.: Prentice-Hall, 1975.

O'Connor, James R. *The Fiscal Crisis of the State*. New York: St. Martin's Press, 1973.

School Finance in Transition. Washington, D.C.: National Conference on School Finance, 1973.

Schools, People, and Money. Washington, D.C.: President's Commission on School Finance, U.S. Government Printing Office, 1972.

Thurston, Lee M., and Roe, William H. *State School Administration*. New York: Harper & Row, 1957.

6

Education: A Fluctuating
Federal Interest

The history of American education during the middle decades of the twentieth century (particularly the 1950s and 1960s) was one of almost continuous controversy over the question of the federal government's role in financing education. Certainly, there have been few, if any, domestic political issues that have generated more discussion and more nondecision debates about who should pay the costs of education than this one. In spite of some federal legislation, such as the National Education Defense Act of 1958 and the Elementary and Secondary Education Act of 1965, the question of the rightful place of the federal government in education is still involved with racial, religious, and political overtones. The issue continues to divide American citizens on emotional as well as on philosophical grounds. Unfortunately, as the twenty-first century approaches accompanied by a school financing crisis, taxpayer revolts, and numerous other similar problems, the determination of ideal federal-state-local relations in financing education has not yet been made.

HISTORICAL ROLE OF THE FEDERAL GOVERNMENT

Historically, the federal role in education has been minor; its function was to conduct research, disseminate information and provide consultant and advisory assistance to the other two levels of government. It was to exercise interest in education without direct responsibility or control. However, at various times the federal government has provided some financial support for education, usually eschewing extensive federal controls in the process. In its regular delvings into providing financial assistance, it has appeared to sense momentary belief that inadequate or poor education is a result of inadequate financing. For the most part, it has attempted to assist low-ability states more than higher-ability states, leaving decision making and administrative controls with the individual states themselves.

The legal relation of the federal government to education is largely indirect. Federal courts rule on alleged violations of constitutional rights by the states and their local school districts. However, the impact of such federal court decisions upon education, even though indirect, has been of great consequence and will continue to be so. The nationwide effect of the Supreme Court's ruling in the *Brown* case of 1954 (desegregation), and also subsequent decisions that implemented and helped clarify the intention of the Court, is an excellent example of how even indirect controls may strongly influence schools and their organizational and administrative operations.

Constitutional Role

The Constitution of the United States provides indirectly for the federal government to exercise only a minor role in the three-way partnership of governmental responsibility for education. The Tenth Amendment has been interpreted as legal sanction for state responsibility for this important service of government. The framers of the Constitution viewed with fear the possible disaster of a nationally controlled school system. Their distrust of a strong central power was a break from the philosophy of government in the European countries of their origin. They feared concentration of power, whether it was political or religious. Their main purpose in coming to America—political and religious freedom—seemed to be antithetical to strong centralization of power in a national unit of government.

Very early in our history, the federal government began a policy of deference to the states in matters of education. Even before the Constitution was ratified, the government in power passed the Northwest Ordinance, which provided for land grants to new states to foster education. These grants provided some incentive for the settlement of western lands and was our first act of federal aid to education. As the colonies became states and relinquished their land claims, the newly formed federal government began to establish a policy for their disposition as gifts to the newly formed states to finance state-sponsored public education systems.

A Sound Partnership

Even the severe critics of American education recognize that the state-local-federal tri-partnership in education worked well for over a century. State constitutions and court decisions at all levels recognized and supported this relation. The public schools, recognized as one of the truly great contributions of this country to the world, were developed under the aegis of this partnership system. Their virility and their accomplishments attest to the validity of this relation.

Thus, for most of the duration of the Republic, the constitutionally authorized advisory role of the federal government was accepted and followed, with only minor exceptions. The grass-roots level of school control that has been so commonly described and so vigorously defended seemed to be working well. The United States became a leader in many areas of science and culture; the schools played an important part in that achievement. Even the perennial problem of financing education was solved in most areas of the country, with little or no involvement of the federal government, although it was the largest and the most financially able of the three partners.

To be sure, the federal government vacillated in its role. Periodic and often spasmodic innovations and policy changes came and went without furor or panic on the part of those who were dedicated to preventing change in the federal role. To a great degree, the occasional venture of the federal government into educational matters represented the philosophies of those in positions of power in the federal hierarchy rather than real or permanent changes in the educational philosophy of American society generally.

In recent years, the generally accepted roles of the three levels of government in sponsoring and financing education have been in a state of flux. In particular, the role of the federal government has become more enigmatic; its relation to state and local government has been in an unprecedented state of confusion and controversy. To a great extent, the increasing role of the federal government has come as a result of the accelerating disability of the other two levels to fulfill their traditional responsibilities in the educational structure.

> The structural and functional weaknesses of the states have been a salient factor in precipitating the crisis in inter-level governmental relationships which currently exists. Many of the states for a variety of reasons have virtually abdicated responsibility for the nation's burgeoning urban problems. As a result, metropolitan centers have had to bypass the states and

turn to the federal government for assistance in confronting myriad problems like housing, welfare, air and water pollution, education, and transportation.[1]

Historically, the states and their local school districts have faced almost complete financial responsibility for education. Recently the problem has become too great for their inadequate taxing machinery. At the same time, the federal government has developed a powerful and responsive taxing system, although it has had little except advisory obligation to the broad field of public education.

A New Role Has Developed

Recently, a new concept of the role of the federal government has characterized federal participation in education. An observable trend has developed in increased federal control of public school programs in the provision of special-purpose grants to states and also to local school districts. The rationale for this shift in federal educational policy was referred to in 1967 by Harold Howe II, while he was serving as the United States commissioner of education:

> The 88th and 89th Congresses, responding to the desires of the people, enacted laws enabling the Federal Government to take its place in the local-State-National educational partnership. . . . Toward the end, the Congress has enacted 24 major pieces of education legislation in the past 3 years. These new laws are channels through which billions of Federal tax dollars will go into our elementary schools, high schools, vocational schools, colleges, and universities.
>
> But this money is not simply handed out in the pious hope that it will be put to good use. Each of the education laws . . . is quite specific. Categories and conditions of aid have been established to insure that these funds are spent in an efficient and prudent manner.[2]

It now seems clear that the recent emergence of massive categorical aid by the federal government to education resulted from an inherent lack of consistency in our governmental taxing structure. Not only were the local property tax and the state sales tax regressive, but they were not responsive enough to cover the perennial increases in school costs. The other main source of revenue, the income tax, was largely usurped by the federal government and was not particularly popular or produc-

1. Michael D. Usdan, "Relationships Between Federal and State Systems," in *The School Administrator* (Washington, D.C.: American Assn. of School Administrators, November 1970), p. 7.
2. Harold W. Howe II, as quoted in *Federal Policy and the Public Schools* (Washington, D.C.: American Assn. of School Administrators, 1967), pp. 2–3.

tive when undertaken at the state level. On the other hand, the federal government flourished with its highly lucrative and progressive income tax system. It alone produced more than half of all tax monies collected. The federal treasury appeared to be an oasis on the desert to the fifty almost bankrupt states and their thousands of financially impotent school districts.

Thus, the strengthening of the federal tax structure at the same time that the state and local taxing systems have shown a weakening has resulted in a confusion of roles of the three levels of government in financing education. Michael D. Usdan makes an interesting comment about this relation:

> Our three-level federal system in which powers and functions are shared among national, state, and local governments is in serious crisis and dis- array. The Comittee for Economic Development in its recent report, *Modernizing State Government,* acknowledged that there was "some validity in the facetious comment that our three-level federalism leaves the national government with the money, local governments with the problems, and the states with the legal powers."[3]

Is federal aid in substantial amounts without federal control desir- able and practical? Is categorical aid worth the confusion and the controversy and divisiveness that it seems to produce over time with a proliferation of programs? These and related questions point to a need for clarifying and solidifying the purpose and role of federal pro- grams in education. While no one can predict what the federal role will eventually become, everyone knows that a new pattern is develop- ing—not systematically, perhaps, but inevitably.

CLASSIFYING FEDERAL AID PROGRAMS

It is erroneous to classify a person or several persons as being either completely in favor of federal aid to education or as unalterably opposed to it, although it is often done. The act of providing federal financial assistance to various aspects of education cannot possibly be considered as either pure virtue or cardinal sin. To defend all its parts or to deny all with the same fervor or pomp or power is roughly equivalent to defending all actions of government or all phases of a taxing system with equal vigor. Some of the most vindictive critics of the federal pro- grams permit their children to participate in school lunch programs, attend agricultural colleges, pursue vocational education, and participate

3. Usdan, "Relationships Between Federal and State Systems."

in many other federally subsidized programs. The most radical critic of federal assistance to education can find little to condemn in the tremendously important land grants or in the G.I. Bill of Rights, which provided federal funds for the education of war veterans. Both of these programs were significant federal contributions to education. On the other hand, the most ardent advocate of federal aid can point to some programs that seem to have gone beyond generally acceptable limits in federal usurpation of control or domination of responsibility for education.

Various classifications have been used to differentiate the many programs of federal aid, depending on their purpose or their supporting rationale. Reference is often made to such common and understandable divisions of assistance as *general-purpose, categorical, emergency,* and *aid* for certain groups of our citizens for which this nation itself assumes an obligatory responsibility.

The American Association of School Administrators described the following five kinds of federal aid: (1) aid to promote the cause of education; (2) aid to broaden the scope of education; (3) aid to educate individuals for whom the federal government accepts responsibility; (4) aid to improve the quality of education; and (5) aid to compensate for deficiencies in the school tax base. Such a classification sublimates the purposes that federal financial assistance to schools intends. It is easy to show, however, that some federal assistance serves more than one of these purposes and is therefore not accurately categorized in any one classification.

Still another way of classifying federal aid may involve only three subdivisions: (1) federal aid to states to help promote and finance already established educational programs; (2) federal aid provided by the operation of federal programs that supplement state-established educational offerings; and (3) federal aid made available to nonpublic schools.

SOME IMPORTANT FEDERAL PROGRAMS

The following outline summarizes some important federal activities that have contributed to American education in the last two centuries. The list is not intended to be complete; the total number of such programs is not known, and their total impact on education can never be measured. They are listed here in terms of general purpose rather than in a strictly chronological order. Discussion of most programs is brief, and objective evaluation has not been attempted. Further details are available to the interested reader in the references listed at the end of the chapter.

Federal Educational Activities

1. Ordinance of 1785 (Land Grants)
   1.1 Provided: "There shall be reserved the Lot No. 16 of every township for the maintenance of public schools, within said township."
   1.2 A result of New England colony policy of granting lands to endow education.
2. The Northwest Ordinance of 1787 (Land Grants)
   2.1 Based on the Bill of Rights for Education—"Religion, morality and knowledge being necessary to good government and the happiness of mankind, schools and the means of education shall forever be encouraged."
   2.2 Became effective when Ohio became a state in 1802, with the provision that section 16 of every township should be "granted to the inhabitants of such township for the use of schools." In 1803, Congress provided that control of such land shall "be vested in the legislature of that state." This policy was followed from 1802 to 1848; twelve states received such a grant.
   2.3 When the Oregon Territory was established in 1848, Congress provided for sections 16 and 36 to be given for education to states newly entering the Union; fourteen states received such a grant.
   2.4 Utah (1896), Arizona (1911), and New Mexico (1911) received sections 2, 16, 32, and 36 for education.
   2.5 Results: strengthened the position of the states as responsible agents for education; was a real factor in helping the states build their public school systems; a few states managed their lands and funds wisely while others were guilty of gross mismanagement.
   2.6 A good example of general federal aid to education without federal control; guidelines may have been unwisely omitted, for such would have reduced mismanagement.
3. Other Land and Money Grants (1802 to 1850)
   3.1 Grants of funds in lieu of land grants in Indian territory.
   3.2 Land grants under the Internal Improvement Act of 1841.
   3.3 Saline land grants (beginning in 1802).
   3.4 Grants of 5 percent of the funds received by the federal government from the sale of public lands in the states.
   3.5 Payments to the states of 25 percent of income from national

forests and 37.5 percent received from the extraction of non-metallic minerals for the benefit of roads and public schools.

    3.6   Allocation of surplus federal revenues to the states (1836).

4.   Morrill Acts (Establishment of Agricultural Colleges)

    4.1   Morrill Act (1862) provided federal land grants of 30,000 acres of land for each senator and representative in Congress for establishment of a college or colleges "where the leading object shall be, without excluding other scientific and classical studies, and including military tactics, to teach such branches of learning as are related to agriculture and the mechanic arts—in order to promote the liberal and practical education of the industrial classes in the several pursuits and professions of life."

        4.11   Received much opposition at first; viewed as encroachment by the federal government.

        4.12   Began the policy of federal restrictions and controls; the first categorical aid law.

        4.13   A significant decision by government that made possible a national system of higher education.

    4.2   Second Morrill Act (1890)

        4.21   Strengthened the original act by providing funds to each state "to be applied only to instruction in agriculture, the mechanic arts, the English language and the various branches of mathematical, physical, natural, and economic science."

    4.3   All states benefited from the Morrill Acts; 69 land grant colleges were established in the 48 states and 3 territories.

    4.4   Control over these colleges has been negligible; their curricula have been liberalized well beyond their original emphasis on agriculture and engineering.

5.   Acts Supplementing the Activities of the Land Grant Colleges

    5.1   The Hatch Act (1887) provided for each land-grant college the establishment of experiment stations for the purpose of conducting research in agriculture.

    5.2   The Hatch Act, along with the Adams Act (1906), the Purnell Act (1925), the Bankhead-Jones Act (1935), the Research and Marketing Act (1946), and others, contributed greatly to experimentation in agriculture, with the result that the United States became the most productive of all nations.

6.   Vocational Education Acts

    6.1   The Smith-Lever Act (1914) provided for extension services by home demonstration agents, by 4-H leaders, and by county agricultural agents, and for services and professional training of such teachers.

    6.2   The Smith-Hughes Act (1917) provided about $7,000,000 annually in funds for pre-college-age vocational education; annual appropriations provided for vocational education in agriculture, home economics, and trades and industry.

    6.21 The first special-purpose grants made to public schools by Congress.

    6.22 Strongly influenced public education toward its vocational programs.

    6.23 The act was broadened by the George-Reed Act (1929), the George-Ellzey Act (1935), the George-Deen Act (1937), the George-Barden Act (1946), and the Vocational Act (1963; amended in 1968).

  6.3 George-Deen Act added $12 million annually to same purposes as the Smith-Hughes Act and added distributive education.

  6.4 George-Barden Act increased funds for vocational education; its Title II provided federal funds for practical nursing education; it provided for many federal restrictions and controls.

  6.5 National Defense Education Act (1958); Title VIII amended the George-Barden Act, adding a new Title III authorizing $15 million annually for area vocational schools (for five years).

  6.6 Vocational Education Act (1963): regarded by many as a milestone in vocational education history; provided grants-in-aid to the states increasing from $60 million in 1964 to $225 million in 1967 and each subsequent year; one-third to be spent for the construction of area vocational schools or operating programs for out-of-school youths.

7. School Lunch Programs (1935–)

  7.1 In 1935, the newly established Federal Surplus Commodities Corporation provided for surplus foods to be distributed to schools for lunches for pupils.

    7.11 Expanded in 1940 to include milk.

    7.12 Later the Department of Agriculture began to make cash payments to reimburse part of the food costs of school lunches.

  7.2 The School Lunch Act (1946): ". . . as a measure of national security, to safeguard the health and well-being of the nation's children and to encourage the domestic consumption of nutritious agricultural commodities and other food by assisting the states through grants-in-aid and other means."

    7.21 Distribution was to be on an equalization basis.

    7.22 Required state matching funds on a progressively increasing ratio.

    7.23 Available to both public and nonpublic schools.

    7.24 Amended in 1962 and 1963 to direct more federal funds to areas of low wealth.

7.25 Participating schools were required to (1) serve lunches that meet prescribed nutritional standards, (2) use foods declared by the Department of Agriculture to be in abundance, (3) provide free lunches for children unable to pay for them, and (4) maintain adequate records for federal auditing purposes.

Relief and Emergency Programs

8.1 Civilian Conservation Corps (CCC) (1933–1943): an act designed to relieve unemployed youth by "restoration of the country's depleted natural resources and the advancement of an orderly program of useful public works."

  8.11 For work relief for men 17–22 years of age.

  8.12 Helped restore depleted natural resources.

  8.13 Provided camps where enrollees were housed and provided for low wages while they built dams, bridges, picnic areas, and did other useful work.

  8.14 Carried on organized educational activities that became a kind of parallel school system rivaling state school systems in some respects.

8.2 National Youth Administration (NYA) (1935–1944): Established by executive order of the President.

  8.21 Organized to provide work relief for unemployed youth 16–25 years of age.

  8.22 Provided part-time employment in practical activities.

  8.23 Enabled some secondary school and college students to continue their education; many others learned occupational skills.

8.3 The Federal Emergency Relief Administration (1933)

  8.31 Superseded by the Works Progress Administration in 1939.

  8.32 One of the many "pump-priming" activities of the federal government designed to get money in circulation and bring economic relief to people during the Depression.

  8.33 Conducted programs in school building construction and maintenance, adult education, vocational rehabilitation, and in many other areas.

8.4 Public Works Administration (PWA) (1933)

  8.41 Made grants for public building construction on a 30 percent of cost basis; later 45 percent.

  8.42 Made loans for school construction.

8.5 These emergency programs were inaugurated as relief measures during the Depression of the 1930s. Stimulation of the economy was the main consideration; educational programs and benefits were secondary in importance.

9. Programs in the War on Poverty
   9.1 Area Redevelopment Act (1961)
      9.11 Aimed at areas of poverty.
      9.12 Established programs to alleviate conditions of unemployment by providing for orderly referral of unemployed people who could benefit from occupational training.
   9.2 Manpower Development and Training Act (1962)
      9.21 "The purpose of this act is to require the federal government to appraise the manpower requirements and resources of the Nation, and to develop and apply the information and methods needed to deal with the problems of unemployment resulting from automation and technological changes and other types of persistent unemployment."
      9.22 Aid for vocational education to help solve economic problems.
   9.3 Economic Opportunity Act (1964)
      9.31 "To eliminate the paradox of poverty and pools of long-term joblessness in the midst of plenty in the nation by opening to everyone opportunity for education and training, the opportunity to work, and the opportunity to live in decency and dignity."
      9.32 Provided vocational education and training in the Job Corps; focused on the special needs of a small minority of youths who because of educational deficiency are at a competitive disadvantage in the labor market.
   9.4 Elementary and Secondary Education Act (1965)
      9.41 Considered a "breakthrough" in the controversy over federal aid.
      9.42 Authorized more than $1 billion for education.
      9.43 Contained "titles" authorizing educational programs for educationally deprived children of low-income families, improvement of school libraries and instructional material centers, stimulation of educational research, and improvement of state departments of education.
      9.44 Designed to help bring economic and social equality to blacks, the poor, the underprivileged, and the educationally disadvantaged.
10. High-Quality Education Programs
   10.1 The National Science Foundation (1950)
      10.11 The Foundation was created "to promote the progress of science; to advance the national health, prosperity and welfare; to secure the national defense; and for other purposes."

10.12   Provided no direct funds for school districts or state departments of education.

10.13   Provided for payments to colleges and universities, and to nonprofit research and professional organizations.

10.14   Its programs were established to help increase the number of science and mathematics teachers and provide new instructional materials for public schools.

10.2   National Defense Education Act (1958) (previously referred to as a part of vocational education)

10.21   Purposes: to strengthen national defense by increasing the supply of competent teachers; provided financial assistance to public schools to improve instruction in mathematics, science, and languages; encouraged states to improve guidance programs; provided funds for research in the use of instructional media.

10.22   Its provisions were extended in 1963 to include other areas and functions.

10.3   The Cooperative Research Program (1954)

10.31   Program was established in the U.S. Office of Education to contract with higher education institutions to conduct research, surveys, and studies in education.

10.32   Funds allotted were very limited; results were good in shaping and defining educational research.

Programs of Direct Federal Responsibility

11.1   The Citizenship Act of 1924

11.11   Accelerated the shift of Indian education from predominantly church-operated schools to federally operated schools.

11.2   The Johnson-O'Malley Act (1934)

11.21   Authorized contracts with the states for the education of Indians.

11.3   A variety of educational programs, principally vocational, for adult Indians provided by the federal government.

11.4   Federal programs for veterans include:

11.41   The Vocational Rehabilitation Program of 1943 for disabled veterans emphasized the need for vocational advisory services and vocational rehabilitation training.

11.42   The G. I. Bill of Rights (Servicemen's Readjustment Act of 1944) to encourage the education of war veterans. The bill resulted in benefits to thousands of World War II and other war veterans.

11.43   War Orphans Educational Assistance Act of 1956.

11.44   Veterans' Readjustment Assistance Act of 1952.

12. Federal Programs in Lieu of Taxes
   12.1 The federal government uses three different methods to determine how much it should pay local school districts or other local units of government in lieu of funds lost by the tax-exempt status of federal property.
      12.11 Payments based on the value of the federal property multiplied by the local tax rate (for some types of tax-exempt property).
      12.12 Payments from public lands include 12.5 percent of revenue from grazing fees in national grazing districts, 50 percent of grazing fees on other federal lands, and 37.5 percent of revenues collected from mineral rights on federal lands.
      12.13 The use of Public Laws 815 and 874. Here federal payments are related to the number of public school children that are added to the school district because of federal programs. Public Law 815 provides funds for the construction of school facilities; 874 provides operating funds in eligible impacted areas; the future of these two laws is now uncertain.

The foregoing examples of federal activities in education illustrate the diversity and the extent of such programs. The list could easily be extended, but to no useful purpose. The average reader will note some he can defend assiduously and others whose contribution to American education he would prefer to protest or question. Some will criticize the imbalance that many of these federal activities have tended to create in the public schools, while others will accept them in lieu of more defensible general federal aid to education.

COMBINING AND SIMPLIFYING FEDERAL PROGRAMS

Recent proliferation of federal categorical-aid programs has created some problems for the fifty states and their local school districts, such as the difficulty of obtaining grants for small districts, the inconsistency and delay in funding various programs, burdensome accounting requirements, and indirect federal control of certain aspects of the curriculum, to name only a few.

In an effort to bring some order and system out of the numerous and somewhat chaotic federal programs, Congress passed Public Law 93-380, known as the Education Amendment of 1974. It was intended as a measure to combine and simplify many of the programs already in existence as well as to add some new ones. For example, it extended the Elementary and Secondary Education Act through 1978 and the Emergency School Aid Act through 1976.

Some of the difficulties involved in creating federal legislation to help finance education may be noted in the following description of the 1974 Amendment:

> With a piece of legislation so complex and so broad in scope as the Educational Amendments of 1974—the printed version of the public law runs to 130 pages—a detailed description of it would necessarily reach encyclopedic proportions. . . .
>
> The array of issues it addresses and the numerous new programs it creates make the Education Amendments a remarkable legislative accomplishment, and one of the most complex Federal education laws ever passed. . . .
>
> P. L. 93–380 in any case represents a major advance in Federal support of the Nation's schools, and its impact will be lasting.[4]

Whether or not the 1974 legislation will in fact accomplish its major purposes is open to some question, as indicated in the following:

> By trying to simplify federal aid to education, have Congress and the Administration created an even larger administrative monster for local and state officials? The first year of efforts to consolidate some programs is half over, and as U.S. Office of Education (USOE) officials finish their preliminary review of state plans under Title IV of the Education Amendments of 1974 (the consolidation provision) and educational administrators learn more about their legal responsibilities, there are some doubts about what is happening. "Local and state education agencies would have been far better served by consolidation in fact rather than in name only as is the case under Title IV," the National Advisory Council on Supplementary Centers and Services charged in its final report.
>
> Citing the seven new programs added under the Special Projects Act, the council says that state and local officials "are faced with more categorization of programs" this fiscal year than before consolidation. These new programs involve discretionary funds, but even in the state grant programs, which were the primary object of consolidation, "categorical requirements for administration of the programs are still being used," says Ray Peterson of the Council of Chief State School Officers. Many of the new requirements, which became effective last week, are based on USOE interpretation of the law and place more, rather than fewer, administrative burdens on states, he says.[5]

4. Albert L. Alfrod, "The Education Amendments of 1974," in *American Education* (Washington, D.C.: U.S. Dept. of Health, Education, and Welfare, Office of Education, Jan.–Feb. 1975).

5. *Education U.S.A., Washington Monitor* (Washington, D.C.: National School Public Relations Assn., Jan. 5, 1976), p. 109.

FEDERAL FISCAL ADVANTAGES AND DISADVANTAGES

The federal government's role in financing public education may well be classified as one that began as an advisory and supplementary one but that seems to be emerging as a more forceful and dominant one. In any event, the contribution of the federal government to the present state of development of our public schools has been important in spite of the disadvantages that this unit of government encounters as a partner in our tri-partnership system of education. It is the unit in our hierarchy of governance that is at the greatest distance from the ongoing process of education. By Constitutional design, it was to have only limited interest in educational matters. While education is the only function of the local school district and is an important function of state government, it is only one of many important responsibilities at the national level. The federal government has a myriad of problems and programs that of necessity often upstage the federal interest in education—especially in periods of acute distress or national emergency.

Superior Taxing System

The federal government has certain advantages which are not enjoyed by the other units of the partnership and which tend to give it high moral, if not legal, responsibility to assist in the operation of this important and expensive service of government. Chief among these is its unchallenged rating as the greatest tax collector. Using as it does the highly graduated income tax, it has become a tax-collecting agency without peer in efficiency and effectiveness. Whether or not such massive federal collections should rest comfortably beyond the desperately grasping hand of an underfed educational system (except for minor amounts of categorical support) was a more or less moot question until the deluge of federal programs in recent years revived it.

The federal government uses the graduated income tax as its predominant source of revenue. Total income, with proper deductions for dependents and other tax exclusions, provides a good comparison of the ability of people to pay their obligations to government. The income tax represents a positive segment of our sometimes maligned tax system. It produces large amounts of revenue at a relatively low collection rate. It is collected for the most part by withholding taxes and is therefore a "convenient" tax to pay. It is paid by a high percentage of our citizens, but its evasion possibilities are much too great under certain conditions. Features of the tax can be regulated in such a way as to alter the economic pattern of the country. With all its limitations and unfairness in the treatment of some individuals or companies compared with others, the income tax remains the backbone of this country's tax structure. Inherent inequities in its application are its greatest deficiency; its power to produce large amounts of revenue while using the ability principle of taxation is its greatest virtue.

Occupies Neutral Position

The federal government enjoys a position of neutrality as far as providing educational advantages to one section of the country is concerned, for all our people are citizens of a nation and not just citizens of local communities and states. The national interest requires some means of ensuring universal equality of educational opportunity that is not confined to rich districts, rich states, or any other level of structure. Only federal tax money can be used in any state for education or in any school district, for every American can be viewed at the national level as being as important as every other one. It is much more difficult for state officials in a wealthy state to practice such a philosophy when considering the pupils in another less fortunate state.

LIMITED FEDERAL AID: A REALITY

Federal aid for education is older than the United States Constitution, and various forms of categorical aid have appeared at an accelerating pace since World War II. As conscientiously as one may search for valid opposing arguments, or as boldly as one may decry federal involvement in educational matters, the die is cast—for the moment at least. The rhetoric, the debate, and even the high-tempered controversies have run their course, and federal aid of categorical vintage is now an observable fact of American life. The problem now facing us is how to use it in the best way possible with the greatest possible output for the investment. President John F. Kennedy pointed out the fact that we can no longer afford the traditional luxury of endless debate over all the sensitive questions raised by each new proposal for additional federal participation in education. He stressed the fact that this nation has not come to its position of leadership by avoiding hard problems and that we must now face and solve the problem of federal aid to education, difficult as it may be.

Johns and Morphet made another important point concerning the controversy over federal aid to education in the following quote:

The real reason for the bitterness of this controversy is that it has become involved with a number of other important national issues. Education has become the battleground for testing many important principles of law, theories of government, theories of economics, and philosophical values. The great number of studies made on the Federal aid issue is evidence of its importance. In 1951 Quattlebaum listed 42 governmental commissions, advisory groups, and private voluntary organizations as having made studies of this problem during the previous 20 years.[6]

DISTRIBUTING FEDERAL FUNDS

Although our need to provide federal programs and monies for education in the states has been established for the moment, no definitive decision has been provided concerning the method or process of distribution. The method that is considered to be the most acceptable (general aid) has not yet been authorized by congressional action. Nor has Congress seen fit to distribute federal funds to the states on an equalization basis.

Federal Equalization

Although the battle has been won for equalization of state funds to local districts, no such arrangement has been authorized for distribution of federal monies to the states. Certainly the arguments for equalization are as valid when applied to allocation of federal funds as when applied to distribution of state funds. Not state boundaries any more than school district boundaries should relegate some pupils to poor education, at the same time elevating others to superior education. Place of birth should not arbitrarily determine the kind and amount of education a student should receive, for the principle of equality of educational opportunity applies to all our citizens.

That federal financial assistance should be distributed to the states on an equalization basis is supported by the following:

1. The states have wide differences in their ability to pay for education, regardless of the devices or methods used to measure such comparative figures. This has a great deal to do with the wide range of annual expenditures per pupil, although other factors are involved. Some of the less wealthy states cannot finance an optimum or even an average educational program without excessive taxation, while others can do so with minimum tax effort.

6. Roe L. Johns and Edgar L. Morphet, *Financing the Public Schools* (Englewood Cliffs, N.J.: Prentice-Hall, 1960), p. 362.

2. Modern education does not confine its social or economic benefits to the area covered by the school district, the state, or even the nation. Conversely, the bad effects of poor education follow the recipients wherever they go. The problems created by inadequate education in a poor state accompany the school dropout or the graduate who often moves to a more affluent area in search of job opportunities. Thus, it is to the advantage and interest of even the wealthy states that every state provide a good education for all their citizens. The best-known method of assuring a sound educational program in every state is providing an equalized finance base.

3. A strong and viable educational program in every state strengthens the nation as a whole—its defenses, its economic productivity, and its support of the basic principles of democratic action. Democratic or representative government can function successfully only with enlightened citizens in a society devoid of caste or class structure. Educational opportunity tends to erase or mitigate social class distinction.

Categorical v. General Federal Aid

In 1968, Harold Howe II, then U.S. commissioner of education, sought to clarify the meaning of three kinds of federal appropriations for education:

1. *Block grants.* The term *block grants* has sometimes been used as if it were synonymous with general aid. This is not the way the block grant concept has come to be understood among most people in education. Educators tend to see block grants as being related to the categorical approach but involving broader categories and greater discretion within these categories. . . .

2. *Categorical aid.* This is the approach under which Congress designates the exact purposes for which federal funds shall be used.

3. *General aid.* In its pure form general aid involves only a general expression of purpose or priority by the federal government, such as improving education at the elementary and secondary levels. It also implies far less accountability, reporting, and evaluation.[7]

Many educators have accepted the categorical aid programs of the federal government in the belief that general aid is more desirable but impossible to obtain under present conditions. Various practical realities foredoom any general federal aid programs that might be (and have been) introduced by the Congress:

7. *Education U.S.A., Washington Monitor* (Washington, D.C.: National School Public Relations Assn., Dec. 23, 1968), p. 102.

1. The forms of federal aid that purport to provide universal equal opportunity would require differential amounts of money per pupil among the various states, according to some measure of need. Members of Congress from wealthy states, whose election to office is determined periodically by their respective voting constituencies, can hardly be expected to vote for larger allocations to the needier states than to their own—unless they see education as a national as well as a state responsibility.

2. Since the federal government through recent decisions of the Supreme Court has ordered the end of segregation in this country, members of Congress are constrained to vote against general federal aid, without controls, until integration has been implemented and the "separate but equal" philosophy of an earlier era has suffered complete demise.

3. Agreement is not at present nationwide concerning use or nonuse of federal monies for nonpublic schools. A few states legally provide state funds for nonpublic school purposes, which are usually vetoed by court decisions; others reject the idea. It will be difficult if not impossible to get congressional approval of general federal aid until such monies are used in every state with the same interpretation of church-state relations in financing education.

4. The fear of federal control of education pervades the thinking of the average American citizen when he considers extension of federal support to the states. Thus if additional federal activities are inaugurated, the degree of control must be set at a point where state or local responsibility for education is not in serious jeopardy. History shows that this control level may be at a very low pitch (the land grants of 1787, for example), or it may be set at a high pitch (the Smith-Hughes Act of 1917, for example).

It would seem that the odds against obtaining general federal aid in any substantial amount are high at the moment. Perhaps it is the better part of wisdom, then, to view the practical pros and cons of categorical aid programs that have recently inundated the state and local districts in so short a period of time that there has been difficulty in adjusting to them. In the words of the American Association of School Administrators:

> We would be thoughtless indeed if we were now to sell short the categorical grant-in-aid. Over the years it has proved to be an ingenious device for promoting cooperation among the different levels of government. I cannot emphasize it enough: the categorical grant-in-aid, its attendant problems notwithstanding, has a great record. Through the many cooperative arrangements it has fostered, the categorical grant-in-aid has been a means of encouraging perspective—that has come from the federal government. The managerial ability, the imaginative talent,

and the practical know-how—all this has come from state and local levels. And now, under the Elementary and Secondary Education Act, categorical programs have been devised that can help children in both public and nonpublic schools—and can do so within our constitutional framework.[8]

The chief arguments raised against categorical aid are (1) it tends to give the federal government too much power and control in determining where the money is to be spent, and (2) it often results in imbalances in the curricula and programs that the schools sponsor. There is hope in the belief that just as the states began their appropriations to local districts in categorical grants and later moved to more general aid, so may the federal government move toward more generalized aid programs in the future.

Future general federal aid programs to be most effective must embody certain characteristics: (1) They must not be used to allow state and local support monies to be decreased. The main responsibility for financing education must remain at those levels; federal assistance must assume an "icing on the cake" function. (2) While funds should be based on the principle of equalization, each state should expect to receive some funds, depending on its comparative wealth and need. (3) Funds should be provided for some specific programs that are in the national interest but that may be neglected because of their high costs, inconvenience, or emergency nature—education of the disadvantaged, the handicapped, the exceptional, and others.

As viewed by Wayne O. Reed, writing for the American Association of School Administrators, future federal aid will involve both general and categorical programs:

> I would say that the future will lead us not to categorical aid alone or to general aid alone, but to a judicious mix of the two, arrived at gradually. And the mix will never harden. It will always be fluid. It will change as circumstances change. General aid, when it comes, will be supplemented now and then—whenever necessary and perhaps then only temporarily—with categorical programs designed to counter specific threats to the national welfare.[9]

FEDERAL-STATE-LOCAL FINANCE SHARING

To what degree should each level of government participate in financing public education? The answer to that very reasonable question has never

8. *The Federal Interest in Education* (Washington, D.C.: American Assn. of School Administrators, 1967), p. 9.
9. Ibid., pp. 12–13.

been made with any consensus. Should the 56–40–4 proportion of local-state-federal sharing, which formed a rough plateau of practice until the recent outbreak of federal programs, be accepted as standard? Are there criteria that can be applied to determine a more realistic and valid basis on which to base each level's partnership responsibility? As the costs of education increase and states and local districts become increasingly less able to finance education, how shall the role of the federal government be determined? The questions in this regard are easy to formulate and numerous; the answers are evasive and almost nonexistent. The problem remains.

It is obvious that the time is ripe for a study to discover answers to the question of government level responsibility for financing education. Arthur F. Corey proposed such a study in 1960 and reiterated it in 1966:

> The present moment would be a propitious time for the initiation of a national study which would bring together our best leadership, with an adequate staff of technicians, to study the problems involved in integrating large-scale federal support into state systems of school finnace. . . . A group like this should ignore traditions and develop a workable blueprint for a national program of school support which would involve the systematic integration of local, state, and national resources.[10]

Governmental Responsibilities Change

From the beginning of this nation, education has been part and parcel of state government. It has been its direct responsibility, but the onus for financing education has chiefly been relegated to the local school districts. Certain operational realities indicate little likelihood of more than nominal change in this condition in the immediate future.

Operation of our schools has been accompanied by two opposing ideas—a decentralizing emphasis in the face of strong support for centralization. This paradox arises from continued enunciation of the merits of local, decentralized control of the educational system at the same time that local inadequacies have brought the state and its centralization tendencies into more responsible action in financing our schools, in certifying our teachers, and in standardizing our curricula. Changing demands of society for more governmental services, including education, put additional pressures upon government for more controls, more definitive guidelines, and stricter regulations, with commensurate loss of local power.

10. Arthur F. Corey, "The Essentials of a Modern School Finance Program," in *Local-State-Federal Partnership in School Finance* (Washington, D.C.: National Education Assn., 1966), p. 17.

The shifting of responsibilities of the three levels of government for educational needs and services is not a new phenomenon. For example, financing education, once a local function only, is now largely a local-state form of partnership responsibility; and promotion of pupils at certain grade levels was once virtually a state-controlled operation, but now it is completely within the jurisdiction of the local district. As shifts come in functional responsibilities, changes come also in the degree of centralization emphasis. Just as any growth or increase in state financial support for education may represent some degree of encroachment upon local control, so additional federal support increases the possibility of centralization of power and lessening of state and local autonomy in operating public schools.

State and federal regulation or power over public school operation have increased slowly but surely in the last decade or so. As districts reach out to become recipients of state and federal revenues, which are more equitably imposed and more economically collected than those at the local level, they must weigh the advantages received against the possibility of power losses that could be sustained.

Partnership Proposals Vary

No compelling or research-oriented rationale exists for determining the proportion of public school costs to be paid by each level of government. The anti-federal-aid advocates would divide the responsibility between the local units and the state. The strong supporters of average practice, or status quo adherents, would leave the proportions at somewhere near the 56–40–4 percentages that were in effect before the recent increases in federal government participation. There are a comparative few who would continue to maintain the unrealistic position that the finances should be provided almost completely at the local level to assure local control of education. A rapidly increasing number of our citizens, including some who are knowledgeable about school finance, are advocating complete state support of education in order to simplify and improve equalization. Some support has been engendered for still another comparative relation of the members of the tri-partnership in education— equal percentage participation by each. Among those who have advocated something close to this proposal was the late U.S. Commissioner of Education James E. Allen. His plan for the U.S. Office of Education was to increase the federal share to 25 or 30 percent by 1980.[11]

Some strong arguments exist in favor of much greater participation of the federal government in financing education. Chief among these is

11. *Phi Delta Kappan* (September 1969), p. 54.

that most state and local units do not seem to possess the financial muscle necessary to do the job as it should be done. In confronting such a problem, school administrators look longingly at the possibility of securing greatly expanded federal financial support, as indicated in the following:

> The federal government should pay one-third of the cost of public education. This thought was expressed repeatedly by speakers at the American Association of School Administrator's (AASA) convention at Atlantic City (1969). Their request represents a dramatic boost in federal aid since the current support is about 8 percent. A few speakers . . . called for even more drastic change. They would virtually eliminate local support for schools.[12]

FEDERAL AID IN LIEU OF TAXES

Federal aid to education does not represent a purely altruistic position by an affluent "uncle" to some financially inept relatives (states and local school districts). Rather, some federal programs have been organized and implemented because of the financial obligations that the federal government has to the states. A prime example is the obligation the former has to make payments in lieu of the taxes that would ordinarily be paid on the tremendous amount of land that it owns, particularly in the western states. About one-third of the land area of the county is owned by the federal government, thus removing it from the reach of state, county, or school district property taxes.

INCREASED GOVERNMENTAL SERVICES

It is impossible to understand and support the point of view that favors extended federal financial support for education unless one understands the change in philosophy about governmental services that has pervaded the country in the last several decades. The "hands off" and "government do as little as possible" view of the earlier years of our existence as a country is no longer acceptable, desirable, or practicable. Traditionally the federal role was accepted as one of maintaining law and order, providing for some degree of protection to the individual and his property, and in general maintaining a laissez faire policy toward most other

12. *Education U.S.A.* (Washington, D.C.: National School Public Relations Assn., Feb. 24, 1969), p. 141.

problems. Such a policy was defensible and worked for the maximum development of individual initiative and growth. Economists and political scientists supported this policy, and it served the country well for a long period of our early history.

The "let alone" policy of government is no longer defensible. The continuously increasing complexity of our social institutions, our economic order, and our political organization has resulted in comparable and increased services of government. The dangers of unlimited extension of such services are great, however. Thus, determining the services that should be provided by each level of government and those that should be left to the individual is now of paramount importance. The assumption here is that each unit of government is responsible for providing those services that will result in maximum social benefits to the greatest possible number of our citizens. The prevailing point of view in this regard was well expressed by Wyatt in the following:

> We must come to view government as a part of our economy, rather than as a burden that the economy itself must carry. Opponents of adequate school financing seem to be waging a campaign to discredit not only school taxation and school financing, but taxation and even government itself. They tend to belittle people who are engaged in education, in recreation, in sanitation, or any governmental area, and to label proposed expenditures for park systems, highways, or perhaps our schools as lavish and wasteful, rather than as an investment in human resources. It seems to me that we must develop among school people, and among the people generally, something of a new concept of the place of government in the economy.[13]

EDUCATIONAL LEADERSHIP NEEDED

It seems likely that the present ferment in education that is related to the controversial role of the federal government will disappear when a proper mixture of educational leadership at all levels is consummated. At the moment, no one is prepared to prescribe the ingredients and additives necessary for maximum results from our tremendous monetary investment at all levels of government. In the past, American ingenuity has been noteworthy for its ability to solve the problems of our society when they have arisen. Solving current problems attached to the increased participation of the federal government in education should be no exception to this well-established practice. In the meantime, if the

13. Robert H. Wyatt, "A Program of Action," in *Financing Education for Our Changing Population* (Washington, D.C.: National Education Assn., 1961), pp. 41–44.

FIGURE 6.1 Percentage of State Land Owned by the Federal Government, June 30, 1969

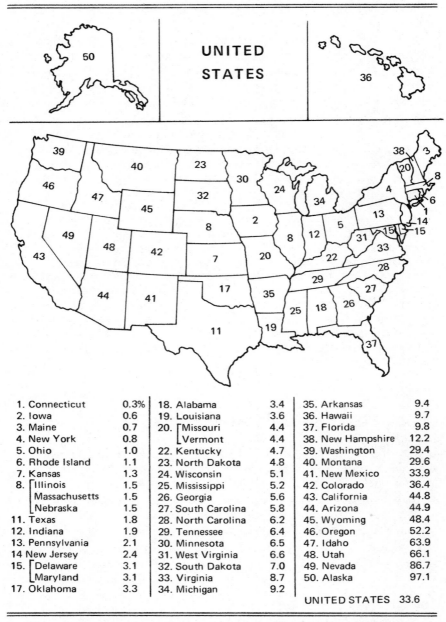

1. Connecticut	0.3%	18. Alabama	3.4	35. Arkansas	9.4
2. Iowa	0.6	19. Louisiana	3.6	36. Hawaii	9.7
3. Maine	0.7	20. ⌈Missouri	4.4	37. Florida	9.8
4. New York	0.8	⌊Vermont	4.4	38. New Hampshire	12.2
5. Ohio	1.0	22. Kentucky	4.7	39. Washington	29.4
6. Rhode Island	1.1	23. North Dakota	4.8	40. Montana	29.6
7. Kansas	1.3	24. Wisconsin	5.1	41. New Mexico	33.9
8. ⌈Illinois	1.5	25. Mississippi	5.2	42. Colorado	36.4
Massachusetts	1.5	26. Georgia	5.6	43. California	44.8
⌊Nebraska	1.5	27. South Carolina	5.8	44. Arizona	44.9
11. Texas	1.8	28. North Carolina	6.2	45. Wyoming	48.4
12. Indiana	1.9	29. Tennessee	6.4	46. Oregon	52.2
13. Pennsylvania	2.1	30. Minnesota	6.5	47. Idaho	63.9
14 New Jersey	2.4	31. West Virginia	6.6	48. Utah	66.1
15. ⌈Delaware	3.1	32. South Dakota	7.0	49. Nevada	86.7
⌊Maryland	3.1	33. Virginia	8.7	50. Alaska	97.1
17. Oklahoma	3.3	34. Michigan	9.2		

UNITED STATES 33.6

SOURCE: U.S. Department of Commerce, Bureau of the Census, *Statistical Abstract of the United States, 1970,* 91st ed. (Washington, D.C.: U.S. Government Printing Office, 1970), p. 192.

interests of boys and girls are to be considered in their proper perspective, the massive difficulties now before us should not be allowed to curtail seriously or thwart the purposes of the federal commitment, or reduce its thrust. The problems of education and the national, state, and local interest in solving them have never been greater. The programs now in operation, as well as future ones, will have important consequences for education for many years to come. No state or local school district should fail to take advantage of the programs that are now available and that will continue to be so. This will require leadership, imagination, and dedication from school people at all levels of operation if maximum individual and social benefits are to be obtained.

THE CHALLENGES OF FEDERAL AID

Federal involvement in education has shown an upward turn since the frustrating years of the Depression. Beginning with the emergency and war preparation programs of the Depression and World War II years, federal activities continued to expand to meet the educational needs of an increasing population and also demands for better-trained personnel for national defense and for a planned trip to the moon. More recently, federal programs have been accentuated to win a national "war on poverty," to eliminate racial discrimination, and to maintain the solvency of the parochial school system.

The last decade has brought many dramatic and far-reaching changes in federal aid to education. These changes have generated problems and challenges that state and local educational institutions have never before faced. While most of these problems are solvable over time, they have resulted in the creation of a state of quiet but discernible criticism of the manner in which many of the federal activities have been conducted. Congressional slowness in funding some programs, rigidity of purpose, loss of local and state control, indecision and frequent reversal of direction, and general lack of communication have combined to lessen the effectiveness of many of the recent federal programs in education, even though their results have generally been highly beneficial.

Federal programs and assistance of any kind or in any amount would likely be accompanied with problems under the best of conditions, for they tend to change the traditionally accepted relation of local, state, and federal agencies to education. Some informed people in educational administration stress their belief that such changes would be beneficial to education and are long overdue. Many writers decry the perpetual continuance of a once relevant localism in education.

The textbook arguments that once justified establishment by local school boards of strictly local objectives, local curricula, and local standards with little regard for the broader community are no longer valid or defensible, they say. Goldman pointed to this in the following in his discussion of "repressive localism":

> Among the greatest irrelevancies of our educational system today are the boundary lines which clearly circumscribe certain areas for education. These boundary lines have tended to shelter local school districts from the problems of the "larger community." The resulting localism prevents schools from mounting significant and relevant efforts toward solving problems which are statewide or national in scope.[14]

Lieberman pointed to the imminent demise of our present system of local control of education:

> One of the most important trends in the next few decades is likely to be the decline of local control of education. Such a development is long overdue. Local control of education has clearly outlived its usefulness on the American scene. Practically, it must give way to a system of educational controls in which local communities play ceremonial rather than policy-making roles. . . .
>
> An autopsy of local control reveals several reasons for its demise. In the first place, mobility and interdependence have completely undermined the notion that local communities ought to have a free hand in educating their children. Second, national survival now requires educational policies and programs which are not subject to local veto. Third, it is becoming increasingly clear that local control cannot in practice be reconciled with the ideals of a democratic society. Finally, local control is a major cause of the dull parochialism and attentuated totalitarianism that characterizes public education in operation.[15]

THE FUTURE OF FEDERAL AID-TO-EDUCATION PROGRAMS

Concerning the future of federal assistance to education, it now seems to be apparent that:

1. The widespread and complex involvement of the federal government in helping to finance public education programs is not likely to diminish or disappear in the near future. There is some evidence,

14. Samuel Goldman, "The Question of Relevancy," in *Preparing Educators to Meet Emerging Needs* (Denver: Designing Education for the Future, March 1969), p. 153.
15. Myron Lieberman, "Local Control of Education," in Sheldon Staff and Herbert Schwartzberg, eds., *The Human Encounter* (New York: Harper & Row, 1969), p. 320.

however, that the specific programs to be sponsored or financed may change often as they are influenced by changing philosophies and changing leaders in the three branches of the federal government.

2. Federal, state, and local experience in working with current and future programs will help immeasurably in solving some if not all of the fermenting problems that now loom as big hurdles in establishing a defensible federal-state-local partnership in the sponsorship of public education.

3. If order is to be established in the administration of federal programs, it will be necessary to center primary responsibility in fewer educational agencies at the national level. The United States Office of Education is the logical agency to administer most if not all of the federal programs directly related to education.

4. Additional federal financial programs need not—indeed, should not—greatly increase the degree of control over education at the national level. However, there is need to give national purpose to education. The confining boundaries between school districts, counties, and states that were of such consequence half a century ago are now imaginary and meaningless. Funds for education, regardless of their source, should be directed toward achieving national as well as state and local community goals of education.

5. Although categorical aid contributes greatly to the educational program, the goals of education demand that some form of general aid should be recognized as desirable. This should be initiated at the earliest possible time to help dissolve the barriers preventing equal educational opportunity for every American citizen regardless of color, race, creed, or place of residence.

The opinions of people concerning the role of the federal government have changed greatly in recent years. Enlarged and increased federal responsibility for education was once defended largely by a "liberal" segment of the social milieu. While still somewhat controversial, it is now supported by a majority of our citizens regardless of political party affiliation, race, religion, or any other designation. As the programs and official responsibilities of the public schools increase, greater participation and support are required at each of the three levels of government. As the costs of high-quality education continue their spiral upward, it is inconceivable that the solutions to the increasing problems of education should rest on only one or two of the parties concerned—the states and the local school districts. For the system to work as intended, each partner must assume some share of the additional responsibility for the cost of the cradle-to-the-grave educational programs that citizens have been demanding and probably will continue to demand in the years ahead.

That the role of the federal government in education will change with the passage of time appears to be certain. The direction of such change, however, is not as evident. One can only guess as to whether it will involve greater emphasis on categorical aid programs—as are emphasized currently, or whether some sort of breakthrough will be made to inaugurate general aids in an attempt to equalize educational opportunity among the several states. Conner refers to "a new and evolving national posture" for the federal government in the years ahead in the following:

> As education has become more clearly identified with the nation's well-being, the schools have become more visible in the political arena. Perhaps at no time in our history has education occupied such a prominent place on the agenda of the United States Congress. The growing awareness of the federal government's responsibility for education reflects a new and evolving national posture. This deeper involvement in community, state, and national life has brought to the schools new challenges, but it has brought, too, perplexing problems and issues that must be viewed and treated with new perspective.[16]

IMPACT OF FEDERAL AID TO EDUCATION

It is difficult to assess objectively the impact that federal aid has had on American education. Berke and Kirst in their study of the financial factors that affect public education and their analysis of the impact of federal school aid in California, Massachusetts, Michigan, New York, and Texas, came to some generalizations concerning this that are worth considering:

1. In the most urbanized areas there was a unique crisis in educational finance caused by a general deterioration in their fiscal situation combined with higher demands and costs—for education and for other public services—than existed in neighboring communities.
2. Central cities received more federal education aid than their suburbs, but the amounts were too small to compensate for the suburban advantage in local wealth and state aid.
3. There were significant differences in the patterns of individual programs.
4. If fiscal capacity to support education is seen only in terms of property value per pupil, there is little compensating effect through federal aid.

16. Forrest E. Conner, *Federal Policy and the Public Schools* (Washington, D.C.: American Assn. of School Administrators, 1967), p. 1.

5. If one takes the proportion of poor and minority pupils in a district as one proxy for educational need . . . federal aid tends to be significantly related to educational need.
6. Over the four-year period of their study, amounts of federal aid reported by individual school districts varied erratically because of the bizarre timing of federal fund appropriation and administration.
7. The failure to concentrate funds on the students most in need of compensatory education has frequently resulted in a superficial veneer of fragmented programs and new equipment, rather than in an integrated, high impact intervention to achieve major educational change.
8. Although federal aid is intended to provide strategically useful funds for educational purposes not otherwise receiving adequate support, the amounts of aid are simply too small in view of the problems that confront education.[17]

THE UNITED STATES OFFICE OF EDUCATION

The federal government's main thrust in performance of its educational function as envisioned by the framers of the Constitution has come through the operations of the United States Office of Education. The federal government has exercised much of its advisory role through the promotion of research and leadership in education that the Office has supplied.

The Office of Education was founded in 1867, with Henry Barnard as its first commissioner. Its functions were to be:

1. Collecting such statistics and facts as would show the condition and progress of education in the several states and territories.
2. Diffusing such information respecting the organization and management of schools and school systems, and methods of teaching, as would aid the people of the United States in the establishment and maintenance of efficient school systems.
3. Otherwise promoting the cause of education throughout the country.

Our chief concern with the Office in this discussion is its relation to the financing of education. For many years it had very little responsibility in such matters—its chief function being that of making research studies, surveys, consultation and field studies, and the like. Since World War II with emergence of the federal government as a somewhat active

17. Joel S. Berke and Michael W. Kirst, *Federal Aid to Education: Who Benefits? Who Governs?* (Lexington, Mass.: Lexington Books, D.C. Heath and Co., 1972), pp. 2–4.

"partner" in financing education, the Office has become an important grant-dispensing agency for the large sums of money made available by numerous laws providing such funds to the states and local school districts. The influence of the Office has increased as its role in disbursing funds has increased. Likewise, the controversy over its role in education has grown as its influence and disbursing power have grown. Strangely enough, even with the increased status of the Office, much of the federal money for educational programs is still disbursed by other agencies of government.

Selected Readings

Berke, Joel S., and Kirst, Michael W. *Federal Aid to Education: Who Benefits? Who Governs?* Lexington, Mass.: Lexington Books, D. C. Heath and Co., 1972.

Educational Responsibilities of the Federal Government. Washington, D.C.: National Education Assn. Educational Policies Commission, 1964.

Federal Policy and the Public Schools. Washington, D.C.: American Assn. of School Administrators, 1967.

Financing Education: Who Benefits? Who Pays? Washington, D.C.: National Education Assn., National School Finance Conference, 1972.

Freeman, Roger A. *Federal Aid to Education—Boon or Bane?* Washington, D.C.: American Enterprise Assn., Inc., 1955.

Friedman, Burton D., and Dunbar, Laird J. *Grants Management in Education: Federal Impact on State Agencies.* Chicago: Public Administration Service, 1971.

Pierce, Truman M. *Federal, State and Local Government in Education.* New York: Center for Applied Research in Education, 1965.

Schools, People, and Money. Washington, D.C.: President's Commission on School Finance, U.S. Government Printing Office, 1972.

The Federal Government and Public Schools. Washington, D.C.: American Assn. of School Administrators, 1965.

Thomas, Norman C. *Education in National Politics.* New York: David McKay Co., Inc., 1975.

Unit 3

THE JUDICIAL SYSTEM AND SCHOOL FINANCE REFORM

What has now become clear is that the courts have provided only an opportunity, not an answer; a starting point for reform, not a solution to the unfairness and irrationality of educational funding in America.

Joel S. Berke,
Answers to Inequity,
1974

7

The Courts and School Finance

Traditionally, major changes in formal education have developed rather slowly. School personnel and the general public have often been reluctant to foster or even to yield to change and innovation on a significant scale. The fault for such resistance has not always been due to satisfaction with the status quo, however. A general attitude of conservatism on the part of governing boards of education, inadequate budgets, small school attendance areas, restrictive rules and standards for state and regional accreditation, lack of financial support and public approval of educational research, lack of qualified personnel who are oriented to change, and other unfavorable conditions have often served as impediments to rapid changes and improvements in public schools.

STATE FINANCE PROGRAMS OFTEN OUTDATED

Over the years, major changes and improvements have usually been difficult to effect in state school finance programs. Legislative action is almost always necessary and this process normally involves disturbance of the state's taxing and funding systems. Changes almost always require additional funds with attendant taxpayer criticism and resistance. As a consequence, public schools are often in some form of financial crisis. Under such emergencies the machinery for school financing is patched or added to with little effort being directed toward major revamping or the replacement of obsolescent finance programs. Thus, many of the states have been financing mid- and late-twentieth century schools with early twentieth century finance patterns.

Nowhere in the broad spectrum of activities in education is there a better example of recent reversal of attitude toward change than in public school finance. Although periods of crisis do not always appear to lend themselves well to the difficult process of changing and innovating, evidence concerning what is now being done in school financial theory and practice contraindicates such a view. For many years the American public has been aware of an impending crisis in our public and also our private schools. Taxpayer revolts against increased bond or even current-expenditure levies, early closing of schools because of depleted budgets, severe reductions of school services, and other similar happenings have become commonplace. Inadequate revenues have been distributed inequitably, and the burden of providing such funds has been shared with little regard to fairness to individual taxpayers. Although the three levels of government have shared in the funding of education, the proportionate burden of this responsibility has been in negative relation to their tax-collecting ability. Yet while these and many other financial problems plagued the schools, little constructive action was taken until the pressure of some recent court actions made such action imperative.

COURTS OFTEN GENERATE CHANGE

One has only to read the history of education to be reminded of the many times the courts of this country have altered the course of education. The *Kalamazoo* case of 1874 established a legal system of taxation for funding secondary education; the *Brown* case of 1954 pushed aside the indefensible doctrine of "separate, but equal" facilities and opportunities for minorities; the "one-man—one vote" decision of 1965 changed the organization of state legislative bodies and ultimately obliterated the requirement that voters must pay property taxes in order to vote in certain school elections; and more recently, in 1971 the *Serrano* v. *Priest* and other similar court decisions that followed put legal pressure on state legislatures to revise their state finance formulas to effect greater equity and equality for the students in all school districts within a particular state. Thus, it is evident that state and federal courts have considerable influence on many of the aspects of school operation.

COURT DECISION GUIDELINES

Generally, the courts tend to reflect the values and attitudes of a majority of the people toward the issues and questions on which they are ruling. Numerous recent court decisions illustrate the changing attitude of the general public toward some legal principles involved in financing education. While this generalization is not always true, it should help school administrators in anticipating the results of potential court action in matters dealing with public school finance.

Over an extended period of time, certain general guidelines and principles have emerged out of the numerous state and federal court decisions about financing education. Some of the most important of these include:

1. The courts are generally inclined to construe statutes concerning taxation strictly. They usually favor the taxpayer over the school district. A Florida court, for example, pointed out that "in deciding questions relating to procedure employed by a governmental taxing agency one must bear in mind at the outset that laws providing for taxation must be construed most strongly against the government and liberally in favor of the taxpayer."[1]
2. School finance funds, including tax monies, are state and not local funds. Local school districts are agencies of the state and are in reality acting for the state. The courts are therefore inclined to require the same care and efficiency in the administration of school funds that is required for other state agencies and institutions.
3. The courts have held consistently to the opinion that school taxes need not be imposed so that a direct relation exists between the benefits an individual taxpayer receives and the amount of taxes that he pays. In the words of one court, "The benefits are intangible and incapable of pecuniary ascertainment, but it is constitutionally sufficient if the taxes are uniform and are for public purposes in which the whole city has an interest."[2]
4. The legislature of each state has complete power to control public school funds and to determine how the public schools shall be financed, subject only to the restrictions imposed by the constitution of the state involved. Consequently, the legislature has wide discretion in determining how school funds shall be apportioned so long as the basis for such apportionment is just and not arbitrary.

POWER OF THE COURTS

Most Americans are aware of the fact that education is a state function with some responsibility delegated to the local school unit. They know,

1. Lewis v. Morley, 204 So. (2nd) 197 (Fla.).
2. Morton Salt Co. v. City of South Hutchinson, 177 F. 2d 889–10th Cir. 1949.

too, that each state's legislative body exercises plenary power over its own educational system. However, they sometimes disregard or under-emphasize the subtle but strong power the judicial system has over educational matters. As a consequence, the average person is often startled when a major court decision shows the effect a higher federal or state court brings to bear on the educational systems of the several states.

Until the early 1970s most higher courts refused to interfere or to rule in certain types of school finance cases with the rationale that the methods used to collect and distribute public funds to local school districts were a legislative and not a judicial problem. For example, in *Sawyer* v. *Gilmore*[3] the Supreme Court of Maine said, "The method of distribution of the proceeds of such a tax rests in the wise discretion and sound judgment of the Legislature. If this discretion is unwisely exercised, the remedy is with the people and not with the court."

No one seriously questions the philosophy of the *Sawyer* court—least of all the courts that have ruled on similar disputes. None of the courts have indicated any real intention to rewrite state school finance laws to meet the conditions they may have ruled against—although some have threatened to do so. The function of the courts to interpret laws and constitutions does not go that far. They have, however, sometimes given states a reasonable time in which to make the court-required changes through the normal channel of legislative action.

EQUAL PROTECTION AND THE COURTS BEFORE 1971

Perhaps the most publicized of the court cases before 1971 that involved the provision of unequal revenues per pupil in different school districts in the same state was that of *McInnis* v. *Shapiro* in Illinois in 1969.[4] The complaint was that there was inequality in the provision of funds in various school districts in the state. The complaint was dismissed by a three-judge court even though it recognized the wide range of expenditures among Illinois school districts. The court ruled that the Illinois plan for financing public education reflected a rational policy consistent with the mandate of the Illinois Constitution. It stated that the unequal expenditures per pupil did not amount to an invidious discrimination, and that the laws that permit these unequal expenditures are neither arbitrary nor unreasonable. It further ruled that equal edu-

3. The Supreme Court of Maine in Sawyer v. Gilmore, 109 Me. 169, 83A 673 (1912).
4. McInnis v. Ogilvie [Shapiro], 394 U.S. 322, 89 S. Ct. 1197.

cational opportunity was not a constitutional requisite and that it (the court) could not decide the issue.

The plaintiffs appealed the case (now *McInnis* v. *Ogilvie*) to the United States Supreme Court. The Court, without hearing the case, affirmed the decision of the lower court. It reemphasized judicial lack of power or authority to change state school finance programs. It said, "The courts have neither the knowledge, nor the means, nor the power to tailor the public moneys to fit the varying needs of these students throughout the state. We can only see to it that the outlays on one group are not invidiously greater or less than that of another. . . ."

The *McInnis* decision was noteworthy in the fact that the United States Supreme Court by its ruling appeared to view the problem of providing equal educational opportunity only in terms of the question of racial discrimination. In contrast, educational advocates of equal protection had projected their thinking to include all children and youth eligible for such by constitutional guarantee under the Fourteenth Amendment. Hence, educators were disappointed at the failure of the Court to take positive action to alleviate the disparities in the *McInnis* case.

DEVELOPMENT OF EQUAL PROTECTION THEORY

While the courts were refusing to take positive positions concerning the equal protection questions being raised regarding inequitable state school finance systems, certain school finance scholars and researchers were engaged in developing a rationale and defense against such inequities in nearly all of the states. Arthur E. Wise, John E. Coons, William Clune, and Stephen Sugarman were some of the leaders who argued that the quality of education within a state should not be a function of wealth, race, or geography. Wise, in recommending that school resources be distributed equitably according to degree of social or economic disadvantage borne by school students, suggested three forms of school finance revision: (1) state collection and distribution of all school revenues to local school districts; (2) equalization of tax bases of local school districts by redrawing district lines; and (3) manipulation of equalization formulas. Coons, Clune, and Sugarman emphasized the "power equalization" theory that was first enunciated by Harlan Updegraff half a century ago with its argument that equal tax effort should generate equal resources in all school districts. The positive effect of their scholarly work, along with that of many other school finance authorities with similar concerns, was soon to be noticed with the court decision in *Serrano* v. *Priest* in 1971 and the avalanche of similar decisions that followed quickly in other states.

SERRANO V. PRIEST

History indicates that occasionally an important, landmark event may occur that may either reverse the direction of thinking or enforce and implement dormant ideas to the point where they become acceptable or even popular. Such an event occurred on August 30, 1971, when the California Supreme Court ruled that John Serrano's complaint against the state's public school financial pattern was justifiable and that said pattern must be revised to make it constitutional.[5]

At the time the *Serrano* suit was brought to court, educational expenditures per person in California ranged from $274 in one district to $1,710 in another, a ratio of 1 to 6.2. In the same year, two districts in the same county (Beverly Hills and Baldwin Park) expended $1,223 and $577 per pupil. This inequity was due to the difference in the assessed valuation of property per pupil to be educated ($50,885 in Beverly Hills and $3,706 in Baldwin Park—a ratio of nearly 14 to 1). The taxpayers in Baldwin Park paid a school tax of 54.8 mills ($5.48 per $100 of assessed valuation) while those in Beverly Hills paid school taxes of only 23.8 mills ($2.38 per $100 of assessed valuation). Thus, a tax effort in the poorer district of twice that in the wealthier one resulted in school expenditures of only 47 percent of that in the wealthier district.

The disparities in school funds available per pupil that led to the *Serrano* lawsuit could have been duplicated in nearly all of the fifty states. It should be noted that the differences in ability to pay for education in Beverly Hills and Baldwin Park were not exceedingly great when compared with the extremes in the entire state or with those that could have been found in other states. Had the case been concerned with the extremes then existing in all of California, they would have been about fifty to one, about fourteen to one in New York, and six to one in Utah. Thus, the issue in *Serrano* was concerned with differences in ability—not necessarily in the size of those differences.

In *Serrano*, the California court considered questions related to the comparative wealth of districts, the classification of education as a fundamental interest, and whether or not the financing system was necessary to the attainment of any compelling state interest. In a 6 to 1 opinion, the court declared the state's public school financing system to be uncon-

5. Serrano v. Priest, 5 Cal. 3d 584, 96 Cal. Rptr. 601, 487 P. 2d 1241 (1971).

stitutional. It declared that dependence on local property taxes was the "root of the constitutional defect." It noted what school finance analysts have long known: under such a system, with heavy reliance on property taxation, school districts with a low value of taxable property per child cannot levy taxes at high enough rates to compete with more affluent districts; in many instances they cannot even provide funds for a minimum program of education.

The following statement summarizes the rationale of the court in the *Serrano* v. *Priest* decision:

> The California public school financing system, as presented to us by the plaintiffs' complaint supplemented by matters judicially noticed, since it deals intimately with education, obviously touches upon a fundamental interest. For the reasons we have explained in detail, this system conditions the full entitlement to such interest on wealth, classifies its recipients on the basis of their collective affluence and makes the quality of a child's education depend upon the resources of his school district and ultimately upon the pocketbook of his parents. We find that such financing system as presently constituted is not necessary to the attainment of any compelling state interest. Since it does not withstand the requisite "strict scrutiny,' it denies to the plaintiffs and others similarly situated the equal protection of the laws. . . . If the allegations of the complaint are sustained, the financial system must fall and the statutes comprising it must be found unconstitutional.[6]

The *Serrano* decision was the result of demurrer hearings held to test in court whether or not the plaintiff's complaint had merit sufficient to justify the time and expense of a formal trial. The California Supreme Court agreed that the plaintiff had a legal cause for action and was therefore entitled to a trial. The Court returned the case to the Los Angeles Superior Court for formal trial. The latter court filed its decision on April 10, 1974 stating that the California system of financing its public elementary and secondary schools violated the equal protection provisions of the California Constitution. It pointed out that it made no difference that the system of paying for education might provide an adequate education for all children of the state.

The trial court held that the California system of financing public education violated the equal protection of the law provisions of the California Constitution because a disparity of tax money to support education existed among the districts of the state. According to the court, it made no difference that the existing system might provide an adequate education for all the children of the state. There was a disparity in the amount of money available for the education of children among the districts which was constitutionally significant because it permitted some school districts to offer a higher quality of education than others.

6. Ibid.

This differential treatment of children was in the area of the fundamental interest of education and was not justified by any compelling reason. Therefore, the court reasoned, the disparity must be corrected and such correction must take place in a reasonable period of time.

While the trial court asserted that providing a school finance law was a responsibility of the California legislature, it took the liberty of suggesting four possible plans to meet the requirements of equal protection: (1) full state funding with statewide imposition and control of real property taxes; (2) reorganization of the 1,067 then existing school districts into about 500 districts with boundary realignments to equalize assessed valuations of real property between all school districts; (3) retention of the school district boundaries but the removal of commercial and industrial property from local taxation for school purposes; and (4) school district power equalizing which has as its essential ingredient the concept that school districts could choose to spend at different levels but for each level of expenditure chosen, the tax effort would be the same for each school choosing such level, whether it be a high-wealth or a low-wealth school district.

In making its demurrer decision in 1971, the California Supreme Court looked past all previous contrary decisions of other courts, including some of those made by the United States Supreme Court. Previous rulings in such states as Michigan, Virginia, Texas, and Illinois had implied that the equal protection clause of the Fourteenth Amendment did not apply to school financing patterns. Thus, *Serrano* became a landmark case—the first major decision by a higher court ruling against a state's school finance program on the basis of violation of equal protection for all the school pupils of a state.

CONSEQUENCES OF *SERRANO*

The following statements are representative of the reactions of school finance scholars and writers to the *Serrano* decision:

> Despite the fact that the school finance systems of every state but Hawaii were subjected to fundamental challenge, the decision was widely hailed on all sides. The press, legislative groups, educators at all levels in the administrative hierarchy, and taxpayer organizations were all enthused. Liberal civil rights adherents rejoiced at the apparent triumph of egalitarianism and conservative property owners rejoiced at the apparently impending demise of the local property tax. . . .[7]

7. Paul D. Carrington, "Equal Justice Under Law and School Finance," in *School Finance in Transition* (Gainesville, Fla.: National Conference on School Finance, 1973), p. 162.

Many members of the educational community view the recent court decisions with a degree of skepticism. Rather than being a great promise for the future in the field of educational finance, the end results of *Serrano* may bring a leveling of the growth curve of revenues provided for education. The possibilities of a period of retrenchment may not be too remote. Taxpayers throughout the nation are rebelling against the local property tax. The cost of, and demand for, all governmental services are increasing; and many citizens are quite concerned about the spiraling costs of educational programs and services.[8]

As often happens when major court decisions are made there are rumors and misunderstandings concerning just what the court said in its ruling. *Serrano* was followed with some inaccurate statements and faulty interpretations concerning what the California Supreme Court had actually said in condemning the finance law in that state. The following statement clarifies some of the misunderstandings that developed:

> Since the *Serrano* decision is a major factor in setting the criteria for education finance reform, it is important to be clear about what the court did and did not say. The court did not say that equal dollars had to be expended per child. It did not explicitly rule out plans providing more funds to higher cost pupils—such as disadvantaged, vocation, gifted, or handicapped students—as long as the distribution of these funds is not related to district wealth. Finally, the court did not exclude the property tax as a basis of education finance, but rather said that the level of educational expenditures could not be a function of district wealth. Thus a statewide property tax with redistribution of the revenues raised on the basis of any of a number of criteria, except district wealth, may be permissible.[9]

Not all school finance authorities or taxpayers agree that the results of the *Serrano* decision will all be positive as they relate to future state school finance programs. Some fear that the reversal of the *Rodriguez* case in Texas (similar in disparities and in its trial court decision to *Serrano*) by the U.S. Supreme Court, along with problems involved in implementing the requirements of the courts, may neutralize or even negate the generally predicted positive effects of *Serrano*. The following two statements are representative of a type of "wait and see" attitude that some writers think to be necessary before post-*Serrano* effects on school finance reforms can be made with a reasonable degree of assurance:

8. K. Forbis Jordan and Kern Alexander, *Constitutional Reform of School Finance* (Lexington, Mass.: Lexington Books, D.C. Heath and Co., 1973), p. 16.

9. Betsy Levin et al., *Paying for Public Schools* (Washington, D.C.: The Urban Institute, 1972), p. 8.

The millennium in school finance may appear to have arrived for those who have advocated greater equalization for years. . . . The harsh facts are that "Rome was not built in a day" and the revolution in school finance programs will not be accomplished over night. . . .[10]

The consequences of the breakthrough in the *Serrano* decision have been almost overwhelming to matters of school finance. Within five months after its announcement, three other states had received similar court rulings, and numerous others have followed since. States that formerly seemed to be satisfied with maintaining their traditional financing programs began to study and restyle them with a zeal well beyond any previously demonstrated. State after state joined the bandwagon, "entertaining" litigation and court decisions against the status quo. Most of them encouraged, or even demanded, formal studies to modernize their school financing formulas. Such prompt state action was considered necessary in the face of an apparent legal threat of nationwide school tax and funding reform. The traditional local property tax, which had formed the chief framework for financing education in some states, appeared to be doomed; although the *Serrano* decision did not condemn property taxes per se, it did condemn the results of the unfairness that resulted from their use in California. State officials faced with apprehension the prospect of providing equitable school finance formulas with required reduction or elimination of the local property tax. They viewed with alarm the possibility of *Serrano*-type litigation in their states. Consequently, organization of studies to correct formula inequities before court action became popular.

Van Dusartz v. *Hatfield* (Minnesota)

In October 1971, only six weeks after *Serrano*, Minnesota became the second state to have its system of financing education declared unconstitutional. A federal district court judge accepted the California arguments and findings as being equally applicable in Minnesota. According to him, "the level of spending for a child's education may not be a function of wealth other than the wealth of the state as a whole." He ruled that the court recognizes that pupils in publicly financed schools have a right under the equal protection guarantee of the Fourteenth Amendment to have money spent on them "unaffected by variations in the taxable wealth of their school districts or their parents." The court said:

This is not the simple instance in which a poor man is injured by his lack of funds. Here the poverty is that of a governmental unit that the

10. Jordan and Alexander, *Constitutional Reform of School Finance,* p. 14.

State itself has defined and commissioned. The heaviest burdens of this system surely fall defacto upon those poor families residing in poor districts who cannot escape to private schools, but this effect only magnifies the odiousness of the explicit discrimination by the law itself against all children living in relatively poor districts.

Robinson v. Cahill (New Jersey)

On January 19, 1972, the New Jersey Superior Court of Hudson County ruled that the state's educational financing system created inequities that violated the state constitution's educational provisions and also the equal protection clause of the Fourteenth Amendment. The court said that pupils living in districts with low assessments of property per child were being discriminated against and that such a system likewise discriminated against taxpayers who shoulder unequal burdens in providing funds for education. It also declared that it was not suggesting "that the same amount of money must be spent on each pupil in the state. The differing needs of pupils would suggest to the contrary."

In April 1973, the New Jersey Supreme Court by unanimous vote declared the state's system of financing public education to be unconstitutional, saying that it failed to fulfill an 1875 mandate in the state constitution concerning equal educational opportunity. The court did not declare the state's local property tax to be unconstitutional but it did rule that any system that continued to rely primarily on local property taxes for financing public schools would be so declared.

The Court gave the state legislature until January 1975 to approve a new program for public school financing with less dependency on local property taxes, or face further court action. The directive to the state involved the establishment of a finance program for a "thorough and efficient" public school system. It further stated that if the legislature failed to guarantee all pupils equal tax support it would issue an order for that purpose—a strong threat of court enactment of taxing legislation. Since the case was tried in state courts and the rulings were based on compliance with the state constitution, the case was never heard by the U.S. Supreme Court despite numerous attempts to appeal the case.

The January 1, 1975 deadline for a new school finance program was not met. The New Jersey Supreme Court then held that the existing state aid program would be in force for the 1975-76 school year. Despite numerous attempts on the part of the governor and the legislature, as of January 1976 the State had not yet defined a "thorough and efficient" school system nor met the mandate of the Court for a new school finance formula.

Spano v. *Board of Education* (New York)

Of the numerous court cases decided since *Serrano* concerning the financing programs of the various states as they are related to the equal protection clause, the first to decide against the charges of the plaintiffs who instigated the suit came in New York. Andrew Spano and other residents and property holders in Lakeland Central School District No. 1 sued the board of education and various state officials because of the alleged unfairness of New York's legislative and constitutional provisions for levying and distributing school tax funds. Although the charges were much the same as in *Serrano,* the court based its decision on two previous cases (*McInnis* v. *Ogilvie,* Illinois, 1969; and *Burruss* v. *Wilkerson,* Virginia, 1970). While acknowledging that there may be inadequacies and unfairness in state school financing systems, the New York Supreme Court indicated that in its view changes to correct such inequities should be within the prerogative of the legislature rather than the court.

Rodriguez v. *San Antonio Independent School District* (Texas)

In 1970, three urban school districts in Texas brought suit against the Texas board of education and the state commissioner of education to determine whether or not the Texas system of allocating state funds for education was unfair. This case was based on the charge that underassessment in many rural school districts of taxable property resulted in their obtaining disproportionate amounts of state funds. As a result of this suit, Texas became the third state, in an apparent domino effect of the *Seranno* case, to have its system of financing education declared unconstitutional. In late 1971, a federal court ruled that its financing system violated both the federal and the Texas constitutions. The court went a step beyond the California and Minnesota decisions by giving Texas two years to reorganize its school financing system with the threat that if the legislature should fail to act, the court "will take such further steps as may be necessary to implement both the purpose and spirit of this order."

The *Rodriguez* case was accepted for review by the United States Supreme Court and thus became the first of the recent "equal protection" cases to be so considered. On March 21, 1973, the Court by a vote of 5 to 4 reversed the lower court decision and thus nullified *Rodriguez* and also the *Van Dusartz* case in Minnesota. This vote negated all related pending federal court actions but did not directly affect actions of a similar nature in state courts.

That the Court did not support or agree with the disparities so evident in the case is indicated in the following statement by Justice Powell:

> We hardly need add that this Court's action today is not to be viewed as placing its judicial imprimatur on the status quo. The need is apparent for reform in tax systems which may have relied too long and too heavily on the local property tax. And certainly innovative new thinking as to public education, its methods and its funding is necessary to assure both a higher level of quality and greater uniformity of opportunity. These matters merit the continued attention of the scholars who already have contributed much by their challenges. But the ultimate solutions must come from the lawmakers and from the democratic pressures of those who elect them.

None of the court cases, including *Rodriguez,* attempted to answer the difficult question of relationship between cost and quality in education. Their concerns were strictly with resource input as indicated in the following statement:

> In *Rodriguez,* there is no specific grievance about the educational outcome, but only about the level of financial effort by the state. The question can and should be asked, what are these dollars really likely to accomplish for the plaintiffs?

The question of course evokes a consideration of the controversy surrounding the Coleman Report of 1966 on the relation between quality and cost of education. Professor Coons and his associates dismissed that controversy by asserting that, whatever the relation, the poor should have the same right as the rich to be disappointed by the results of school spending . . .[11]

While this action of the Supreme Court in effect supported property taxation as the chief source of local school financing, it is doubtful that it will stop the momentum now generated in the several states for school finance reform. Strangely enough, the Court found current methods of financing education chaotic and unfair, but it could not say "that such disparities are the product of a system that is so irrational as to be invidiously discriminatory." On the other hand, Justice Thurgood Marshall, in his dissenting opinion, charged that the Court's decision "is a retreat from our historic commitment to equality of educational opportunity."

In spite of the reversal in the ruling of the Supreme Court in *Rodriguez,* the great progress already apparent in school finance reform will probably inspire most states to model their new school finance programs around the universally accepted principle of equitableness, as declared in *Serrano,* regardless of the decision of the Supreme Court.

11. Carrington, "Equal Justice Under Law and School Finance," p. 167.

Since *Rodriguez* was tried in federal courts, it was to be expected that its reversal by the U. S. Supreme Court would shift similar cases away from the federal court system to state courts. It is important to note that the state courts have continued to challenge and rule against the great disparities in school finance programs that were in operation in many of the states. The best evidence available indicates that the frustration and disappointment experienced by the *Rodriguez* reversal will have only minimal effect on progress toward the school finance reform movement generated by *Serrano v. Priest.*

Other Related Court Decisions

The National Education Association noted other recent court decisions involving state school finance programs in the following:

> State court decisions in some 14 states have declared unconstitutional those systems of school financing that make the level of education a child receives a function of the wealth of the district in which he resides. However, interpretations of the *Serrano* decision vary from state to state.
>
> On December 16, 1974, the Washington State Supreme Court, in a split decision, upheld the state's system of relying on property taxes and special levies for school funding. The majority decision stated that "the validity of a statewide uniform system of public schools is unaffected by variations in district size or tax base or by a partial reliance on local funding." Then, on December 26, 1974, at the opposite end of the nation, a superior court judge ruled that Connecticut's system of school financing was in violation of the state constitution. The judge declared that the system of distributing funds to towns according to pupil population did nothing to correct inequities stemming from disparity in wealth of communities. . . .[12]

The domino effect of the first school finance court cases was evidenced by the fact that in less than two years after *Serrano* at least eight other similar decisions had been made by the courts. Even though two of these were reversed in appellate courts, the support of court action gave school finance reform almost unstoppable momentum.

In general, but with some noteworthy exceptions, the first state reform programs emphasized fiscal neutrality ("a child's education may not be a function of wealth other than the wealth of the state"), the provision for districts to vary in their expenditures per pupil, provisions to reduce the amount of local effort required, and provision for full state support of allowable local effort. These characteristics can best be

12. *Financial Status of the Public Schools, 1975* (Washington, D.C.: National Education Assn., 1975), pp. 44, 46.

made operative through full state funding or by a district power equalization formula.

PRINCIPLES ESTABLISHED BY
RECENT COURT DECISIONS

The court decisions of *Serrano* and related cases that have followed have seemed to agree, with only minor exceptions, with the following general principles or conclusions:

1. The public education of a child shall not depend on wealth other than the wealth of the state as a whole; this means that the quality of a child's education cannot be a function of the wealth of his parents, his neighbors, or the school district.
2. Taxes levied for school purposes must generate the same total number of dollars per mill of tax in poor districts as in rich districts.
3. Since educational needs vary from district to district, the state does not have to require all of its school districts to spend the same amount of money or offer identical educational programs.
4. Education is considered to be a fundamental interest of the state.
5. Although local property taxes discriminate against the poor, state legislatures are not required to eliminate them in favor of taxes on other sources of revenue.
6. Additional expenditures may be made by schools for programs for exceptional children and compensatory programs for culturally disadvantaged children, and also for other educational needs of children that are significant and worthy of special treatment.
7. There is an implication, although not a direct ruling, that equitability must be established in school district capital-outlay expenditures in a way the same as that required for current expenditures.
8. No specific plan or plans have been mandated to achieve equitability in school finance formulas; states will be allowed a reasonable period of time to revise their laws and bring them within court guidelines.

POST-*SERRANO* PRESSURE FOR
REFORM

The court decisions resulted in the generation of extreme pressure on most state legislative bodies to bring reform to their school financing programs. Now these bodies face two important questions: (1) What effect will the decision of the U.S. Supreme Court in the *Rodriguez* (Texas) case have on state actions to improve their programs? (2) What should be the nature and direction of the resultant reforms in state finance programs now that the equal protection clause has been reinterpreted?

It is easier to formulate an answer to the first question than to the second. *Serrano* provided a breakthrough in its interpretation of equal protection, and the torch for school finance reform has been permanently lighted. Undoubtedly, the numerous studies in the fifty states will produce important changes with or without the benefit of any future court decisions. It is inconceivable that the changes and improvements already foreseen or those yet to evolve will be negated by the actions of any or all courts that react to litigation of the problem. On the other hand, the possibilities for change offer so many alternatives that no one can predict accurately what financial reform should or will encompass. Some of the prerogatives open to legislatures include full state funding with elimination of local tax levies, use of statewide property taxes, higher state income taxes or sales taxes or both, assumption by the state of all capital-outlay costs, raising school expenditures in poor districts with or without decreasing expenditures in more affluent ones, provisions for additional local revenue to supplement a state-funded school program, and advocacy of greater federal participation in financing education.

In the past there have been numerous attacks on school finance theories and practices that have generated efforts for improvements of varying proportions. For example, the excessive taxpayer burdens in some districts and the lack of adequate revenue to support desirable educational programs in some poor districts led to provision for flat and percentage grants in the early 1900s. The second quarter of the century saw the establishment and implementation of crude foundation programs. The 1950s and 1960s fostered improved state equalization formulas. During that period the federal government sponsored categorial aid programs to help the country rebound from the shock of Sputnik. Since 1954, as a result of the *Brown* segregation decision by the Supreme Court, emphasis and improvement have been pointed in the direction of providing equal rights for minority groups.

Thus, striving for school finance improvement is a never-ending struggle in the fifty states of this country. Only occasionally, however, does the effort become so concerted and so visible that it becomes classified as a "reform" movement. Such a reform effort began in the early 1970s as a result of the numerous court decisions that ruled that their respective state school finance laws were unconstitutional. Nearly all the states began a strong post-*Serrano* effort to provide greater equality in the allocation of their resources in order to insure equal protection of all children and youth—as guaranteed by the Fourteenth Amendment.

SIGNIFICANT FINANCE STUDIES

The landmark *Serrano* decision in 1971 generated an epidemic of studies concerning state school finance programs. The Education Commission of the States estimated that by the summer of 1972 more than a hundred studies were being conducted in forty-nine states and that more than thirty *Serrano*-type cases were pending in state and federal courts. Many more similar studies and court cases have emerged since that time. Because of *Serrano*, and in spite of the 5-4 vote of the United States Supreme Court in reversing Rodriguez in March 1973, several states passed new and improved school finance laws in the early 1970s in an attempt to meet court objections and to provide a greater degree of equality of educational opportunity.

The President's Commission on School Finance

One of the principal results of the growing national interest in solving the persistent problems of financing education was the creation of the President's Commission on School Finance in 1969. In its report of March 1972, it made the following principal recommendations:

1. Each state should assume responsibility for raising and allocating the funds required for education but leave control of education at the local level.
2. State governments should assume responsibility for financing substantially all of the nonfederal outlays for public education, with local supplements permitted up to a level not to exceed 10 percent of the state allocation.
3. State allocations should include differentials based on educational need such as for education of handicapped and disadvantaged students.
4. The federal government should assume only a supplementary role to the states in financing education.
5. States should reorganize their school districts to provide more nearly equal tax bases.
6. Additional federal funds should be provided to help solve the unique problems of large city school districts.
7. Consideration should be given to financial assistance to nonpublic schools.

8. Programs in career education should be given greater financial assistance and priority.

The degree to which the commission's recommendations will be carried out is yet to be determined. However, the importance of executive department interest in the problems involved in the current revolution and reform movement in financing education cannot be questioned. The commission's study has added interest and stimulation to the work of other organizations that are seeking answers to the prodigious financial problems now facing the schools of this country.

The National Educational Finance Project

The National Educational Finance Project was launched in 1968 under the sponsorship of the Committee on Educational Finance of the National Education Association and the chairmanship of Roe L. Johns. It was charged with making "a nationwide study of the financing of public education beginning with pre-first grade education, continuing through junior college and including adult and continuing education." The leaders of this study pointed to seven factors that were causing state programs for financing public education to be inadequate to meet the demands that the pressure of contemporary expectations for the schools generated:

1. A growing awareness of the importance of providing an adequate education for all citizens.
2. An increasing recognition of the need for differential educational programs for individuals and groups having special learning needs.
3. A developing understanding of the importance of human capital to the well-being of a "brain-intensive" economic system.
4. A burgeoning use by the federal government of appropriations earmarked for educational programs, that is, categorical aids designed to accomplish specific purposes deemed in the national interest.
5. A growing disparity between the revenue available to the schools from traditional sources and the amount of money needed to mount programs that satisfy social demands.
6. An expanding population that needs to be educated in the public schools. This condition results from population growth and from rapid extension of free public education at both ends of the traditional age range.
7. A complex of population shifts, which has produced a "flight to suburbia" from the cities by relatively affluent, middle-class Americans and a movement to core cities by poorly educated and unskilled members of minority groups, so that the cities are faced with a great influx of "high-cost" citizens (in terms of their consumption of

public services) at the same time that the revenue potentials of the cities are declining.[13]

The NEFP made its report to the nation in a series of regional conferences that began in the fall of 1971. The importance of this study—coming in the chaotic period following the *Serrano* decision in California—was recognized immediately. The project, published in five volumes with an additional summary volume for laymen, was the most comprehensive and potentially significant study of school financing in recent years.[14] Some of its most salient findings include:

1. People in all parts of the United States continue to have great confidence in the public school system despite its financial and other problems.
2. An urgent need exists for the various states to move more energetically and thoroughly into the planning role for financing education.
3. An immediate need exists for a substitute for the property tax, much maligned as a source of revenue for public education.
4. More than half the states had lawsuits pending against state school financial systems similar to cases already decided in California, Minnesota, Texas, and New Jersey.
5. State financial systems need to be improved to make them more equalizing. Most, if not all, states need to move into equalization programs that consider local district ability to pay as well as variations in unit costs and pupil costs.
6. New measures are being used to determine and compare the fiscal ability of school districts to finance an educational program. The assessed value of property per child to be educated will lose its validity with the gradual demise or minimization of the property tax. Newer measures of comparative ability will include income.
7. Nonproperty taxes tend to disequalize educational opportunity among local districts as much as property taxes do.
8. In practice, the cost differentials for various classes of pupils vary considerably. Using $1.00 as a base for comparative costs of pupils in grades 1–6, the currently existing cost per pupils in grades 10–12 is $1.40, kindergarten $1.30, grades 7–9 $1.20, physically handicapped $3.25, and vocational-technical pupils $1.80.

---

13. Roe L. Johns and J. Alan Thomas, "Introduction," in *Dimensions of Educational Need* (Gainesville, Fla.: National Educational Finance Project, 1969), pp. 4–5.

14. *Dimensions of Education Need*, vol. 1; *Economic Factors Affecting the Financing of Education*, vol. 2; *Planning to Finance Education*, vol. 3; *Status and Impact of Educational Finance Programs*, vol. 4; *Alternative Programs for Financing Education*, vol. 5; and *Future Directions for School Financing* (Gainesville, Fla.: National Education Finance Project, 1971).

9. There is need to give financial consideration to cities to compensate for their higher percentages of high-cost children.
10. Federal aid to education should be general rather than categorical.

An incidental value resulting from the NEFP study came from the special attention some of its leaders gave to the organization of a professional group of scholars to study and debate the problems of school finance. Beginning in the late 1950s the Committee on Educational Finance of the National Education Association sponsored annual conferences on school finance. These conferences brought together scholars, researchers, and practitioners to study and report on problems and trends in financing education and to discuss significant research findings in the field. Because the National Education Association dropped its sponsorship of these conferences, the annual meetings from 1973 to 1975 were sponsored by the Institute for Educational Finance of the University of Florida. In 1975, some of the directors of the National Education Finance Project were instrumental in organizing the American Education Finance Association which will sponsor future annual conferences. The Association publishes *The Journal of Education Finance*, a quarterly journal for the publication of articles from educators, economists, and others concerned with problems and issues in educational finance.

The Advisory Commission on Intergovernmental Relations (ACIR)

The Advisory Commission on Intergovernmental Relations, an agency of the national, state, and local governments, was established by Congress in 1959 to study and recommend improvements for intergovernmental coordination and financing of public services. The commission has dealt with problems involving relations among the branches of government. Its many reports of studies have been highly informative.[15] Most of them have been about fiscal and tax problems as they affect the three levels of government.

An example of the work of this advisory commission is its report of a study President Nixon requested on the problems of property tax reform, school finance, and alternative revenue sources. In early 1973, this 26-member commission issued its report, which argued that states have the fiscal capability of financing education and that increased federal funding of education should be delayed until the United States

15. For example, see *State Aid to Local Government* (Washington, D.C.: Advisory Commission on Intergovernmental Relations, April 1969).

Supreme Court has ruled on the constitutionality of using local property taxes for financing education.[16]

The studies, reports, and recommendations of the advisory committee offer some hope for successful resolution of the problems involved in intergovernmental administration of public services, including education. Its uniqueness in being representative of the federal, state, and local levels of government and its record of study in its first decade of existence give promise of potential effect in the months and years ahead on many of the problems of financing education.

The ACIR has shown considerable interest in plans and proposals for financing education since the court cases concerning equal protection. It has proposed a model that would require states to assume "substantially all elementary and secondary education costs. Its proposal for equality would cross state lines. If such a plan can not be effected, it recommends equalization across metropolitan areas. Its financing method would use the power equalization principle with a uniform property tax and with the state "recapturing" excess funds in wealthy districts. Its alternate to this plan would be full state funding.

STATE SCHOOL FINANCE STUDIES

The Fleischmann Commission Study

In 1969, the governor of New York and state education leaders appointed a state study commission to make a two-year analysis of the problems of financing education in that state. Listed officially as the New York State Commission on Quality, Cost, and Financing of Elementary and Secondary Education, the "Fleischmann Commission" (named after its chairman, Manly Fleischmann) became its more popular designation. This important study, directed by Joel S. Berke, noted in its 1972 report that the fiscal crisis in public education faced a "double-edged dilemma; first, a failure to raise adequate revenues through equitable means, and second an inability to allocate revenues in an effective and equitable manner. Its main recommendations were (1) use of a statewide property tax for school support, with school districts having a five-year period to adjust their current local rate to the new level; (2) an equalization plan to level the expenditures of all districts to a degree that approaches the level of the more affluent districts; (3) an outlay

16. An advisory group representing seven important educational organizations later expressed disagreement with the conclusion of ACIR on the states' funding capabilities.

by districts of 50 percent more for disadvantaged students than for normal or average ones; and (4) greater federal support for education in New York schools.

The Fleischmann Study indicated that inequities in education in New York were largely a result of socioeconomic and racial factors. (This would argue for large weighting factors covering those areas in the state's school finance program).

The biggest problem in the state is the high correlation between school success or failure and the student's socioeconomic and racial origin. The higher on the socioeconomic scale a child is, the more likely he is to succeed in school. While children from affluent backgrounds score well on standardized tests, graduate from high school and attend college, children from low-income and minority backgrounds fail in school in numbers which far exceed their proportion of the state's total population. In spite of high expenditures and quality improvements, New York State is not providing equality of educational opportunity to its students as long as the pattern of school success and school failure remains closely tied to a child's social origin.[17]

Other State Studies

Although a complete and accurate description of all state finance studies and reforms would be impossible to compile, some indication of the extent and importance of these may be obtained from the following:

> One thing is clear, however—the momentum for reform of the inequitable allocation of educational resources and tax burdens that has accelerated since the *Serrano* decision was not stopped by *Rodriguez*. It has been undoubtedly slowed since federal courts will not be prodding legislatures to action. However, many legislative bodies are already in action. Florida, Kansas, Maine, Michigan, Minnesota, Utah, and several other states have passed significant reform legislation. Nearly every state has a school finance commission at work.[18]

> In Florida, a comprehensive school finance reform bill passed by a wide margin. The bill includes a number of important provisions, including a limit to the property tax rates that can be levied by any district, adjustment of allocation to meet pupils' needs, a recognition

17. Report of the New York State Commission on the *Quality, Cost, and Financing of Elementary and Secondary Education*, vol. 1 (New York: Viking Press, 1973), p. 4.

18. R. Stephen Browning and David C. Long, "School Finance Reform and the Courts After *Rodriguez*," in John Pincus, ed., *School Finance in Transition* (Cambridge, Mass.: Ballinger Publishing Co., 1974), p. 101.

of the higher cost levels of urban areas, and state assumption of all future capital outlay needs and existing local bonded indebtedness.

Maine passed a roughly similar law within a few weeks of Florida. . . .

In Kansas and Utah, major reform laws were passed in the 1973 session. Both are based on the power equalizing approach, guaranteeing that equal tax effort will result in equal school revenues in each district in the state.[19]

According to Berke and Kirst, school finance reform laws in six states (Maine, Florida, Utah, Kansas, California, and Minnesota) produced nine principles which they share in whole or in part: (1) greater state assumption of school costs and, therefore, a shift away from the local property tax; (2) a lessening in the range of expenditure variation among districts; (3) greater equalization of tax burdens from district to district; (4) the retention of a degree of local choice in setting tax rates; (5) upper limits on local property tax rates; (6) allocations of educational resources in relation to educational need; (7) adjustments of state aid in proportion to cost of living; (8) state assumption of some or all construction costs; and (9) reform of property tax assessment procedures.[20]

In 1975, the National Education Association summarized the progress of state school finance reform in the following:

Since 1971, fourteen states have substantially revised their school finance systems: Arizona, California, Colorado, Florida, Illinois, Kansas, Maine, Michigan, Minnesota, Montana, New Mexico, North Dakota, Utah, and Wisconsin. . . . New Jersey is soon expected to meet the mandate of the *Robinson* v. *Cahill* case to produce a "thorough and efficient" school finance plan. The 14 reform states increased their over-all share of school funding from about 43 percent in the last year before reform to 51 percent in the first year after reform. Specifically, Arizona, Colorado, Kansas, Minnesota, Montana, and North Dakota raised their state share of school funding by more than 10 percent. . . .

The pattern of school finance reform among these states indicates a trend away from heavy reliance on Strayer-Haig-Mort foundation programs toward a greater degree of equity through power equalization plans combined with local property tax relief.

Some states that have instituted reforms are evaluating these reforms and revising school finance formulae to provide for greater equalization. Also governors in a number of states have proposed increased school aid in fiscal 1975: Georgia, Idaho, Indiana, Minnesota,

19. Joel S. Berke, *Answers to Inequity* (Berkeley, Calif.: McCutchan Publishing Co., 1974), pp. 26–27.

20. Joel S. Berke and Michael W. Kirst, "How the Federal Government Can Encourage State School Finance Reform," *Phi Delta Kappan*, (October 1973), p. 242.

North Dakota, Oregon, and Washington. The governor of Texas proposed a $1 billion increase in state aid with distribution based on taxable property values; in South Dakota, a state income tax to finance a major increase in state aid for greater equalization; in Alaska takeover of basic school support; in Illinois, $375 million for school construction; and in Utah, free textbooks.[21]

Selected Readings

Alexander, Kern; Corns, Ray; and McCann, Walter. *Public School Law, 1973 Supplement* (Cases and Materials). St. Paul, Minn.: West Publishing Co., 1973.

————, and Jordan, K. Forbis, eds. *Constitutional Reform of School Finance*. Lexington, Mass.; Lexington Books, D. C. Heath and Co., 1973.

Benson, Charles S.; Goldfinger, Paul M.; Hoachlander, E. Gareth; and Pers, Jessica S. *Planning for Educational Reform—Financial and Social Alternatives*. New York: Dodd, Mead & Co., 1974.

Callahan, John J.; and Wilken, William H. eds. *School Finance Reform: A Legislator's Handbook*. Washington, D.C.: National Conference of State Legislatures, February 1976.

Coons, John E.; Clune, William H. III, and Sugarman, Stephen D. *Private Wealth and Public Education*. Cambridge, Mass.: Harvard University Press, 1970.

Financing the Public Schools—A Search for Equality. Bloomington, Ind.: Phi Delta Kappa, 1973.

Johns, Roe L., and Morphet, Edgar L. *Planning School Finance Programs*. Gainesville, Fla.: National Educational Finance Project, 1972.

Meltsner, Arnold J.; Kast, Gregory W.; Kramer, John F.; and Nakamura, Robert T. *Political Feasibility of Reform in School Financing; The Case of California*. New York: Praeger Publishers, 1973.

Pincus, John A., ed. *School Finance in Transition*. Cambridge, Mass.: Ballinger Publishing Co., 1974.

Understanding Education's Financial Dilemma. Denver: Education Commission of the States, 1972.

21. *Financial Status of the Public Schools, 1975*, p. 40.

8

Public Funds and Nonpublic Schools

Since the early separation of church and state functions in this country, the predominant philosophy of government has supported the belief that some services required by people can be supplied better by the public sector than by the private sector. Education is a notable example. Relatively few people would favor removing the responsibility of government for this important public service. At the same time, however, privately sponsored schools have been encouraged for those groups and individuals who are willing to support them financially after they have participated in financing the public school system.

The illegality of direct government support for private and parochial schools is well established in the codes of the various states and at the federal level. However, a few state governments are beginning to repudiate this principle by enacting legislation that provides some state-collected tax funds for use by nonpublic schools. The courts, particularly the U.S. Supreme Court, have failed to agree with the efforts of the States to provide direct financial support for such schools.

Those who favor direct public aid to nonpublic schools base their arguments on the following points:

1. Parents should have freedom of choice in the education of their children. They cite the case of *Pierce* v. *Society of Sisters* (268 U.S. 510) as a guarantee of such choice. Said the court, "The fundamental theory of liberty under which all governments in this union repose excludes any general power of the State to standardize its children by forcing them to accept instruction from public teachers only."
2. There is no evidence to support the fear of divisiveness in education caused by the existence and operation of nonpublic schools.

3. The failure of nonpublic schools would create a tremendous impact on the financing of public education; from the economic point of view it would be better to finance nonpublic schools to the extent necessary to keep them solvent.

Opponents to direct aid to nonpublic schools argue that:

1. Parochial aid represents a backward step, since this country once maintained such a system of education but has since repudiated the concept.
2. Private schools tend to discriminate against students in terms of race and religious background.
3. Such a practice violates the First Amendment.
4. Solution of the problem should be based on principle and not on economic implications.

NONPUBLIC SCHOOL ENROLLMENT TRENDS

The National Education Association noted some significant changes in the relative enrollments in nonpublic schools as compared to public schools in the years 1950 to 1974:

> Until the late 1950s, enrollments in private elementary and secondary schools increased proportionately faster than enrollment in the public schools. The private-school share of total enrollments rose from 11.8 percent in fall 1954 to 14.9 percent by fall 1959. Since 1959, the percentage has decreased to an estimated 9.7. Between fall 1965 and fall 1974, private elementary-school enrollment (grades K-8) decreased from 4,9000,000 to 3,500,000, and private high-school enrollment (grades 9-12) decreased from 1,400,000 to 1,300,000.[1]

The decline in enrollments in nonpublic elementary and secondary schools that became significant during the decade from 1965 to 1975 has become a matter of some concern to many Americans. Taxpayers have anticipated the placing of additional tax burdens upon them as more and more nonpublic schools have become insolvent and have returned their students to the mainstream of public education. Political leaders at all levels of government have become interested in potential ways and means of solving this difficult problem. At the same time, the courts have consistently ruled against almost all plans to find legal

1. *Financial Status of the Public Schools, 1975* (Washington, D.C.: National Education Assn., 1975), p. 10.

methods of providing public resources to aid nonpublic schools in order to keep them operable.

Enrollments in nonpublic elementary and secondary schools decreased from 6.3 million in 1964 to 4.8 million in 1974. Those figures, however, do not describe the problem adequately. Nonpublic school enrollments are concentrated in certain states and particularly in large cities. Failures of nonpublic schools in such states as Oklahoma, North Carolina, and Utah—states with less than 3 percent of their school students enrolled in nonpublic schools—would not cause tremendous financial adjustments. On the other hand, major closings of nonpublic schools in Rhode Island, Pennsylvania, and New York—states with more than 15 percent of their students enrolled in nonpublic schools—might cause large financial burdens on the public schools.

It would seem that the states with the highest percent of students attending nonpublic schools would be the biggest losers if public monies were to be diverted to these schools. However, in one of those states (New York) the Fleischmann Commission in its post-*Serrano* report estimated that it would be $415 million cheaper for the State to refuse such assistance and pay the additional school costs for students who moved from defunct nonpublic schools to public schools. The Commission was opposed to providing public funds to nonpublic schools.

THE LAW AND CHURCH-STATE RELATIONS

Determining an acceptable relation of church and state has concerned this country since it founding. The early New England colonies, except for Rhode Island, made the Congregational church their official church, while the colonies south of Maryland were Anglican. New York had a "mutiple establishment" pattern of church-state relationship. Only Rhode Island, Pennsylvania, and Delaware had no officially established church. Vestiges of church-state relations have continued to exist in one form or another since that early partnership beginning.

Legal Provisions for Separation

"No person, demeaning himself in a peaceable and orderly manner, shall ever be molested on account of his mode of worship or religious sentiments, in the said territory." The foregoing statement and Article VI, Section 3, of the U.S. Constitution were important antecedents to the adoption of the First Amendment that was included in 1791 in the Bill of Rights—ten amendments that delineated the rights of individuals.

Article VI provided that "no religious test shall ever be required as a qualification to any office or public trust under the United States."

Separation of church and state received its real supporting foundation from the First Amendment, which says that "Congress shall make no law respecting an establishment of religion, or prohibiting the free exercise thereof." The intended meaning is clear and defensible enough, but how to provide the proper and complete application of the principle is highly controversial. The Fourteenth Amendment, often referred to as the due process amendment, was established in 1868 for the purpose of granting citizenship to Negroes. In the years since that time, it has been interpreted by the courts as applying the First Amendment to the states. It provides that "no state shall make or enforce any law which shall abridge the privileges or immunities of citizens of the United States; nor shall any State deprive any person of life, liberty, or property without due process of law, nor deny any person within its jurisdiction the equal protection of the laws."

The Courts and the Child-Benefit Theory

The Supreme Court of the United States has ruled a number of times on the legal relation of church and state as intended by the amendments to the Constitution. For the various state legislative bodies and for the people generally, the Court's decisions have had varying degrees of palatability. The complete lack of support by the states for the federal position is at least partially vindicated by the general lack of unanimity among the Court members themselves in many of these decisions, some of which were made by the narrowest possible vote by the Court itself.

In 1930, in *Cochran* v. *Louisiana State Board of Education* (281 U.S. 270), the United States Supreme Court upheld the practice of Louisiana in providing free textbooks, paid for by tax funds, for pupils attending nonpublic schools. In the view of the Court, this was not a violation of the First or Fourteenth Amendments and was therefore legal because of its "child-benefit" theory. According to this theory, the children and not the churches they represented were the beneficiaries of the funds expended. This view of the problem was never supported by more than a few of the states. Most of them viewed the child-benefit theory as the "hole in the dike" of Jefferson's figurative wall of separation between church and state.

In the 1947 *Everson* verdict, the U.S. Supreme Court by the closest possible margin, 5 to 4, held that using New Jersey tax funds allocated to school districts in New Jersey to reimburse parents for the cost of bus fares to attend nonpublic schools was legal and not in violation of the First or Fourteenth Amendments. Seeking the protective cloak of the child-benefit theory, the Court regarded the action as a safe, legal, and expeditious process of public welfare legislation.

A few of the states have reacted in support of the *Cochran* decision; about half of them have accepted the essence of the *Everson* verdict. Alaska (1961), Wisconsin (1962), Oklahoma (1963), and Delaware (1966) "have struck down enactments authorizing free bussing of children attending denomination schools."[2] Pennsylvania (1967) and Connecticut (1960) upheld some variations of the *Everson* decision. The reluctance of states to accept the child-benefit theory in operating their own schools is indicated in the following.

> A review of legislation nationally shows that 26 states prohibit or permit no aid to nonpublic schools. The statutes of eight states permit or provide textbooks for nonpublic students. Twenty-seven states permit or provide for transportation for nonpublic school students on public school buses. Six states provide auxiliary service and five states have tuition grants available for nonpublic elementary and secondary school students.[3]

In this connection, it should be pointed out that nearly all of the 50 state constitutions contain provisions that prohibit spending public funds for sectarian purposes. With rare exceptions these provisions have been followed, and the defense against using state funds for operating nonpublic schools has been relatively airtight until recent years.

Federal Aid and Nonpublic Schools

The many proposals of members of Congress for federal support to public education have habitually become involved with the always controversial issue of providing federal funds for nonpublic schools. Generally, however, in the face of increasing pressures to provide funds to "save the parochial schools from financial disaster," the line has been held. As with many other issues, however, each skirmish on the issue has found the defense lines weakened and more vulnerable to future conflicts.

Some Dents in the Armor

One of the first real dents in the armor of those who decry using state funds for parochial schools came in Pennsylvania. In 1968, that state

2. National Education Assn. *Research Bulletin* 45, no. 2 (May 1967), p. 44.

3. David H. Hurtzman, "The Pennsylvania Case," *Compact* 3, no. 4 (Denver: Education Commission of the States, August 1969), p. 34.

passed an act authorizing the state superintendent of public instruction to contract for the purchase of secular education services from nonpublic schools located in the Commonwealth of Pennsylvania for its students. It provided that certain revenues from state harness racing should go into the nonpublic elementary and secondary education fund for the financing for all of these expenditures. No public school funds were involved.

Because the Pennsylvania legislation was controversial and had potential influence on other states, litigation was expected, and it soon materialized. Suit was brought in June 1969 against the state superintendent of public instruction and the state auditor general. The plaintiffs, of which there were many professional and religious groups, charged that the legislation violated the First and Fourteenth Amendments to the U.S. Constitution. Late in 1969, a federal court ruled on the case:

> Catholic educators are hailing a federal court decision in Pennsylvania as a legal breakthrough supporting state aid to nonpublic schools. The ruling upheld the nation's first state aid law for nonpublic schools by dismissing a suit challenging the constitutionality of the 1968 Pennsylvania statute. The 2 to 1 majority decision approved the state statute which provides for $21 million this year and $41 million next year in state aid to nonpublic schools. The court said the law neither creates nor supports the establishment of religion.[4]

Supreme Court Rulings

Catholic acclaim of the decision in Pennsylvania was short-lived. In June 1971, the U.S. Supreme Court overruled the district court decision and declared the Pennsylvania law to be in violation of church-state separation policies. The decision was accompanied, however, by a contrary one as far as public support of nonpublic colleges and universities in Connecticut was concerned.

In these rulings, the Supreme Court acted simultaneously on three appeals of cases that were each concerned with the use of public funds for nonpublic schools. These cases included *Tilton* v. *Richardson* (public funds for higher education in Connecticut), *Lemon* v. *Kurtzman* (public funds for providing educational services in nonpublic elementary and secondary schools in Pennsylvania), and *DiCenso* v. *Robinson* (public funds to provide supplements to the salaries of teachers in certain nonpublic elementary schools in Rhode Island).[5]

4. *Education U.S.A.* (Washington, D.C.: National School Public Relations Assn., Dec. 8, 1969), p. 86.
5. 312F. Supp. 1191 (1970), 310F. Supp. 35 (1969), 316F. Supp. 112 (1970).

In considering the three cases, the Court looked at a number of issues: (1) Is aid to church-related colleges and universities constitutionally different from similar aid to church-related elementary and secondary schools? (2) May the state or the federal government or both provide direct aid to nonpublic schools, or must it confine such to indirect assistance like that already approved in the *Everson* and *Cochran* cases? (3) To what extent do these cases support or violate the Establishment Clause requiring avoidance of excessive government involvement or entanglement with religion?[6]

In many respects, the Court seemed to be inconsistent in its decisions in these three cases. While in *Tilton* it sustained the Connecticut law for public aid to colleges and universities, in *Lemon* it rejected the Pennsylvania law to aid nonpublic elementary and secondary schools; and it also rejected the Rhode Island plan for supplementing teacher salaries in nonpublic schools. The cases seem to have been determined on the basis of the Court's belief that there is less likelihood of state involvement or entanglement in the affairs of a church-related college than in a church-related elementary or secondary school.

Controversial Nature of the Issue

Evidences of the controversial nature of many other state and federal plans for using or not using public funds for nonpublic schools is shown by the following representative examples of many laws and court rulings:

- A New York law that would have provided $33 million a year to church-related schools for teacher salaries, instructional materials, and other costs of instruction was declared unconstitutional by a three-judge federal panel in 1971.
- The U.S. Supreme Court ruled against tax benefits for any private segregated school set up in Mississippi to avoid integration.
- Ohio's law permitting aid to nonpublic schools was upheld by the Ohio Supreme Court in November 1971, but in October 1972 the U.S. Supreme Court affirmed the decision of a federal district court that had ruled against the state's making direct grants to parents of children attending nonpublic schools.
- In 1969, the California legislature made profit-making enterprises not connected to their tax-exempt purpose (religion) subject to the state's 7 percent tax on net income.

6. Given emphasis in 1970 when the Supreme Court in *Walz* v. *Tax Commission* (397 U.S. 664) upheld by an 8 to 1 vote a constitutional and statutory provision in New York exempting church property from taxation.

- The West Virginia Supreme Court ruled in 1970 that county school systems must furnish bus transportation to parochial school students.
- The Maine Supreme Court ruled against church-state-related legislation. The court pointed out that financial conditions created by closing parochial schools was not the issue—the Constitution, not economics, was at stake.
- According to a recent study, 33 states report varying degrees of assistance to religious schools. Most of them provide fringe benefits, however; only a few of them provide direct aid. The federal government provides nonpublic school aid to many districts through the operation of the Elementary and Secondary Education Act.

The proponents of plans to allocate state monies to nonpublic schools, especially in New York and Pennsylvania, have made numerous attempts to enact such laws in harmony with the types of such aid as the Supreme Court had agreed upon in previous years. At the same time they have endeavored, with little success, to meet the Court's objections in previous cases. For example, after the *Lemon* v. *Kurtzman* decision in 1971, the advocates of parochiaid tried to enact legislation that met three criteria established by that court for determining whether or not a law meets the Establishment Clause requirements: (1) the statute must have a secular legislative purpose; (2) its principal or primary effect must be one that neither advances nor inhibits religion, and (3) the statute must not foster excessive government entanglement with religion.

In June 1973, in *Sloan* v. *Lemon*, the U. S. Supreme Court held that Pennsylvania's Parent Reimbursement Act for Nonpublic Education was unconstitutional. The Act provided funds to reimburse parents for some of the tuition expenses they paid to send their children to nonpublic schools. On the same day the Court held unconstitutional a New York statute that provided funds for nonpublic schools serving low-income families. The funds were to be spent for the maintenance and repair of buildings, tuition grants and certain tax benefits for low-income parents of students attending nonpublic schools.

The major arguments presented against the Pennsylvania and New York laws were (1) providing state funds for nonpublic schools violates the First Amendment to the Constitution; (2) such allocation of funds could have a serious effect on the capability of the public schools to discharge their responsibility; (3) such funding would divert money from public education to private education; (4) this funding would tend to renew the conflict over church-state relations; and (5) such funding would increase the number of students in nonpublic schools and change the mix of students in public schools.

The Supreme Court in reviewing *Sloan* v. *Lemon* (Pennsylvania) and *Committee for Public Education and Religious Liberty* v. *Nyquist* (New York), by margins of 8-1 and 6-3 respectively, rejected both statutes. It held that the "maintenance and repair provisions violate the Establishment Clause because their effect, inevitably, is to subsidize and advance the religious mission of sectarian schools." It held that the tuition reimbursement parts of both statutes "fail the 'effect' test for the same reason as those governing the maintenance and repair grants. It ruled that the tax benefit to parents of nonpublic school children did not fit the pattern of property tax exemptions sustained in *Walz* v. *Tax Commission* (in the view of the Court these tax exemptions tended to reinforce the separation of Church and State and to avoid excessive government entanglement with religion). The controlling factor, in the view of the Court, was that although both statutes would aid all nonpublic schools, 90 percent of the students affected were attending schools controlled by religious organizations. Thus, the statutes had the practical effect of advancing religion.

The decisions in *Lemon* and *Nyquist* invalidated similar laws in other states. The decisions decreased the options left to be tried to find legal ways of allocating public funds to nonpublic schools. The consistency of the Court in recent years in rejecting nearly all forms of such aid leaves church-state financial relations without much legal chance for a solution that would be satisfactory to proponents of such aid. The courts appear to be adamant in their rejection of such a relationship.

Some of the remaining alternatives open to the proponents of spending public money for the operation of nonpublic schools are indicated by Doerr in the following:

> If the tax credit tuition reimbursement plan (a proposal in Congress to provide federal income tax credits to reimburse parents for nonpublic school tuition) is struck down, the parochiaid lobby may attempt to seek an amendment to the United States Constitution to allow such aid. Alternatively, it may fall back on "shared time" or "reverse shared time" plans. These involve having public schools take over part of the nonpublic school teaching load, either by bringing nonpublic students into the public schools for part of the day or by sending public school personnel into specially leased space in the nonpublic schools. The latter plan, known as "reverse shared time," is currently being challenged by Americans United in federal courts in Michigan, Kentucky, and New Hampshire, and by the American Civil Liberties Union in Oregon.[7]

7. *School Finance in Transition* (Gainesville, Fla.: National Conference on School Finance, 1973), p. 152.

SUMMARY OF THE CONTROVERSY

The case for using public funds to help finance nonpublic schools is made in the following:

> Failure of the government to provide financial aid to private nonprofit schools will place a costly burden on hard-pressed public school systems. This was the prediction made by Msgr. James C. Donohue, director of the Division of Elementary and Secondary Education, U.S. Catholic Conference, to the House of Representatives General Subcommittee on Education. Donohue pointed out that closings and cutbacks in Catholic schools over the past two years have resulted in an estimated increase in public school taxes of at least $315.8 million a year. Enrollment in Catholic elementary and secondary schools dropped 500,000 during the two-year period. Children leaving Catholic schools "do not vanish," Donohue said. Instead, they enter public schools, creating a need for more teachers, classrooms, equipment, and materials. The solution to the problem, the Catholic educator said, does not lie in refusing public assistance to nonpublic schools but rather in providing them the "relatively modest" supplementary aid they need to stay in buisness.[8]

The case against using public funds to help finance nonpublic schools is made in the following:

> Parochiaid, then, could rather quickly cost Americans billions of dollars annually and destroy our public schools. But the financial and social costs of parochiaid would be even higher. Splintering and balkanizing education into a multiplicity of larger or smaller sectarian, racial, ethnic, ideological, and other sorts of enclaves would surely reduce overall educational efficiency and raise overall educational costs.
>
> Socially, this fragmentation would increase the divisions and centrifugal forces straining the seams of our society. Government sponsored and supported sectarian segregation in education in Northern Ireland is an obvious example of where this can lead, since parochial schools tend to closely approach 100% denominational homogeneity of faculties and student bodies.[9]
>
> What would be the financial and social costs of a policy of no public aid for nonpublic schools?
> First of all, nonpublic schools are not going to close wholesale if public aid is not granted them. Further, they will probably continue their slow and gradual decline until they reach a lower plateau. According to the Notre Dame study done for President Nixon's Commission on School Finance, total nonpublic enrollment is expected to decline approximately 46% between 1970 and 1980. This decline will involve a Catholic school enrollment drop of about 52% for the decade and a

8. Ibid., p. 112.
9. Ibid., pp. 154–155.

non-Catholic nonpublic enrollment decline of about 2.5 million students by 1980. Some of this decline will be due to lower birth rates, but the bulk of it will be due simply to changing parental preferences.

This nonpublic enrollment decline, which began around 1965, should produce no burdensome costs, however. Birth rates have dropped so sharply in the last five years that transfers from nonpublic to public schools are being and can be readily absorbed.[10]

Financial Overtones

The relation of church and state applied to education has serious overtones related to school finance. Some of these become more apparent each year. For example, the high and constantly increasing costs of education for nonpublic schools have caused the sponsoring agencies to take a serious look at the operation of such institutions. Their argument that some governmental financial assistance may be required to keep their operation solvent so that they can continue to supplement and abet the educational programs of the public schools has substance and support. Their contention is that nonpublic school bankruptcy will, if left alone, bring hundreds of thousands of abandoned students back into the public education system, at a very high cost.

Despite the obvious fact that nonpublic school failures will result in higher costs of public education, most citizens prefer to view the church-state issue on the basis of principle rather than economics. Either "solution" to the problem has its limitations, its defenders, and its critics. Consequently, litigation in this area of financing education is becoming more common and controversial than ever before in history. Unfortunately, even though many courts have ruled on the problem, there is no clearly determined answer to whether or not certain statutes adopted in some of the states are contraventions of the First or the Fourteenth Amendments. The dilemma that the church-state conflict has engendered is summed up by the American Association of School Administrators in the following statement made just after another Supreme Court decision against certain programs of state aid to parochial schools: "To predict what the future holds for the nonpublic schools with their 6 million elementary and secondary children would be purely speculative at this point. The ultimate solution poses vexing questions not only to private school administrators but to their public school counterparts as well."[11]

10. Ibid., p. 155.
11. *Hot Line* 4, no. 7 (Washington, D.C.: American Assn. of School Administrators, July 1972), p. 1.

Selected Readings

Alexander, Kern; Corns, Ray; and McCann, Walter. *1973 Supplement to Public School Law* (Cases and Materials). St. Paul, Minn.: West Publishing Co., 1973.

———, and Jordan, K. Forbis. *Constitutional Reform of School Finance.* Lexington, Mass.: Lexington Books, D. C. Heath and Co., 1973.

Reischauer, Robert D., and Hartman, Robert W. *Reforming School Finance.* Washington D.C.: The Brookings Institution, 1973.

School Finance in Transition. Gainesville, Fla.: National Conference on School Finance, 1973.

Schools, People, and Money. Washington, D.C.: President's Commission on School Finance, U. S. Government Printing Office, 1972.

Wilson, Charles H., Jr. *Tilton v. Richardson: The Search for Sectarianism in Education.* Washington, D.C.: Assn. of American Colleges, 1971.

Unit 4

IMPROVING STATE SCHOOL FINANCE PROGRAMS

Serrano *and* Rodriguez *are now household words and have been major factors in the quiet but intensive revolution in school finance theory and practice that is now taking place in various states. Long overdue, the struggle toward attainment of greater equality of educational opportunity for the youth of America now seems assured.*

Percy Burrup
*Financing Education in a
Climate of Change,* 1974

9

Pre-*Serrano* School
Finance Systems

As pointed out in a previous chapter, in the early history of public education the various states seemed content to accept responsibility for education but were reluctant to assume major responsibility for financing it. Local school districts—usually of small size and often with limited resources—bore responsibility of financing education for many years without state assistance. It is true that the states generally provided ways and means of legalizing local school property taxes, but grants, equalization funds, and a general state-local "partnership" arrangement received little attention until the second quarter of this century.

This system of operating an educational program was somewhat satisfactory and workable in most school districts during the time in American history when there was extreme local pride in the public schools and limited competition for the property-tax dollar. This was true, perhaps, because of satisfaction with limited curricula, low costs, and little state control and interference. But its obvious weakness soon rose to the surface and demands for change and for some form of state financial support began to permeate legislative halls. Even though American citizens continued to hold fast to their historic conviction that public schools should function as locally controlled institutions, they began to advocate the idea of some form of state support for financing education in order to equalize educational opportunity and equalize the burden of paying for continuously expanding school programs.

Much of the early inequality and inequity in financing education was caused by the fact that school districts varied greatly in size and in wealth, from large city districts to very small common school districts operating only one- or two-room schools. With such extremes the taxable property base per person to be educated varied tremendously from one district to another. This, of course, resulted in similarly large variations in property tax levies. This unfairness was slow in disappearing. The American Association of School Administrators reported, for example, that as late as 1955-56 the local levies in a county in Iowa varied from a total millage rate slightly over 2 mills in the wealthiest district to a total millage rate of 154 mills in the poorest district.[1]

Reduction of the number of school districts in a state gradually reduced the range of variation in ability of its districts to finance education. But school district reorganization and the elimination of many small and inefficient districts was a very slow process until the 1940s and 1950s. Such reorganization was hampered by three major conditions: (1) the operation of permissive reorganization laws that required the exercise of local initiative and voter approval—a requirement that by its nature was unpopular and resulted in few successes; (2) bitter resistance by voters in low-levy school districts against merging with districts that required higher millages for school operation; and (3) reorganization issues were usually settled on the basis of emotional feelings of citizens to their local school and community with little consideration of the potential educational benefits of such reorganization.

Mandatory legislation reorganizing school districts has always been a possibility for quick action in such matters, but its implementation has been infrequent. With a few exceptions, such as Utah in 1915, West Virginia in 1933, and Nevada in 1956, most state legislatures appeared to be content to wait until the people concerned made the first move under provisions of permissive legislation to reorganize schools.

The semipermissive legislation that was adopted in many states during the 1940s and 1950s did much to reduce the number of local school districts, but the process has not yet been completed, for some states still operate with large numbers of districts that need to be combined with others in order to provide greater equality of educational opportunity.

LOCAL DISTRICT FUNDING

Full local district funding was the first of all school finance plans. Over the years it has proven to be the least desirable and the least effective in producing equality of educational opportunity among the districts within a state. Its operation as the sole producer of school revenue terminated near the turn of the twentieth century with the beginning

1. *School District Organization* (Washington, D.C.: American Assn. of School Administrators, 1958), p. 84.

of state grants and other allocations to local districts. Its almost exclusive use in the years preceding the use of flat grants and foundation programs preceded any modern-day philosophy of equal educational opportunity or equal sharing of the burden of taxation. The place of a child's birth determined to a large degree the quality and the quantity of his education. The place of one's residence and the extent of his investment in real property were major factors in the calculation of each taxpayer's burden in financing education.

As an example of the unfairness of the local district funding system, consider the following example comparing three mythical districts. It is assumed that assessment practices are the same in all districts and that "weighted pupil units" is a fairer measure of each district's financial need than the number of pupils to be educated.

District	Assessed Valuation	Weighted Pupil Units	Assessed Valuation per WPU
L	$10,000,000	1,000	$10,000
M	20,000,000	1,000	20,000
H	40,000,000	1,000	40,000

L — the district with the lowest AV/WPU
M — the district with the median AV/WPU
H — the district with the highest AV/WPU

v — assessed valuation of all taxable property
p — total number of weighted pupil units
l — required mill levy
e — expenditure per weighted pupil unit

The formula for this form of school finance (local district funding) becomes:

$$1 = \frac{ep}{v}$$

Thus, it is evident that the higher the assessed valuation (assuming the same number of WPUs), the lower the tax levy, assuring wealthy districts a low levy and poor districts a high levy. (See Model 9.1).

Inequities that result in strong dissatisfaction with this method of financing education are obvious. In the example, District H obtains the $800 per weighted pupil unit with a tax rate of only 20 mills, but District L is required to levy 80 mills for the same revenue. In states where the relative ability of local districts to finance education by use of the property tax varies by as much as 100 to one, or more, the result becomes ridiculous. Generally speaking, such a system is workable only

MODEL 9.1.   Local District Financing

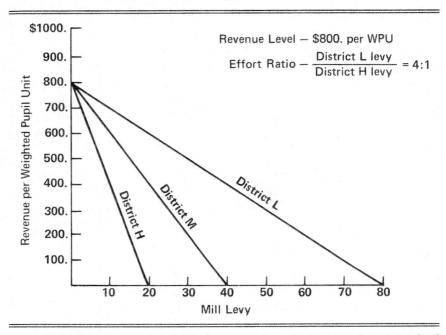

Revenue Level — $800. per WPU

Effort Ratio — $\dfrac{\text{District L levy}}{\text{District H levy}}$ = 4:1

For MODEL 9.1., assume that the three districts have the same number of weighted pupil units and that each is financing an expenditure program of $800 per weighted pupil unit.

in states with a very small number of school districts with little variation in their ability to support education.

EARLY STATE ASSISTANCE TO LOCAL DISTRICTS

As the costs of education increased and as competition for the revenues generated by a local property tax became greater, it was logical and necessary for local districts to obtain some financial assistance from state government. This support emerged principally as flat grants and categorical aids until the theory of foundation programs and equalization was discovered and implemented.

Although state financial support for education is largely a twentieth century development, Mort reported that about one-fourth of public school revenue in 1890 came from state sources. He did not differentiate between the funds derived from federal land grants and those obtained from strictly state sources.

Flat Grants

In the early attempts of states to assist local districts in financing their schools, flat grants were used extensively. These grants were usually funds per pupil, funds per teacher, or percentage grants. They were provided as a form of relief to local taxpayers with no real intent of providing equalization. Their effect on local districts was usually non-equalizing, except with the use of percentage grants which do not change the ratio of tax effort among districts either toward or away from equalization of tax effort. To illustrate this, assume that districts A and B have the following characteristics:

District	Assessed Valuation	Paid by State	Budget Needs	Mill Levy	Weighted Pupil Units
A	$6,000,000	nil	$240,000	40	600
B	5,000,000	nil	100,000	20	400

Under local district funding, since District A is required to levy 40 mills for its program and District B needs a levy of only 20 mills, the effort ratio (ER) is expressed as 2:1. The purpose of equalization is to create an effort ratio of 1:1. All attempts to provide state aid should be directed toward reducing the ER to that value.

Suppose, in the above example, the state provides $100 per weighted pupil unit as a flat grant. District A's requirements from local property taxes now become $180,000 and District B's become $60,000, requiring levies of 30 mills and 12 mills, respectively. The effort ratio now becomes 2.5:1. Thus, the flat grant is nonequalizing in its effect upon the two districts, for it has actually increased, rather than decreased, the ER.

As an example of state percentage grants, assume that the state pays 40 percent of the budget needs of each district. Under this arrangement, District A is now required to raise $144,000 by using a property tax levy of 24 mills and District B $60,000 using a levy of 12 mills. Thus, the ER remains at 2:1 and the percentage grant has been neither equalizing nor nonequalizing in its effect upon these two districts. This type of grant is seldom used in modern school finance programs. There is little to recommend it when compared to other models that have some degree of equalizing effect in their application.

Model 9.2 shows the effect of a flat grant of $200 per weighted pupil unit upon the same three districts shown in Model 9.1.

District	State Funds per WPU	Local Funds per WPU	Total Funds per WPU	Mills Tax Levy	Total Funds per M/WPU
L	$200	$600	$800	60	$13.33
M	200	600	800	30	26.67
H	200	600	800	15	53.33

MODEL 9.2.   State Flat Grants

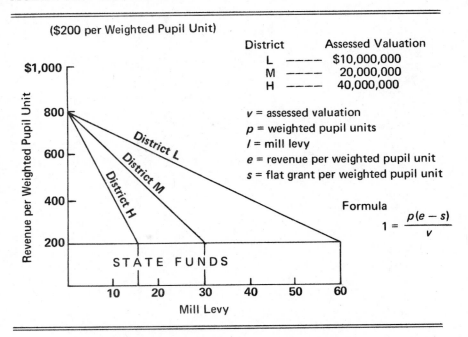

($200 per Weighted Pupil Unit)

District		Assessed Valuation
L	-----	$10,000,000
M	-----	20,000,000
H	-----	40,000,000

v = assessed valuation
p = weighted pupil units
l = mill levy
e = revenue per weighted pupil unit
s = flat grant per weighted pupil unit

Formula

$$l = \frac{p(e - s)}{v}$$

In this model, the flat grant of $200 per weighted pupil unit leaves each district with the need to provide the additional $600 by a local property tax levy varying from 60 mills in District L to 15 mills in District H. Since the state is providing one-fourth of the revenue of each district, the grant has the same effect as any percentage grant—the ratio of highest tax levy to lowest tax levy remains the same as without the grant (in this example 4:1) and no equalization is effected. If examples are used with varying numbers of weighted pupil units (or other base on which the grant is made), the effect of the grant is usually non-equalizing.

Even though flat grants do not usually accomplish the purpose for which they are intended, they obviously reduce the burden on taxpayers in all districts and are therefore a first step in replacing the outmoded system of complete local financing. For example, in the model, District L has had its tax burden lessened by 20 mills, District M has had its tax burden lessened by 10 mills, and District H has been able to reduce its tax by 5 mills. In terms of percentage decrease each has reduced its required mill levy by 25 percent.

Even though flat grants are generally not equalizing to local school districts, they are still being used in some state school finance formulas—usually in combination with other equalizing state allocations. Tradition continues to play an important role in financing education even though there are far better methods of allocating state funds to local districts.

Flat grants were first provided by states to local districts on an incidental and haphazard basis. Gradually, however, the states developed theories and guidelines for such appropriations. Thurston and Roe noted the crudeness with which these funds were being allocated in the early part of this century:

> A look at the state aid plans in effect in the various states shows that the great majority of the states have taken steps that are definitely designed to assure reasonably adequate educational opportunities for all children in properly organized school districts. Close investigation, however, shows that these plans are really a curious combination of refined methods of financing based upon logical principles, mixed with crude and awkward schemes of disbursement.[2]

As one takes a serious look at the various state plans or systems of allocating funds to local districts, he may very well ask some pertinent questions concerning the processes used and the supporting rationale. What purpose is the state trying to serve with such allocations? What processes will best serve the purposes and objectives that are being sought? What guidelines are defensible in making such allocations? These and many other questions need to be answered before value judgments can be made on any of the programs being considered.

Equalizing Grants

Most states now use the equalizing grant in allocating some or all of their state money to local districts. Such grants are made in terms of the tax-raising ability of the local districts. Some states use combinations of grants—equalizing, percentage, flat, and variations of these—but the trend is toward allotting higher percentages of all state funds on an equalization basis. For example, "Every State aid dollar in Rhode Island equalizes. More than $90 of every $100 of State aid equalizes in Georgia, Idaho, Kentucky, Maine, Michigan, Nevada, New York, Ohio, Tennessee, and Utah."[3]

While the equalizing-grant method of allocating state funds has been used for a long time in some states it is relatively new in many of them. Nineteen states increased the percentage of total aid that was distributed by equalizing grants in the period between 1953–54 and

2. Lee M. Thurston and William H. Roe, *State School Administration* (New York: Harper & Row, 1957), p. 84.

3. *State Aid to Local Government* (Washington, D.C.: Advisory Commission on Intergovernmental Relations, April 1969), p. 41.

1967–68. Most of the state funds allotted to local districts take the form of nonrestrictive general-purpose grants. While some standards or guidelines are usually provided for the districts receiving these grants, it is intended that their use be determined by the local school boards, with little or no restriction by the state. States, for the most part, put the onus on the receiving districts for proper and wise use of such funds. At one extreme, the states of Idaho, New York, Ohio, and Wyoming give discretionary power to local boards for expending at least 99 percent of their state funds.[4]

The percentage of state funds allocated to local districts on a categorical, or special-purpose, basis is now somewhat less than 15 percent, and it decreases every year. Some of the best-known of these funds are those for transportation, special education, and building purposes. In 1968, Alexander estimated that, by number, 76 percent of the total number of state school funds could be classified as special-purpose, even though they included only 15 percent of the money distributed.[5]

The states do not want to absorb all of the yearly school cost increases at the state level. Consequently they often devise ways and means short of mandated levies to keep local effort as high as possible in order to keep state increases within bounds. Traditionally, this has been done by "reward for additional tax effort" or by "reward for performance." Cubberley's finance proposals included a kind of reward for effort, but this not only was in effect nonequalizing but often actually increased the degree of inequality in many instances. His plan was to provide more funds for those districts with more teachers and those with schools with enriched or extended school services. Since the more wealthy or able districts usually already had more of both, the incentive plan was a benefit to them but of little help to the poorer districts. As a result, the states have used various kinds of programs to aid districts that make the tax effort to go beyond the foundation program—supplementary or leeway programs that usually have some degree of equalization built into them.

Most state school finance plans are not set up in pristine simplicity; they often combine several kinds of state aid in varying mixes. North Carolina, for example, pays the total cost of a basic program, plus categorical aid for such programs as vocational education, driver education, and others. Programs beyond the foundation must be supported solely by the local district. Utah requires the local coverage of a required foundation program levy—if a district has such—to revert to the Uni-

4. Ibid., p. 42.
5. S. Kern Alexander, "Trends and Issues in School Finance," in *Interdependence in School Finance: The City, the State, the Nation* (Washington, D.C.: National Education Assn. Committee on Educational Finance, 1968, p. 150.

form School Fund, to be used to help finance the minimum program in other districts.

THE EQUALIZATION PRINCIPLE

The work of Strayer and Haig in introducing the foundation program principle of financing education was a major breakthrough in school finance theory. It now seems improvident that such a simple and defensible principle should not have been discovered and applied much earlier in school finance history. But its relatively late appearance near the end of the first quarter of this century is matched by the even slower rate at which it was adopted by the states. For years knowledgeable people had observed and deplored the disparities, the inequities, and the injustices that existed in American society in terms of unequal wealth, unequal incomes, and unequal opportunities. Similar inequities in educational opportunities and in sharing the costs of education seem to have been accepted with the same feeling of frustration and an inability to change the existing situation.

The birth of the foundation program concept provided a means of removing some of the heretofore disparities in school revenues and expenditures. But changes come slowly and some states were reluctant to apply the principle to their school finance program to any great degree. While the principle is not perfect and has many limitations, its application would have eliminated, or at least reduced, much of the unfairness of revenue distribution that still exists in many states. Improved finance formulas involving extensions and improvements of Strayer-Haig-Mort foundation programs have been visible and available yet their utilization has often been sporadic or nonexistent. Adoption of the foundation concept is a necessary and first step to the even more defensible program of power or open-end equalization now being advocated by most people in the field of school finance theory.

IMPROVING STATE EQUALIZATION PRACTICES

The theory of the foundation program to achieve equalization of educational opportunity is relatively simple; however, its practical application is often complex, usually unnecessarily so. The formula that each state uses involves three essential conditions: (1) calculation of the "monetary need" of each school district necessary to obtain a state-guaranteed minimum program, measured objectively in terms of the number of weighted pupils (and other measures of need)—to be financed at the level of support that the state will guarantee; (2) determination of the amount of local school revenue that can be expected with a state-established uniform tax rate levied against the equalized assessed valuation of all taxable property within the district; and (3) determining the state allocation by finding the difference between the district's established need and the revenue obtainable from its required local tax effort.

Complications arise in applying the theory to practice for a number of reasons: (1) Not all pupils require the same number of dollars of expenditure, even under a commitment to the principle of equality of opportunity, for handicapped children are more expensive to educate than normal ones and children who attend very small schools and those who attend very large ones are more expensive than those in medium-sized ones. (2) Wide variations exist in the assessment practices in the districts of a state, even when all are presumed to be assessed at uniform rates. (3) The quality of the teaching staffs may vary considerably, as determined by educational preparation and experience, thus varying the costs of instruction among the districts. (4) The dollars provided do not purchase the same amount or quality of goods and services in all districts, thus favoring some districts and penalizing others. (5) Some states operate many different kinds of school districts with differing taxing responsibilities and restrictions.

The net result of these and other differences among districts is that finance formulas usually include provisions to try to offset inequalities. Weightings for school size differentials, such as sparsity and density factors, special consideration for exceptional children, allowances for transportation costs, and provision for additional funds for better-qualified teachers are some of the most common adjustments in formulas that add to their complexity but also increase their validity and effectiveness.

FOUNDATION PROGRAM VARIATIONS

The foundation program concept can be applied with a number of variations, such as with or without local options to go above the state guaranteed minimum program, with or without state matching of local optional revenues, or in combination with flat grants and/or categorical allocations. Some of these possibilities are illustrated in the following simplified models.

Model 9.3 is composed of two parts. Model 9.3a illustrates the foundation program constructed with the mill levy necessary to produce the state program in the richest district with no surplus being generated. Model 9.3b illustrates the same program with a required levy high enough to produce a surplus in the wealthiest district which may or may not be recaptured by the state—depending on the philosophy of the state in this regard.

Model 9.3a is a mandatory foundation program comparing the three districts L, M, and H with assessed valuations of $10,000,000, $20,000,000, and $40,000,000, respectively. A required mill levy of 20 mills is applied, with no surplus above the foundation program. There is no provision in this model for board or voted options to go above the mandated

MODEL 9.3. Foundation Program (Without Local Options)

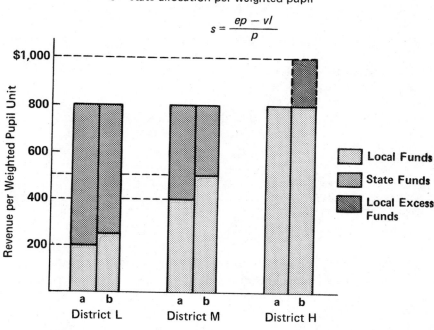

a —— Local Levy of 20 Mills
b —— Local Levy of 25 Mills (with surplus in wealthy district)

v = assessed value of taxable property
l = mandated tax levy
e = revenue per weighted pupil unit
p = number of weighted pupil units
s = state allocation per weighted pupil

$$s = \frac{ep - vl}{p}$$

program. Hence, it is an unequalized minimum as well as maximum program. It illustrates the application of a simple form of foundation program where equality of educational opportunity, as measured by equal dollars of total revenue per weighted pupils, is achieved; at the same time local property taxpayers share the burden equitably. In its simplest form (without local capability of supplementing the program) it makes "perfect" equalization of a minimum-maximum program; it provides no opportunity for districts to enrich the state-mandated program. It is usually unsatisfactory unless accompanied by provisions for local extension of the program beyond the foundation level unless it is equalized at a high enough level to provide adequate funds for all districts.

District	State Funds per WPU	Required Tax Levy	Local Funds	Total Funds per WPU	per M per WPU
L	$600	20 M	$200	$800	$40
M	400	20 M	400	800	40
H	Nil	20 M	800	800	40

Model 9.3b illustrates the use of the foundation program concept when the required local levy produces more revenue in some districts than the state guaranteed level per weighted pupil unit. The surplus may be left with the local district or it can be used (recaptured) by the state to help equalize the costs in other districts. The argument in favor of its being kept where it is produced is that since it is coming from a so-called wealthy district the taxpayers there are already providing proportionately higher percentages than in poorer districts to the state coffers through sales taxes, income taxes, and the like. On the other side of the argument is the observation that even with state recapture, the local district taxpayers are paying the same property tax rate as is being paid by those in all other districts. Model 9.3b illustrates a foundation program (without state recapture of surplus local funds raised by a 25 mill local levy)

District	State Funds per WPU	Required Tax Levy	Local Funds per WPU	Total Funds per WPU	per M per WPU
L	$550	25 M	$250	$800	$32
M	300	25 M	500	800	32
H	Nil	25 M	1,000	1,000	40

Model 9.3b with recapture becomes the same as Model 9.3a except that equalization has been effected in all three districts but with a 5 mill higher local levy being required.

Model 9.4 illustrates a foundation program with board leeway options not supported with state funds. It assumes the same three districts as before, with the following characteristics:

District	Assessed Valuation	Required Levy	Board Leeway
L	$10,000,000	20 M	10 M
M	20,000,000	20 M	10 M
H	40,000,000	20 M	10 M

It shows that the equalizing effect of a foundation program guaranteeing $800 per weighted pupil unit with a required levy of 20 mills is eroded with each district using a 10 mill (unsupported) tax levy beyond the foundation program. Such a plan reduced the inequalities shown in our earlier models but falls far short of complete equalization. The lower the base of the foundation program and the greater the leeway above it, the greater are the inequalities that result from the use of this model.

MODEL 9.4.   Foundation Program with Unmatched Board Leeway

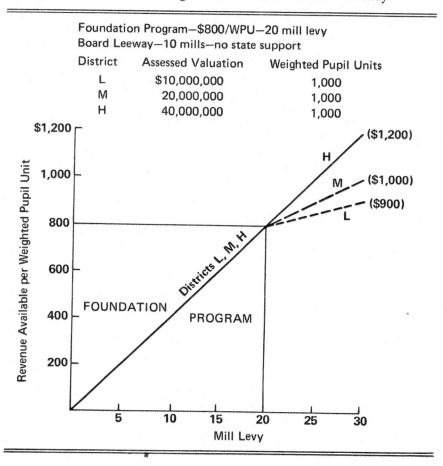

Foundation Program—$800/WPU—20 mill levy
Board Leeway—10 mills—no state support

District	Assessed Valuation	Weighted Pupil Units
L	$10,000,000	1,000
M	20,000,000	1,000
H	40,000,000	1,000

District	Foundation Program Funds per WPU			Leeway Program Funds per WPU			Total Program Funds per WPU		
	State	Local	Total	State	Local	Total	State	Local	Total
L	$600	$200	$800	Nil	$100	$100	$600	$300	$900
M	400	400	800	Nil	200	200	400	600	1,000
H	Nil	800	800	Nil	400	400	Nil	1,200	1,200

Thus, District L has $30 available per weighted pupil unit per mill levied; District M has $33.33, and District H has $40.

All the school finance models used in this text are shown in their simplest form. It should be noted that differences in the numbers of weighted pupil units, differences in local levies to be made, differences in the amount of state funds to be provided, and the possibility of numerous combinations of these programs would increase the inequities shown in these models.

In practice, school finance formulas are much more complicated than the models. They often are arranged as a combination of more than one type. For example, prior to 1973 the State of Utah used a program with a fairly high state guarantee for its foundation program with a required 16 mill levy; the board leeway program of 12 mills brought reduced guaranteed revenue per mill per distribution unit and an additional 10 mills of voted leeway generated a further reduced guaranteed revenue per mill per distribution unit. While nearly all districts used the full 12 mill board leeway program, the voted leeway was reduced to a point where it provided little state revenue and only about one-fourth of Utah's forty districts used any part of this deflated program.

Models 5 and 6 show the effect of some combinations of flat grants and foundation programs, with or without school board and voted options combinations is almost unlimited. The various states have used varying to go above the state-guaranteed program. The kind and number of such combinations of such programs is almost unlimited. The various states have used varying combinations to suit their own school finance philosophy.

It should be emphasized that whatever system or process a state may use in financing education the state should support the program to a greater extent in poor districts than in wealthy ones. It serves no useful purpose for a state to provide board options and taxpayer-voted options to go above the state program—except to widen the gap between the wealthy and poor districts and thus produce a nonequalizing effect in the finance program.

As the straight line in Models 5 and 6 that relates local tax effort and revenue per weighted pupil is flattened by a reduction of state support, the net effect of such becomes evident. For example, in Model 6, District H can obtain $1,400 per weighted pupil unit with a total levy of 40 mills while District L obtains only $1,100 with the same levy.

MODEL 9.5. Combination Flat Grant, Foundation Program and Unmatched Board Leeway

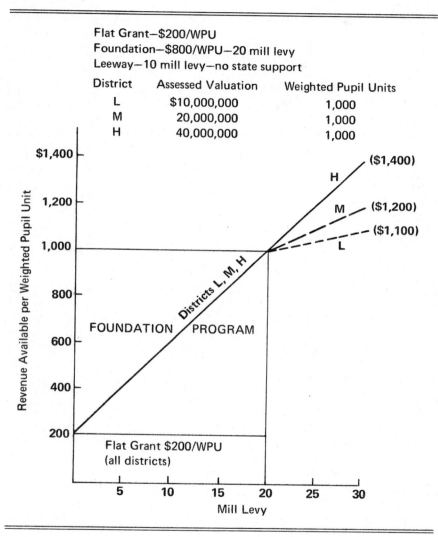

Flat Grant—$200/WPU
Foundation—$800/WPU—20 mill levy
Leeway—10 mill levy—no state support

District	Assessed Valuation	Weighted Pupil Units
L	$10,000,000	1,000
M	20,000,000	1,000
H	40,000,000	1,000

While they each would receive $1,000/WPU for a 30 mill levy, the unsupported voted leeway in this model has thereby added a non-equalizing factor. With the district power equalization principle now being emphasized (state support at the same rate at all tax-rate levels) there would be no such discrimination between districts that use leeway levies above the foundation program.

MODEL 9.6. Combination Foundation Program, Board Leeway with reduced support, and Voted Leeway with no state support

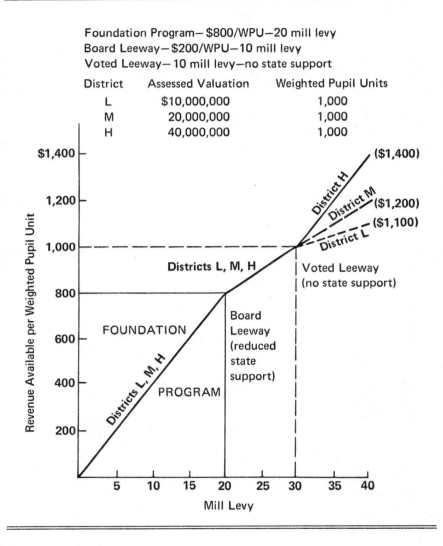

Foundation Program—$800/WPU—20 mill levy
Board Leeway—$200/WPU—10 mill levy
Voted Leeway—10 mill levy—no state support

District	Assessed Valuation	Weighted Pupil Units
L	$10,000,000	1,000
M	20,000,000	1,000
H	40,000,000	1,000

STATE SUPPORT OF PUPIL TRANSPORTATION COSTS

The generally accepted philosophy of free public education in this country places great emphasis on the need and desirability of universal equality of educational opportunity. Complete equality can never be attained so long as some students live next to the school building and others live at places far removed from it. Since school buildings cannot be made equally accessible to all, the individual states are obligated to provide whatever assistance they can to those whose residence is unfavorably situated in relation to school facilities.

The early school buildings of this country were built as near as possible to the clientele they served. In spite of that, many pupils living on farms and in sparsely settled areas often had long distances to travel to obtain the benefits of formal schooling. As the schools began to grow in size and importance, it became increasingly necessary to solve the problem of easy access to the school. Boarding schools and family-sponsored transportation by wagon, horseback, boat, or other means represented early attempts to solve this problem.

The daily transportation of millions of boys and girls to public schools in thousands of school districts now constitutes an important part of the big and expensive business of education. It has been estimated that about one-third of all pupils now attending our public elementary and secondary schools are being transported to and from school at public expense. Approximately 4 percent of our total current expenditures for these schools comprises transportation costs.

Financial Responsibility

Originally, the cost of getting pupils to and from school was considered to be an obligation of the parents of the children being served. As the size of school attendance areas increased and as schools began to be consolidated, the local districts began to provide such services. The first state to pass legislation to provide such services was Massachusetts, in 1869. By the turn of the century, only three or four states had made provision for state financing of pupil transportation services.

As districts were given responsibility for administering the local property tax for educational purposes, gross inequalities in ability to support schools began to appear. The need for state support for financially inadequate districts became evident with pupil transportation costs as it did with all other parts of the school finance program.

This is not the place to debate the question of state responsibility for providing transportation without cost to students—if such a position still needs debate. The premise here is that if the state causes the school to be established and requires certain of its citizens to attend, it *must* assume primary responsibility for getting the students to the place where formal education can take place. It is also assumed that the principle of equality of educational opportunity presupposes that the states will help most those districts having the greatest need.

Effect of School District Reorganization

Since the 1930s, many of the states have become increasingly concerned with helping local districts finance pupil transportation. This problem was accentuated with the increased state activity in reorganizing school districts and consolidating school attendance areas, which received considerable emphasis during the 1940s and the 1950s. These school district reorganization practices have resulted in the closing of many small schools, particularly in rural areas. As these schools were closed, it was necessary to transport students to larger units. Thus, increased demands were placed upon transportation facilities, and a greater portion of the budget was required for such services.

The individual states have been the chief instigators and promoters of school district reorganization. The decrease in number of school districts from more than 125,000 to fewer than 16,000 in the last thirty years did not just happen; it came as the result of concerted effort by educational leaders in nearly all states. The same states, then, directly or indirectly obligated themselves to alleviate the unfairness accentuated by the demise of many small schools. Where distance and transportation had been no special problem, by the creation of larger districts many pupils were left living far from school doors.

Equalization of Transportation Costs

Inequalities in district-assessed valuation per student to be educated are found among the districts within the boundaries of every state. Likewise, transportation costs and the ability to pay for them vary a great deal. Table 9.1, comparing two districts in the same state, is illustrative. If we assume a total levy of 36 mills for current expenditures, it is quite unfair for District *B* to have to spend 33⅓ percent of its budget to get its pupils to and from the schoolroom when District *A* is required to spend less than 3 percent for the same purpose. How can District *B* be expected to operate a comparable program with 24 mills of tax, compared with 35 mills in District *A*? Equality of educational opportunity can never become a reality where such disparities are permitted. The answer lies in state allocations to local school districts with equalization the goal.

Most states allocate transportation aid to local districts based on some relation between amount of service provided and cost of that service at the local level. In a few states, however, the extent of local transportation need does not necessarily influence the amount of state aid.

The student of school finance might well ask some pertinent questions

TABLE 9.1   Variations in Transportation Costs in Two Districts

	District A	District B
1. Transportation costs for one year	$91,000	$134,000
2. Number of pupils transported	3,500	2,000
3. Per pupil cost of transportation	$26	$64
4. District's assessed valuation	$91,000,000	$11,200,000
5. Local tax levy required to pay entire transportation cost	1 Mill	12 Mills

at this point: Why have states been so slow in applying the principles of equalization to the allocation of state funds to local districts for education—and particularly, for pupil transportation? Why does practice in this important area of school financing lag so far behind well-accepted theories and principles? There are a number of answers to these questions, including the following:

1. In many states the small-district system of education minimized the need for such services until recent years. Since most of the early mergers of districts and consolidations of school attendance areas were locally inspired and motivated, the solutions to transportation problems also came at that level without benefit of state support or legal basis. Thus, local school boards, in the absence of statutes, proceeded on their own, without experience, to set up and finance transportation programs. Gradually, statutes were enacted to give legal basis for transportation systems and their financing.
2. State legislatures and courts have very reluctantly dropped the tradition that held that the local school district and the parents of children who receive the services should assume most if not all of the cost of this service.
3. The states themselves have not had sufficient funds available for all aspects of the educational program for which they have been responsible.
4. The method used in allocating state funds for transportation in one state does not necessarily fit the needs in any other state. Thus, each state must learn by its own experience the best approach to this problem in terms of its own special conditions.

State Allocation of Funds

Traditionally, each state has enjoyed almost complete freedom in the way it has allocated funds to local school districts. Some states chose to leave the financing of education almost completely to each local dis-

233

trict; others used grants of varying kinds to alleviate local overburden; still others used equalization programs of varying degrees of complexity.

Allocations of state money to local districts have usually been made on the basis of the number of pupils to be educated and in terms of the ability of the district to finance a minimum or foundation program. Equality of educational opportunity has been interpreted to mean providing the same amount of money for each pupil who is to be educated. Gradually, however, financing formulas have recognized that it costs more to educate some pupils than others. Among the earliest changes in this regard was providing more money per pupil for those who lived in rural areas, where the unit cost of education was higher and where transportation was an important cost factor. Later, the provision of additional funds for educating exceptional children, especially the physically and mentally handicapped, became acceptable and desirable. Today, one of the great needs is for special financial consideration for the large city and metropolitan districts, where deprivation, tax overburden, and racial and ghetto-area problems have increased the unit costs of education well beyond those in average districts.

Espousal and implementation of programs with unequal amounts of money per pupil is fertile ground for confrontation and litigation. In 1968, test suits were made in at least three states, where the plaintiffs demanded more state money for inadequate schools because of a state's constitutional obligation to provide all children with equal educational opportunity. They were seeking to prove that more money must be spent on certain pupils to provide them with the same education that others receive.

In one form or another, the issue of equal protection of all citizens as provided by the Fourteenth Amendment has often been a matter of litigation. In 1954 in the famous *Brown* case, the Supreme Court required equal rights for the education of all our citizens regardless of race. By 1962, geographic discrimination was eliminated in the legislative reapportionment decision. By 1965, the Court had determined that financial ability could not be used to deny criminals equal protection of the law. By 1968, the issue of unequal protection of students by unequal expenditures of money for children attending different school districts had reached the courts.

Noting the wide disparities in expenditures of money per pupil in every state, school finance students had long anticipated legal action contesting such a system. As early as 1954, notice was taken of the terseness of judges of the U.S. Supreme Court when they noted that education was included within the equal protection clause of the Fourteenth Amendment: "In these days, it is doubtful that any child may reasonably be expected to succeed in life if he is denied the opportunity of an education. Such an opportunity, where the state has undertaken to provide it, is a right which must be made available to all on equal terms."

With the shock of the *Serrano* v. *Priest* decision in California now a matter of history, unparalleled confusion now exists in the realm of public school finance. Although legislatures have been given indirect warnings to provide new models for financing education, little direction has as yet been provided to assist them in their overthrow or improvement of our traditional, but obsolescent, manner of financing public education.

Court cases have not solved the problem of providing equal financial opportunity for all children within a state; they have simply opened the door for debate and reform. Certainly they have raised more questions than they have answered. What direction should states now take in financing their educational programs in the light of implied condemnation of the property tax as a source of locally provided revenue for schools? How can other taxes be used to replace or reduce property taxes, with control of education still kept at the local level? To what extent do these court decisions mandate standardization and uniformity of school programs? Do these decisions obliterate consideration of weighted pupils in determining expenditures?

STATIC SCHOOL FINANCIAL PATTERNS

Evidence of massive resistance to changes in school financial practices is observable in all fifty states. Such resistance is not always the fault of educators, however. The following are examples of a few ideas and practices that states and school districts have used and continue to use well beyond determination of their ineffectiveness or obsolescence.

1. Some states still require local school districts to rely almost completely on a local property tax as the source of funds for education in spite of the unfairness and regressiveness of such a means.
2. In spite of sound theories of equalization that have evolved during the last half-century from the thinking of numerous school finance specialists such as Strayer, Haig, Updegraff, and Mort, some of the fifty states have not yet incorporated these principles in their school finance programs.
3. Although it can be documented that education is really an investment in people, many legislative bodies give a strong impression that the cost of education threatens the economic capability of those who provide its funds.

4. It has been known for a long time that small schools are more expensive and less productive educationally than larger ones. But local pride and resistance to change are still effective in thwarting those who favor large and viable school organization patterns.

5. Despite our belief in the principle of equal protection for all our citizens as guaranteed by the Fourteenth Amendment to the United States Constitution, many different groups of people are denied this right by failure of state and local governments to provide sufficient funds to educate them. Students who are handicapped or gifted, or aspire to vocational training, or who are not of the dominant culture may not always have a reasonable chance to reach their potential as citizens.

6. Even though our pride in "free education" seems to be a sincere expression on the part of nearly all our citizens, in practice in many places such a designation is almost mockery. Numerous fees and incidental charges in many of our schools discriminate against children of low-income families and relegate them to second-class citizenship.

Selected Readings

Berke, Joel S.; Campbell, Alan K.; and Goettel, Robert J. *Financing Equal Educational Opportunity.* Berkeley, Calif.: McCutchan Publishing Corp., 1972.

Cohn, Elchanan, and Millman, Stephen D. *Economics of State Aid to Education.* Lexington, Mass.: Lexington Books, D. C. Heath and Co., 1974.

Coons, John E.; Clune, William H. III; and Sugarman, Stephen D. *Private Wealth and Public Education.* Cambridge, Mass.: Belknap Press of Harvard University Press, 1970.

Grubb, W. Norton, and Michelson, Stephan. *States and Schools.* Lexington, Mass.: Lexington Books, D. C. Heath and Co., 1974.

Johns, Roe L., and Morphet, Edgar L. *The Economics and Financing of Education,* 3rd ed. Englewood Cliffs, N. J.: Prentice-Hall, 1975.

——; Alexander, Kern; and Stollar, Dewey H., eds. *Status and Impact of Educational Finance Programs.* Gainesville, Fla.: National Educational Finance Project, 1971.

Murphy, Jerome T. *State Education Agencies and Discretionary Funds.* Lexington, Mass.: Lexington Books, D. C. Heath and Co., 1974.

The Realities of School Finance. Washington, D.C.: American Assn. of School Administrators, 1971.

10

Needed Reforms in Financing School Facilities

The uncomplicated and seemingly satisfactory nineteenth-century system of financing public school capital outlays with funds raised almost solely by local property taxes is obsolete and impractical for present-day use. Before the 1900s there was little need for extensive state participation in this important aspect of financing education. Most school districts had been able to finance their own capital outlay expenditures without assistance. Their school building problems had not yet reached the magnitude they have attained in recent years. There were many reasons for this, including the following among many others: (1) A smaller percentage of the school-age population attended school. (2) Building costs were much lower for a number of reasons: they were much less pretentious, labor costs were much lower, and they had fewer special areas and expensive equipment in them. (3) There was no accumulation of need for buildings as there has been during much of this century. (4) Since extensive changes and innovations were minimal, relatively few facilities or buildings were discarded because of obsolescence. (5) The assessed value of taxable property per child to be educated was much more favorable in terms of the taxes to be raised than it is now.

As the need for state involvement increased in the early years of this century, a few states made feeble gestures toward helping finance school district capital outlays. About half a dozen southern states provided emergency funds that were made available to hardship districts least capable of providing school buildings with local tax funds alone. Today more than forty states provide some form and amount of state financial assistance for local capital outlay and debt service costs.

COMPLETE LOCAL SUPPORT

One of the strong traditions that began to develop early in school finance history was that capital outlay costs were of local concern only, in spite of strong and almost universal acceptance of state responsibility for education. The soundness of such a position is open to serious debate, but traditional acceptance of this local responsibility with almost complete indifference on the part of state governments is a matter of open record. In spite of recommendations for state participation in capital outlays by such finance planners as Updegraff and Mort, the main concern of most authorities in the Strayer-Haig era of influence was with state support of current operational costs only. The place of favor and right of first consideration were amply supported by the fact that current expenditures included about 85 percent of the total school budget with only 15 percent being spent for capital outlay.

Complete local support for financing capital outlays was a defensible and practical method of collecting the money to build and equip new school buildings for many years in the early history of this country. But the rationale for such a method of collecting capital outlay and debt service funds has virtually disappeared in the face of newer and certainly fairer methods of financing education. Some of the changes in school finance philosophy include support of the following statements:

1. Since responsibility for education is legally a state function, responsibility for its financing rests firmly upon each state.
2. There is no justification for financing capital outlays on a different basis from that of financing current expenditures. If state financing of current operations is defensible and fair, so also is state financing of capital outlays.
3. There is no defense for the traditional method of financing school facilities by relying completely on a regressive and unfair local property tax when more equitable tax sources are available at the state level.
4. It is false economy to indebt school districts for long periods of time with excessive interest costs.
5. It is paradoxical to provide adequate funds for current expenditures for all districts and then deny some of them good educational programs because low assessed valuations and state-imposed limitations on debt service maximums deny them the fiscal ability to provide satisfactory facilities.
6. Just as no district, regardless of its wealth, should enjoy pecuniary advantages over another in the obtaining of current operation funds, neither should any district enjoy resource advantages over another in the provision for school facilities.

Complete local responsibility for financing the current expenditures of school districts was eliminated in most states in the early part of this century with the advent of state grants of various kinds to local districts. But progress in financing the building of school buildings has not yet made such progress, for such financing is still almost completely a local responsibility in most of the states. In terms of the Coons, Clune, and Sugarman version of fiscal neutrality, the kind, number, and even the quality of school buildings and facilities available to most school children is still a function of the wealth of their parents, neighbors, and the school district in which they live. Financing school facilities is more than half a century behind our practices in financing current expenditures and the gap is widening rather than decreasing.

The school finance court decisions in the early 1970s were concerned largely with inequities and inequalities in financing current expenditures. Only by implication can it be said that they were requiring the same improvements in financing capital expenditures. Our problems in improving the latter are tremendously greater than they are in improving state finance programs for current expenditures. The problem of overcoming tradition and then directing attention and action toward equalization in financing capital outlays will require much time, effort, and money. The inequities in this area are great, as indicated by Governor Rampton of Utah in his 1972 address to the Utah Conference on School Finance. He said, "If we think there are inequities in state systems for funding current expenditures of public schools, wait until we examine the way we finance school buildings."

FACTORS RESTRICTING LOCAL RESPONSIBILITY

A big factor working against local responsibility for building school facilities, especially before recent reorganization emphasis, was the low assessed valuations of literally thousands of small school districts. Regardless of the statutes and the willingness of people to tax themselves, bonding small districts to build school buildings was often mathematically impossible. In some school districts, for example, the cost of a new building might well exceed the assessed valuation of the entire district, while in other districts in the same state a small tax levy would be adequate to build needed buildings on a pay-as-you-go basis. Such inequity is a violation of our concept of providing equality of educational opportunity for all children within a state.

Another argument against complete local responsibility for construction of school buildings is that such costs would then be paid almost entirely by property-tax-payers. Some people would then escape paying their share of these capital outlay costs. While the property tax at one time in our history may have been a reasonably fair measure of taxpaying ability, it is not such today. Using property tax payments exclusively for capital outlays repudiates our long-held belief in taxing people in terms of their ability to pay for education. Only state participation in such costs can provide relief or correction for this inequity. Such relief should be provided on an equalization basis. This would bring some relief to property-tax-payers and would broaden the tax base to include tax revenues from many different kinds of taxes, an absolute necessity in any defensible tax system.

STATE SUPPORT: A TREND

In recent years, it has become evident that changes would have to be made in our method of financing capital outlays. Unsolved problems have been accumulating in many financially weak districts that were unable to meet their own building needs. These needs were accelerated after World War II with the result that there was an increased demand that states come to the rescue of local districts with defensible plans to provide substantial amounts of capital outlay money, with little if any increase in state control.

Even though much progress has been made in eliminating the strong tradition of state "hands-off" policy in providing funds for capital outlay, the idea persists in many parts of the country. In spite of admitted inadequacies of the local property tax, the trend toward using other more realistic and defensible forms of taxes for financing construction of school buildings and other facilities, especially at the state level, has been slow in gaining full momentum.

LOCAL CAPITAL-OUTLAY FINANCE PLANS

During the many years of almost exclusive local support for financing capital outlays, several different plans and procedures have evolved in the various states. Chief among these have been pay-as-you-go, use of tax reserve funds, and bonding.

Pay-As-You-Go Financing

Pay-as-you-go financing, which has been feasible in some large and relatively wealthy school districts, is an ideal way to finance capital outlays. It is the quickest and perhaps the easiest way of getting the necessary resources from the private sector to the public sector of the economy. It eliminates expenditure of large sums of money for interest, the costs of bond attorney fees, and election costs. It is convenient and tends to reduce the time required to obtain school facilities. This is particularly important in periods of high interest rates. As the costs of education have risen year after year, fewer districts have been able to take advantage of this method without creating hardship for some of its property-tax-payers.

Pay-as-you-go plans usually do not produce adequate revenue to finance school plant construction because of two factors: (1) relatively low assessed valuations in small and average-sized districts compared with the high cost of building, and (2) low tax levies due to restrictive legal limitations and high tax rates on property for obtaining the revenue for current expenditures. Many school districts that successfully used this plan in the years of relatively low cost construction have found it impracticable in recent years.

Building Reserve Plan

The accumulation of tax funds to be held in reserve for future building needs has been practiced in a few states; in some others it is illegal. This plan provides for spreading construction costs over a period of time *before* the buildings are erected as contrasted with bonding, which spreads the cost over time *after* the schools are constructed. At first consideration, this reserve plan would appear to be a good method of solving this financial problem. However, there are a number of legitimate, and also some controversial, objections to this process, such as:

1. The accumulated funds paid by taxpayers before the money was needed will have cost them the use of such funds with interest that might have been earned, and in many instances they may be funds that were borrowed by taxpayers at rates considerably higher than those available to the school district if these accumulated funds were to be invested until they were needed.
2. Changes in the membership of the board of education or changes in the apparent needs of the school district or both may sometimes result in diversion of these reserve funds to purposes other than those for which they were collected.
3. Some of the taxpayers who paid into the reserve fund may never receive the attendant benefits because they move from the school district.
4. Inflation tends to erode the value of the reserve and reduce its pur-

chasing power, rather than increase it as a result of interest accumulation.

5. Some argue, rather feebly, that all those who use the buildings should pay their fair share of the cost of such facilities; this is possible only when the costs are paid over a long period of time and thus is not possible when pay-as-you-go or pay-in-advance procedures are used.

The validity of this so-called intergeneration-equity philosophy is open to question. If one espouses the point of view that each generation should pay for the benefits it receives from use of school facilities, he is rejecting the ability-to-pay principle of financing education and reverting to the benefit principle, an untenable position that has long since been rejected in school finance theory. At this point, too, it seems reasonable to assume that each generation will be called upon to make sizeable payments for school facilities without concern for which generation is getting more or less than its share of benefits.

Although it is usually illegal to combine funds from the current-expenditure budget and the capital-outlay budget, except under certain legally established conditions, the effect of high tax rates in one area is that taxpayer resistance often forces lower tax rates in the other. Thus, the high rates necessary for pay-as-you-go or pay-in-advance payments for capital outlay may force lower rates for current expenditures, resulting in district curtailment of educational programs and services, or other presumed economies brought about by such things as reduced salary increases or increased pupil-teacher ratios.

Some districts that use the building reserve plan make a practice of earmarking certain voted revenues that are accumulated in a sinking fund to finance capital outlays. In practice, the plan is much like the pay-as-you-go process.

Under certain conditions, surpluses may be transferred from current expenditures at the end of a fiscal period to building reserve funds. The use of building reserves is usually subject to prior approval by the eligible voters of a district. In some states its potential utilization is limited to new construction; in others it may be used for any construction including renovation and remodeling.

Bonding

The most common of all local programs for financing capital-outlay and debt service expenditures is bonding. The process involves obtaining taxpayer favor for the district to issue long-term bonds to obtain funds to construct buildings and provide other facilities. Bond retirement involves levying property taxes to obtain funds to repay the principal and accrued interest. Bonding practices are required in districts with low assessed valuations of property, where tax revenues are not large enough to finance building costs on a current basis, and where the accumulation of reserve funds is either impracticable or illegal.

The principal advantages of the bonding system of raising school construction monies are:

1. Relative stability may be maintained in the tax levies necessary for construction. The tax burden is usually small enough each year so that it does not disturb the taxing plan for current-expenditure revenue.
2. Most districts can bond for large enough amounts to meet their building needs, while pay-as-you-go financing does not usually provide this opportunity.
3. School buildings and facilities necessary to operate a new program can be obtained when they are needed. Waiting for new construction until the required funds are in the school treasury would result in the denial of many educational benefits to the unfortunate students who were going through the school program when the facilities were needed but not provided.
4. The generations of people who get the greatest use of the facilities would be the ones to pay for them.

There are also some disadvantages to the use of a bonding process for school building construction. Some of these drawbacks include:

1. Greater total cost of the facilities due to the necessity of paying large amounts of interest. However, the position of most school finance authorities is that the interest cost is small when compared with the benefits obtained by the almost immediate procurement of school facilities when they are needed.
2. Deferred payments often result in the construction of larger and more elaborate facilities than are needed; cash payments tend to reduce the desires of those who supply the funds at the time of purchase.
3. Bonding puts the entire cost of school construction on property-tax-payers.

CAPITAL-OUTLAY FINANCING SINCE WORLD WAR II

A number of events and conditions made necessary a reconsideration of the roles of the state and local school districts in financing capital outlays after World War II. In the first place, the building needs of school districts had increased for a number of reasons including the following:

1. The backlog of needed school buildings had been increasing and had reached a phenomenal high by the end of the war. The economic effects of World War I, the Depression of the 1930s, and World War II had each taken its toll in unbuilt school buildings. From 1914 until 1945 there had been few years when current building needs had been met.
2. A sharp upturn in birthrates during and immediately after the Second World War necessitated sharp increases in the number of school buildings to be built.
3. During the long periods of inertness in the construction of school plants and particularly during and after World War II, changes in educational objectives and instructional procedures rendered many school buildings obsolescent, with urgent need for their replacement.
4. School reorganization programs, particularly during the late 1940s and through the 1950s, had done much to create school building needs. Larger plants were needed to accommodate larger groups of pupils at the same time that the small buildings in sparsely populated areas were no longer located where they were needed.
5. The accelerated mobility of people, with the largest group moving toward the suburbs with low potential for building its required facilities, and the migration of minority groups, particularly from the South to urban centers in the North, were primary factors in creating imbalances of facilities.

A second important condition that helped force changes in school construction responsibilities was that as the districts faced increasing pressure to build new schools, many intervening factors reduced their ability to do so without additional state or federal financial assistance:

1. Increased costs of education, including construction costs, made the financing of capital outlays with accumulated reserves, or on a "pay-as-you-go" basis, less feasible than ever before. Many districts that had used one or both of these methods in earlier years now found them totally impossible to implement.
2. The indebtedness limitations that most states had placed on local capital-outlay levies had become unrealistically low in many instances. These tax levy ceilings had been placed on local districts to protect property owners from excessive taxation when they were suffering from the financial penalties accompanying the worst modern depression, that of the 1930s. The result of these limitations was that in many districts where the people were willing to incur indebtedness for adequate capital outlays, state restrictions made such solutions impossible.

The pros and cons concerning state restrictions upon bonding power tend to counterbalance each other. According to Knezevich and Fowlkes:

> Although legal restrictions on incurring indebtedness are onerous, they are not necessarily bad in themselves. Those that promote better management, such as the requirement that only serial bonds can be issued, are commendable. Statutory or constitutional requirements which promote the careful regulation of the school's debt can make bonds easier to market and command a more favorable rate of interest. Legal restrictions, such as holding the debt limitation of schools to an unrealistically low percent of the assessed valuation of property, can result in the impairment of the fundamental purposes of the school district.[1]

3. State requirements for voter approval for districts to incur long-term indebtedness made such approval difficult or impossible to obtain. Requirements such as a two-thirds favorable vote necessary for approval and the requirement that a real property tax payment be made by all eligible voters made it particularly difficult to vote bonds in some school districts for the large sums necessary to finance capital outlays solely by local property taxation.

Bond Elections Have Failed

Some indication of the difficulty of passing a bond issue under restrictive state voting requirements is indicated by the fact that of the 175 bond issues on which Californians voted in 1967-68, 96 of them failed. Of the 96 that failed, 79 were favored by a majority vote even though they fell short of the required two-thirds.

Recently, courts have been acting against state laws that restrict voting eligibility to real property owners exclusively. For example, courts voided such laws in Arizona and New York in 1969.

Some other factors have been influential in school bond election failures. High interest rates, the difficulty of borrowing money, and the excessive tax on real property have combined to produce a form of taxpayer rebellion. The problem is referred to in the following:

> The financial crisis that is crippling many school districts around the country is showing no signs of easing up. A new report from the U.S. Office of Education (USOE) declares that voter rejection of public school bond issues, on the rise since 1966, hit a new high last year. USOE reports that only 56.8% of the school bond issues voted on in 1968–69 were approved, compared with 74.72 in 1964–65. The bond

1. Stephen J. Knezevich and John Guy Fowlkes, *Business Management of Local School Systems* (New York: Harper & Row, 1960), p. 215.

TABLE 10.1 Number of Public Elementary and Secondary School Bond Elections Held and Number and Percentage Approved: United States, Fiscal Years 1963-1972

Fiscal Year Ending June 30	Number of Elections		Approved (in percent)
	Held	Approved	
1963	2,048	1,482	72.4
1964	2,071	1,501	72.5
1965	2,041	1,525	74.7
1966	1,745	1,265	72.5
1967	1,625	1,082	66.6
1968	1,750	1,183	67.6
1969	1,341	762	56.8
1970	1,216	647	53.2
1971	1,086	507	46.7
1972	1,153	542	47.0
1973*	1,273	719	56.5

SOURCE: *Bond Sales for Public School Purposes, 1971-1972,* DHEW Publication No. (OE) 73-11406 (Washington, D.C.: U.S. Department of Health, Education, and Welfare, Office of Education, 1972), p. 2.
*U.S. Office of Education, *Digest of Educational Statistics, 1973,* p. 60, Table 72.

issues approved totaled $1.7 billion—$631 million less than in 1968 and the lowest total since 1962. They amounted to only 43.6% of the $3.9 billion proposed, another new low. The average net interest cost for fiscal 1969 rose to a new high of 4.88%, up from 4.57% in 1968. USOE says the cost of borrowing through school bond issues has increased almost 57% since 1963 and continues to rise with some districts now paying well over 6% interest.[2]

LOCAL SCHOOL BONDING PRACTICES

Local school districts that are in need of large capital-outlay funds find it necessary, like individuals, to borrow money from some source to be repaid with interest over a relatively long period of time. Typically, the individual borrowing money for himself signs a short-term note and receives the amount of the loan in cash or credit to be repaid at an established or agreed-upon rate of interest over a predetermined period. The process is much the same for a school board needing capital-outlay funds. The board, after receiving formal voter approval from the school

2. *Education U.S.A.* (Washington, D.C.: National School Public Relations Assn., July 1, 1970), p. 224.

patrons (required in nearly all states), issues and sells bonds to one or more competing companies on the basis of the lowest bid for interest rates. Usually the principal and interest on these bonds is to be paid by a previously agreed-upon plan, usually over a 10-, 20-, or 30-year period.

Registered bonds, as the name implies, require that all payments must be made solely to the registered owners on record with the school district that issued them. Thus, they are nonnegotiable, while coupon bonds are payable to the holder whenever they become due. Most authorities regard the coupon bonds as better than registered bonds because of their negotiability, lack of need of registering, absence of problems in transferring, and the lack of need of keeping meticulous records, which are required with registered bonds.

Bond Attorney

The increasing complexity of state requirements for bonding and the increasing legal and financial problems facing the school administrator make it almost mandatory for school districts to employ a bond attorney when a bond issue is contemplated. His experience and training will provide the school board and superintendent with advice and legal information necessary to complete this important aspect of financing the construction of school facilities. His services include securing legally accepted affirmation of bonding by the voters, proper and advantageous sale of bonds to the best interest of the school district, and many other important services.

Bonding Power

Bonding is not an implied power that school districts may use at their discretion and convenience. It is rather a power that must be expressed in the body of state law. The legislature has full power to determine the conditions required for bonding and the limits of bond issues available to each district. Likewise, it has plenary power to determine the qualifications of voters, how the bonds are to be sold, and any other pertinent conditions surrounding the transaction. However, the statutory conditions concerning bonding are often directory rather than mandatory, and courts usually support bond business where substantial compliance with the law has existed. While strict compliance is expected, the intent of the statutes is to determine the will of the voters. Consequently, the legality of bond elections and sales is usually determined by whether or not the procedures have determined what the people actually wanted. Recent decisions by the United States Supreme Court have changed some, and probably will change more, state requirements for bond issue approval.

Bonds Are Debentures

School district bonds are debentures acknowledging a debt that the school district owes to the bondholder; they do not have collateral backing or ordinary mortgage rights, however. They are not mortgages in the typical sense of the word, for they do not permit bondholders to foreclose and take over the physical assets of a district in the event of default in payment. The various lawmaking bodies and the courts, while recognizing that taking possession of school property by an unpaid bondholder would be against the interests of the people in general, protect the bondholders by requiring that certain tax funds be earmarked and set aside in special funds or accounts for bond redemption. Knezevich and Fowlkes noted that very few districts have ever defaulted in the paying of bonded indebtedness.[3]

BOND TYPES

There are several ways to classify bonds: according to the agency (municipality or state) issuing them, the degree of security protecting bondholders, or the procedure to be used in paying them. The most common way of classifying them is by the method used to pay or retire the bond principal. Under this classification, there are two main types: serial bonds and straight-term bonds.

Serial Bonds

The advantages offered by the serial type of bonding are such that its use is required in most of the states. This kind of bond provides for payment of accrued interest each year and also for retirement of part of the principal each year on an amortized basis. This reduces the total interest cost, since interest is charged only on the unpaid balance of the principal. It also affords an extension of further bonding capacity as the amounts on the principal are paid. It is not necessary under this type of bonding to amass large surpluses or sums of money in a sinking

3. Knezevich and Fowlkes, *Business Management of Local School Systems*, p. 215.

fund in anticipation of bond maturity at a later date. Taxes can be held to the total amount required to pay the predetermined costs of debt retirement each year. Such a plan is inflexible and may cause problems in periods or situations with unanticipated declines or reductions in yearly tax receipts for such purposes.

Straight-Term Bonds

Straight-term bonds that mature at the end of the bonding period have very little real value to a school district. Although they are said to have been important and useful in financing capital outlays in years past, their history has been one of mismanagement and poor planning. Hence, they are not used extensively today. There is little to be gained by a district's delaying retirement of a debt until the end of the bonding period. The arguments were forcefully stated by the Bond Buyer in the following:

> The debt retirement plan should provide for: (1) the retirement of principal at least as rapidly as the capital assets acquired with the proceeds depreciate; (2) declining debt service on existing debt, otherwise the almost inevitable sale of emergency or unanticipated issues will result in debt service having a decidedly upward bias; (3) a maturity schedule that does not add undue rigidity to the budget.[4]

A variation of the straight-term bond saw the development of legal requirements for establishing and maintaining "sinking funds" for the payment of bonded indebtedness. These requirements called for the proceeds of debt retirement tax levies to be placed in a specific fund for payment of the bond principal at maturity. The usually anticipated problems of administering reserve funds—proper and safe investment, protection against mismanagement, and avoidance of making loans or transfers to other accounts—have continued to materialize in the administration of these kinds of bonds.

Callable Bonds

Bond amortization plans are usually rigid and prevent adjustment over the period of their retirement. Bonds that are sold during a period of high interest rates may thereby become a severe debt if interest rates drop appreciably during the life of the bond issue. For that reason, "callable," or "refundable," options are available to the school district at the time of the original issue of the bonds. These provide for pre-

4. "Preparing a Bond Offering," *The Bond Buyer* (1962), p. 9.

mature payment of the debt, with reissue of the bonds at a more favorable rate of interest. Since this feature protects only the school district from falling interest rates (with no protection to the bonding company for increasing rates), the cost of such an option makes callable bonds a little more expensive than ordinary serial or straight-term bonds.

Bond Sales

Bonds are most often issued in $1,000 or $5,000 amounts. They are sold through competitive bidding. Interest rates are determined by the economic conditions at the time they are sold, the extent and degree of competition in the market, the bond rating, and the length of the term for which they are issued. Bonds are attractive investments because of their exemption from federal and state income taxes.

Amortization Schedules

The preparation of the best schedule for a district to retire a bond issue depends on whether or not additional bonds will be involved before the issue in question is repaid. It requires no particular skill to amortize one issue over a period of years, keeping total interest and principal payments (and consequently tax levies) at a nearly constant figure. The problem is rather complicated, however, in districts that require frequent bond issues of varying amounts and with varying bond interest rates.

Long-range planning in school districts involves anticipation of school construction and bonding for several years ahead. Although there is no mathematical or exact rule for amortizing bond issues, a few practical guidelines may help the school administrator in planning such when frequent issues are expected:

1. The bond principal should be retired as soon as possible in order to reduce bond interest cost and to increase future debt capacity.
2. Bond levies should ordinarily be kept somewhat constant, with the highest levy being set at the time of voter approval and with legal reserves being kept reasonably high. (Taxpayers often resent frequent increases in tax rates, particularly when they come as a result of poor planning or lack of foresight by the school board.)
3. Promises made by school personnel concerning bond-redemption tax levies should be made only on the basis of careful long-range planning. Such promises should be kept.
4. Surplus sums of money held in anticipation of bond payments should be invested within the restrictions of state law.

5. Bonds should be refunded whenever it is to the financial interest of the district to do so.
6. School boards should utilize consultant help from finance authorities in planning long-range bonding programs.
7. Bond and debt service levies should not be so high that taxpayer resistance forces a reduction of the levy for current expenditures.
8. The people should be kept informed concerning the long-range construction and bonding plans of the school district.
9. Indices of amortization that have been derived by authors in business and mathematics can often be used to advantage in preparing complex amortization schedules.
10. So far as possible, provision should be made in bond payment schedules to anticipate future school facts and figures that affect fiscal matters: Changes in projected school population, expected fluctuations in property assessment values, economic trends, and changes foreseen in the policies of the community and state toward indebtedness and future educational needs are a few of the most important matters to consider.

STATE CAPITAL-OUTLAY FINANCING

Even though the states did little to help in financing local public school capital outlays until the second quarter of this century, it was not due to lack of such suggestions or proposals by finance authorities that delayed action for so long in this matter. For example:

> Updegraff had proposed in 1922 a varying percentage of state support of capital outlay related to actual cost and local taxpaying ability. Mort had suggested the possibility of capital outlay support as a fixed percentage of current expenditure. Adams in 1928 suggested depreciation, local taxpaying ability, and uniform local tax effort as components of a state capital outlay program for Kentucky. Grossnickle tested Mort's hypothesis in New Jersey in 1931, concluding that debt service was 14 percent of current expenditure. Weller in 1940 favored a standard unit of housing, average cost, and attendance as components of a state formula for capital outlay support. These and postwar concepts, such as Lindman's equalized matching formula and Barr's index of capital need and taxpaying ability, played a major part in the postwar development of state support for capital outlay.[5]

5. W. Monfort Barr and W. R. Wilkerson, "State Participation in Financing Local School Facilities," in *Trends in Financing Public Education* (Washington, D.C.: National Education Assn., 1965), pp. 224–5.

Early State Capital-Outlay Programs

Since an initial action of Delaware in 1927 that provided for significant state support for local district debt service costs in the foundation program, most of the 50 states have made some progress in this aspect of school finance. By 1965, about 80 percent of the states had used some method of assisting local districts in financing capital outlays and debt service. Legislative grants and appropriations, including, for example, a part of the foundation program, state loans, state guarantees of local indebtedness, and state purchases of local district bonds, are the most important devices or ways used by the various states to help local districts finance capital outlays. An indication of the extremes among the states in financing such expenditures can be seen from the following:

> State participation in financing local facilities ranges from Delaware's major support to California's billion dollar loan plan, from the Pennsylvania State School Building Authority to Indiana's and Kentucky's "do it yourself" holding companies—originated in the 1920's—from Florida's, Washington's, and New York's scientifically conceived state grant programs to South Dakota's purchase of local bonds and Oregon's support of construction of junior colleges only. In 1965, state school officers in only 10 states responded, "We have done nothing in the way of state support or loans for local school construction in postwar years."[6]

Current Programs

The United States Office of Education has done much to stimulate the various states to provide plans for helping local districts to finance capital outlays—especially since World War II. In 1951, it proposed that each state should include capital-outlay financing in its foundation program for current and long-range building programs. State departments of education were to establish specific programs and help administer them. Current funds were to be used and reserves were to be established when practicable.

A few states have adopted a policy of making loans to the districts for capital-outlay purposes. The conditions of repayment usually include a standard effort for each district. The districts unable to repay said loans with a preestablished degree of tax effort receive the unpaid part of the loan as a state grant. The plan works well but may sometimes result in overburdening some districts with tax effort in order to meet stated requirements for eligibility to use such loans. Such handling of loan grants provides a degree of equalization, for the more wealthy

6. Ibid., p. 225.

districts would have no chance to default in repaying their loans, but poorer districts would often find it impossible to do otherwise.

The current situation on state financing of local district capital outlays indicates that:

1. Emergency state grants often precede regular appropriations or provision for capital-outlay funds in the state's foundation program. Relatively few districts share in the use of such emergency funds. The success of these plans is largely measured by the objectivity of the guidelines and standards required for participation. Over time, these emergency programs very often develop into more or less permanent patterns for such diversion of funds for school construction.

2. Only a few states include capital outlays as a part of the foundation program. Flat grants, incentive funds (such as matching funds or reorganization grants), emergency grants-in-aid, special grants to financially feeble districts, repayable loans, building authorities, and equalized foundation grants are the main ways used to allocate state funds to local districts for financing capital outlays.

3. There is little similarity among the methods used by the states for providing capital outlays and debt service funds to school districts; state appropriations and state loans are probably the two most used methods. While flat grants and incentive grants help all districts, they are not equalized and therefore tend to be limited in scope and in their effect on solving the capital-outlay problem. Some of these grants have been utilized to encourage school district reorganization and attendance area consolidation. Matching grants used by some states have given greater aid to wealthy than to poor districts, and on that basis they are not satisfactory.

4. Many states use more than one main program or device in getting state school money converted into local buildings: some allow local districts to accumulate funds for future building needs.

5. The state usually supervises rather carefully the expenditure of state monies for local school building construction, as it does with other state funds. The state often provides such supervision even when no state funds are directly involved in local school construction. This often involves required state approval of plans for new construction, observance of state-established building standards, and the services of state school building consultants in the planning of local schools.

6. Building authority plans offer a temporary solution to the problem of obtaining adequate buildings in some school districts. However, many of the financially weaker districts are hard pressed to provide funds for the high cost of such building authority rentals. There seems to be no more reason for the state to subsidize weak district

rental costs than to subsidize and liberalize the construction practices involved in building their own buildings in the first place. As pointed out by Johns and Morphet, "The question might well be raised as to whether the state is gaining anything from a long-range point of view by establishing indirect procedures for doing something that could be done even better by setting about to solve the problem directly."[7]

The use of school building authorities is an oblique attack on the problem of providing adequate school buildings. Under this plan, the building company constructs a building and rents it to the school district. The chief virtue of the plan is that it provides facilities for use by financially weak districts that could not bond to build their own because of low assessed valuations and unduly restrictive debt limitations.

School building authorities, while provided for in some of the states, have not always proved desirable for all school building purposes. Adequate planning, construction of school plants with modern educational specifications, and the difficulties involved in fitting changing programs to rigid or inflexible facilities are some of the problems that this kind of program calls forth.

7. Some degree of increased control and supervision of local districts seems to accompany the provisions of state funds to help pay local school building costs. Local school boards and citizens sometimes interpret the provisions some states attach as guidelines and standards for school construction as usurpation of some of the authority commonly vested in the local school board.

Actions at the federal level of government brought the seriousness of the nation's school building problem into focus shortly after the close of the Second World War. The National School Facilities Survey of school building needs in the early 1950s dramatized the size of the problem. The passage of Public Law 815 in 1950, which provided federal capital-outlay funds for school districts in areas impacted because of federal installations and defense projects, was substantial evidence of federal recognition. The study showed that tax relief at the local level was necessary if school districts were to be able to meet the challenge of providing adequate and satisfactory facilities for good-quality and expanded educational programs.

One of the satellite studies of the National Education Finance Project was the National Capital Outlay Project. As its title indicates, it was a survey of practices used in the several states to finance school construction in the public schools. It was conducted by Indiana Uni-

7. Roe L. Johns and Edgar L. Morphet, *The Economics and Financing of Education*, 2nd ed. (Englewood Cliffs, N.J.: Prentice-Hall, 1969), pp. 386–7.

versity with the assistance of several other midwestern universities and the U.S. Office of Education. Barr and Jordan summarized the purposes and the results of this study in the following:

> The purpose of the National Capital Outlay Project was to survey the legal bases, procedures, and practices which the 50 states, as of 1968–69, utilized in providing funds for elementary and secondary school construction, related debt services, lease-rental arrangements, and lease-purchase of facilities; and, further, to analyze the underlying theories of the above arrangements, the rationales, and the programs for intergovernmental transfer of funds related to capital outlay. The final phase of this satellite project consisted of the development of alternative fiscal models for allocation of funds, ranging from complete local support to complete state and Federal support of public school facilities.[8]

STATES UNABLE TO MEET THE PROBLEM

The postwar school building needs found most of the states grossly unprepared to offer immediate and defensible solutions to the problem. Some of them sought solutions by making grants from accumulated surpluses; others provided equalized matching plans, and still others experimented with including capital-outlay monies as a fundamental part of their foundation programs. Variety in the solutions to the problem and inadequacy of funds were the chief ingredients of such state-local partnership plans. Barr and Wilkerson summarized the developments in this program up to 1965 in the following short paragraph:

> Alabama's foundation program, New York's equalization plan, Delaware's assumption of the major proportion of capital outlay, and Ohio's developing program, supplemented by miscellaneous programs in eight other states, constituted the base from which state programs in at least 40 states had been launched in 1965.[9]

DEBT LIMITATIONS LIBERALIZED

In addition to the many direct methods that the states used to facilitate construction of needed school buildings—the grants, the loans, the

8. W. Monfort Barr et al., *Financing Public Elementary and Secondary School Facilities in the United States* (Bloomington, Ind.: National Educational Finance Project, 1970).

9. Barr and Wilkerson, "State Participation in Financing Local School Facilities," p. 224.

creation of building authorities, the inclusion of such costs in foundation programs, and others—there were indirect provisions that allowed some local districts to solve their own problems. One of the most important of these indirect provisions was the liberalization of school district debt and tax-levy limitations. Debt limitations, usually expressed in some percentage of the assessed value of taxable property, were changed in one or more of several possible ways. Some states changed from a percentage of assessed value to a similar percentage of true value as the total debt limitation of a school district. Others increased the limit by a stated dollar amount; still others provided for additional tax-rate levies.

The matter of relating a school district's debt limits to a specified percentage of the assessed valuation is open to serious question, as Barr and Garvue have indicated:

> Debt limits should not be related to the amount of local assessed evaluation. A more appropriate overall limit for financing capital outlays would be a limit of 25 percent of school revenue allocated to reserve funds, debt service, lease rental, and current construction. Experience has shown that this, or even higher allocation of public school revenues for school building purposes is feasible [and] prudent, and does not adversely affect bond ratings.[10]

THE FEDERAL GOVERNMENT AND CAPITAL OUTLAYS

Participation of the federal government in programs to aid school districts with their capital-outlay expenditures is of relatively recent origin. The almost universal opinion that school plant construction was exclusively a local problem was not interrupted with federal relief until the emergency programs of the Depression years were undertaken. Between 1933 and 1943, the federal government paid about 57 percent of the cost of construction, through the PWA and WPA, of 12,500 public school buildings. The Civil Works Administration and the Federal Emergency Relief Administration added over $63 million for construction and improvement of educational facilities. The NYA assisted with 18,000 school improvements and financed 3,700 new schools, units, or additions.[11]

Federal aid to education is often opposed because of fear of federal control, as well as for some other reasons. If it is assumed or admitted

10. W. Monfort Barr and R. J. Garvue, "Financing Public School Capital Outlays," in *The Theory and Practice of School Finance* (Chicago: Rand McNally & Co., 1967), pp. 276–7.

11. Lee M. Thurston and William H. Roe, *State School Administration* (New York: Harper & Row, 1957), p. 170.

TABLE 10.2   Federal Provisions for Local School District Capital Outlays, 1933–1963

Program	Year	Kind of Aid
Public Works Administration (PWA)	1933	Made grants for the construction of school buildings (on a 30-percent-of-cost basis).
Works Progress Administration (WPA)	1939	Conducted programs in school building construction
Lanham Act	1941	Money for school construction in areas affected by defense activities.
Federal Property and Administrative Services Act	1949	Disposal of war surplus property to schools and other institutions at low cost.
Public Law 815	1950	School building funds for districts in impacted areas.
National Defense Education Act (NDEA)	1958	Grants and loans for remodeling science laboratories and purchasing equipment.
Vocational Education Act	1963	Some funds for construction of vocational schools.

that federal control follows federal funds for local district current expenditures, no such acknowledgment is made when the funds are used for the construction of school facilities. For example, PWA and WPA constructed many school buildings in the 1930s and then released them to local school boards with no federal control over their use.

General federal aid has been described at various times as a strongly political issue, with racial and religious overtones. But federal aid for the construction of local school buildings was advocated in the political campaign of a decade ago by both dominant political parties. Both candidates for the presidency spoke in favor of such aid as the beginning point and least controversial aspect of federal aid. In spite of that, no significant bill for federal aid for school building construction has yet been enacted.

CURRENT FINANCING PRACTICES

The various methods now in use to finance school capital outlays are not yet what they should be, but they are an improvement over pre-World War II practices. Barr and Garvue made an excellent summary of the "departures from common practices prior to World War II":[12]

12. Barr and Garvue, "Financing Public School Capital Outlays,' p. 276–7.

1. Cooperative financing of school facilities by local districts and state governments has been developed in 80 percent of the states.
2. Debt limits have been liberalized in many states.
3. State and local authorities, state commissions, and other agencies have been utilized in several states to provide school facilities funds by issuing revenue bonds.
4. Federal support for school facilities has had little impact except in scattered communities on an emergency basis.
5. Property taxation for school facilities has been supplemented by state grants of funds from nonproperty tax sources.
6. Only a few states have incorporated state grants for capital outlay in their state foundation programs.
7. States have utilized both appropriations and bond issues as sources of funds for state grants or loans for local school facilities.
8. Assessment practices and levels have been improved in several states.
9. Use of reserve funds and pay-as-you-go plans for financing school facilities have proved significant in many areas of the nation.
10. States have tended to withdraw from the field of property taxation.
11. State permanent school funds and retirement funds have provided an increased market for school bonds.
12. Several states have taken positive steps to increase the desirability of school bonds by providing assistance in preparing issues for local districts, by substituting state for local credit, by guaranteeing local bonds, by purchasing local bonds, and by state grants and loans.
13. Use of new building materials and building techniques have contributed to prudent construction of school facilities throughout the nation.
14. The belief that cost of financing school facilities is a fixed percentage of current expenditures is no longer valid.

Selected Readings

Barr, W. Monfort; Jordan, K. Forbis; Hudson, C. Cale; Peterson, Wendell; and Wikerson, William R. *Financing Public Elementary and Secondary School Facilities in the United States.* Bloomington, Ind.: National Educational Finance Project, 1970.

———, and Wilkerson, William R. *Innovative Financing of Public School Facilities.* Danville, Ill.: The Interstate Printers & Publishers, Inc. 1973.

——— "State Participation in Financing Local Public-School Facilities."

In *Trends in Financing Public Education.* Washington, D.C.: National Education Assn., 1965.

Future Directions for School Financing. Gainesville, Fla.: National Educational Finance Project, 1971.

Schools, People, and Money, The Need for Educational Reform. Washington, D.C.: President's Commission on School Finance, U.S. Government Printing Office, 1972.

Wilkerson, W. R. "Alternatives in Capital Outlay Financing," *Guide for Planning Educational Facilities.* Columbus, Ohio: Educational Facility Planners, 1969.

11

Post-*Serrano* School
Finance Alternatives

The *Serrano* v. *Priest* decision, important as it was in setting the stage for school finance reform, was not the first strong signal for such need. For several years prior to Serrano's welcome appearance on the American scene, taxpayer resistance to the continually increasing costs of education had been slowly building to revolt proportions. Wide disparities in tax levies and school revenues had been changing school finance problems from local to state to national concerns.

At the same time, school finance scholars were collecting and presenting evidence of the fact that none of the state school finance programs in existence provided the equal educational opportunity they were devised to provide. The foundation program concept with the panacea expectation with which it was accepted prior to mid-century had fallen short of the objectives its proponents had set for it. Equalization programs with local options that provided little or no state support eroded the effect of the foundation program concept as a guarantor of equal protection of school students in different districts. As implemented, it left the wealthy districts with more total funds per student than poor ones with consequent disparities in curricular offerings as well as in tax burdens.

SERRANO: AN EXTENSION OF EQUAL RIGHTS

Since the beginning of this country as a nation, factors have been at work extending and protecting the rights of American citizens. Soon after the ratification of the Constitution the Bill of Rights was adopted to provide greater and more specific protection of individuals. Since that time, society itself has been making slow, but consistent, progress in improving and equalizing the rights of individual citizens in numerous ways. As early as 1874, in the now famous *Kalamazoo* case, high school students were provided an education on the same taxing basis as elementary students. In the *Brown* case of 1954, black citizens were to be granted equal educational opportunities with whites. By the mid-1960s the country had eliminated or reduced geographic discrimination in legislative bodies, by deciding that "the value of one's vote could not be diluted or debased when compared with the votes of others in the same circumstances," and had determined that lack of financial ability could not be used to deny criminals equal protection of the law.

Some important American historical events increased the need for, and helped accelerate, implementation of plans for greater equality of educational opportunity and equal protection for school-age citizens. Industrialization increased the discrepancies in the financial ability of school districts and states to finance education. The Depression of the 1930s with attendant defaults in the payment of property taxes, greatly reduced incomes, and other economic distresses emphasized the need for increased state support of floundering school systems. World Wars I and II emphasized the extremes in unequal education that were being provided in various sections and school districts throughout the country —including such things as extremely unequal rates of nonacceptance of potential military servicemen because of education deficiencies. Sputnik, in 1957, produced evidence of the need to improve public school educational programs if the United States intended to remain competitive in the matter of exploring outer space. These are only a few of this country's indicators of need to equalize and improve educational opportunities for our school-age children and youth.

Thus, it is evident that although *Serrano* appeared to be an abrupt reversal of popular public and court opinion, it was in reality an extension of the trend toward providing greater protection of the rights of citizens in many aspects of the constitutional guarantee of equal protection for all Americans. It was not—as some have thought—a completely new or novel idea without precedent.

As expected, there were many direct and consequential results of *Serrano* and the other similar court decisions and finance studies that followed. The early 1970s saw great activity in the courts, in school board meetings, and in legislative halls. One of the most noticeable results was a revival and reemphasis of certain tenets of school finance philosophy and theory of an earlier era sponsored by such almost forgotten theorists as Updegraff and Morrison. Some of their ideas of how to provide equality of educational opportunity—not popular in their introductory stage and not given an opportunity for practical develop-ment—began to appear anew and with increased recognition of their potential. Morrison's ideas concerning greater state control and virtual elimination of local districts now seemed logical to many who favored full state funding of public education. Updegraff's concept of reward for effort now reappeared under the title of power or open-end equaliza-tion. Rather suddenly, these half-century old ideas hidden away in the textbooks of that era seemed to offer the best solution to perennial problems in school finance.

In the aftermath of *Serrano,* there appeared to be only two plans of state school finance programs that would meet the conditions now being implied by the courts. These were: (1) full state funding, and (2) district power equalization. These two plans are not equally acceptable to all states or to all people. The long and cherished tradition of local control of education seems to be threatened with such radical departures from past practices, especially with the almost revolutionary concept of full state funding. Certainly, few states could function as one district as in Hawaii. Although it had been known that flat grants, percentage grants, foundation programs with or without local options, or any com-bination of these methods did not achieve the equal protection now be-ing mandated by the courts, few states were ready for the full and complete changes in school finance theory that now seemed imminent.

FULL STATE FUNDING

The idea of full state funding of education certainly should not be considered radical or unacceptable to the people in those states which were (and are) providing more than half of their public school revenues from state sources. Earmarked state property taxes, sales taxes, income taxes, and others were common and could be expanded if full state funding were to be adopted. However, the difficulty of accepting the idea of full state funding in those states that provide much less than half the public school revenues presents a much greater problem. Many voters and decision makers look askance at increased state support with the possibility of increased state control over local schools.

At various times in American history, exponents of complete state financing of education have stated such a proposal with little popular support. Some, including James B. Conant, have suggested that the time may now be ripe for accepting and carrying out this arrange-ment. They point out that more than half a century of state effort to equalize educational opportunity and school tax burdens by state-local partnership finance formulas has not achieved this goal. They reason that all states could attain this objective if they collected and controlled the disposition of all school funds.

There are three different degrees of state participation that are possible for financing and operating public schools: (1) the foundation program approach, with state funds added to local tax funds to produce a state-guaranteed level of school support; (2) complete state support, with elimination of locally raised funds but with state basic programs increased to adequate levels; (3) state operation of public schools, with substantial reductions in the administrative and operational responsibilities of local school boards. Lindman noted the possible results of complete state support of education:

> Perhaps the most obvious result of complete state support or of state operation of schools would be the equalization of school tax burdens. Even if the legislature chose to continue property taxes for the support of schools, there would be a uniform statewide school property tax rate. The proceeds from this tax would be combined with other state tax revenues to provide sufficient funds to operate all schools in the state.[1]

He pointed out that complete state support of education would not, however, provide complete equality of educational opportunity, with all students having equal access to educational programs suited to their needs and talents. "Without the local property tax to supplement programs financed from state and federal sources, local program adaptation would be dangerously curtailed. Experimentation with innovative school procedures would be drastically limited if it had always to wait for state or federal appropriations."[2]

Models 11.1 and 11.1a are illustrations of two forms or plans for full state funding of education—with minor adjustments. Model 11.1 is full state funding without allowance for local options. In it all districts would receive the same number of dollars per weighted pupil unit. Its limitation rests in the fact that the state legislature would determine by itself the maximum dollars per pupil to be provided. Local needs, local desires, and local initiative would be ignored under this type of financing. Model 11.1a provides almost full state funding with limited local options to go above the state-sponsored program. While this plan purports to provide for local preferences, it is nonequalizing and favors wealthier districts, as do all finance plans where local effort is not state supported.

1. Erick L. Lindman, "The Conant Plan—Shall the States Take Over the Financing of Schools?" in *The School Administrator* (Washington, D.C.: American Assn. of School Administrators, February 1970), pp. 11–12.
   2. Ibid.

MODEL 11.1. Full State Funding 11.1a. Almost Full State Funding with Local Levy Option (10 M)

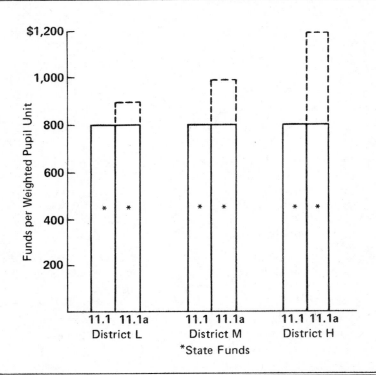

*State Funds

Model 11.1. Full State Funding

District	Assessed Valuation	State Funds per WPU	Required Local Levy
L	$10,000,000	$800	Nil
M	20,000,000	800	Nil
H	40,000,000	800	Nil

As indicated, this provides exactly the same amount of revenue per weighted pupil unit in each district. This has some serious limitations, such as: (1) it makes the state-determined program a minimum as well as a maximum program; (2) it provides no way for a school district to enrich its program beyond that which the state mandates; (3) it removes fiscal responsibility from the control of local school boards; and (4) it may tend to jeopardize local school programs when the state's revenue will not seem to support full state funding at a desirable level.

Model 11.1a. Almost Full State Funding
with Minimum Local Options

Additional Local Levy	Local Funds per WPU	Total Funds per WPU	Total Funds per M per WPU
Dist. L — 10 M	$100	$900	$90
Dist. M — 10 M	200	1,000	100
Dist. H — 10 M	400	1,200	120

When this model is used, the result is nonequalization among districts of varying taxable wealth per weighted pupil. Thus, in the example, when all three districts use the maximum ten mill levy the net effect is that District L has available only $90 per mill per weighted pupil unit while District H has $120 per mill per weighted pupil unit. By the use of nonsupported local optional levies, the equalization accomplished with full state funding has been neutralized to some degree. Of course, if the state provides funds for nearly all the cost of school district programs with only minimal local optional levies, the disequalizing effect of the latter may not seriously upset the over-all equalization that the program produces.

Ramifications

Full state funding under any plan raises some questions about an attendant increase in state control of local schools and a corresponding decrease in the power and authority of local school boards. There are those who feel that recent increases in state support of local school revenues have already reduced the role of local school boards in administering schools to an undesirable and irreversible point. Others suggest the fact that the high degree of local control of half a century ago may not either be possible or desirable in today's world with its increased mobility of people and with the great reduction in the number of operating school districts, particularly since the 1930s.

Full state funding—as the name implies—places the burden for providing a good public school program strictly and completely upon the state itself. There is little promise that the typical legislature, in the face of extreme pressure for state funds from all state institutions, would provide the money year after year necessary to provide the high level educational program desired by the citizens of its various school districts. Determining the amount of money necessary for education could very well become an "average practice" minimum program devoid of the utilization of local incentives.

Full state funding is an acceptable plan for districts that would be "leveled up" to expenditure levels or standards above their previous position. But "leveling down" or even forcing some districts to remain at such a high rate and with the increased leverage of professional and labor organizations in establishing salaries, it is doubtful that leveling down or maintaining the status quo could be operable in any state—if, indeed, such were found to be necessary or desirable. Hence, the state itself would be forced to find a system or method or rationale for providing funds above the established amount for expensive or high expenditure school districts.

Probably the biggest deterrent, and certainly the most negative aspect of full state funding, is related to two potential problems: (1) the state would exercise the power to determine the amount of revenue in every district with little regard for the educational needs or desires of the local citizenry, and (2) there is no way to determine upon a rational and objective basis which districts should be given the funds necessary for them to be "lighthouse" districts. Since local districts would make no tax effort on their own to finance education, the state would be without legal framework or device with which to determine which schools or in what amount state funds should be allocated to "deserving" districts.

It is likely that full state funding would lead to the extended use of sales and income taxes with less emphasis upon the property tax. There is much to be said in favor of this change. But the plan tends to discourage, if not obliterate, local initiative and special tax effort to provide better schools than that legislated by the state. Thus far, the states have found no satisfactory substitute for the incentive grants that have been used to provide innovative and better programs than are financed in districts where there is no expressed desire to extend local district effort to obtain such excellence.

Plan Adoption is Inevitable

That full state funding may be inevitable for financing education in some of our states in order to meet the requirements of the court decisions was indicated by Rossmiller:

> Movement toward a much higher level of state support for public elementary and secondary schools appears inevitable. It should be evident, however, that full state funding will not be a panacea for all the ills which afflict elementary and secondary education. Full state funding would eliminate or reduce some problems, but probably would aggravate other problems. In fact, full state funding might create problems which do not presently exist. It should also be evident that full state funding can be accomplished in a variety of ways. Each model has advantages and disadvantages and none are perfect. This nation has 50

state school systems and each is somewhat unique. Movement toward full state funding undoubtedly will occur on a broken front, and is likely to vary according to the situation which confronts each state.[3]

Advantages and Disadvantages

Numerous advantages of full state funding are claimed by its advocates. They say that it would:

1. Meet the requirement of the court decisions that the education of a student should be dependent only upon the wealth of the state and not upon the wealth of the parents or the school district.
2. Equalize the revenues among school districts and at the same time provide greater equity among the taxpayers of the state.
3. Reduce interdistrict competition for state funds that lead to the possible elimination of small and inefficient school districts.
4. Relieve local districts of the problem of obtaining funds so that more local effort could be devoted to the improvement of the curriculum.

Those who point to the disadvantages of full state funding say that it would:

1. Result in a loss or reduction in the amount of local control of the educational program.
2. Result in loss of revenue in many districts now making additional tax effort to support better school programs and would in reality result in a leveling down process.
3. Curtail innovative and high cost programs regardless of their need or worth.
4. Put public schools in more direct competition with other state agencies, such as higher education institutions, for state revenues.
5. Make a minimum program the maximum program by not providing a way for any district to go beyond the state-mandated and state-supported program.
6. Penalize districts with comparatively high salaries and operational costs.

Full State Funding Not Defined Accurately

Part of the problem in considering the philosophy of full state funding lies in its definition in practice. If taken literally, *full* state funding has

3. Kern Alexander and K. Forbis Jordan, eds., *Constitutional Reform of School Finance* (Lexington, Mass.: Lexington Books, D. C. Heath and Co., 1973), p. 72.

some distinct limitations in its application to several districts within a state (as pointed out in this chapter). However, if the term *almost full* state funding is used, there could be options available to local districts that could mitigate or eliminate most of the disadvantages of this system of financing education. This latter definition is the one most commonly used even though it is incongruent with the term itself.

Would Create a Centralized System

Although current systems of financing education generally result in local competition for financial resources, full state funding would likely result in having professional organizations of teachers negotiating at the state level as the major thrust for greater expenditure of funds for education. Local needs, local desires, and local problems of a unique nature would likely become subordinate to the collective bargaining process with the end result that it would create centralized school operations in contrast to the decentralized pattern now in existence in all states except Hawaii.

DISTRICT POWER EQUALIZATION

An alternative to the full state funding model that would meet the requirements of recent court decisions is that of district power equalization, a more popular name for open-end equalization. By definition, DPE refers to the principle that each local district mill levy should produce the same number of dollars of total school revenue per mill per weighted student in every district, and the last mill to be levied should produce the same total funds as the first one. It was advocated in 1922 by Updegraff but it found little support until the early 1970s. Its later popularity came largely as a result of the court decisions and lack of support for full state funding as a means of providing equal protection as mandated by numerous court decisions and recommended by several school finance studies.

Power equalization is sometimes viewed by its critics as a process or means of depleting a state's financial resources. Thus far, there is little evidence to support this view. Its value lies in the fact that it is extremely effective in its obliteration of financial advantages of one district over another in providing the funds required to produce a quality education program rather than simply providing a minimum or foundation program.

MODEL 11.2   District   Power   Equalization   11.2a.   Reduced   Percentage
Power Equalization

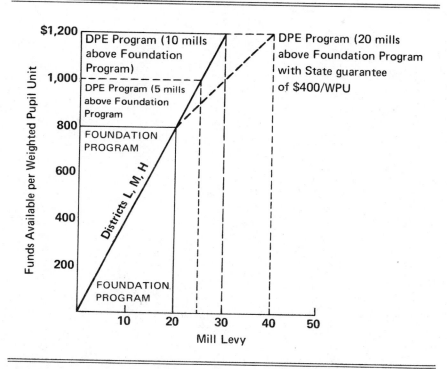

Model 11.2 illustrates district power equalization with full state
support for each mill of tax levy. Model 11.2a shows the same principle
but with all levies above those of the foundation program supported by
the state at a fractional part of the original amount. This, of course,
flattens the graph line (see model) thereby decreasing the state percentage and increasing the local percentage of revenue produced. The
program remains equitable, however, so long as the level is kept above
the amount the wealthiest district could produce locally or if all surpluses were recaptured by the state.

It should be noted that the steeper the line in a DPE formula
graph the greater the so-called raid on the state treasury and the less
the effort required at the local level. Thus, such increased costs by this
process would probably cause a state to flatten the DPE line and thereby
increase the local district's share of the cost of the educational program.
By this process the state should be able to control the degree of deple-
tion this program would bring to its treasury.

The following is a simplified example of how an equalized percentage or power equalization program might function.

Foundation Program

Dist.	Assessed Value/WPU	Mill Levy	Guaranteed Amount/WPU	Revenue/WPU Local	Revenue/WPU State	Local-State Ratio
A	$50,000	10	$1,000	$500	$500	1:1
B	40,000	10	1,000	400	600	2:3
C	10,000	10	1,000	100	900	1:9
D	5,000	10	1,000	50	950	1:19

Program Above the Foundation

A	50,000	2	200	100	100	1:1
B	40,000	2	200	80	120	2:3
C	10,000	2	200	20	180	1:9
D	5,000	2	200	10	190	1:19

In the above example, four mythical districts of widely varying assessments of taxable property per weighted pupil unit are compared in the calculation of a foundation program with an equalization program of $1,000 per weighted pupil unit with a required local levy of 10 mills. District A has its local revenue matched by the state on a 1:1 basis, District B on a 2:3 basis, District C on a 1:9 basis, and District D on a 1:19 basis. This, of course, is a simple foundation program. If each district goes 2 mills above the foundation program on a DPE basis, District A gets a $1,200 per WPU program with $600 local and $600 state revenue; District B has the same program with $480 local and $720 state revenue; District C has $120 local and $1,080 state revenue; and District D has $60 local and $1,140 state money. Thus, in a power equalization program the state is required to continue its degree of partnership with each district for the full program. By this process, financially weak districts (such as District D in the above example) are able to offer as good a program (in terms of cost) as wealthier ones. This is the essence of the American philosophy of equality of educational opportunity.

At first glance it may seem that this creates a standard program for every district within a state. Such is not the case, however, for each local district would have the right and the responsibility to determine what the local tax rate would be over and above the mandated foundation program levy. In this way local control is assured and state partnership responsibility is mandated. To illustrate this, suppose that District A elected to levy one mill above the mandated foundation program, District B decided on a 2 mill increase, District C a 4 mill program, and District D a 5 mill increase. The result of this would be as follows:

Optional Program Above Foundation Program

District	Increased Tax Levy	Guaranteed Amount per WPU	Local Revenue	State Revenue	L-S Ratio	Total per WPU
A	1 M	$100	$50	$50	1:1	$1,100
B	2 M	200	80	120	2:3	1,200
C	4 M	400	40	360	1:9	1,400
D	5 M	500	25	475	1:19	1,500

It can be seen that equal levies bring equal dollars in all districts, but each district is free to choose the level at which its program will be supported. This preserves the element of local control in decision making, but at the same time it requires the state to support the entire program to whatever level the law permits local districts to operate.

As previously indicated, fear of local determination of mill levy increases under this program being high enough to deplete state treasuries is the greatest deterrent to adoption of this form of district power equalization. However, studies conducted in some states that have used the concept to a limited extent do not seem to justify such apprehension. For example:

> The state share for any district thus varies according to the need and ability of the school district. Therefore, on superficial theoretical analysis, people have concluded that a completely open-end EPM (equalized program matching) grant without a ceiling on per-pupil expenditures would lead to a raid on the state treasury. Better theoretical formulations and the experience of the past decades have proved this conclusion to be faulty.[4]

Studies by Benson and Kelly in Rhode Island and by Daniere in Massachusetts as well as theoretical analysis by Daniere and by Pauly showed that an EPM grant would not increase educational funds much beyond that experienced in other states during the same period. In Rhode Island, state funds did increase faster than in other states; that is, state funds substituted for local funds without great increases in total funds for schools. Thus, one might claim or not claim that there was a raid on the state treasury.[5]

The merits of district power equalization philosophy are readily discernible. Local control of the extent the educational program goes above the state minimum rests with each individual school board but

4. Eugene P. McLoone, "Modernizing State School Finance Programs: Six Selected Areas," in *Interdependence in School Finance: The City, the State, the Nation* (Washington, D.C.: National Education Assn. Committee on Educational Finance, 1968), p. 23.

5. Ibid., p. 24.

the state cannot escape its proportionate financial responsibility. Districts are motivated to make adequate tax effort, for if they spend less they lose more. Complete equalization is possible in spending as well as in tax effort. If there is a high enough ceiling on local tax options, the inequalities encountered between wealthy and poor districts, which are obvious in a typical foundation program with unsupported local options, disappear. The only restriction to an adequately financed program thus becomes the willingness or unwillingness of the people at the local level to tax themselves within reasonable tax limits. With the state matching the local district on a predetermined basis in terms of local ability, the previously unrealistic tax requirements for a quality education program in a poor district are reduced greatly or even eliminated.

The power equalization principle is not new nor does it represent a revolutionary departure from school finance theories and practices of the last few years. As mentioned in chapter 5, Harlan Updegraff introduced the concept in 1922 but it was not widely accepted at that time. The author advocated it to the Education Committee of the Legislative Council for the State of Utah in 1964. Under its more descriptive title "open-end equalization" it was considered by various educational organizations in Utah as a possible recommendation for legislative action. The principle was rejected, however, because of its potential threat as a drain on the state treasury. It was considered to be an equalizing principle not likely to be understood and supported by many people outside the ranks of school finance authorities.

The 1973 Utah Legislature enacted a limited power equalization program into law.[6] Under that law, each of the State's forty school districts receives the same number of dollars per weighted pupil unit per mill of tax levy up to the state required levy of 28 mills. Unfortunately, the power equalization principle was not applied to the voted leeway option of 10 mills beyond the equalized program. However, only about 25 percent of the districts use any part of this leeway and none of them use it to the legal maximum. This leeway program receives virtually no state support and thus is disequalizing in its effect upon school districts.

DETERMINING THE BEST FINANCE PLAN

There are many defensible plans available to states for the allocation of funds to local districts. Various combinations of equalizing grants, adaptations of the foundation program principle, and varying degrees of power equalization may be used in ways to utilize the advantages and eliminate the disadvantages of each. The state may use categorical or special purpose funding to encourage the introduction or stimulation of innovative programs. It may use instructional programs or units as the basis for determining the size of state allocations to local districts, or it may set up state standards or guidelines and use state committees to negotiate with local districts for budget plans that meet the peculiar or unique needs of districts not met by other financing methods. Thus, the number of potential state financing patterns is almost unlimited.

While the choice of financing programs is great, at this point in school finance reform there are no perfect systems for distributing state funds to local school districts. Each plan has limitations and falls short of equalizing financial resources to the complete satisfaction of all the people concerned. Some systems are better than others and some states make greater efforts to improve than others. With the inequalities and the inequities that exist in almost every state plan there is no room for any degree of complacency in viewing school finance reform in any state. Certainly, there is little justification for maintaining or preserving traditional methods until a panacea formula is discovered, or invented.

It has been estimated that the various states use nearly 400 kinds of state aid to local districts, including such kinds as the minimum program, transportation, salary-schedule allowances, and shared state taxes. No way is generally accepted as the best, in terms of its popularity over all other plans, for organizing the state-local partnership plans for financing education. Programs now in existence vary from Hawaii's one-district system, where the district covers the state and is the sole taxing and financing unit for the operation of all its public schools, to programs in which state-level allocations to local districts involve only a relatively small part of the total funds available to local districts. All other states come somewhere in between these two extremes.

It is safe to assume that school financing plans of the future will emphasize greater state involvement and proportionately less local responsibility. Since the property tax is the only realistic source of local revenue, and since its utilization has already reached a saturation point, it is evident that state tax sources will have to be increased to meet the surging costs of education. Of the big revenue producers, primarily only the sales tax is left to state government. This tax, with moderate support from state income taxes, produces about three-fourths of the total revenue for state government. These taxes are probably destined to bear the brunt of tax increases, which appear to be necessary now and in the future to finance the high-quality education programs that nearly all our citizens demand.

One of the embryonic ideas on future state financing of education, whether through complete state financing or some degree of state-local partnership, involves state equalization of services rather than of dollars. One of the chief problems in state allocation of funds revolves around the incontrovertible fact that equal dollars provided to unlike districts result in unequal units of service. Similar amounts of money never result in equal purchases of instructional services, since some districts must pay much higher salaries than others. The costs of school buses, of gasoline, or of any other required services or supplies vary considerably in all the districts of all the states. The fairest measure of equalization, then, would be the program that equalizes the required school supplies and services in all school districts. Such a principle needs no justification; however, much more research and experience will be required before it replaces present-day equalization of dollars among the school districts of any state.

REEMPHASIS ON WEIGHTING FACTORS

Determining the funds necessary for operating a school program, regardless of the process or formula used, is a function of the "need" of the school district. This so-called need is related first of all to the number of pupils to be educated. There are many other determinants of need, but the number of pupils in average daily attendance (or the pupils enrolled) forms the basic unit of measurement. Although schools have used, and continue to use, the idea of providing equal dollars for all children in the state as the measure of equality of educational opportunity, such a concept is really not defensible. Equal dollars per student do not produce equal products or equal results. Unequal educational opportunities are guaranteed when funding does not consider such common variables as racial origin, physical and mental handicaps, socioeconomic backgrounds, language deficiencies, and many other unequal characteristics of students.

In addition to differing student characteristics, the cost of an educational program is related to such existing variables as the size of the school district and the size of the school attendance area, for the cost of educating 25,000 pupils is not necessarily exactly 100 times that of educating 250 pupils. Similarly, the cost of operating a high school of 500 pupils may not be the same as that for financing 500 elementary pupils. Schools with a high percentage of disadvantaged pupils cost more than those with a lower percentage do. Sparsity factors make the cost of education in small rural communities higher than in average-sized towns. On the other hand, the unique problems of our large cities and metropolitan areas make the cost of education proportionately higher, even though some might expect decreased costs as a result of large numbers of pupils to be educated.

Weighting factors are perhaps our best measures of the amount of additional resources and services needed to provide all students—regardless of their personal or environmental handicaps, with reasonably equal educational programs. Fortunately, there are few of our citizens who continue to challenge the humanistic view that children with physical or mental handicaps, or who attend school in indefensibly small or extremely large and disadvantaged schools, should be the recipients of educational programs that are more costly than so-called normal ones.

Although some have thought that the weighted-pupil concept was a direct discovery of the *Serrano* era of school finance reform, only its degree of acceptance in recent school finance programs is new. Mort and Reusser pointed out the age of this fundamental principle more than a quarter of a century ago:

> The weighted-pupil unit (or its mathematical equivalent—the weighted-classroom unit) is the most systematically refined of all measures of educational need and has been in practical use for a quarter of a century in state-aid laws, in expenditure comparisons of various types of districts, and in comparisons of ability to support schools.[6]

The rationale for weighting was aptly expressed by McLoone:

> Today to achieve both vertical and horizontal equity, equal educational opportunity for a pupil to develop to his full potential means a different dollar amount per pupil, that is, resources in whatever amount it takes to overcome environmental (socio-economic) differences among pupils. This recognizes that every pupil, irrespective of native ability or intelligence and the differences these make among pupils, comes to school with a broader or more limited horizon. The difference may be in motivation, preparation for learning in school, verbalization, or similar characteristics, but this difference is one that added resources can or will help alleviate or will overcome.[7]

Many inequalities exist that force states to recognize that the number of pupils by itself does not indicate the operational need of school districts. That being true, it becomes necessary for weightings to be made if fairness and equality of educational opportunity are to be achieved. "But the greatest disparity in the fiscal needs of school districts arises from the composition of their pupil populations. Higher proportions of children with learning disabilities impose massively greater

6. Paul R. Mort and Walter C. Reusser, *Public School Finance*, 2nd ed. (New York: McGraw-Hill, 1951), p. 491.

7. Eugene P. McLoone, "Evaluating the Weighting Factors in Use," in *Trends in Financing Public Education* (Washington, D.C.: National Education Assn. Committee on Educational Finance, 1965), pp. 63–64.

resource demands if those children are to have the same chance at success in school as their more fortunate classmates."[8]

Note that weightings would lose their importance and would not be needed if the schools to be served had the same proportions of variables that appear to require weightings. If 40 percent of the pupils in every school district are secondary school pupils, there would be little need for weighting this factor. If every district had 10 percent of its pupils in small or isolated school attendance areas, there would be little need for weightings here. However, these factors are never constant from district to district. Weighting tends to put the extra costs incurred in providing maximum quality education for pupils with special or more than average problems where they belong, on the state. Many of these discriminating problems if left to local districts are minimized or ignored.

PRINCIPAL TYPES OF PUPIL AND OTHER WEIGHTINGS

In any consideration of the number of pupils as a determinant of the money needs of a district, several important weightings must be considered: (1) the sparsity of pupils in rural areas; (2) the density of pupils in heavily populated metropolitan areas; (3) the grade levels of pupils; and (4) the degree of disadvantage certain classes of pupils may suffer, such as the handicapped or those who require special education services. Consideration should be given, in addition to pupil weighting, to the training and experience of the professional staff members of each district. To consider all pupils of equal worth or cost is no more erroneous than to consider all teachers as of equal worth or cost to a school system.

Sparsity Factors

The need to provide additional funds to help finance the necessary small schools that operate in nearly every state has long been recognized and accepted. State legislatures, mostly rurally dominated until recently, have usually made provisions for the protection of small and expensive schools and districts. The methods used may vary from state to state, but the end results are much the same. Typically, the process used involves

8. Joel S. Berke and John J. Callahan, "Serrano v. Priest: Milestone or Millstone for School Finance?" (Paper delivered at the Convention of the American Society for Public Administration, New York, March 22, 1972), p. 56.

weighting such pupils in the finance formula so as to require the state to pay its proportionate share of the higher cost involved in the education of pupils in small groups. At the same time, some states give the state board of education the responsibility of determining when such privilege may be rescinded or withdrawn, as when some small schools might reasonably be expected to be consolidated or reorganized into larger and more effective and efficient units.

Sparsity weighting factors are difficult to construct without providing some inequalities. For example, the following formula developed by the National Education Finance Project[9] leaves some discrepancies in the funds that would be provided for certain sizes of schools.

Elementary School Size	Weighting Factor
Fewer than 100	1.30
100 — 149	1.20
150 — 200	1.10

Under this formula, a school with 99 students would get a total weighting of 128.7, but a school with 100 students would get a weighting of only 120. All schools with enrollments of 94 to 99 would receive more funds than the school with 100 students. At the high expenditure levels of schools today, this becomes too great a difference for schools of this size to ignore.

In the Utah study[10] an attempt was made to eliminate such inequalities, resulting in complicated formulas but ones in which every additional student enrolled in small, isolated schools would generate additional dollars of revenue. The comparable formula for small, isolated elementary schools in Utah (to compare with the NEFP formula) is:

Elementary School Size	Total Weighting
5 — 12 pupils	27
13 — 20	40
21 — 30	53
31 — 50	53 + (1.4) (ADA minus 30)
51 — 90	81 + (1.2) (ADA minus 50)
91 — 110	129 + (1.0) (ADA minus 90)
111 — 165	149 + (0.3) (ADA minus 110)

By the use of this formula, a school with 165 students would be given credit for 165.5 WPUs. This is smaller than the 166 that would be

9. *Alternative Programs for Financing Education* (Gainesville, Fla.: National Education Finance Project, 1971), p. 272.

10. Percy Burrup, "Utah School Finance Study," mimeographed (Salt Lake City: Education Committee of the Utah Legislative Council, December 1972), p. 21.

given to a school with one more student in a school with no weighting for sparsity. While this may appear to be unnecessary manipulation in order to obtain equality, in a state with many small schools it is an important factor in maintaining harmony and good-will among school boards and administrators who know the size and funding of their neighboring schools.

Density Factors

While the sparsity factor has long been accepted and applied in finance parlance and in practice, allocation of additional funds per pupil to large city school districts is relatively new and has had only limited application. Dealing with municipal overburden, large numbers of disadvantaged and exceptional children, the practical problems and additional costs needed to implement racial integration, the higher salaries and operational costs resulting from strong union organizations—all is a part of the finance problem of large urban or metropolitan areas. The best answer to this complex problem appears to be weighting of pupils. This would guarantee that the state would share in paying for these additional expenses, which are largely beyond the power of control of the districts involved.

The reluctance of people, even many of those who are knowledgeable in school finance matters, to recognize and solve this problem is understandable. For many years, in fact until only recently, the city school districts enjoyed financial and cultural advantages over their rural counterparts. Less reluctance to exploit the property tax, better-prepared teachers and administrators, more cultural opportunities to abet the school program, and less resistance of its citizens to accept change and innovation—all added their part to the natural advantage that city schools enjoyed over rural schools. Hence, the city schools provided much of the leadership for improving the curriculum and for increasing the monies available for education.

But the problem today is not the same; neither is its solution. With the cities losing many upper- and middle-class citizens to suburbia and gaining in their stead less affluent and less well-educated citizens who moved to the cities to obtain employment, the tax base has weakened at the same time that the problems of city school systems are increasing. The problems attending migration of people to and from the core of large cities, such as lower tax-paying ability, increased competition for the tax dollar to provide better police protection, greater social problems in the ghettos, and additional required services of government, have placed the cities at a financial disadvantage for the first time in our history.

The solution to the density problem is not too difficult *if* the required additional money is available and *if* the problem is acknowledged. New York State set a pattern in the early 1960s by providing the large cities with more money per pupil than the finance formula would otherwise have provided. A few other states have tried other ways of achieving the same results.

Burke, in discussing the situation in New York, summarized the problem of using density factors in school finance formulas:

> What we have in big cities is a complex set of conditions making it difficult to muster sufficient support for public education at a time when the educational needs of these cities are more critical than ever before. It was not poverty alone but outdated school district structure, public values, and many other factors which resulted in the deplorable educational conditions found in the rural areas of the state during the first three decades of this century before the state equalization program brought some relief. To the extent that the density correction brings relief it can be defended. Many other aspects of state equalization programs have had no better justification than that.[11]

Grade Level Weighting

Traditionally, weightings for secondary pupils as compared with elementary were widely accepted and put to use. The pupil-teacher ratio was lower, the average salary of teachers was higher, the cost of instructional materials and equipment was higher, and the student activities and out-of-school programs were more extensive and expensive for the secondary level. The validity of the assumption that secondary school pupils should have a weighting when compared with elementary pupils is more seriously questioned now than ever before. The chief argument favoring the weighting is that pupil-teacher ratios are lower in secondary schools, thereby increasing the cost per pupil. There are, however, a number of arguments, some controversial, that build a strong rationale against such weighting: (1) there is little if any difference in salaries in most states between the two levels since single-salary schedules make no differentiation; (2) with the emphasis on the use of instructional media and improved libraries for elementary schools, the differences in costs here have largely disappeared; and (3) activity and field-trip programs are no longer restricted or limited to secondary schools.

11. Arvid J. Burke, "The Density Correction in the New York State School Aid Formula," in *Long-Range Planning in School Finance* (Washington, D.C.: National Education Assn. Committee on Educational Finance, 1963), pp. 136–37.

The evenness of the debate over grade-level weighting was shown by the fact that in 1962–63, 26 states used grade-level weightings and 24 states did not. As summarized by McLoone:

> Almost no research on this topic exists and it is impossible to say which is preferable: weighting secondary-school pupils more than elementary or like treatment of both. While it is true that more is spent on secondary schools than on elementary because of elective and structural considerations, the assumption that high schools necessarily cost more is not valid. Better results at the elementary-school level may be accomplished if the same amount per pupil were spent in elementary schools as is now spent in high schools.[12]

Special Education Weightings

Some aspects of the school's program will be more expensive than others: vocational education and education for physically or mentally handicapped pupils, for example. If one accepts the thesis that public education should be provided for all pupils of the kind and extent that will allow each to develop his maximum potential, it follows that he accepts the corollary that these pupils or their programs must receive a weighting in the school finance plan. Programs in these areas were stalemated or did not even exist until states and school districts gave them weighting commensurate with their needs. Here again, the weightings may take any of many forms, such as special appropriations or grants and weightings of the individual students in such programs.

Teacher Qualification Considerations

Universal high-quality education is being stressed on every hand. It seems to be one of the absorbing concerns of the professional educator at the moment. The prevalence of single-salary schedules throughout the country strongly implies that increased academic preparation and increased experience in the field improve the teacher and thereby improve the quality of instruction. However, in 1962–63 only 19 of the 50 states had provisions in their foundation programs for weighting or consideration of a teacher's training or experience or both.

The finance problem enunciated by this dilemma can be seen very easily. The foundation program provides money for teachers and other operational costs in terms of the number of weighted pupils to be edu-

12. McLoone, "Evaluating the Weighting Factors in Use," p. 64.

cated, and also for other specialized employees or services. But the teacher requirement places the school district in a precarious position. If in the employment of professional personnel the superintendent strives to improve the quality of instruction, he will usually recommend employment of those teachers with the most training and experience—with attendant higher salaries. This leaves him little or no state-equalized foundation program funds for operational costs. These would then have to be paid with local funds. If, however, he employs a less well-qualified teacher, funds from the foundation program can be used for other expenses, but this does little to improve the quality of the instructional program. The net result is that the wealthy districts employ those personnel they think will do most to improve the quality of instruction, but the poorer districts are forced to employ those with least demands on the salary schedule regardless of other factors.

State foundation programs should include, as some do, weightings that consider the qualifications of the professional employees so that the state will pay its proportionate share of the cost of employing a better-qualified staff. Without such, the onus for improving instruction by employing better-trained and more experienced teachers rests strictly on the local district. If it is to the advantage of the local school district to employ personnel with more training and experience, it is also to the advantage of the state to help see that this is possible financially.

To picture the simplest possible use of the teacher-training and experience allowance in the foundation program, assume that Districts A, B, and C in Table 11.1 have equal amounts for all pertinent factors being used except the training and experience of their teachers.

The average teacher index is calculated by placing each teacher's name in the proper training and experience slot on an index salary schedule, adding the index figures for all teachers and dividing that total by the number of teachers. In the example below, District A (which obviously has a predominantly young and not-too-well-trained staff), with an average index of 1.20, is entitled to an additional 20 percent of its total of

TABLE 11.1   Teacher Qualifications as Weighting Factors

District	Assessed Value	Class-Room Units	State-Guaranteed Amt/CRU[a]	Required Levy	Number of Teachers	Average Teacher Index
A	$40,000,000	100	$15,000	15 mills	80	1.20
B	40,000,000	100	15,000	15 mills	80	1.35
C	40,000,000	100	15,000	15 mills	80	1.55

[a]CRU means classroom unit.

TABLE 11.2   New Foundation Program

	District A	
1.	Minimum program need — (100 + 16) (15,000)	= $1,740,000
2.	Local tax effort — (40,000,000) (0.015)	= 600,000
3.	State allocation (Step "1" minus step "2")	= 1,140,000
	District B	
1.	Minimum program need — (100 + 28) (15,000)	= $1,920,000
2.	Local tax effort — (40,000,000) (0.015)	= 600,000
3.	State allocation (Step "1" minus step "2")	= 1,320,000
	District C	
1.	Minimum program need — (100 + 44) (15,000)	= $2,160,000
2.	Local tax effort — (40,000,000) (0.015)	= 600,000
3.	State allocation (Step "1" minus step "2")	= 1,560,000

80 teacher-earned classroom units. District *B* would receive 35 percent of 80 as additional units; and District *C* would receive 55 percent. The calculations for the foundation program would then be according to Table 11.2.

District *C*, with its better-trained and more experienced (and therefore more expensive) staff of teachers would receive considerably more state money than District *A* or District *B*. The state thereby shares the additional costs of better-qualified teachers. Under such an arrangement, no district would be forced to employ inexperienced and poorly trained teachers simply because they cost less. Teachers with greater experience and more extensive training would then be able to compete for positions in the school marketplace with current-year college graduates and others with limited experience and training.

The arguments favoring weighting teacher qualifications in the foundation program do not go uncontested. It has been pointed out that rural districts and less wealthy districts usually employ less well-qualified personnel than their opposites do. To the extent that this is true, such allowances for training and experience may reduce instead of induce equalization. But even this argument falls flat when it is realized that the only means (without such allowances) the poor districts have of competing with wealthier ones in the employment of the best-qualified teachers would necessarily come through greater local tax effort. With teacher-qualification weighting, however, the possibility of the poor districts increasing the qualifications of their teachers moves up in degree to reality. Concern over what the wealthy districts can do in this matter should be of little consequence, for most of the costs of such improvement in the more or less impoverished districts would come from all the taxpayers of the state rather than from only those who live in the school district.

Miscellaneous Weighting Factors

Many other weighting factors can reasonably be expected in state foundation programs. Notable examples include provision of funds for transportation, administrative and other professional nonteaching personnel, and capital outlay or debt service. Unfortunately, the incidence of such factors is low, and there is too little state acceptance of these in foundation programs. Many of these, however, are covered by special grants or appropriations of a nonequalizing nature. Certainly, greater interest and more state support need to be developed in these areas, especially in providing stronger and more equalized state support for capital outlay and debt service expenditures.

Selected Readings

Alexander, Kern, and Jordan, K. Forbis, eds. *Constitutional Reform of School Finance.* Lexington, Mass.: Lexington Books, D. C. Heath and Co., 1973.

Benson, Charles S.; Goldfinger, Paul M.; Hoachlander, E. Gareth; and Pers, Jessica S. *Planning for Educational Reform: Financial and Social Alternatives.* New York: Dodd, Mead & Co., 1974.

Berke, Joel S. *Answers to Inequity: An Analysis of the New School Finance.* Berkeley, Calif.: McCutchan Publishing Corp., 1974.

———; Campbell, Alan K.; and Goettel, Robert J. *Financing Equal Educational Opportunity.* Berkeley, Calif.: McCutchan Publishing Corp., 1972.

Cohen, Michael A.; Levin, Betsy; and Beaver, Richard. *The Political Limits to School Finance Reform.* Washington, D.C.: The Urban Institute, 1973.

Coons, John E.; Clune, William H. III; and Sugarman, Stephen D. *Private Wealth and Public Education.* Cambridge, Mass.: Belknap Press of Harvard University Press, 1970.

Grubb, W. Norton, and Michelson, Stephan. *States and Schools.* Lexington, Mass.: Lexington Books, D. C. Heath and Co., 1974.

Johns, Roe L., and Alexander, Kern. *Alternative Programs for Financing Education.* Gainesville, Fla.: National Educational Finance Project, 1971.

Pincus, John A., ed. *School Finance in Transition.* Cambridge, Mass.: Ballinger Publishing Co., 1974.

The Realities of School Finance. Lexington, Mass.: Lexington Books, D. C. Heath and Co., 1973.

UNIT 5

DISTRICT
AND SITE-LEVEL
FINANCE OPERATIONS

*While the administrator should not become so
engrossed in financial details that he neglects
to keep abreast of educational developments,
neither can he ignore the financial implications
of instructional programs without endangering
the welfare of the school system.*

Stephen J. Knezevich,
*Administration of Public
Education,* 1969

12

Administering
the School Budget

The consequential innovations that are currently receiving such emphasis in curricular and administrative aspects of education have their counterparts in school finance theories and practices, including budgeting and accounting. Present budgetary practices are the result of a long evolutionary development—a development that in recent years has been accelerating rather than becoming stabilized or decelerating. The traditional principles and practices of budgeting, which seemed to be so well established and proved, are nonetheless now being supplanted or supplemented by more sophisticated and meaningful systems of interpreting and explaining the educational program of the school.

EVOLUTION OF BUDGETARY
PRACTICES

Historians report that budgetary practices originated and received their greatest early development in England. Knezevich and Fowlkes construe budgetary development as having been part of a movement toward Parliament's securing control over the king in matters dealing with finance.[1] They noted that budget practice was used in England more than two centuries before its use by the United States government and that the British government was practicing full-fledged budgeting by 1822. As developed in England, budgeting involved budget preparation

1. Stephen J. Knezevich and John Guy Fowlkes, *Business Management of Local School Systems* (New York: Harper & Row, 1960), p. 18.

by the executive branch of government, approval of the budget by the legislative branch (with amendments when deemed necessary or appropriate), authorization of tax levies by the legislative branch to meet the expected expenditures, and administration by the executive branch of government. Johns and Morphet noted the importance of these developments in budgetary theory:

> This may seem like a very simple and natural arrangement. But it took hundreds of years for the people to wrest from ruling monarchs the authority to levy taxes and to determine governmental expenditures. . . . The budget is not just a document containing a list of receipts and expenditures but it is a process by which the people in a democracy exercise their constitutional right to govern themselves.[2]

Budgeting Developed Slowly in America

Seemingly boundless wealth in the early history of America thwarted the early development of sound budgetary practices in government. Petty jealousies between members of Congress and the executive branch of government also contributed in large measure to the slow metamorphosis of budgeting practices in this country. The first law providing for a national budget was passed in 1921; it set the pattern for the present budgetary procedures of the federal government.[3]

Budgetary practices became common in business and industry before local boards of education accepted them generally. Until the end of the first quarter of the twentieth century, public school budgetary practices were unrefined and not standardized to any appreciable degree. As with many other innovative practices, urban school systems developed budgetary patterns and routines before rural schools did. Gradually the various states enacted laws that established guidelines and specifics required of all districts in the receiving and disbursing of school funds. The extent of these requirements and the degree of detail of accounting have increased until such practices have become somewhat standardized for similar kinds of districts within each state.

Financial Problems Encourage Budgeting Practices

Institutions have established sound budgetary practices following the occurrence of serious financial problems. As long as revenues are plenti-

---

2. Roe L. Johns and Edgar L. Morphet, *Financing the Public Schools* (Englewood Cliffs, N.J.: Prentice-Hall, 1960), p. 392.

3. Ibid., p. 393.

ful, institutions—state, local, and national—are relatively slow in accepting the challenge of establishing and following budgetary practices. On the other hand, when expenditures increase proportionately faster than income, then school districts, businesses, or even households turn for possible solutions expectantly to increased dependence on a more strict accounting for funds received and spent, in other words, elementary budgeting practices.

THE BUDGET

Because everyone uses the word budget in government, in business, in industry, in education, and even in the home, it is presumed to be commonly understood. Technically, however, *budget* may mean different things to different people. Certainly, the purposes for which budgets are prepared and the degree of adherence to budgetary detail and administration vary considerably among the people and agencies that use them.

Definition

Perhaps each person using the term *budget* has his own definition of what it means. Although accepted definitions are numerous, all assume that budgeting involves at least four elements: (1) planning, (2) receiving funds, (3) spending funds, and (4) evaluating results—all performed within the limits of a preestablished time factor. Thus, budgeting is planning, receiving, and spending funds over a particular period, usually a year for school districts. The evaluative aspects cover examining previous budgets in order to build better budgets for succeeding periods.

Roe defined the educational budget as "the translation of educational needs into a financial plan which is interpreted to the public in such a way that when formally adopted it expresses the kind of educational program the community is willing to support, financially and morally, for a one-year period."[4] Some other examples of acceptable definitions of budgeting include the following: "A budget may be defined as a specific plan for implementing organizational objectives, policies and programs for a given period of time. It embodies (1) descriptions of organizational activities and services requisite to attainment of organizational goals;

4. William H. Roe, *School Business Management* (New York: McGraw-Hill, 1961), p. 81.

(2) estimates of expenditures and their allocations; and (3) forecasts of fiscal resources available to support the plan."[5] And "In public education, budgets are . . . more than 'merely matters of arithmetic,' i.e., adding up the proposed expenditures and the anticipated receipts for a given period. The budget must be regarded as the fiscal translation of the educational program."[6]

Importance of Budgeting

Few people question the importance of budgeting in the public schools, in the branches of government, in business, in industry, or in any activity that involves receiving and expending large sums of money. Its importance in school districts increases as its function develops from purely mechanical and mathematical accounting to appraisal and translation of the educational program into meaningful terms. In the words of Simpson and Lake:

> If the budget is a living thing, it is not solely a document with a great number of méchanical attachments. If school budgeting is to implement social policy, it must be a continuous process whereby the people of a democracy seek, through gradual development and within their means, to set their sights on what schools can do to raise the level of living. Thus conceived, school budgeting helps education to become the expression of broad social policy.[7]

Purposes of Budgetary Practices

The school district budget serves a number of important functions: (1) It projects the proposed school program and educational plan of the district for the next fiscal period. (2) It shows the sources of funds, anticipated expenditures, and allocation of authority for administering budgetary items. (3) It serves to inform the public about the educational program of the school. (4) It provides a guide for evaluating a year's program and a means of comparing school services with those that have

---

5. Leon Ovsiew et al. "Budgeting," in Warren E. Gauerke and Jack R. Childress, eds., *Theory and Practice of School Finance* (Chicago: Rand McNally & Co., 1967), p. 209.

6. Knezevich and Fowlkes, *Business Management of Local School Systems*, p. 17.

7. Alfred D. Simpson and Ernest G. Lake, "The Budgetary Process," in R. L. Johns and E. L. Morphet, eds., *Problems and Issues in Public School Finance* (New York: National Conference of Professors of Educational Administration, 1952), p. 324.

been offered in other years. (5) It provides the motivation for careful planning, for establishing systems of control, and for wise and effective expenditure of funds. (6) It points out the relationship of the state, federal, and local units of government in supporting education.

Budgetary administration varies with state laws and with administrative interpretation of its function. To some it may be the master to be followed with strictness and complete propriety; to others it is a guide to be followed without blind submission to its arithmetic regardless of cause and effect on the educational program that school administrators propose for the benefit of boys and girls.

BUDGETARY PRINCIPLES

Certain basic principles concerning preparation and administration of the budget are accepted by students of public school finance. These include, as a minimum, the following:

1. The superintendent of schools should administer the school district budget. In this, he is responsible for preparing the budget document; he should involve administrative and other school staff members, and also citizens and groups in the community in its preparation; and he should present and defend the tentative budget to the school board and the public. It is his responsibility to administer the budget and to be held accountable for the results that it produces.

2. The school board has legal responsibility for the formal adoption of the budget; it should hold the superintendent responsible for its administration.

3. Preparation of the budget is a continuous process, which should proceed in three phases: (1) determination of the educational plan, (2) calculation of the cost of the proposed program, and (3) determination of the plan for obtaining the necessary revenue.

4. The proposed budget should be reviewed in an open hearing where all citizens have an opportunity to study it and make recommendations and comments concerning it; the hearing should be held soon enough for adjustments to be made by the board should they choose to do so as a result of public reaction; the final budget should be operable on the first day of the fiscal year to which it applies.

5. The approved budget should be included with the minutes of the board meeting as official verification of its acceptance.

6. Continuous appraisal by all parties concerned is necessary in order to assure yearly budgetary improvements.

PREPARATION OF THE BUDGET

Responsibility for the preparation of the tentative budget document rests with the superintendent of schools and his administrative staff. This in no way suggests that he should ignore other school employees in its preparation, nor does it suggest that he must do all the detailed work required. As executive officer of the board he is charged with supervising its development and with full accountability for the end product.

The Budget's Three Dimensions

Traditionally, since its first use by De Young, the school district budget has been represented by an equilateral triangle, the base of which is the educational program, with one side the cost of the program necessary to attain or produce that program, and the other side the revenue plan. In theory, the educational plan is determined first. It is then converted into cost terms, and finally the determination of the sources of required revenues is made. The rationale for such a sequence is that our educational programs are to be planned for the peculiar needs of the pupils without letting the available funds be the guide and master, or limiting factor, in determining the bounds of the educational program.

In the past, the affluent school districts were able to follow sound principles and accepted procedures in preparing the budget. Where revenue limitations were not too restricted, the process worked well. In the districts with restricted revenue, budget building was sometimes reversed in sequence of preparation; the revenue was determined and then school officials decided what kinds of programs and services could be purchased for the amount of the expected revenue. This procedure often resulted in including programs and services that were inexpensive rather than those that represented the real needs of the pupils. Such planners resemble the prospective consumer in the restaurant, the variety store, or some other place who reads the menu or price list always from right to left. He may find himself purchasing goods or services that do not meet his dietary or other needs simply because they are less expensive than those that would be appropriate.

Determining the Educational Program

The educational program is directly related to the purposes and objectives of the school. Unfortunately, the aims and objectives of educational institutions are not always clear or well defined. This makes determination of programs and services very difficult. The superintendent finds himself faced with a myriad of problem questions, such as, What services of the school should be increased next year? Should the school provide more guidance services, or should it put more emphasis on equipping teachers with more and better facilities and instructional media? Should more emphasis be put on expensive programs such as driver education, or should the social science offerings be increased? Should the school provide for kindergartens and for special education classes? To what extent should the pupils participate in paying the costs of education with incidental fees and charges? These and countless other questions must be answered in preparing the proposed educational program to be sponsored by each school district.

The superintendent, regardless of the complexity of his problems, must work with his staff and with the school board and parents in the community to determine the proposed educational objectives and program for the subsequent fiscal year and for several years ahead. Those superintendents who suggest to their boards of education that, since there is a potential increase of 5 percent in school revenue, each area of the budget will automatically be increased by that amount are making at least three errors: (1) they are presuming that the previous budget was perfect and that therefore, since costs have increased, each part of it must be increased by the same amount; (2) they are ignoring the need for evaluating the past year's budget and for examining and resolving such imbalances as it may have had; and (3) they are denying those with an interest in the school—teachers, staff members, school board members, pupils, and the general public—their rights and responsibilities of continuous evaluation of the public school program.

The superintendent working with the board of education is responsible for involving people in determining educational policies and objectives. He should use all his public relations know-how to get committees of representatives of the PTA, the press, radio, television, and other media or groups to participate in such policymaking. Final decisions, however, regarding proposed program changes and innovations must rest with the board of education, acting with the advice and recommendations of the superintendent and his staff.

Preparing the Budget Document

The educational plan for budgetary purposes is valueless until converted into dollar costs. Under the direction of the superintendent, those who will be responsible for specific parts of the educational plan determine the needs of these programs. Sound budgeting theory dictates that teachers and other school personnel should be provided with forms and figures indicating budget allotments and expenditures for one or more past years and with blanks for estimates of next year's needs. Some districts will ask for cost estimates; others make such estimates in the district office after staff members have indicated the quantity and kind of needs.

With increasing frequency, districts are using another aspect of budget building by school personnel. In addition to having teachers and others suggest what they *need* for the following year, many progressive districts ask them also to submit requests for those supplies and facilities required for an optimum or superior program, or even for an alternative program. The administration is thereby, in effect, asking school personnel to indicate by their *wants* or *desires* what, if granted, would provide the best possible program that each individual can at that moment envision. Teachers who in past years may not have received the supplies and equipment they requested may not be too anxious to make the extra effort to determine what they could use effectively, if such were to be available. However, regardless of the final disposition of the individual's requests according to needs or desires, the experience of having each school employee determine how much money should be allocated and for what it should be spent to provide the best possible educational program is a very much worthwhile experience in itself. Such a problem as determining the kind and frequency of use of instructional media that would be used under an ideal budget arrangement will cause the teacher to evaluate carefully the many alternatives available in the teaching process. And then there is always the possibility that the requested optimum program may be accepted and implemented in the final budget document.

It should be remembered at this point that as school districts move in the direction of program budgeting and systems analysis of the school program, the determination of alternatives in arriving at the completion of educational objectives is a necessary requirement. From that point of view, the school employees will be much more deeply and personally involved in the determination of budgetary requirements.

Unfortunately, the extent of involvement of teachers and other staff members in determining the educational program and allocating resources to attain the school's objectives is minimal in practice. For various reasons, many school administrators use the previous year's budget as the sole basis for the budget for the next year. In this way, inequities and imbalances tend to become perpetuated. Some administrators find that district office determination of budget needs is not only easier and less frustrating but more acceptable to many teachers and staff members who treat the business of budgeting with apathy or indifference.

James noted the popularity of the percentage increase method of budgetary calculations in the following:

> An extensive examination of school budgets over more than a decade, in many states during this period of rapid increase in school expenditures, leads me to conclude that line items of expenditures increase at about the same rate.
>
> The two inferences I draw from this observation are that increases in the total budget are allocated across line items, not on a rationally selective basis, but on a flat percentage-increase basis; and that the reason this is so is that insufficient information is available at the policy-making level to provide a more rational basis for allocating funds.[8]

In the districts that follow the staff-participation method of budgetary preparation, the principal of each of the various attendance areas combines the budget requests of all staff members working under his direction, checks them for omissions, duplications, or errors, and then submits them (usually in combined form) to the school district office, where they are summarized and combined into totals for the district. From these reports and from similar requests from district employees, a tentative budget document is prepared.

The tentative budget is presented to the board of education at a regular meeting for its study and recommendations for changes. The board is free to make whatever changes it desires within the limits of the statutes governing such practices in the state. The tentative budget is then accepted, summaries are prepared, and the board of education and the superintendent and his staff prepare for a budget hearing.

The budget does not stand by itself. It is related to many other records involved in the school district's business affairs, such as salary schedules, insurance policies, and inventories, and is influenced by them. Many of these schedules should accompany the budget document as it is presented to the board for study and adoption. They aid greatly in interpreting the message that the budget conveys. Ovsiew and Castetter made an excellent and inclusive list of such materials:

> Suggested materials to accompany the budget: asterisked items suggest materials that should be included in the budget document.
> * Letter of transmittal
> * Statement of introduction, especially relating budget to the school philosophy
> * Justifications

---

8. H. Thomas James, "Modernizing State and Local Financing of Education," in *A Financial Program for Today's Schools* (Washington, D.C.: National Education Assn. Committee on Educational Finance, 1964), pp. 56–57.

- Curriculum review, by unit, divisions, and departments
- Audited statements of funds
- Bonding schedule
- Recapitulations of sections of the budget
- Salary schedules
- Statistical summary of salary program, showing experience, training, and classifications
- Statistical summary of other pertinent data, such as
  - Enrollment, showing trends and projections
  - Numerical adequacy of staff
  - Average daily attendance
  - Pupil-teacher ratio in instruction
  - Per pupil costs by budget categories
  - Enrollment by curriculum in the high school
- State-aid provisions, indicating changes
- Insurance in force
- Transportation schedules
- Property tax experience, including relationship to assessments, market values, per cent of collection, and millage limits
- Non-property tax experience, by type levied and by potential
- Cost experience, by trends in prices of selected items
- Retirement and social security schedules
- Expenditure and revenue items for 2 to 3 previous years
- Policy statements mandating expenditures
- Unmet needs report
- Items mandated by new laws or official directives
- Inventory report
- Budget transfers during previous year
- Summary of germane committee reports
- Comparative costs data with selected school districts[9]

The Budget Hearing

Superintendents have long since discovered that there is little interest in budget hearings if no effort is made to summarize and interpret the massive lists of figures and minute details of the budget document. In preparing for a hearing, the superintendent and his staff must exercise ingenuity in devising an interesting and informative way of presenting the pertinent facts about the budget so that they can easily be understood by lay citizens. The use of audiovisual materials—charts, film strips, films, transparencies, and the like—help greatly in elucidating and explaining points that are of most interest and concern to school patrons.

9. Ovsiew and Castetter, *Budgeting for Better Schools*, p. 52.

Not all states have laws that require a formal hearing before adoption of the annual school district budget. In those that do, the board and the administrative staff present and explain the tentative budget, listen to the suggestions and criticisms of school patrons, and make necessary justifications of questioned items or policies. Final approval of the budget usually rests with the school board in fiscally independent districts. In fiscally dependent districts, a city or county board usually must pass on the total budget levy authorized by the school board, relating it to the tentative budgets of other agencies of government under its general jurisdiction. In such districts, the city or county board usually has the power to require a reduction of the budget levy if necessary, but detailed alterations are left to the board of education within the accepted total levy approved.

General Provisions of the Budget

Budgets should provide for classification of receipts and expenditures in line with the accounting system that the state and the local school district require. For the most part, these classifications should be in line with those recommended by the U.S. Office of Education.[10] The budget should provide for separating general expenditure funds from the bond and debt service funds. The current-expenditures budget should provide for emergencies by a contingency fund. Provision should be made, where possible, for a cash surplus at the beginning of the fiscal period to minimize the need for borrowing money until local tax money or state allocations are received.

School administrators often find it advantageous to provide a comparison of the new-budget items with similar considerations of the past year or two. There is much to be said in favor of a written explanation and justification of some budget items. The unexplained arithmetical figures found on any budget may mean little to the uninformed person who views them without perspective or rationale. This is particularly true when more than typical changes are being made in specific items. Critics of unexplained items or changes often become supporters of these same items or changes when they understand the reasons behind them.

Some administrators and students of budegtary practice urge the establishment of priorities in the spending plan of the school district. Their defense rests on the fact that such priorities can only be established after much study of the relative value of alternative parts of the

10. Charles T. Roberts and Allan R. Lichtenberger, *Financial Accounting* (Washington, D.C.: U.S. Office of Education, U.S. Dept. of Health, Education, and Welfare, 1973).

school program. The practical advantages of this procedure would be obvious when expected revenues are less than what has been counted on or when costs exceed expectations.

ADMINISTRATION OF THE BUDGET

Once the budget is formally adopted, it becomes effective on the first day of the new fiscal period. The superintendent (by law in some states and by assignment only in some others) is the administrative officer charged with carrying out the programs that the budget authorizes. Unfortunately, some school districts try to differentiate between the strictly educational responsibilities of the superintendent and the fiscal policies, which are supervised by a clerk or business manager who is responsible directly to the board of education. The dilemma that such an arrangement creates is antithetical to the purposes of the school. A dual head to a school system, with one administrator in charge of the instructional program and the other guarding the treasury, can work satisfactorily only under ideal conditions, and these seldom exist. The board of education should, and usually does, recognize that the superintendent as its executive officer must be in charge of the entire school operation. The official in charge of the business functions of the school, regardless of his title, must be directly responsible to the superintendent. Only with such an arrangement can the board hold the superintendent accountable for the educational program of the school district.

Expending Money

Once the budget is formally adopted, the various line items and amounts are posted to the official accounting forms and funds of the district. The new budget then becomes a daily guide for the necessary expenditure of school funds. Work plans and expenditure policies must be established so that the money can be expended for the purposes for which it was intended without undue red tape or unnecessary inconvenience. The purpose of the budget is not to save money; rather it is to help spend it wisely and expeditiously when needed. All school employees need to know the policies and specific procedures to be followed in carrying out the budgetary plan. It should not be hoped or planned that complicated or time-wasting procedures will be such that they will discourage proper expenditure of the necessary funds to operate any and all aspects of the school program that have been approved.

Evaluation of the Budget

No person, least of all the school administrator, expects a perfect budget. He knows that careful planning and evaluation may reduce but never completely eliminate the need for making changes in his current budget. The board of education can do this when necessary by operating within the legal requirements for such adjustments. Of course, if the budget is changed at will with impunity, it becomes a meaningless document of questionable value to the school district.

The superintendent is responsible for seeing that the budget is more than just an accounting system built and administered around a legal requirement to make guesses or estimates about receipts and expenditures. He has the obligation to demonstrate that the budget is a well-conceived monetary summary of the educational plan of the school district for specific time. He must be able to demonstrate that it is constructed around the specific purposes or objectives of the school and the plans, services, personnel, and systems to be used in achieving those objectives.

Each succeeding budget should be an improvement over the previous one in terms of utility and effectiveness. It should indicate steady progress toward achieving its main processes and purposes, such as more consequential involvement of school personnel and citizens in its preparation, more concerted effort to avoid program imbalance, more conferring and more effective rationale to defend budgetary items, greater effort toward continuous planning, and greater emphasis on program budgeting with the provision for alternative programs to meet specific objectives.

One of the important lessons school administrators learn is that the budget is the business of all the people in the district and not just the official concern of the superintendent and the school board. This concept has been a long time in receiving wide acceptance. School patrons cannot be expected to support financial claims against them without some degree of understanding of purpose. In reality, budget critics often become budget defenders when they understand the objectives the school is attempting to achieve and the financial limitations under which it operates.

The superintendent is responsible for keeping the board of education informed on the operation and effectiveness of the budget. He usually issues financial reports to the board on a regular basis showing the total expenditures to date, balances in the chief accounts, and anticipated problems in keeping within main budget item limitations. He concerns himself with some determination of the extent to which the budget has been effective, what improvements should be made in the next budget, what imbalances have been created between programs that are overfinanced compared with those that are underfinanced, and many other similar and necessary subjective as well as objective evaluations of budget performance. He takes special note and reports from time to time to the board concerning the ever present problems of protecting the school's funds against dishonest, unethical, or careless handling by school personnel. Experience has taught him that any precautions or guidelines he may use to protect public funds, as well as to protect the reputation of the people using them, will be effort well spent.

The Budget Calendar

School administrators recognize that to be maximally effective, budget building must be a continuous process. They recognize a need to follow a fairly specific budget preparation calendar. The details to be followed and the actual time to be assigned to budget preparation is a function of the size of the school district, the number of employees involved in budget preparation, and the degree of difficulty encountered in obtaining three-sided balance in the budget triangle. Regardless of these factors, however, budget building should start as soon as the current budget is put into operation.

The fiscal year in most school districts starts on July 1 (in order to confine it to only one academic school year). On that day the current year budget begins, and the superintendent and his staff start planning for the next year. The details involved in the preparation of a new budget will not be the same in all districts since the legal requirements and the number of staff members responsible for budget planning will not always be the same.

The budget calendar would probably be organized with certain minimum requirements included. Fixed dates, or at least suggested dates, should be predetermined for the completion of certain actions, such as when new program requests must be recommended, when required supplies and instructional materials must be reported, when the initial and tentative budget document will be presented to the board of education (sometimes provided for in the law), and when and where budget planning and budget hearings will be held. Although the school district must follow whatever budget preparation requirements are written in the state code, other performance dates and deadlines are usually directory and need not be followed to the letter if it seems in the best interest of the school district to deviate from such proposals. In any event, the superintendent makes a serious mistake if he procrastinates budgetary preparation to the point where approaching deadlines interfere with conscientious budget-building practices.

SYSTEMS ANALYSIS

Essentially, systems analysis is the comparison of alternative means of carrying out some function, when those means are rather complicated and comprise a number of interrelated elements. Such analysis could often be called "economic analysis," since the aim is to find the best use of one's resources, but the word *systems* is useful in calling attention to the complex nature of the alternatives being compared.[11]

During the early 1950s, many of the leaders in educational administration became vitally interested in developing basic theories involved in the practice of their profession. New kinds of textbooks were written, and theory classes in school administration began to appear in the curricula of the graduate programs at many of the progressive colleges and universities. The rationale for this departure from the past was that research and practice in educational administration were too heavily involved with empiricism. The front-line thinkers in the field noted, rather apologetically and almost unbelievingly, that the discipline up to that point had almost completely ignored theory in the study and practice of school administration.

A New Look at Administration

The development of theory in educational administration, with an emphasis on the science of administrative behavior, was accompanied by the beginning of what has become known as systems analysis, or the systems approach, a new way of looking at the functions involved in administration. According to the AASA Commission on Administrative Technology, the beginnings of the systems approach are not known precisely but can be traced to the first efforts to introduce science into the management of organizations, some crude efforts of which occurred at the beginning of this century.[12]

The systems approach and systems analysis, in various contexts, have become increasingly popular and prestigious as terms and practices, but their definitions remain elusive and subjective, as indicated in the following:

The term [*system*] may be used to gain some measure of recognition for the user. There may be little concern for its preciseness in describing accurately what the concept means. . . . New approaches to management decision making, such as systems, may be expressed in many ways

11. J. A. Kershaw and R. N. McKean, *Systems Analysis and Education* (Santa Monica, Calif.: Rand Corp., October 1959), p. 1.
12. *Administrative Technology and the School Executive* (Washington, D.C.: AASA Commission on Administrative Technology, 1969), pp. 17–18.

and applied in a variety of contexts. In addition, a full range of terminology associated with technology has developed as new applications have increased and spread. This has resulted in a lack of standardization of terms, creating difficulty for those interested in identifying and describing the emerging technology.[13]

Systems analysis is a broad and general term. It is difficult to define in terms of specifics. For example, one author refers to it as "providing a framework that promotes commonalities in approach . . . [and] encourages interdisciplinary dialogues and combats the myopic fractionalization of contemporary scholarship." Another writer describes it as "orderly analysis of the differentiated component elements and processes within an organization; the relation of each element and process to the other, and all to the missions of the organization; and the perception of the organization as unified, possessing dynamic qualities, and having defined boundaries."

Hartley summarized the problem of terminology and definition concerning the systems approach:

> Systems approaches to planning are not blessed with clear terminology. Different writers and policy makers use terms interchangeably. In addition to general systems theory and such economic concepts as input-output and cost-benefit analyses, several other analytical techniques from management science deserve mention. One writer found forty different code names and acronyms for management controls or approaches such as PERT (Program Evaluation and Review Techniques) and OR (Operation Research).[14]

The concept of systems analysis is based on the premise that a school offers a variety of viable programs, each of which can be determined. Hartley describes it as "part of the new generation of interrelated management procedures that seek to enhance organizational rationality."[15]

Program Budgeting

Program budgeting is planning, assessing, and providing for resource allocations to support alternative programs that an institution may offer to reach its specific objectives. A form of program budgeting (not to be confused with computer programming) has been used to a very limited extent in business and industry for about a quarter of a century.

13. Ibid., p. 18.
14. Harry J. Hartley, *Educational Planning-Programming-Budgeting* (Englewood Cliffs, N.J.: Prentice-Hall, 1968), p. 36.
15. Ibid., p. 5.

The plan was little known, however, before its successful introduction into the federal government structure in the early 1960s.

Program budgeting is not synonymous with performance budgeting. The former provides for choices between alternative ways of achieving a goal or objective and is therefore oriented toward intensive planning. It focuses on the output of the school rather than the input. On the other hand, performance budgeting, as the name implies, indicates great pressure on management to perform efficiently without having been offered alternatives. "Program budgeting is a subunit of a more comprehensive approach to the study of organizational activities, which, for lack of a more descriptive term, may be called systems analysis."[16]

It should not be assumed that program budgeting is a subtle or clever plan or device to curtail expenditures or to facilitate retrenchment of programs. It is concerned with effectiveness of the various ways in which the school can organize to achieve its goals; it is neutral about reducing the total costs of education. It is aimed at securing optimum results by allocating the school's resources to productive programs and denying them to less productive ones. Its relation to economics is shown in the following:

> The program budget is a product of political economy, combining economic and political rationality, with emphasis on the former; it is the connecting link between the program structure of a school and its available resources; and it is the focus for organizational planning, encompassing goal setting, resource allocation, evaluative review, and revision of objectives.[17]

School districts have not yet widely accepted program budgeting. Its basic structure is difficult to augment, for the necessary expertise is often lacking, especially in small districts. Undoubtedly, however, this new concept, with improvements and refinements, will be used extensively in educational planning and budgeting in the years ahead.

THE FEDERAL GOVERNMENT AND SYSTEMS ANALYSIS

While serving as secretary of defense for the United States in 1961, Robert McNamara introduced some aspects of systems analysis to certain difficult problems facing the Department of Defense in the government of the United States. His avowed purpose was to facilitate a more deliberate and considered choice of department goals or objectives, a

16. Ibid.
17. Ibid., pp. 6–7.

more systematic relating of means to ends, and more precise evaluations of the outcomes of certain programs.[18]

Many new concepts were introduced in the department during the period 1961-65, one of which was the Planning-Programming-Budgeting System (commonly referred to as PPBS). While the new approach was controversial, the success of the department in using and developing it resulted in causing President Lyndon B. Johnson in 1965 to instruct twenty-one nondefense departments to institute similar planning techniques by 1966.[19]

PLANNING-PROGRAMMING-BUDGETING SYSTEMS

A planning-programming-budgeting system is an integrated system devised to provide administrators and other school staff members with better and more objective information for planning educational programs and for making choices among the alternative ways for spending funds to achieve the school's educational goals or objectives. It is probably the most promising new method or device ever introduced to improve school budgetary procedures and practices. Originally, this new phenomenon was known as a PPB system; later it became PPBS—its most widely known and recognized alphabetical form. Recently, some who have felt that "evaluation" was not stressed sufficiently added an *E* to the acronym, making it PPBES. The Association of School Business Officials were not yet satisfied with the designation and substituted ERMD (Educational Resource Management Division), which it felt was more descriptive of this new approach to budgetary planning.

THE CONCEPTS OF PPBS

The planning-programming-budgeting system (PPBS) is a way of extending the planning period and duration of a program budget, often for from five to ten years. Its chief thrust is in the direction of replacing broad and traditional objectives with specific and measurable ones. It involves a cycle in planning that includes (1) establishing objective goals, (2) determining the financial cost of alternative plans for reaching the objectives, (3) evaluating the results, (4) improving the objectives, and (5) adding to and improving the alternative plans to reach the revised objectives.

PPBS is another indication of the need for greater accountability

18. *Administrative Technology and the School Executive*, pp. 28–29.
19. Ibid., p. 68.

in education. It emphasizes the well-known fact that taxpayers are no longer willing to accept increased expenditures unless there is measurable evidence of an increase in the quality of the product. In economic terms, they are asking for a closer relation between input and output. The PPBS concept is a device for distributing limited resources (input) in the public sector to provide the greatest possible returns in services (output).

An Integrated and Innovative System

"PPBS is not a new machine or piece of hardware. It is an intellectual technology and is part of the systems approach to administration."[20] It is an extension of systems analysis (a scientific way of devising alternative plans for reaching an objective). With main emphasis on the outputs of the school, the system requires specific identification of the products and services that society demands of its schools. It is an integrated and innovative system, with the objective of supplying the administrator with better planning and programming in order to make maximum use of limited resources.

Main Requirements

The research division of the National Education Association enumerated a series of documents that "are major tools of a PPB system":[21]

1. The program structure and statement of objectives.
2. Program analyses (cost-effectiveness analyses) and memoranda.
3. The multi-year program and financial plan.

In the preparation of these documents the PPB system requires:

1. Clarifying and specifying the ultimate goals or objectives of each activity for which a government budgets money.
2. Gathering contributing activities into comprehensive categories or programs to achieve the specified objectives.
3. Examining as a continuous process how well each activity or program has done—its effectiveness—as a first step toward improving or even eliminating it.
4. Analyzing proposed improvements or new program proposals to see how effective they may be in achieving program goals.
5. Projecting the *entire costs* of each proposal not only for the first year but for several subsequent years.

20. *NEA Research Bulletin* 46, no. 4 (Washington, D.C.: National Education Assn., December 1968), p. 113.
21. Ibid.

6. Formulating a plan, based in part on the analysis of program cost and effectiveness, that leads to implementation through the budget.

What PPBS Is Not

One of the best summaries of what PPBS is not is the following statement by the research division of the National Education Association:

> We may know what PPB is, but let us make sure that we know what it is not. It is not revolutionary. Its ingredients are largely not new except in the way they are organized or presented. It is not a substitute for judgment, opinion, experience, or wisdom. The decision maker still has to make the decision, and he has to use his intuition, knowledge, judgment, etc. It is not an attempt to computerize the decision-making process. Computers do not make decisions; they are just useful tools. It is just not another way to save money. As a matter of fact, it will cost a great deal of money to fully implement it. It is not just another budget, and it surely is not the answer to every problem involving every issue. But if PPB is successful, it will be successful because it provides a better format to decision makers through which they can make more intelligent, rational decisions.[22]

THE PUBLIC SCHOOLS AND PPBS

In spite of the great potential of PPBS and systems analysis approaches to budgetary responsibility, schools have been slow in adopting any form of program budgeting. The reluctance of schools to move into this field is understandable, however, for the program is new and there are few who have a clear conception of how it can be applied. It has been noted that PPBS is "now seeping into the educational community with promises of great potential, especially for the administrator who must decide how to divide limited funds among competing projects."[23]

Lack of Acceptance Decried

The AASA Commission on Administrative Technology deplored the slowness with which schools and the U.S. Office of Education are mov-

22. *NEA Reserach Bulletin* 47, no. 3 (Washington, D.C.: National Education Assn., October 1969), p. 95.
23. *Education U.S.A.* (Washington, D.C.: National School Public Relations Assn., May 6, 1968), p. 201.

ing into program budgeting and PPBS. It expressed the belief that business, industry, and government have made greater progress in budgeting than education has. The commission was convinced that in education there is more talk than action towards implementing PPBS.[24] Burkhead referred to the fact that the U.S. Office of Education failed to discuss program or performance budgeting in its recommendations for financial accounting.[25]

Adoption Requires Readiness

Despite the loud acclaim that has been given PPBS, it is evident that the school districts of this country are not going to be ready to inaugurate such a system in the near future. The AASA Commission on Administrative Technology listed four conditions that must be satisfied before school districts will be ready for such an innovation:[26] (1) a restatement of educational objectives in a program format that facilitates the use of indicators and more precise output measurement devices in education; (2) generation of a supply of alternatives for reaching an objective; (3) reclassification of budget accounts now used in individual states or recommended nationally to reflect program and output-oriented classifications; and (4) employment of specialized workers with systems analysis capability.

CALIFORNIA AND PPBS

The PPB system idea seemed to have great promise for education, especially in the late 1960s after its apparent success in the operations of the federal government. One of the best examples of the enthusiastic and early acceptance of the idea at the state level came in the state of California. Kirst reviews "the rise and fall of PPBS in California"—a part of which review is cited:

> Among the groups intrigued with PPBS was the California legislature. In October, 1966, this body . . . established the Advisory Commission on School Budgeting and Accounting. This citizens' commission appeared to be the first step in state-mandated installation of PPBS in California's 1,056 school districts.

24. *Administrative Technology and the School Executive*, p. 68.
25. Jesse Burkhead, "The Theory and Application of Program Budgeting to Education," in Gauerke and Childress, eds., *Trends in Financing Public Education* (Washington, D.C.: National Education Assn., 1965), p. 183.
26. *Administrative Technology and the School Executive*, pp. 87–88.

Seven years later, the California legislature made a 180-degree turn and abandoned PPBS. All that remains is an accounting system that provides some program information at a very high level of aggregation. Filed in the state archive's are the elaborate PPBS manuals developed at a cost of several million dollars. State Education Department officials never use the word PPBS in public. Local school people have long forgotten the inservice training sessions on PPBS that were so prominently featured statewide in the late 1960s.[27]

Kirst explains why the California experience with PPBS was unsuccessful in the following:

Once the vocal opposition coalesced, the support for PPBS proved to be very shallow. It appears that legislators want public school accountability, but only if the particular accountability techniques used do not provoke organized opposition extending beyond professional educators. The California experience makes me suspect that accountability will be confined to technical issues and performance reporting. Much of the data will either obfuscate or avoid areas with significant value conflict. Consequently, parents and laymen will rarely become concerned or involved.[28]

Perhaps some lessons can be learned from the experience with PPBS in California and in other states, such as:

1. PPBS, while it can promise effectiveness if successfully implemented, requires considerable money, experienced personnel, time, and general support of school personnel and patrons in order to be made operable.
2. PPBS can, and often does, place too much stress on detailed measures of educational output.
3. The System is not a panacea for a school's or a state's financing and accounting programs.
4. More study and understanding are required before the System can be made to work effectively in helping solve the budgetary and accountability problems of public education.

PPBS AND THE FUTURE

Considerable interest exists among many of the national leaders in school finance in how to resolve the problems that accompany the introduction of systems analysis, or PPBS, into a school system. Accordingly, research and study in this field have been accelerated. Several important studies

27. Michael W. Kirst. "The Rise and Fall of PPBS in California," *Phi Delta Kappan* (April 1975), pp. 535–38.
28. Ibid.

have been made in some states, counties, and local school districts that may help to make the outlook for PPBS innovation less doubtful than it is today.

Although it is obvious that the PPBS concept of budgeting has not yet been developed to the point where it can be universally adopted by school districts, school administrators everywhere recognize the need to improve budgeting practices and to relate them more closely to programs. The demand for higher-quality education with accompanying increase in school costs, the demand for more system and efficiency in dealing with the public treasury, and the results of successful experience with program budgeting are potent forces that are moving schools towards considering systems analysis and PPBS. It seems safe to predict that in the years immediately ahead many school districts will follow the lead of federal and state governments, as well as many areas of business and industry, in moving into program-planning-budgeting systems.

PPBS Research and Study

As an example of some of the extensive research that has been conducted in the use of PPBS, the Research Corporation of the Association of School Business Officials entered into a three-year agreement in 1968 with the U.S. Office of Education for experimentation and development of a model or design for an integrated system of program planning, budgeting, and evaluation for local school systems. The sponsors of the project counted on at least three important results of the study: (1) the development and dissemination of a conceptual model of program planning-budgeting-evaluation design; (2) demonstration of an operational system in a county public school system; and (3) encouragement and motivation for other local school systems to investigate and use the model developed in the study.

The federal government has given some encouragement and motivation to states and local school districts to begin study and implementation of program budgeting. The Elementary and Secondary Education Act stresses intensive planning and evaluation of the results of programs in terms of their objectives.

An example of such motivation to study implementation of PPBS was the so-called 5–5–5 Project. Five states (California, Michigan, New York, Vermont, and Wisconsin), five counties (Dade of Florida, Davidson of Tennessee, Los Angeles of California, Nassau of New York, and Wayne of Michigan) and five cities (Dayton, Denver, Detroit, New Haven, and San Diego) were involved in this project. The project was financed by a grant to George Washington University from the Ford

Foundation. The project provides some information on the processes, the potentials, and the issues involved in instituting an integrated system for planning public services and the facilities to provide them. Other studies of a similar nature, but on a smaller scale, are being conducted in a number of states and local school districts.

NEED FOR BUDGETARY IMPROVEMENT

While schools have been rather slow in joining the ranks of PPBS innovators, the success of program-planning-budgeting in many governmental units indicates the possibility that future legislative actions may very well be influenced by information produced by such systems. Those who view the seemingly awesome task of making such a break with budgetary practices of the past may find themselves forced to change their goals and objectives of education to fit this more functional process of measuring the output of the school with its constantly increasing input.

Selected Readings

Aliota, Robert F., and Jungherr, J. A. *Operational PPBS for Education.* New York: Harper & Row, 1971.

Administrative Technology and the School Executive. Washington, D.C.: American Assn. of School Administrators, 1969.

Hartley, Harry J. *Educational Planning-Programming-Budgeting.* Englewood Cliffs, N.J.: Prentice-Hall, 1968.

Lindman, Erick L., ed. *Approaches to Program Accounting for Public Schools.* Los Angeles: University of California at Los Angeles, September 1968.

Managing Public School Dollars. New York: American Institute of Certified Public Accountants, 1972.

Mushkin, Selma J., and Cleaveland, James R. "Planning for Educational Development in a Planning, Programming, Budgeting System," in *Interdependence in School Finance:* The City, the State, the Nation. Washington, D.C.: National Education Assn. Committee on Educational Finance, 1968.

Ovsiew, Leon, and Castetter, William B. *Budgeting for Better Schools.* Englewood Cliffs, N.J.: Prentice-Hall, 1960.

13

Accounting and Auditing

Schools are maintained for the purpose of providing a high-quality educational program, which means that they are operated to spend money —but it must be spent for the right purposes. Getting maximum benefits for the money expended, rather than saving money, is the function of the business administration of a school district. Certain key words and expressions are associated with this responsibility, such as *economy, judicious spending, honesty, protection of property,* and *protection of individuals.*

In addition to the responsibility the school has for spending school funds wisely to provide high-quality education, it has the challenge of protecting school funds and property, as well as of protecting the reputation of those involved in disbursing school monies. There is little to question or to criticize when there are accurate and verified financial records of a school's operations. On the other hand, shoddy or inadequate records often serve to impugn the actions of those who have been careless in keeping records of their stewardship, even with no intent to be dishonest.

Everyone accepts in principle that the business of education, which is the largest and most important in the nation, should use the best possible system of collecting, expending, and accounting for the large sums of public money required to educate our citizens. And yet, the history of accounting for such funds, especially at the site-level unit of organization, has not been a particularly outstanding one. Far too many examples of shoddy practices and even malfeasance have been brought to light to allow educators to point with pride to the record of schools in accounting for school funds. But such malpractices have done much to cause states and local school districts to require better accounting systems, with stronger guidelines and defensible legal requirements, for operating school business than ever before.

THE SCHOOL ACCOUNTING SYSTEM

Efficiency and effectiveness in school financial practice require a sound system of accounting for income and expenditures. Permanent records of all financial transactions are an integral part of a system of reporting the reception and disposition of the public funds required for operating schools. Legality of practice and the quality and effectiveness of the school board's stewardship of all funds are documented and supported by accounting records. Questions of integrity and propriety in the handling of public funds can be erased or supported by the records that are kept of the monies at the disposal of a school district. Thus, a system of accounting, which was once something of a luxury in some small school systems, is now a practical necessity in all schools.

Purposes

One of the main purposes of an accounting system for a business in the private economy is to determine its fiscal condition. Determining whether a company has made a profit or a loss, and how much, is fundamental to good business operations. Without such information, determination of dividends or profits or losses to stockholders cannot be made. But schools in the public sector have no concern whatever with the profit motive. Their goal is directed toward providing valuable services for their clientele. School pupils and their parents always sustain a momentary loss rather than experience a gain with the "company." What purposes, then, does the school have as a nonprofit organization, and what values will it receive in utilizing a modern accounting system? Briefly summarized, a school district employs an efficient accounting system in order to:

1. Protect public funds from the always present possibility of loss from carelessness, expenditure for the wrong purpose, theft or embezzlement, or the malfeasant actions of school officers.
2. Provide a systematic way to relate expenditures to the attainment of educational objectives through the operation of a budget and related reports and processes.
3. Provide an objective method of appraisal of the performance of school personnel in attaining the school's objectives.

4. Meet the legal requirements of the state and other governmental units for reporting basic information for comparisons, reports, and reviews.
5. Provide local school patrons with important information concerning the fiscal and academic activities and needs of the district.

Principles

The business of school administration is to receive, spend, and account for taxpayers' dollars for education in the most effective and efficient way in order to produce maximum educational benefits at minimum cost. Clearly, financial management of the schools is a means to an end, but that does not minimize its importance. Schools cannot achieve their instructional goals without the wise expenditure of public monies. Prudent disposition of funds requires that responsible school personnel adhere to some generally accepted principles of school accounting.

School accounting practices and principles have shown an evolutionary development over the entire period of school operation in this country. The modern accounting system in a typical large school district today is scarcely related to the unstandardized and inadequate "system" used in school districts of an earlier era.

The National Committee on Governmental Accounting developed a number of standard principles and procedures for governmental accounting that have general application to school accounting. Their standards included such principles as would (1) be compatible with legal requirements, (2) use the double-entry and general-ledger accounting system, (3) use uniform terms and standard classifications, (4) use as few different funds as possible, within legal and accounting requirements, (5) make "a clear segregation . . . between accounts related to current assets and liabilities and those relating to fixed assets and liabilities," (6) use the budgetary control principles, and (7) use the accrual basis of accounting principle.[1]

In spite of recommended principles and attempts to standardize practices, there are differences and variations that appear in every school accounting system. Each business administrator uses those accounting procedures that will help him most in implementing and accounting for the school's program. There are, however, certain general principles that may well be applied to form the basis for an adequate and effective accounting system in every school.

1. For further information, see Stephen J. Knezevich and John Guy Fowlkes, *Business Management of Local School Systems* (New York: Harper & Row, 1960), pp. 34–38.

1. *Accuracy.* There is little value in any accounting system that is not accurate. While audits are useful in discovering and reporting errors, they are a very poor substitute for original accuracy. More errors than an absolute minimum (which should be discovered and corrected immediately) not only make financial reports ineffective or useless, but may jeopardize the reputation of the administration or ruin the positive image that the school business administrator may otherwise have created for himself.

2. *Completeness and Currency.* Incomplete records of transactions and accounting records that are in arrears provide little help to the superintendent in his attempt to follow a budget, explain a fiscal transaction, or defend a policy concerning future budgetary allocations or expenditures. This means also that any information that the administrator or the school board needs should always be readily available. The actual fiscal condition of the school district should be known at all times. Regular reports of income, expenditures, encumbrances, unencumbered balances, and other useful kinds of information should be made periodically.

3. *Simplicity.* School accounting practices and procedures are intended to provide information to administrators, school boards, the state, and local citizens. As such, they are valuable if understood and worthless if not. Simplicity therefore is a necessity in school accounting practices. Their purpose is to explain to a relatively unsophisticated clientele what the school has done, how much it cost, where the money came from, what the total costs were, and what the fiscal condition of the district is at any particular time. There is no intent or purpose to deceive or to confuse anyone by extremely complicated accounting systems or professional jargon in explaining some of the district's expenditures or other transactions.

4. *Uniformity.* Comparisons of costs between school districts are misleading unless the items being compared are uniform and to some degree standardized. Account classifications and funding practices must be the same in all types of districts if comparative costs are to be valid and useful. State reports sent to the U.S. Office of Education are presumed to be made with sufficient uniformity to make them useful for such purposes.

STANDARD ACCOUNTING PRACTICES

Until recent years, in spite of much effort, little success was achieved in standardizing school accounting practices for American schools. According to Knezevich, "For over 100 years uniformity in terminology and procedures in fiscal material resource management has been a much sought after goal."[2]

The United States Office of Education has exerted a leading role in establishing recommended practices in school accounting procedures. Handbooks in 1940, 1948, and 1957 led the way in promoting uniformity in reporting school financial transactions. The 1957 handbook was particularly important in this regard. It was "the product of the cooperative efforts of five nationwide education associations and the Office of Education over a period of more than two years. Hundreds of individuals constituting a broad cross section of American education shared in its development."[3] The committee preparing the handbook selected items that provided information based on four criteria: (1) importance to a local district in the operation of its school system; (2) importance to local school districts throughout the country; (3) need for financial comparisons among local school districts; and (4) information that can be maintained as a record with reasonable effort.[4]

The U.S. Office of Education suggests that universal use of the standard accounts and terminology of the 1957 handbook will (1) help to insure appropriate initial recording of financial data; (2) improve the accounting for school funds; (3) improve school budgeting; (4) establish a sound basis for cost accounting; (5) improve the accuracy of local, state, and national summaries; (6) facilitate comparisons of financial information among communities and among states; (7) enable local and state educational authorities to obtain more suitable needed information for policy determination; (8) improve the accuracy of educational research; and (9) facilitate and improve reliable reporting to the public on the condition and progress of education.[5]

The 1957 handbook recommended the use of three chief receipt accounts: Revenue Receipts, Nonrevenue Receipts, and Incoming Transfer Accounts. It also suggested the use of fourteen important expenditure accounts: Administration, Instruction, Attendance Services, Health Services, Pupil Transportation Services, Operation of Plant, Maintenance of Plant, Fixed Charges, Food Services, Student Body Activities, Community Services, Capital Outlay, Debt Services, and Outgoing Transfer Accounts. The 1957 handbook was revised in 1973. This revised edition, *Financial Accounting: Classifications and Standard Terminology for Lo-*

2. Stephen J. Knezevich, "Resource Management and Educational Logistics," in Warren E. Gauerke and Jack R. Childress, eds., *The Theory and Practice of School Finance* (Chicago: Rand McNally & Co., 1967), p. 186.

3. *Financial Accounting for Local and State School Systems* (Washington, D.C.: U.S. Office of Education, U.S. Dept. of Health, Education, and Welfare, 1957).

4. Ibid., p. vii.

5. Ibid., p. xvi.

cal and State School Systems, is designed to serve the same users as the 1957 handbook served.

The 1973 handbook serves as a vehicle for program cost accounting at the local school and intermediate unit levels. It was planned so that when programs are identified and benefits can be measured, a full program, budgeting, and evaluating system can then be operated. The original (1957) handbook answered the need for a cost-accounting system that satisfied the legal and stewardship requirements connected with handling public funds, but the classification structure prohibited the ability to accumulate costs of programs.[6]

The value of the 1973 handbook is indicated in the following:

> New challenges and opportunities for the Nation's educational systems have caused researchers and educational decisionmakers to focus on new questions or at least look at old questions in different ways. The revised handbook makes it possible to organize data in a manner to permit the interrelating and combining of data elements that results in wide ranges of information. The goal of comparability is strengthened and achieved in the process.[7]

In addition to having the data classifications arranged for fund accounting and fund reporting, the manual has as one of its components additional dimensions of classifications, not financial in nature and incorporated from other handbooks in the series, which provide not only a means of relating resources and processes with cost, but, which also contain the elements of a design for a comprehensive system of educational information. The financial record made when acquiring resources can be duplicated and filed under each dimension for future analysis manually or can contain a code for each dimension and be filed electronically. In each case, the initiating acquisition request is used as the control for relating resources and processes with cost.

These classifications as they are defined and coded, do not constitute a system. Their items are grouped into mutually exclusive categories, sets, or dimensions. In system arrangements, some of the classifications are related in such manner as to become subclassifications of others. The procedure for filing and retrieving these dimensions becomes the system.[8]

The chart of accounts in the 1973 handbook was structured to enable planners to budget, program, and evaluate the resources, processes, and effectiveness of the school's objectives—in anticipation of the establishment and operation of PPB systems in school districts. The

6. Charles T. Roberts and Allan R. Lichtenberger, *Financial Accounting* (Washington, D.C.: U.S. Office of Education, U.S. Dept. of Health, Education, and Welfare, 1973),p.1.

7. Ibid.

8. Ibid., pp. 2–3.

adoption of such systems has been much slower in development than anticipated, in fact, such adoption in the near future seems highly unlikely because of the experiences of some states in unsuccessful attempts to initiate PPB systems. Since most school districts are still operating with the accounting system recommended by the 1957 handbook, the following summaries of receipt and expenditure accounts and code numbers are included here.

RECORDING SCHOOL RECEIPTS AND EXPENDITURES

The word *revenue*, like many other words, has a general as well as a specific meaning. The money received by a business during operation is often referred to as its revenue, an example of the broad and general definition. In school accounting procedures, however, *revenue* is used in its more specific sense to distinguish it from *nonrevenue* or *transfer accounts*. Here, *revenue* refers to money received by a school district that represents additions, but not exchanges, to assets that do not at the same time incur a comparable obligation to be paid at a later time.

Revenue Receipts (Series 10–40)

Under Revenue Receipts are recorded all revenues from local, intermediate, state, and federal sources. The chief local source is local property taxation. Other possible local sources are non-property taxes, tuition fees, earnings from permanent funds and endowments, earnings from investments and rentals, net receipts from revolving funds, gifts, bequests, and state and federal appropriations.

Nonrevenue Receipts (Series 50–70)

Those receipts that require that a future obligation be met or that merely change the form of an asset are called nonrevenue receipts. The money received from loans, bond sales, sales of property, and insurance adjustments fall in this category.

Incoming Transfer Accounts (Series 80–90)

Incoming transfer accounts are those funds which are received from other school districts for services rendered to them. They include tuition from other districts for pupils attending the receiving district. They also include transportation money received from other districts and other items such as health service funds.

The main items for the Receipts Accounts for a school district would include the following subdivisions:

Revenue Receipts (10–40 Series)
Series 10. Revenue from Local Sources
        11. Taxation and Appropriations Received
        12. Tuition from Patrons
        13. Transportation Fees from Patrons
        14. Other Revenue from Local Sources
Series 20. Revenue from Intermediate Sources
Series 30. Revenue from State Sources
Series 40. Revenue from Federal Sources

Nonrevenue Receipts (50–70 Series)
Series 50. Sale of Bonds
Series 60. Loans

Series 70. Sale of School Property and Insurance Adjustments
Incoming Transfer Accounts (80–90 Series)
Series 80. Amounts Received from Other School Districts in the State
Series 90. Amounts Received from School Districts in Other States

Other accounts or divisions are used when necessary or convenient. The coding system gives school accounting practices in a particular school the value that comes from comparing similar costs and receipts in other districts within the state as well as in other states. Receipt Accounts use the numbers from 10 through 99.

TABLE 13.1 Expenditure Accounts (100–1499 Series)

Prior to 1957	Recommended by 1957 Handbook	
General Control	Series 100.	Administration
Instruction	200.	Instruction
Auxiliary Services	300.	Attendance Services
	400.	Health Services
	500.	Pupil Transportation
	900.	Food Services
	1000.	Student-Body Services
	1100.	Community Services
Operation of Plant	600.	Operation of Plant
Maintenance	700.	Maintenance of Plant
Fixed Charges	800.	Fixed Charges
Capital Outlay	1200.	Capital Outlay
Debt Service	1300.	Debt Service from Current Funds
	1400.	Outgoing Transfer Accounts

THE USE OF CLEARING ACCOUNTS

School accounting systems provide for clearing accounts (revolving funds) in order to avoid distorting receipts and expenditures when there is a double handling of money. The use of such funds is common to most people. The practice involves receiving money from the operation of some activity (student-body activity or food services, for example) and then spending it for the same activity at a future time. If "Receipts" is credited when the money is received and "Expenditures" is credited when the money is spent, both accounts have been increased beyond their true state and the books do not then show either account as it actually is. To illustrate: If a school district spends $500 to set up an account for a particular purpose and then is repaid the $500, it is as if nothing has happened as far as "Receipts" and "Expenditures" are concerned. Neither account should be increased by $500, but the transaction should be shown through a clearing account. If, however, the activity does not repay the $500, such amount must be charged to the appropriate expenditure account. Clearing accounts make it possible and convenient to report the complete story of transactions involving the double handling of money without involving the "Receipts" and "Expenditures" accounts.

The 1957 handbook refers to seven kinds of transactions that include most of those included under clearing accounts: (1) activities financed wholly or in part by revenue produced by the activity, (2) prepayments or advancements, (3) abatements, (4) exchanges of one asset or liability for another asset or liability, (5) interfund transfers, (6) current loans, and (7) insurance adjustments.[9]

ENCUMBRANCE ACCOUNTING

Encumbrance accounting is important to any budgetary system. A commitment, such as a contract for services or a purchase order, decreases the available funds for other expenditures just as much as a check issued or an actual payment in cash. As soon as some action involving future payments of money is made, the proper account should be thus encumbered by that amount. Without such an up-to-date record the administrator may not always remember when the cash balance of a particular account has already been committed to another purpose. Encumbrance accounting serves the purpose of keeping the administrator informed concerning expenditure commitments. It is a necessary part of the ac-

9. *Financial Accounting for Local and State School Systems*, p. 105.

counting system of every school district. Proper use of such an accounting device will not only help to keep the accounts in balance, but it may save the administrator from the embarrassment that accompanies a second expenditure of money from an account that has already been depleted by a previous obligation. Encumbrance accounting is important enough for some states to require it of all school districts.

COST ACCOUNTING

Cost accounting has been an important element in business institutions for a long time. While used to some degree in most larger school districts, the practice has never reached such popularity in smaller ones. The argument that it is not needed in schools because the profit motive is lacking holds little weight, for all schools are faced with the necessity of getting the greatest possible benefit out of the least possible expenditure.

Cost accounting provides the necessary information to determine answers to a number of pertinent questions concerning various aspects of the school program. For example: What are the relative costs of various programs—the athletic program as compared with the physical education program? What is the cost (loss in state allocations of money) due to nonattendance of pupils? How do the costs of elementary education compare with those for secondary education? Speculation or guessing concerning the comparative costs of programs is of little value, but judgments based upon the expenditures may produce the evidence necessary to evaluate them more objectively.

The business of education is replete with examples of need for sound judgment in decision making. Fortunate indeed is the school administrator whose accounting system provides the information necessary to allow him and the school board to make decisions on the basis of adequate, reliable, and relevant facts and figures from a cost accounting system. No other basis can be considered as valid.

Cost accounting has two primary values: (1) it provides information for in-school choices and decisions in the expenditure of funds, and (2) costs for the same services can be compared with those of other schools. Too often, school personnel have seen the importance and value of the latter but have failed to recognize that potential in-school values of cost accounting exceed those that might come from comparisons with other school systems.

MACHINE ACCOUNTING

Much is being said in educational circles about the mass exodus of school districts from painstaking accounting for school funds by hand (with a limited use of typewriters, adding machines, and the like) to the much more glamorous and efficient business of machine accounting or data processing. Our interest here is related to the high cost of equipment necessary to install automatic data processing (ADP) or electronic data processing (EDP) equipment. At present the initial costs are prohibitive to the point that only large districts can afford such equipment, or for that matter can even afford to purchase such services from other districts, higher education institutions, the state department of education, or a private institution or business.

The advantages of the use of punched card machines and computers in school accounting have been summarized by the United States Office of Education and also by other groups. Perhaps the main advantage that accompanies machine accounting of this type is that it helps to eliminate or reduce the repetitive entry and reentry of information into books or simpler machines, thus conserving the time of the accountant. The same basic principles of accounting must be used, however. According to the USOE, "all these processes are simply techniques to replace the paper and pencil."

As useful as machines and computers are to the school finance accounting field, it is well to remember that even though they save much valuable time and have the value of instantaneous "memory," they are not a panacea and likely will not revolutionize the field of school finance in small school districts. Muller aptly expressed the point: "You will recall that in the 1930s the radio was going to revolutionize education . . . and in the 1940s films were going to revolutionize education . . . and in the 1950s television was going to revolutionize education. Now in the 1960s we hear that *computers* are going to revolutionize education."[10]

RECEIVING AND DEPOSITING FUNDS

The school accounting function begins with the receipt of funds from the county treasurer or other tax agency that collects local property taxes

10. L. A. Muller, "Education and the New Technology," in Edgar L. Morphet and David L. Jesser, eds., *Planning for Effective Utilization of Technology in Education* (Denver: Designing Education for the Future, August 1968), p. 30.

and from the state agency that allocates funds to local districts. There must be agreement between the instruments showing receipts of funds and the amount of such monies received.

The typical school board has control of its own budget and has custody of its own funds. Local property taxes are usually collected by a county tax collector, who transfers the rightful share to the school board treasurer(s) in his county. In some states the law requires that the school district pay the county for the collection of such taxes, but this practice is not particularly popular. The school board treasurer deposits tax warrants, state allocations, and all other school district monies in the bank or banks that the school board has designated as its depository.

The school board uses the same criteria for the selection of a depository for its funds as an individual would use when establishing his own account. Since the typical school district seldom has funds to invest, any difference in the interest rates available is only a secondary concern in the selection of a bank. Quality of service, financial standing, convenience to the board, and the integrity of its officials are the most important factors to be considered.

EXPENDING SCHOOL FUNDS

General authorization for the expenditure of funds comes from the budget and the minutes of the board of education. Under the direction of the superintendent, charges and obligations are made against the district accounts as provided by these two documents. Some boards of education authorize charges against the district by sole action of the superintendent but with full accountability to the board, while others require either preapproval or ratification at a board meeting of all expenditures or encumbrances above a predetermined amount.

Invoices received by the district office are checked for accuracy, approved by the responsible official, and then directed to the business office for payment. Other documents that legalize the payment of monies from the school treasury include such items as contracts, time cards, and legal claims by government (social security payments, for example). All original documents must show evidence of proper authorization and satisfactory acceptance of services rendered or goods received before such can be authorized for payment.

All original documents that serve as supporting evidence of money received or expended must be filed as official records of fiscal transactions. They become the supporting records from which audits can be made. Usually, the requisition, purchase order, and invoice or voucher for a particular transaction are clipped together and filed, forming a complete record of the events that authorized that particular expenditure. The original documents—receipts, contracts, invoices, checks and warrants, deposit slips, requisitions, purchase orders, payrolls, and other similar documents—provide the information necessary for entries in the ledger and journals maintained in the accounting system.

FINANCIAL REPORTS

The board of education and the general public are kept informed concerning the fiscal operations of a school district by various kinds of financial and statistical reports made by the business office. Typically, these include monthly reports of receipts, expenditures and encumbrances, and balances in all main budgetary accounts. The monthly report forms the basis for future commitments of funds. It allows the board to anticipate further encumbrances and points the way to budgetary control practices that avoid overexpenditures or even underexpenditures in specific accounts or funds.

The annual financial report is sometimes required by law as a newspaper report to the public. It includes a record of the district's fiscal operations for the previous school year. The amount of detail included is often subject to controversy in view of its high cost. While a statistical summary serves a useful purpose in keeping the public informed, it is doubtful that the complete detail of the district's fiscal transactions is worth the cost of its publication.

Other reports are made as deemed important and relevant by the superintendent or the school board. Reports including summaries of transactions made with the use of charts, graphs, pictures, and other visual devices have proven to be popular and effective in telling the financial story of the district. Many superintendents consider such reports to be one of the very best public relations devices at their disposal.

State reports, fiscal as well as statistical, are a requirement for most school districts. The value of such reports can hardly be overemphasized. They form the basis for legislative action and for information that various state agencies and groups use to debate the cause of education. The states submit a summary of these reports and other information to the U.S. Office of Education, which combines them and thereby provides comparative financial information that is then available to all the school districts of the nation.

AUDITING

When protection of property and money is being considered, as well as protection of the reputation of the employees involved, the administrator and the board of education turn to the audit for support. Auditing is usually the final or culminating act in the business of protecting the assets of the school district, and for that reason it is used in some form and to some extent by all school districts.

An audit is a systematic process or procedure for verifying the financial operations of a school district to determine whether or not property and funds have been or are being used in a legal and efficient way. It provides a service that no business—least of all an institution receiving and expending public funds—can afford not to use on a more or less regular basis.

Purposes

The purposes of auditing are the same now as they always have been, but the emphasis has changed dramatically. While discovery of fraud and detection of errors were the main functions of auditing in its earlier years, it has other, more important functions today, as indicated in the following statement by Knezevich:

> Detection of fraud is no longer considered even one of the main purposes of an independent audit. The aims of present day audit are to verify (1) that the financial operations are proper, legal and mathematically accurate, (2) that all financial transactions have been recorded, and (3) that the transactions are accurately reflected in accounts and statements drawn therefrom in accordance with accepted accounting principles.[11]

In spite of the foregoing, it seems likely that the average citizen, perhaps even the average school administrator, views the audit as simply a means of discovering financial shortages or misuses of public funds. That, however, is becoming less and less its main value to the school district. On a comparative basis, only a very small percentage of school audits disclose any acts of dishonesty in handling school money. On the other hand, every audit does result in some protection to the honest school officials who have been responsible for the fiscal management of the district. In addition, the audit shows the degree or extent of observance of state and district laws and policies, shows the financial condition of the district and the adequacy or inadequacy of accounting procedures, provides suggestions to improve the system, and gives an official review of the operations of the school system for the period of

11. Knezevich, "Resource Management and Educational Logistics," p. 203.

the audit. These are the values that make the audit worth its cost and that defend state legislatures in their statutory requirement of school district audits at periodic intervals.

Kinds of Audits

Audits or appraisals of school finance practices and records are of several kinds, but their purposes are the same—to satisfy state and local district requirements, to protect school funds, and to help establish public confidence in the operation of the schools. All types of audits form a basis for more efficient management of school monies, and at the same time protect the school and its employees from what might otherwise be legitimate criticism of the school's handling of public funds.

The most common kinds of school audits in general use are internal, state, and external. These may be subdivided in turn according to when the audit is conducted and its extent, or degree, of completeness.

Internal Audits

Internal (continuous) audits are conducted by technically qualified personnel already employed by the school district. They may be preaudits, current audits, or even postaudits. The last-mentioned usually are used in years when districts, in the absence of legal requirements, do not authorize an external audit. Internal audits function as an integral part of a control system that some districts use to assure school patrons of proper and careful management of school monies. By themselves, internal audits cannot guarantee such management, and they are in no sense a jusifiable alternative to the more professional external audits that are required at regular or periodic intervals in the various states.

State Audits

It has been pointed out that states are paying a high percentage of the cost of public education in most states. It is also known that school funds in reality are state funds. It follows, then, that the states have a direct interest in the management of local school district funds and therefore have a right, as well as a responsibility, to know how school finances are managed. Accordingly, the states require periodic audits of local district funds to ensure that the law is being observed in their utilization. The nature and extent of the audit varies considerably from one state to another. Those states that have many districts with limited resources and those that have many other institutions requiring state audits usually restrict the extent of state-required audits. Some states concern themselves only with local district observances of state laws governing expenditure of school monies. A few states require such an audit only every three or four years. Many states solve this problem by requiring that independent auditors perform this function on a yearly or other regular basis.

External Audits

External audits are those conducted by qualified agencies or individuals (usually certified public accountants). They are usually of the postaudit variety and may or may not be complete audits. The typical district will not require a complete external audit every year because of the cost factor, but this varies with the district's policy and the state's requirement.

External auditing practices follow state laws established for such purposes as well as certain other generally accepted accounting procedures. Complete year-end audits will usually include the following actions:

1. A study of the minutes of the meetings of the board of education. These records are the official authorization for all transactions that occur in the operation of the schools. The financial records of the school must be reviewed in terms of their agreement with the school board minutes and the legal requirements and regulations provided in state laws.
2. Verification of all receipts from all sources—revenue, nonrevenue, and transfer funds. This action includes a check on the allocation of receipts to the current-expenditure fund, to capital outlay, and to debt service accounts.
3. Verification of expenditures—requisitions, purchase orders, vouchers, and checks issued.
4. Review of the entries in the journal, ledgers, payrolls, and other similar books of entry and disbursement.
5. Reconciliation of bank statements, accounts, and investments.
6. A review of all subsidiary records, deeds, supporting documents, inventories, insurance policies, trusts, sinking funds, and numerous other records related to the operation of the school.
7. While some districts tend to disregard the audit for the student

activity and other internal accounts, these should be a part of every external postaudit. No school official should accept internal audits as meeting the audit requirements for such accounts and use as reasoning that they are not under the direct control of the board of education. There has been a tendency in the past to minimize or disregard the importance of spending taxpayer's money for such audits. In the average school district, these accounts are more likely in need of review and audit than the regular district-level accounts.

Thus, it is evident that a complete audit means exactly what the name suggests. In the words of Knezevich and Fowlkes, it is a "detailed study of the system of internal control of all books and accounts, including subsidiary records and supporting documents, to determine the legality, mathematical accuracy, complete accountability, and application of accounting principles."[12]

There are other kinds of audits in addition to the complete audit. For example, special audits (considering some particular phase or part of the school operation) are used when suspicion of error or fraud may be involved. Such an audit may be for other than a full fiscal year and may sometimes cover parts of more than one fiscal period.

The kinds of audits that school districts use are sometimes differentiated according to when they are to be made. For example, preaudits occur before the transactions actually occur, continuous audits occur during the length of the complete fiscal period, and postaudits occur after the fiscal period has elapsed.

The preaudit is an informal system to prevent unauthorized, illegal, or questionable use of school funds. It is an administrative procedure to protect the school from spending money for the wrong purpose or from the wrong account. In practice, it becomes a system of administrative control to assure school officials that embarrassing, unwise, or even illegal transactions are prevented. A certain amount of preauditing takes place in every school's operation where care is taken to prevent unwise expenditures of money. The officials of the school may not think of their informal preventive or protective measures as being preaudits, but they are, nonetheless.

The continuous audit is much like the preaudit carried through the entire fiscal period. Large districts may have a more formal organization, with a controller or other official to perform this function. It is important that this function should be conducted for the good of the educational program and that it should not become a position popularly referred to as "watchdog of the treasury," with its negative connotation.

12. Knezevich and Fowlkes, *Business Management of Local School Systems,* p. 144.

Selecting an Auditor

Boards of education may sometimes wish to employ an auditor on the basis of the size of his fee. Other factors are usually much more important in such a selection. The accountant's competence, reputation, experience with similar assignments, availability, and ability to get the job done in a reasonable time are very important. Competitive bidding for the assignment should never be used. Such a process is analogous to competitive bidding for the position of teacher or school superintendent.

Occasionally, some problems arise between the auditing agency and the school district. In no sense is the auditor being placed in a position of evaluating the judgment of the board of education in the use of school monies. It should be made clear to the auditor before he accepts the assignment that his function is to verify what has happened in the school operation and report his findings to the board—not to the individual who has been in charge of fiscal operations. As a technical expert, the auditor provides fact-finding and advisory services only. He should have a free hand in performing his services, and the records of the school district and the informational services of the school employees should be at his disposal. These matters seldom are cause for difficulty if an understanding is had before the beginning of the audit.

It is very important that the board of education and the auditor agree on the extent of the audit to be made and establish some reasonable relation between this assignment and the estimated cost. A complete audit on a per diem cost basis might go well beyond the need of the school district or its ability to pay.

Audit Reports

If, as generally assumed, it is important to require audits of a school's fiscal operations, it is equally important that formal reports of such studies should be made to the school board. Typically, such reports should include:

1. A letter of transmittal, including the general contractual agreement, the procedures followed, and other general information.
2. A specific statement of the scope of the audit and any limitations it may include.
3. A statement of the general and specific findings of the audit, along with the implications of such.
4. A list of recommendations for any improvements, additions, or deletions in the accounting system, together with the rationale for such recommendations.

5. A schedule of tables, figures, and summaries of pertinent information concerning school operations, including inventories, insurance policies, deeds, and the like.
6. Comparisons of school operations with those of other years, including receipts, expenditures, special accounts, and related information.

Administrators and Audits

No wise administrator advises his board of education to avoid or postpone periodic audits of all school district fiscal operations. The cost is little when compared with the service it may provide for improving and evaluating school business operations. No professional educator should leave his position or accept a new one where he is responsible for the management of school funds until some kind of formal audit, preferably by a certified public accountant, has been performed. The reputation of a school administrator, and to a lesser degree a teacher, is inextricably related to how the public views his management of public funds. An audit protects the prudent and detects the imprudent. It is therefore a necessity and not a luxury. A comprehensive audit by a qualified agency is the public's best possible assurance of the honest and efficient operation of school fiscal affairs.

PROTECTING SCHOOL FUNDS

The school ordinarily does not impose on itself the rigid legal and system-oriented rules for receiving and expending money that banks and many other businesses usually use. Unfortunately, some administrators and teachers have had little or no training in business and have not placed the necessary emphasis on this aspect of the educational program. No system, and no individual, can afford to handle public funds without strict compliance with fundamental and sound business practices—regardless of the amount of funds under his jurisdiction. Strict observance of basic accounting principles and the bonding of all school employees who manage school funds are absolute needs in any and all schools.

SURETY BONDS

The chief purpose of bonding school officials is sometimes misunderstood. Bonding is not done, as some suppose, because of questions about the integrity of the incumbent officials concerned. Rather, bonds are placed on officials because of the nature of the office itself. Bonding protects the school district against fraud or loss, but it also provides motivation to the official to be more businesslike in handling funds under his jurisdiction. Surety bonds are of three main types: fidelity, public official, and contract. There are many varieties and special forms of each of these.

MANAGEMENT OF CASH RECEIPTS

The receiving and disbursing of school district funds offer few problems for the money that goes through the normal fiscal cycle. Receipts for income, board authorization for the payment of verified invoices and other obligations, two signatures on checks for all expenditures, regular internal and external audits, and periodic reports to the board of education all add their evidence of the careful and legal management of school district funds.

But there is less approval of some methods of handling cash receipts—lunch money, fees, store sales receipts, student activity funds, and many others. School officials should establish guidelines, policies, and procedures to protect these incidental funds as well as to protect the reputation of those who handle them. Personal integrity is important, but so are records. The accounting system for such funds should follow acceptable guidelines, such as a centralized account for all student activity funds, receipts issued for all monies received, early deposit of cash receipts with only minimum amounts of cash left in the school safe at any time, an unlocked-safe policy when protecting small amounts of money of less value than the safe door, all payments made by two-signature checks issued only after proper authorization, accurate and complete records of all transactions, supervision of all accounting systems by a faculty member or administrator, continuous internal auditing by qualified personnel, and regular external audits.

Selected Readings

Adams, Bert K.; Hill, Quentin M.; Perkins, Joseph A. Jr.; and Shaw, Philip S. *Principles of Public School Accounting*, Handbook 11-B. Washington, D.C.: U.S. Government Printing Office, 1967.

Casey, Leo M. *School Business Administration*. New York: Center for Applied Research in Education, 1964.

Financial Accounting for State and Local School Systems. Washington, D.C.: U.S. Government Printing Office, 1957.

Jarvis, Oscar T.; Gentry, Harold W.; and Stephens, Lester D. *Public School Business Administration and Finance.* West Nyack, N.Y.: Parker Publishing Co., 1967.

Jordan, K. Forbis. *School Business Administration.* New York: The Ronald Press Co., 1969.

Knezevich, Stephen J., and Fowlkes, John Guy. *Business Management of Local School Systems.* New York: Harper & Row, 1960.

Roberts, Charles T., and Lichtenberger, Allan R. *Financial Accounting.* Washington, D.C.: U.S. Office of Education, U.S. Dept. of Health, Education, and Welfare, 1973.

Tidwell, Sam B. *Public School Fund Accounting.* New York: Harper & Row, 1960.

14

School Property Management and Insurance

Instructional and administrative personnel would be severely handi-capped and their contributions to the educational program greatly minimized in the absence or short supply of appropriate materials and equipment. This is particularly true in the modern school with its em-phasis on instructional media and educational technology. The days of providing teachers with only limited supplies of absolute necessities were not difficult ones for the school purchaser—who often was the teacher himself. But purchasing, storing, and distributing the vast array of machines and materials needed by the school staff today is another matter. Instructional devices, aids, office supplies and equipment, cus-todial materials and machines, and even the large amount of gadgetry used in food service preparation and in libraries (now known as instruc-tional materials centers) have revolutionized education and the manage-ment problems of the business offices of school districts.

The costs of such devices have increased in relation to the changes from such essentials as chalk, paper, pencils, textbooks, and a few maps and charts to the proliferated list so necessary today, which includes radios, recorders, television sets, projectors, teaching machines, com-puters, globes, charts, mockups, models, adding machines, cameras, duplicating machines, and numerous other items. It is doubtful that the average school patron, often somewhat conspicuous by an occasional visit to a school, is aware of the technological revolution that has taken place in education since he himself attended a public school. Unfortun-ately, this may cause him to be critical of the costs of instructional materials and machines. Certainly, he will not be fully aware of their tremendous value to the program of the school.

THE BUSINESS OFFICE

The school business office is often spoken or written about as if such an "office" always existed in a school system. Very often indeed there is no such place as an entity by itself; the office referred to is usually in reality only a part of the broad and all-inclusive function of the superintendent of schools. The superintendent in most small school systems is, in effect, the business manager, the purchasing agent, and perhaps even the accountant for the district. In some instances, he may also be the high school principal and even a part-time teacher. But regardless of the existence or the nonexistence of a specified business office in a school district, the purposes to be served and the problems encountered in school business management are much the same in all of them.

The superintendent of schools is directly responsible to the school board for the educational program in all its aspects. In small districts, he performs most of the functions of the business manager himself, sometimes with little, if any, clerical assistance. In medium-sized districts, an assistant superintendent or an official clerk may be assigned as the business manager. In the larger districts, the office has a staff of assistants, clerks, and office workers who perform the business functions of the school, usually under the direction of an assistant superintendent.

DELEGATING RESPONSIBILITY

In today's complex school community regardless of its size, the superintendent's chief responsibility is to provide educational leadership. Regardless of his ability or his stamina, he cannot possibly perform all of the generally accepted functions of the superintendency by himself. He must therefore delegate to others some of the duties of his office. Since the business aspects of the school are clearly secondary to the educational, he should delegate some of the former duties to capable employees but keep for himself direct leadership responsibility for the academic program. In delegating responsibilities to the members of his staff, he should remember that he is employed as an educational leader and not as an office clerk or purchasing agent, although he is responsible for supervising the work of all departments of the school operation.

Having selected someone to assist in performing the business management affairs of the school district, the superintendent is then free to devote his time and ability to improving the educational program in his school district. He cannot, however, escape responsibility for the conduct of the business affairs of the district. He must know what is being done, and he must keep himself in a position in which he remains qualified to advise and to confer with those who perform the functions of the business office. There is no school district large enough, wealthy enough, or with a large enough district office to jusify the superintendent's ignoring fiscal and material resources management.

Knezevich and Fowlkes emphasized the point of this argument in the following:

> But delegation of authority does not in any way justify ignorance of the principles of the functions and duties delegated. The chief adminitrator does not get rid of his responsibilities by this action, for the chief executive is held accountable for the acts of assistants. Top management has the further responsibility to consult with and review the progress and efforts of assistants. . . . It can be concluded that the principles of sound business management must be known by the large-system superintendent upon whom falls the burden of performing many of the details of business management.[1]

THE BUSINESS MANAGER

Occasionally, a newly appointed superintendent of schools discovers that the board of education has an employee, a treasurer, a clerk, a purchasing agent, or even a business manager who is directly responsible to the board but not to the superintendent. His office is viewed as a sort of "watchdog of the treasury." In effect, he is responsible for the money and the superintendent is responsible for the educational program, a real dichotomy in school administration. Although some districts in this country and in Canada make claims for the virtues of such an organizational pattern, few candidates for the superintendency would take a serious look at such a position. The objective of the school system is not to save money; it is rather to spend it wisely for the necessary goods and services a good educational program needs. The person in charge of the school must be in charge of the financial program, subject only to the board of education and the state code. All employees of the district must be responsible to the superintendent of schools, and he in turn must be accountable to the board.

Knezevich and Fowlkes raise their emphatic objection to the unorthodox separate arrangement in the following:

> Authority in school business affairs was one of the last responsibilities to be entrusted to professional school administrators. . . . The vestigial remains of board execution of business affairs and the reluctant delega-

1. Stephen J. Knezevich and John Guy Fowlkes, *Business Management of Local School Systems* (New York: Harper & Row, 1960), p. 4.

tion of authority in this area are still apparent in many school systems. One vestige of such board executive activity is the secretary or treasurer to the board of education. The secretary or treasurer to the board enjoys special status and his position often makes him coordinate with the general superintendent. The functions performed by such individuals include such activities as operation of business affairs, preparation of board agendas, and recording and keeping the minutes of board meetings. . . . If the superintendent of schools is the *chief* executive officer of the school system is there a need for an independent board of education secretary or treasurer? The answer is *no*.[2]

In fairness to boards of education, it should be pointed out that tradition is often the reason for such an arrangement as dual responsibility to the board for the operation of the schools. Over time, it is possible to change this arrangement by education and an exercise of patience and understanding on the part of the administrator. With the right attitude and working relation, too, it may be that even this paradoxical situation may be made workable.

FUNCTIONS OF THE BUSINESS OFFICE

The functions of the business office increase as the size and demands of the school district increase. Some writers have designated the so-called business management assignment of this office "fiscal and material resources management" in an effort to describe its function more comprehensively and accurately.

Regardless of the size of the school district, there are certain services that must be provided as a part of its business administration function. Some of the most important of these include providing supplies and equipment; operating and maintaining the school plant—cleaning, lighting, heating, and repairing; transporting pupils—purchasing and maintaining school buses, providing bus services; providing school food services—employing and supervising personnel, purchasing food supplies.

SUPPLIES AND EQUIPMENT

Increasing pressures on school administrators for economical use of the school tax dollar and mounting demands for additional quality and

2. Ibid., p. 14.

quantity in educational programs emphasize the necessity for public school administrators to take a critical look at their entire fiscal operations. The objective of producing high-quality education at minimum cost has never been emphasized more than at present. The emphasis now being exerted on accountability, the main thrust of the systems analysis–program budgeting–PPBS syndrome, and the negative reaction of taxpayers in their so-called revolt, all point to the need for operating schools more efficiently without reducing their quality. Since salaries of personnel account for a major share of the total cost of education, and since cost cannot be reduced without decreasing the number of personnel employed, the superintendent must turn to economical purchase and efficient use of school supplies and equipment to try to effect savings and avert waste.

Financial accounting systems treat supplies differently from equipment. Procurement of supplies represents a charge against the current operating expenditures of the district, but equipment (except replacement equipment) is a capital-outlay expenditure. It is therefore important to distinguish between the two terms. This was done by the U.S. Office of Education in its 1973 financial accounting manual:

A supply item is any article or material that meets any one or more of the following conditions:

1. It is consumed in use.
2. It loses its original shape or appearance with use.
3. It is expendable; that is, if the article is damaged or some of its parts are lost or worn out, it is usually more feasible to replace it with an entirely new unit rather than repair it (which is not true of equipment).
4. It is an inexpensive item, having characteristics of equipment whose small cost makes it inadvisable to capitalize the item.
5. It loses its identity through incorporation into a different or more complex unit or substance.

An equipment item is a movable or fixed unit of furniture or furnishing, an instrument, a machine, an apparatus, or a set of articles that meets all of the following conditions:

1. It retains its original shape and appearance with use.
2. It is nonexpendable; that is, if the article is damaged or some of its parts are lost or worn out, it is usually more feasible to repair it rather than replace it with an entirely new unit (which is not true of supplies).
3. It represents an investment of money which makes it feasible and advisable to capitalize the item.

4. It does not lose its identity through incorporation into a different or more complex unit or substance.[3]

The differentiation between supplies and equipment is sometimes very difficult to make. In the interest of consistency, schools and many other institutions sometimes use a fixed standard of cost as the arbitrary determinant of the classification of the materials used in the operation. Thus, a material costing $5 per single unit might be classified as a supply, while one costing more than that would be called equipment. Standardization and consistency in whatever distinction is made is important if cost comparisons are to be made from year to year or from one district to another.

PURCHASING

The direct charge of accountability now being emphasized in education may well start with the purchasing and procurement of school materials. It is among the first of the school's business operations to be studied and improved when the sometimes insistent pressure of public opinion is directed toward economizing school business operations. The increased size of schools and the recent influx of almost countless devices, machines, and gadgets necessary to implement innovative programs have combined to multiply the problems involved in purchasing supplies and equipment for a modern school program.

Purchasing supplies and equipment is not just the simple process of ordering something from a vendor, although some people are inclined to view it as such. Involved in the complicated process of purchasing are such problems as determining what is needed and in what quantity and quality, synchronization of the time of need and the time of delivery, providing the quality of the product needed without overspending the amount budgeted, storing what is required without keeping too much money invested in inventories, keeping unsuccessful bidders happy when they cannot compete successfully, and satisfying school personnel when recommended brands of items are not purchased or deliveries are late or some other reason prevents delivery of essential materials or equipment.

Great as the purchaser's problems are, planning and efficiency of operation will solve most of them. Written policies concerning the use of requisitions, of purchase orders, and of statements of standards or

3. Charles T. Roberts and Allan R. Lichtenberger, *Financial Accounting* (Washington, D.C.: U.S. Department of Health, Education, and Welfare, 1973), pp. 93, 108.

specifications are mandatory for efficient procurement and use of materials.

The problems involved and the procedures used in purchasing materials for schools differ somewhat from those usually encountered in business and industry. Businesses tend to specialize to some degree in certain kinds or types of products, while schools require a great variety of items spread widely over many areas. In private business, and to some degree in industry, procurement of necessary supplies and equipment is usually restricted within limited fields of a highly specialized nature. The materials required are usually selected, designed, or developed by technical staffs and passed on to the procurement officers. In general, however, school purchasing agents do not have the benefit of these specialized aids. They must therefore devise their own methods of evaluating quickly and properly the characteristics of almost innumerable items that appear on their requisition lists. In so doing, they must satisfy the needs of the various teachers at all levels of education and in many special departments.

It is obvious that in all puchasing, economy, speed, and accuracy are important. The measure of efficient purchasing in any organization is having a particular item in the right place at the right time, having been procured at a fair price. If this ideal is to be realized, it is essential that a procurement program be established that will provide adequate supplies and equipment that meet the immediate and long-range needs of the local school program.

Much has been written in textbooks and periodicals in recent years to provide school administrators with help in establishing workable and efficient purchasing departments and in improving those already in existence. The California Association of Public School Business Officials has indicated that despite differences in the size of school districts, and regardless of the character of materials procured or the sources from which they are obtained, some principles of purchasing procedures are commonly recognized as sound. Purchasing practices in a school district should:

1. Accomplish a definite objective in the shortest possible time and in the easiest manner consistent with accuracy and efficiency.
2. Provide simplicity to speed operations and reduce possibilities of error.
3. Establish procedures that are definite and understandable, to obviate friction, duplication, and confusion.
4. Fix responsibility for each step of performance.
5. Establish procedures that are sufficiently elastic to allow for expansion as the district grows.
6. Provide a system of procurement that is inexpensive and consistent with the job to be done.

7. Ensure that the system is adequate to perform with satisfaction the task for which it was created.

Policies Governing Purchasing

Effective school purchasing requires a systematic purchasing organization that is operated by established procedure. The first step in establishing such an organization is for the board of education to adopt written policies concerning purchasing. Such policies are extremely valuable, not only to the board, school staff, and pupils, but also to the patrons of the school. They bring clarity and understanding to school operations. Carefully considered and well-written policies are the basis for all board functions. They legalize actions and relieve employees of the responsibility of making policy decisions under the pressure of time or expediency. They help interpret institutional purposes and facilitate speed and accuracy in translating policy into action. They clarify the relationships of school board, superintendent, and staff to and among each other in the matter of providing materials for the school program.

To supplement the policies that the school board has adopted, the superintendent of schools or the assistant superintendent in charge of the business office should establish regulations concerning the procurement of materials that will serve as detailed guides for staff members. If the purchasing policies of a school district are to achieve the desired level of effectiveness, they must be generally known and understood by all persons who are affected by them. This necessitates that the most effective communication devices possible be used to make the information available to staff personnel and to vendors and interested patrons in the community.

Jordan and Brock suggest that purchasing policies and procedures should provide guidelines in the following areas:[4] (1) purchasing structure; (2) purchasing personnel; (3) establishing specifications; (4) selecting vendors; (5) purchasing procedures; (6) receiving and inspecting supplies; and (7) storing, inventorying, and distributing supplies.

Standardization

Many of the supplies that a school district uses can be of a standard size and quality without loss in effectiveness. Where such standardization is possible, the use of standard lists has certain advantages, includ-

4. K. Forbis Jordan and Dale E. Brock, "Principles of Public School Purchasing," *American School Board Journal* 49 (August 1964), p. 14.

ing reducing unit costs through buying larger quantities and through competitive bidding by vendors. Even when the personnel concerned help determine the standards and specifications of materials to be used, there will sometimes be justifiable reasons for buying special supplies or supplies with nonstandard specifications. Important as standards are in procuring supplies and equipment, no worthwhile school program should suffer unduly because of inability to use standardized materials.

Standardization practices usually result in a number of benefits to school districts. Standardization:

1. Allows lower costs from bids on large quantities of one item.
2. Reduces and facilitates repairs and replacements.
3. Reduces inventories, thereby reducing storage costs, and at the same time increases the amount of school funds available for other purposes.
4. Speeds delivery of materials or equipment.
5. Reduces the number of materials and equipment for which specifications must be written.
6. Reduces the work of the purchasing department, including that of business office record keeping.

One of the problems involved in determining the standards of quality that should be established, and therefore of price, is determining what quality in a product is required to achieve a particular function for a particular period. This is the same problem that the purchaser meets when buying an automobile for his personal use. He must decide whether a secondhand car of a certain quality will provide the proper amount and quality of service for the duration of his known needs, or whether additional investment in a new car will prove to be more economical in the long run. The school district purchasing agent facing the same problem may often be tempted to procure the least expensive item in order to provide for purchases of other items. All too often this results in employee dissatisfaction, poor performance, high repair costs, early replacement, and an unwise and uneconomical expenditure of school funds.

In determining the standard of quality, the purchaser should consider: (1) length of term for which the product is to be used, (2) the comparative service that each potential choice is known to have given, (3) prestige factors involved if any, (4) the extent of safety hazards involved if any, (5) the availability of the products under consideration, (6) initial cost and also upkeep costs, and (7) disposal problems and costs.

Specifications for materials to be purchased often require much time and effort in preparation if they are specific. When possible, districts take advantage of the standard specifications already prepared by private companies or by the Federal Bureau of Standards. The use of brand-name products will save the time of the business office in soliciting quotations and in ordering the product. It also provides some foreknowledge of the quality of the product being purchased. It has one important disadvantage: the user is often required to use one brandname product when his experience and his personal bias would strongly suggest the purchase of a different one, often at little or no additional increase in cost.

Quantity Purchasing

School districts usually try to buy in large quantities to save on original cost and to reduce office work and delivery problems. This kind of purchasing policy requires a knowledge of needs and assures the business office of budgetary control in all supply and equipment accounts. At the same time, the practice could result in tying up the funds of the district in unnecessary inventories, and also requiring large areas of district facilities for storage. It may also occasion early purchase of certain materials that later become undesirable because of teacher preference changes or because better materials are invented or discovered. This may result in having to use supplies or items of equipment that are outmoded, obsolescent, or not as effective as newer items. There is no standard rule for the purchaser to follow in equating quantity orders with more frequent orders. Experience with the products, as well as with the desires and working policies of school staff members, is necessary to determine the best policy for each district in quantity purchasing.

Bidding

Most states or local districts or both have rules and regulations concerning the need for competitive bids for the purchase of school supplies and equipment. Ordinarily, purchases or contracts for services for more than a stipulated amount or cost must be by bid. Here again, determining the maximum amount that does not require a bid is difficult. If the amount is low, little saving is possible, for advertising for and receiving bids is expensive to the district and also to the vendor. Low maximums also tie the hands of the purchasing agent, who may otherwise have the opportunity of making frequent small purchases at a saving. On the other hand, placing the maximum too high allows and encourages the district to purchase most, if not all, required materials without the formality and the savings of competitive bidding.

Bidding requires advertising, establishment of specifications, obtaining sealed bids or offers to supply the materials at a certain price, and board of education determination of the successful bidder. Bids are let to the bidder under a general policy of "lowest-best bid." This is not always the lowest bid in terms of unit cost. Other factors to be considered are quality of product, quality of service, ability of the vendor to provide the product or service or both (usually covered by a performance bond), time when delivery can be made, and reputation and fiscal responsibility of the vendor.

SUPPLY MANAGEMENT

Once the supplies have been ordered and received, the neophyte purchasing agent may think his problem is solved. But the problems of receiving, storing, and distributing supplies loom large in the average school district. The supplies or inventory have little value unless available when needed. The chief problem involved in receiving supplies is concerned with checking purchase orders against the goods received, noting the differences if any, calling any errors to the attention of the vendors, certifying delivery, and authorizing payment. This is the work of a careful and well-trained person. Irresponsibility in the receiving of supplies may cost the district money through errors in shipment or untold difficulties with vending companies. One of the advantages to be gained by receiving all purchases at the district or a central receiving warehouse is that it eliminates the possibility of careless checking often found when many individuals perform this service.

Supply Storage

In large school districts, the problem of supply storage often looms large. The district must decide between a central storage facility or several site-level facilities. The advantages of these two methods tend to balance out. Central storage provides for better district control and accountability and reduces the number of employees involved in storing and distributing supplies. The decentralized system assures more school unit control and guarantees availability of materials whenever needed but with less experienced employees involved in their handling.

As pointed out before, our primary concern is for the fiscal implications of the school's operation. The details of storage, distribution, and use of school supplies are therefore beyond the purview of this brief treatment. However, it is within the purpose of this work to suggest certain policies and procedures that do affect the costs of education. The following list of six requirements for an effective storage system seems pertinent:

1. All supplies must be stored in spaces that are free of destructive factors such as excessive heat or cold, moisture, vermin and insects, and fire hazards.
2. All storage areas must be accessible for both incoming and outgoing supplies.
3. All supplies must be so stored as to be readily available when needed.
4. All storage materials must be administered under the rule that old stock is used first.
5. A current inventory should be kept for each storage area.
6. Responsibility for proper operation of storage areas must be specifically assigned and clearly understood by all involved.

Distribution of Supplies and Equipment

Each school district will have its own special system for the distribution of supplies and equipment. The essential characteristics of any system will involve use of requisitions, records of distribution, and stock or inventory records.

The policy involved in the distribution of school supplies in the modern school is much different from the old and traditional policy of an earlier era. No longer are supplies stored in the darkest corner of the basement under the strongest lock and key system, and available only on certain days or at certain hours and distributed on the basis of a permanent short-supply philosophy. Instead of this, modern philosophy encourages and practices a policy of putting supplies where they can be seen and can be obtained with the least possible inconvenience to the teacher or other staff members. Modern administrative policy recognizes the value of materials in helping the staff achieve the purposes of the school. It is economically foolish to employ a teacher at a good salary and then deny that person a chance to succeed by limiting the supplies, the devices, and the other aids so essential to the educational program. The fear of waste with open shelves of readily accessible supplies that dominated the "lock and key" policies of earlier schools has proved to be groundless. Today's teachers use more supplies and greater varieties of them, but there is little if any evidence of their misuse.

SCHOOL INSURANCE

The main purpose of the school is to provide its pupils with high-quality education of the variety and quantity that will improve their behavior and competence as law-abiding and self-supporting citizens in the social milieu. But that purpose is not all-inclusive; the school's first responsibility involves maintaining the safety and protecting the health and well-being of all who attend. Education has relatively little value to the seriously injured pupil or to the one whose physical or mental health has been jeopardized or ruined through neglect or negligence on the part of anyone in the school community.

Too often in the past, school employees have given only limited attention to protecting the safety and maintaining and improving the health of their pupils. These activities, they reasoned, were the responsibility of other agencies of government and of the home. They often found their own academic or administrative responsibilities too compelling and too time-consuming to permit them significant involvement in the primary safety and health concerns of students.

Increasing Safety Hazards

The potential and the real hazards to the health and safety of pupils in the school complex are greater than is commonly believed. As schools have become larger, many of the dangers to its members have increased. From the automobile-motorcycle-bicycle triad of hazards outside the school itself, to the playground heavily stocked with potentially dangerous equipment, to the overcrowded classrooms, gymnasiums, and laboratories, the danger to life and limb manifest themselves on every hand. As a result, the importance of eliminating safety hazards, protecting the health of pupils, and providing adequate kinds and amounts of insurance is much greater today than ever before in the history of American education.

Most schools are not negligent in their attempts to provide pupils with a safe and hazard-free environment, but a few are. Every school, regardless of its safety record in the past, should constantly be reviewing and improving its policies and procedures to protect the safety and well-being of all members of the school community. In addition to the desire to protect schoolchildren, school staff members should remind themselves often of the fact that courts will look very critically on an institution whose members, who are required to be there by edict of the state, have not been given the greatest possible personal protection while in attendance.

While most schools do a great deal to protect the safety of people, there are other risks against which the board must protect itself. There is always the danger that buildings and property may be damaged, altered, or destroyed, or that some of their vital parts may be stolen, in spite of the best protection the school can provide. In addition, school personnel may become involved in tort action in the courts. It thus becomes increasingly necessary for boards of education and school administrators to know and observe state laws concerning safety precautions as well as to exercise their best judgment in providing insurance protection as it is related to all aspects of the school program.

Insurance Defined

Insurance, by definition, is a method and process of providing for cooperative sharing of the risk of financial or other loss in the event of some unfortunate incident. Here, we are concerned primarily with insurance protection against loss of life, acts of criminals, the alteration or destruction of school property or damage thereto, the liability of school personnel for tort action, and the personal welfare of school employees.

Insurance has been called a necessary expenditure to provide for benefits for an incident or emergency that the purchaser hopes will never occur. The risk taker (school or individual) purchases insurance from a professional risk bearer (the insurance company) as financial security in the event that some undesirable event occurs. No person looks forward hopefully to the burning of his home or his children's schoolhouse so that he or the school board will collect the insurance. The insured is merely trying to soften the financial blow that results after a catastrophe in the hope that the loss will not damage him permanently.

School Board Responsibility

The school board's responsibility for operating schools carries with it stated as well as implied powers necessary for the protection of public funds and property. It is taken for granted, too, that schools and their pupils must be given reasonable protection from interruption and loss from emergencies, disasters, or other less serious losses. The legal responsibility for such protection rests solely with the board of education in each school district, except in states in which such protection is provided at the state level. This is an important obligation and one that the board can ill afford to ignore or minimize. At stake are several needs; protection of the state's and local district's large investment in school buildings and property; financial protection for individuals in the event of injury, tort action, or death; and public protection against interruptions in the normal school process in the event of emergencies.

Just as a prudent individual protects himself against financial loss from fire in his home or place of business, so a responsible board of education will protect a community from the same risks with its school buildings. This is best accomplished by buying insurance in amounts commensurate with the size of the investment the district has in such properties.

Basic Principles

Since it would usually be unwise economically for a school district to provide insurance to protect it from all the possible risks such an enterprise might face, school boards are often faced with the problem of selection of those items or assets for which they are most obligated to provide insurance protection. There are a number of basic safety measures that school boards can use to help cover many of the areas or items of low-risk to aid and abet the insurance program considered necessary for high risk facilities and operations. These would include such things as loss prevention through good building design, safety programs, regular inspections of buildings, the provisions of adequate and modern fire-fighting equipment, and the accumulation of reserves to pay for any losses sustained.

As thousands of school boards have dealt with their insurance problems over a long period, certain basic rules or principles have evolved, such as the following:

1. A well-organized and conscientiously administered safety and loss-prevention program is not only inexpensive but also very effective in reducing injuries and property losses through accidents. Such a program is needed for humanitarian reasons, and it also is the best and least costly kind of insurance.

2. The board of education has a moral and legal responsibility to provide protection for its employees, its students, and its patrons against the ordinary accidents that often occur within the jurisdiction of the school. Once a discretionary power of the board, the provision for a well-conceived insurance plan is now a mandatory duty of every board of education acting within the legal framework and guidelines provided in each state.

3. The board of education has a moral (and sometimes a legal) obligation to formulate in writing its policies and regulations concerning the safety and protection of all those in the school community.

4. The insurance program of a school should be the result of careful study of risks involved, past experiences in the district, and the recommendations of consultants. The field of insurance is so broad and complex that school administrators cannot hope to advise their boards concerning such needs solely on the basis of their own knowledge and experience.

5. The insurance program should not be static and unchangeable, but should reflect changing needs and risks. To continue an insurance program year after year without evaluation and change or adjustment is a practice that only the inexperienced, the careless, or the uninformed pursue.

MAIN TYPES OF INSURANCE

Insurance on almost any risk can be purchased if cost is of no concern to the purchaser. Thus, insurance may be available for almost anything and everything the school board may want to insure. The establishment of insurance priorities is therefore highly important to the board. The following is a list of some of the most common kinds of insurance that a typical school board would want to consider. No priority is intended, for that would vary from one school to another.

1. *Fire.* Insurance on the building and its contents against loss from damage by fire; common to all school districts; may use coinsurance, blanket insurance, specific or specific-schedule insurance, or self-insurance.
2. *Extended Coverage.* Insurance that is added to fire insurance policies to cover miscellaneous risks, usually windstorm or tornado, smoke, loss by vehicular or aircraft damage to buildings, hailstorm, or riot damage; often difficult to obtain and expensive in riot-prone areas.
3. *Glass.* Insurance against loss of windows or door glass; usually too expensive for buildings with extensive window areas; some schools are experimenting with plastic windows that are nonbreakable in order to reduce high insurance costs.
4. *Boiler.* Insurance for protection against property damage, injury, and death due to boiler or pressure-tank explosions; a *must* for high-pressure boilers but not so necessary for low-pressure ones now being used in many schools.
5. *Floater.* Insurance to protect all valuables and equipment used by the school; originally was inland marine insurance, which protected property in transit from one location to another.
6. *Crime.* Protection against loss by burglary, robbery, or theft.
7. *Automobile; Bus.* Protection against damage or destruction and liability for damage and injury to others caused by district-owned automobiles or buses.
8. *Liability.* Protection against bodily injury or damage caused by accidents due to the negligence of employees or those sustained

on school-owned property; also protection to the school board in states that have waived the immunity rule for school boards.

9. *Workmen's Compensation.* State protection from loss to the employee because of injury or death resulting from his employment.

10. *Surety Bonds.* Protects the school district against loss or damage through dishonesty of employees.

11. *Accident.* Protection for pupils for injury sustained in the activities of the school.

FIRE INSURANCE

Financial protection of the large investment that every school district has in buildings, equipment, and other property is an absolute necessity. The serious predicament of the small school with inadequate or no insurance that loses its only building to fire is not easy to contemplate. If such an event should occur, no amount of explanation or rationale based on the board's opinion that insurance costs were beyond its budgetary provisions would satisfy the local citizenry, replace the school building, or in any way provide for the future school program. Thus, fire insurance is a necessity in order to protect the capital assets of a school district.

Rates Are Increasing

The ability of a school board to purchase fire insurance on public school buildings can no longer be taken for granted. Recent increases in vandalism and arson that have resulted from the militancy of students, and particularly from out-of-school dissidents, have had their effect on insurance companies and their willingness to insure school and other kinds of buildings. "Schools, once wooed by insurance companies, are now either flatly rejected or asked to pay higher premiums and to accept increased deductibles." This indication that some insurance companies may have overreacted to campus unrest does not alter the possibility that social problems of the day may have a deleterious effect on schools and on their efforts to protect the assets required for their operation. The penalties, difficulty in getting adequate property insurance and being forced to pay high rates for coverage, fall on districts with a record of few claims just as they do on districts with a record of many and high damage claims.

The current problem of securing insurance coverage is greatest in urban areas, particularly in those cities where vandalism is not new.

Some of these city school systems have been forced to close their doors for a short time after policies were cancelled or their renewal refused. Some of the larger cities use self-insurance; smaller city school districts are almost forced to count on greater state or federal financial assistance to help solve this threatening problem.

Determining Insurance Needs

Neither overinsurance nor underinsurance represents an economical expenditure of funds for a school district. Overinsurance is a financial waste, for the district can never collect more than the actual loss of a building. On the other hand, insurance companies never pay more than the value of the insurance policy regardless of a greater amount of loss. It is therefore expedient, for the interests of the school district, for fire insurance policies to be maintained at the right level at all times.

Determining insurable values of buildings involves original cost (excluding the cost of the site, architectural fees, foundations and other noninsurables), depreciation, and replacement costs. The insurable value is the replacement cost (minus noninsurables) minus the value of depreciation for the number of years the building has been in existence. Table 14.1 illustrates how insurable values are determined.

It is essential that school boards should know the insurable value of their buildings when they are insured. The presumed saving that may be made by a board that determines its own values for original purchase of insurance may be lost when fire insurance adjusters determine the value of claims on fire loss. The value of using qualified appraisers and professional services in determining insurance needs is obvious.

Fire insurance rates are determined in terms of the risks involved. The type of construction of the building, adequacy of the fire depart-

TABLE 14.1   Calculating Insurable Values of Buildings

Building	Initial Cost	Noninsurable Cost	Insurable Cost
A	$1,000,000	$140,000	$ 860,000
B	3,500,000	330,000	3,170,000
C	4,000,000	410,000	3,590,000

Building	Replacement Cost	Depreciation Age (Years)	Rate	Amount	Insurable Value
A	$1,500,000	10	0.02	$ 300,000	$1,200,000
B	4,000,000	10	.03	1,200,000	2,800,000
C	4,500,000	12	.025	1,350,000	3,150,000

ment and its water supply, kind and age of equipment, distance from the department to the school, and fire alarm systems are all determinants of the rates school districts must pay for insurance. Non-fire-resistive buildings require higher rates than those that are fire-resistive. Rates are lower for buildings that are near adequate and modern fire departments. Rates are also lower for insurance issued for longer periods; the typical term of an insurance policy for school buildings is either three or five years.

Coinsurance

School districts have generally favored a system of coinsurance for protection against fire losses. Coinsurance involves a sharing of the risk between the school district and the insuring company. "The coinsurance concept was developed as a result of investigation which showed that the aggregate sum of partial losses paid by insurance organizations exceeded the aggregate sum of total losses."

Coinsurance policies are usually written with either 80 percent or 90 percent coverage. This means two things: (1) If the school district maintains its required coverage (the 80 or 90 percent of insurable value which it chose), the rate will be less than if it allows its coverage to be less than the agreed-on percentage. And (2) if full coverage of the 80 or 90 percent is maintained, the insurance company will sustain the total amount of fire loss up to the value of the insurance; but if full coverage is not maintained, the district will share proportionately in every fire loss regardless of how large or how small it may be. As an example, suppose two districts each have school buildings of the same insurable value and one insures at 80 percent coinsurance and the other at 90 percent. Table 14.2 illustrates the operation of the insurance program in the event of fire loss.

The example shows that it is important for the district to have the correct amount of fire insurance as determined by its coinsurance agreement. Too little insurance causes the district to share in fire losses of any amount. The amount of insurance carried, written as the numerator of a fraction, and the amount required under the coinsurance agreement, which is written as the denominator, represents the fraction of any fire loss that the insurance company will pay. The district must stand the rest of the loss itself. Coinsurance is a plan that uses lower rates as an incentive for districts to carry the maximum amount of insurance that it has agreed to carry. Since any amount less than that agreed on makes the district liable for some fraction of any fire loss, districts are motivated to keep their coverage at the maximum. Since most school building fires do not result in complete loss of the building,

TABLE 14.2   Calculating Losses with Coinsurance Policies

	District A (80 Percent)	District B (90 Percent)
Insurable value of building (Replacement cost minus depreciation)	$3,000,000	$3,000,000
Required insurance coverage	2.400,000	2,700,000
Recoverable amount (with full coverage)		
Complete loss of building	2,400,000	2,700,000
Fire loss of $300,000	300,000	300,000
Fire loss of $6,000	6,000	6,000
Recoverable amount (with $1,800,000 insurance) Ratio of actual coverage to the amount of required insurance	3:4	2:3
Complete loss of building	$1,800,000	$1,800,000
Fire loss of $300,000	225,000	200,000
Fire loss of $6,000	4,500	4,000

less than maximum insurance coverage would never fully protect the district for any of its fire losses.

In light of Table 14.2, it becomes evident that a district must keep accurate and up-to-date records of property values and insurance coverage. Regular appraisals of property by qualified professionals is an absolute necessity. Appraisal services are often available through state agencies or insurance companies, usually at low cost to the school. Certain organizations, such as the National Board of Fire Underwriters, perform useful services that are now available to schools in the improvement of the fire insurance policies and standards necessary to protect public property.

EXTENDED COVERAGE

All the real and imaginary risks to buildings are not covered by ordinary fire insurance policies. For example, the risks of damage from riot, explosion, windstorm, tornado, hail, smoke, or aircraft are not ordinarily covered in such policies. Extended coverage policies, however, provide such insurance with some additional cost. Just what kinds of insurance and in what amounts the district should carry it are judgment factors each school board must decide for itself. Such decisions ideally will be made only after careful study of the experience, over time, of comparable districts in comparable locations and with the recommendations of the administrative staff (made only after consulting some of the leading professionals in school building insurance).

No school board, regardless of its revenue-producing ability, can afford to protect the school district from all possible hazards or risks. The cost would be prohibitive and would represent a degree of misuse of public funds. The insurance carried by a district should be determined on a "degree of risk" basis. For example, a school building near an air-port represents a different degree of risk from that sustained by one located in open country not covered by commercial airlines. Again, fire-resistant (sometimes erroneously referred to as fireproof) buildings in open country represent a much different danger or risk from what frame construction buildings in the same location offer. The responsibility of the school board is to protect itself and its clientele the best it can with insurance, keeping in mind the cost as compared with the risk involved in each unit insured. A good rule of thumb for the board would be to provide adequate insurance on all high risks; establish priorities and exercise sound judgment on all average risks; and, eliminate or minimize insurance on low-risk insurables.

STOCK VERSUS MUTUAL INSURANCE COMPANIES

In planning the insurance program for a school district, the question naturally arises concerning the advisability of dealing with mutual com-panies as compared with stock companies. A stock company is organized as a corporation that issues capital stock to be purchased by investors. Such stock becomes a money guarantee that the company will be able to pay losses even when premiums paid by insured participants are not large enough to cover them. On the other hand, mutual companies, since they do not issue capital stock, must depend on insurance premiums for the payment of losses.

SELF-INSURANCE

Insurance costs are determined by many factors including the probability of loss as determined by experience with large numbers of similar risks under similar circumstances. Thus, the danger of loss of several build-ings in a school district may be slight, particularly if they are scattered at random within the district. Under such conditions, a very large school

TABLE 14.3   Characteristics of Stock and Mutual Companies

Characteristics	Stock Companies	Mutual Companies
Capital stock	Issued to investors	Not issued
Ownership	Stockholders	Policyholders
Losses are paid from	Premiums (and when necessary from capital stock)	Premiums (and some companies assess policyholders for this purpose when necessary)
Risk rests primarily with	Stockholders	Policyholders
Profits go to	Stockholders	Policyholders[a]
Insurance rates	Usually higher in order to pay dividends to stockholders	Usually lower; sometimes subject to assessment to cover high losses
Legally available	In all states	In most states— especially if non-assessable

[a]Considered only as a refund of excessive premium charges; sometimes retained by the company to protect against future losses.

district with a large number of buildings and with adequate financial resources may decide to provide "self-insurance" for its buildings. The board may reason that the risk of loss of one or more buildings is offset by the large sum necessary to pay the insurance premiums over time. It may then proceed in one of three ways: (1) with no insurance— losses to be paid out of tax revenues or from special bond issues; (2) with the provision of insurance only on property with the greatest risk of loss and no insurance on the rest; or (3) with the provision for reserve funds (instead of premium payments) from which future losses will be paid.

The use of self-insurance in protecting schools in the event of fire loss is obviously controversial. The debate concerning it ranges from the argument at one extreme that such a procedure offers no protection whatever to the argument at the other extreme that some districts could and should insure themselves. Consequently, state law and the judgment of the board of education must provide the answer to whether or not to self-insure its buildings.

Knezevich and Fowlkes listed nine bases on which a sound self-insurance program should rest.[5] Summarized, these include: (1) there should be a large number of property units; (2) the amount of coverage per risk should be reasonably small and uniform; (3) hazardous prop-

5. Knezevich and Fowlkes, *Business Management of Local School Systems,* pp. 276–77.

erty units should be insured with other underwriters; (4) the risks covered should be independent of one another; (5) there should be a gradual accumulation of a self-insurance fund and a gradual transfer from commercial underwriters to self-insurance; (6) favorable loss experience during the preceding 10- or 20-year period should be conservatively interpreted; (7) only districts in sound financial condition should plan for self-insurance; (8) self-insurance funds should be kept inviolate; and (9) there must be careful management of self-insurance reserve funds.

STATE-OPERATED INSURANCE ON SCHOOLS

The property owned by local school districts is, in reality, state property. The school operates it as an agent of the state. A few states have emphasized this point by providing in some manner for state-operated or state-financed school insurance programs. There is some evidence that this arrangement reduces the cost of coverage, with no negative effect on the state providing it. In spite of the presumed advantages of such a plan, there has been little stir in this direction. Roe reported that only five states were using such a plan by 1961, even though one was inaugurated as early as 1900 in South Carolina. With the difficulty that some urban schools are having in finding companies willing to insure school buildings at competitive prices, there is some notion that state-operated or even federally operated insurance programs may become necessary in the years to come.

LIABILITY INSURANCE

With the slow, but almost certain demise of the archaic immunity rule of school board liability for tort action in the several states, providing liability insurance becomes a relevant consideration. While the question, "May school funds be legally expended for liability insurance to protect school boards for the torts of its employees in common-law states?" still produces more than a little controversy, there is no such paradox in the states that have abrogated that rule. The law and a moral sense of fairness to pupils require that for their protection all those who have a responsibility for pupils' safety, welfare, and education be insured. In the common-law states supporting the immunity principle, this means liability insurance on school employees at district expense; to the gradually increasing number of states that have cast aside the immunity rule by either court edict or state statute or both, this means liability insurance on school employees *and* school boards at public expense.

Regardless of whether the law mandates or simply approves school district liability insurance on itself or its employees, school boards have moved to provide whatever liability insurance coverage is necessary to protect all those with legal liability. This is a necessary part of the cost of education and one that experienced boards of education will not refuse to approve.

REGULATION OF INSURANCE

It is necessary that the broad and encompassing field of insurance be regulated by some agency of government to protect all parties concerned. Without regulation, the cost of insurance could be placed at almost any point at the same time that some companies could default in their insurance payments to the parties who had suffered losses.

Most states control insurance companies through the office of a state commissioner. Through his office, insurance companies are approved to sell insurance if they meet the state rules and regulations that apply. The possibility of deception or fraud is decreased under this or any other form of state regulation. School boards need to become familiar with the general pattern in their state for control of this important service to school districts and to any other groups or individuals using insurance services. Among many other benefits to be obtained by the school board from such regulatory procedures, there is the value that comes from obtaining a reliable rating of all insurance companies licensed to operate within the state.

Selected Readings

Candoli, I. Carl; Hack, Walter G.; Ray, John R.; and Stollar, Dewey H. *School Business Administration.* Boston: Allyn and Bacon, Inc., 1973.

Jordan, K. Forbis. *School Business Administration.* New York: The Ronald Press Co., 1969.

Knezevich, Stephen J., and Fowlkes, John Guy. *Business Management of Local School Systems.* New York: Harper & Row, 1960.

Lee, Lamar, and Dobler, Donald W. *Purchasing and Materials Management,* 2nd ed. New York: McGraw-Hill, 1971.

Linn, Henry H., ed. *School Business Administration.* New York: Ronald Press Co., 1956.

15

Personnel Administration and School Finance

While in industry and other fields the term personnel refers to those employed in a particular undertaking, the educational field has adapted it to mean the complement of a school—the staff and also the students. Thus, education refers to "employed personnel" and "student personnel."

This chapter is concerned only with the administration of the services of school-employed personnel. It deals largely with the effect salary schedules and fringe benefits have on the rising costs of education. It is not particularly concerned with the "how" or the methods being used to determine those costs. Hence, the important part that negotiations and collective bargaining play in setting salaries, wages, and fringe benefits is recognized but is not discussed nor deemed important to the subject at hand. It matters little to the administrator of a school district budget whether a particular percent of salary increase or the cost of a certain fringe benefit came because of negotiation or because of the work of a teacher salary committee, or by any other process. For that reason, this chapter does not discuss the details of salary determination.

PROBLEMS IN SCHOOL PERSONNEL ADMINISTRATION

Many difficult problems face the administrator and the board of education in the administration of personnel services; most of them are directly concerned with the expenditure of money. Some of the most tenacious of these problems include: (1) determination of the best possible salary schedule in terms of teacher and other staff requirements as well as the funds that are available; this problem involves determining the size of the beginning salary as compared with the maximum, the number and size of increments in each classification, and evaluation of experience in other districts; (2) determination of the other factors that should be used to determine placement of teachers on the salary schedule, for example, merit pay, dependency allowances, and extra pay for extra service; and (3) determination of the policies and procedures to be followed in moving from one salary schedule to another.

Since more than 75 percent of the current expenditures for public education is involved in providing financial rewards for the services of school personnel, the subject of personnel administration is of prime importance in any study of financing education. No school can attain its goals unless it has a corps of competent teachers and other staff members. At the same time, no school can provide the qualified personnel so necessary for its purposes unless sufficient funds are available to provide the adequate salaries and fringe benefits required.

Perennial Nature

Some of the persistent problems involved in personnel administration are of long standing, and their "solutions" have often been found each year in some measure of socioeconomic crisis. Salary increases and the determination of the extent and nature of fringe benefits have a notorious recent history of perennialism and increasing confrontation between teachers and local boards of education.

Personnel administration in the public schools has lagged behind the policies and practices that business and industry generally use. Satisfactory personnel policies, including recognition of the worth and contribution of school personnel to the social as well as the economic well-being of the community, have been minimal or even missing in many public school systems. Although business and industry have recognized for a long time that their success largely depends on qualified and satisfied employees, many schools have not shown positive evidence of this relation.

Changing Personnel Relations

Recent years have seen extensive and dramatic changes in school personnel administration. Educators, long known for their complacency and subordination to the voice and will of school boards and the general public, have risen to assert themselves. No longer content to accept willingly what school boards offer as compensation for services, teachers and their professional organizations are demanding a larger part of the tax dollar in higher salaries, better working conditions, and increased fringe benefits. While many members of this once beleaguered profession, especially those of an earlier era, decry the tactics that have had to be used to attain such improvements, few will deny the effectiveness and the implications resulting from the effort. This is not to presume that the problem is solved, for it is far from that. It is to emphasize that the status of the teacher needs to be improved even though unfortunate and drastic procedures seem to have been the only way open to the profession to obtain economic and social equality in the community. Undoubtedly, the ethics involved in teacher strikes, withholding of services, sanctions, and the like, will be debated by the American people for some time.

Textbooks lauding teachers and teacher organizations for their non-strike policies now appear to be old-fashioned and out of date. The strike, right or wrong, is now a part of the offense used by the profession to attain its objectives. The reversal of previous position in this matter has changed significantly in recent years, as indicated in the following:

> The past school year from August, 1967, through June, 1968, was witness to a veritable explosion in teacher strikes and work stoppages— a total of 114. These strikes accounted for over one-third of the number of teacher strikes and 80 percent of the estimated number of man-days involved in strikes since 1940. They occurred in 21 of the 50 states and in the District of Columbia, and ranged in length from 1 day to more than 3 weeks. . . .
>
> Many editorials in affected communities and nationally syndicated columns viewed striking teachers as heretics; many other editorials viewed them as martyrs. While some citizens applauded the teachers, others sought punitive action against them.[1]

The trend has continued in recent years. However, our concern here is with only one aspect of the problem, the effect of teacher negotiations and strikes on financing education. It requires no figures and very little imagination to predict that the militant actions of teachers will result in higher salaries and greater fringe benefits and even better working conditions for them. There is no desire here to enter the political forum that debates their need or their justification. Neither is there any disposition to contest or to defend the apparently changing ethics of the teaching profession. The position here is very simply stated: the increased militancy of teachers, regardless of form or of justification, will increase the cost of public education, which will necessarily be reflected

---

1. *NEA Research Bulletin* 46, no. 4 (Washington, D.C.: National Education Assn., December 1968), pp. 113–14.

in increases in tax sources and tax levies. The implication of this prospect is that a firmer basis must be formed for more adequate financing of education.

Asnard noted the probable effect of teacher–school board negotiations on the costs of education in the following:

> No doubt, teacher–school board negotiation, in and of itself, will cause educational expenses to rise. It cannot be proven that negotiation has caused or will cause expenditures to increase more than they would have without negotiation. Nevertheless, the implication that there will be an impact on the school budget is clear.
>
> The budgetary impact of other matters cannot be overlooked. The more experienced in negotiation educational personnel become, the greater the realization that for many school personnel this is virgin territory. Therefore, there will be the cost of training personnel in the art of negotiating. Further, if arbitration becomes necessary, there will be added expenses.
>
> Moreover, negotiation will be blamed for much more than its share of the increased costs, when in reality, negotiation will merely accelerate expenditures for education which should have been made in past years.[2]

Expanding Role of Personnel Administration

As the size of the school complex has increased, the need for improving school personnel services also has increased. Likewise, as the number of teachers in a school or community has increased, the voice of the profession has been magnified. To the perennial concerns faced by school boards related to selection and recruitment, orientation, assignment, and payment of instructional and other personnel have been added the relatively new concerns involved with professional negotiations and all of its ramifications. The calmness and matter-of-factness that characterized school personnel administration to the middle of the century has been replaced by an unsureness and seriousness that borders on confrontation between school boards and teachers in today's administration of personnel services.

Nygaard and Roelfs referred to ten factors that justify the expanding role of personnel administration in the public schools:

> Several factors justify the expanding role of personnel administration and indicate no reversal in the trend to the present commitment to quality education. Among these factors are the (1) manpower shortage and the

---

2. Robert R. Asnard, "Negotiation, the School Budget, and the Future," in *Interdependence in School Finance: The City, the State, the Nation* (Washington, D.C.: National Education Assn. Committee on Educational Finance, 1968), p. 172.

short supply of qualified teachers,[3] (2) urbanization and unique problems of financing education in large cities, (3) the growth of teacher union membership and the absence of a unified school employee organization, (4) the employment of sanctions and collective bargaining procedures by teacher groups, (5) the demands and consequences of automation as it will affect both teaching and nonteaching groups, (6) the public's persistent demand for more and better general, technical, and professional education, (7) the increased concern for education of the dropout, the juvenile delinquent, the migratory child, minority groups, and the exceptional child, (8) experimentation on new concepts of staff utilization, (9) national concern for and development in many states of community colleges, adult education programs, and reshaped vocational education programs, and (10) the gradual move toward a longer school year and enjoyment of teachers and other school employees on a yearly basis.[4]

TEACHER SALARIES

Sound personnel policies are needed to insure that expenditure of a major portion of the school budget is earmarked for the essential purpose for which schools are established—quality instruction in the classrooms. . . . The lack of policy in personnel matters leaves the door open for political selection and favoritism, sudden dismissals, individual bargaining, job insecurity, inaccurate communication and misunderstanding within the organization.[5]

Since the chief function of the school is to provide those who attend with human services in the form of high-quality academic instruction, the biggest cost of public education is salaries to instructional personnel. Thus, the problems of school finance are directly related to the problems encountered in personnel administration.

The problems related to providing increases in teacher salaries and also satisfactory fringe benefits are not new to the field of school administration. Teachers have been among the last of the occupational groups to obtain financial compensation commensurate with their training and experience. Salary increases and generally improving fiscal policies of the last few years have, however, brought some hope for a satisfactory outcome.

3. This part of the quotation is no longer true.
4. Joseph M. Nygaard and R. M. Roelfs, "Personnel Policies and Public School Finance," in Warren E. Gauerke and Jack R. Childress, eds.,, *The Theory and Practice of School Finance* (Chicago: Rand McNally & Co., 1967), p. 315.
5. Ibid., p. 312.

Salary Schedules

Salary schedules for teachers are a product of the second quarter of this century. Only a few of the progressive city school systems were using such schedules to any important extent prior to the 1920s. The bargaining policies involving higher salaries for high school teachers than for elementary teachers with the same qualifications, and many other now outmoded practices, preceded the formal salary schedule.

As salary schedules developed, they gradually became the single-salary variety (equal pay for personnel with the same qualifications and experience without regard to sex, grade level to be taught, number of dependents, or other previously used factors). Experimentation with merit pay or dependency provisions or both in salary schedules was conspicuous with its lack of permanent success in satisfying the teachers involved, the school boards, or the general public. At the same time, defense of the single-salary schedule became no less difficult, for mere passage of time without evidence of teacher improvement has always been difficult, if not impossible, to defend as *the* criterion for salary increases.

Merit Provisions in Salary Schedules

Even though it is impossible to defend the philosophy of the single-salary schedule, which ostensibly defends equal salary increases for all teachers in the same classification with the mere passage of time, its opposite—merit pay—has not yet proved its lasting worth in very many instances. The arguments have changed little in the last half-century; the salaries of teachers should be determined by the merit or contribution teachers make to the education of boys and girls. But such merit cannot be measured objectively. Consequently, the subject is under constant research, but its practical application is never realized. This was illustrated by a recent study by the NEA Research Division:

> Only 85, or 7 percent, of the 1,221 teacher salary schedules analyzed by the NEA Research Division for inclusion in its 1969–70 salary schedule studies indicated additional compensation for superior teachers. This kind of provision is usually one of three major types.
>
> The first . . . includes provisions for exceeding the teacher salary schedule by definite dollar amounts. As a rule, these merit supplements are granted either before or after the regularly scheduled maximum has been reached. Requirements for eligibility vary from system to system, but most merit provisions awarding definite dollar amounts are applicable only after the teacher has served several years in the system; many apply only after the regularly scheduled maximum has been reached through normal progression on the schedule. . . .

A second kind of merit provision is the authority retained by the board of education to exceed the schedule for "outstanding" or "meritorious" service by teachers and sometimes by other members of the instructional staff. . . .

The least frequently reported type of merit is a statement granting the board of education power to accelerate the progress of outstanding teachers on the regular schedule by granting double increments, or the like. . . .[6]

Extra Duty Salary Supplements

The practice of adding salary supplements for additional services of teachers is becoming rather popular. Such a practice began with small stipends for coaching some of the important sports—football and basketball in particular. The rationale for this beginning centered around the many extra out-of-school hours required in many athletic programs. From that beginning, the practice has spread to many other fields of activity. There are at least three significant objections to this practice: (1) it often tends to create problems between those who receive such supplements and those who do not; (2) it is difficult to find a teaching area in which such supplements could not be justified if the teacher is making a maximum effort to develop it; and (3) such a practice tends to erase some of the characteristics that education must possess if it is to be a real profession; teachers under this system tend to think in terms of the time required to perform a particular function rather than in terms of units or elements of service.

Salary supplements for extra duties represent one means of avoiding the evils of the lockstep single-salary schedule. Defensible or not, the practice represents an attempt to determine salaries on the basis of services rendered. Its deficiencies come from the fact that it is generally a quantity rather than a quality measurement.

Salary Scheduling Problems

The teacher is a public employee and as such suffers from the undenied fact that salaries paid out of public funds usually are not competitive with those paid in the private sector where the profit motive is in control. Government employees at all levels are victims of the same unwritten law of economics. The salaries paid in the public sector are controlled by boards or administrators that are sworn to protect the

6. *NEA Research Memo 1970–7* (Washington, D.C.: National Education Assn., April 1970), p. 1.

public treasury; in the private sector the individual operator or the board of directors of a business is free to pay whatever is required in the competitive complex in which they are operating. Then, too, the latter can usually measure quite objectively the amount of production of the worker, but the controlling board of education has real difficulty in measuring the increased production of services resulting from the work of higher-paid teachers.

Salary schedules, regardless of their base or structure, must be operable as minimal in nature. Even the poorest teacher, or the teacher with the fewest dependents, or the teacher who is most devoid of training or experience, must be paid a living salary if his services are engaged. Provisions for extra pay for extra service, merit pay, or any other special consideration must be additions to this minimum schedule. While all these addends are controversial and somewhat inimical to the professionalization of education, they add to the total cost of the educational program. Merit-pay provisions have not proved successful except in a few isolated instances. Dependency provisions have been used in a few districts, but they defeat their purpose when a teacher with a number of dependents attempts to obtain a new position in competition with another equally qualified candidate with fewer dependents. On the other hand, extra pay for extra services is increasing in popularity. "The practice of adding supplements to teachers' salaries for guidance of pupil-participating extracurricular activities is widespread, and consequently, there is considerable interest in information on extra pay for extra duties."[7]

TRENDS IN SALARY SCHEDULING

The business of salary scheduling is not static, for innovations and changes are constantly being introduced into the process. Such additions and improvements usually add additional weight to the increasing costs of education and at the same time decrease the unfairness and inequities that have so often been an integral part of salary schedules in the past. Some of the most important discernible trends in salary scheduling include:

1. Retention of the single-salary schedule as a minimum or base scale, with its virtual elimination of individual bargaining for salary purposes; special cost-of-living increments and dependency clauses will be minimized or eliminated.

7. *NEA Research Bulletin* 48, no. 2 (Washington, D.C.: National Education Assn., May 1970), p. 42.

2. Continued interest, with serious consideration given to salaries based on traditional or newer measures of teacher effectiveness or merit; it is likely that specific progress in this direction will be slow, however.

3. Greater emphasis on index salary schedules that will facilitate the salary determination for a differentiated staff and at the same time give more favorable salary consideration to career teachers at or near the top of the salary scale, and wider acceptance of these schedules.

4. More attention, with probably continuing controversy, to salary supplements for the extra services rendered by some teachers— particularly in supervision of extraclass activities.

5. More recognition of the cost-of-living factor in determining salaries at all levels, with greater concern for the demands of teachers for generally higher salaries.

6. More attention to, and application of, the use and benefits to be derived from longer-term contracts for those teachers who desire them; 10-, 11-, or 12-month contracts will likely be offered to many more of the instructional staff than receive these contracts now.

7. Increased annual salary increments at all levels with a slight decrease in the number of increments to reach the maximum salary in most categories.

8. Salary schedules that will continue to be written in such a way as to encourage additional academic and professional education for teachers.

9. More and more districts will make progress in adopting salary schedules by which the career teacher will be able to double his beginning salary in about ten or twelve years.

FRINGE BENEFITS

School districts were generally slow in accepting the functional value of fringe benefits to teachers and other school employees. Business and industry led the way in inaugurating such benefits as retirement plans, tenure, sick-leave privileges, and insurance benefits. For the most part, these are benefits that have entered the educational scene in the last half-century, most of them having been made available only since World War II. In today's competitive market for goods and services, all these fringe benefits have become important parts of the rewards for service of publicly as well as privately employed personnel. Their importance is now recognized as being great, and as necessary to employed personnel in one sector as in the other.

Some of the important aspects of these fringe benefits as they apply to education include the following:

1. School boards, like private employers, have discovered that fringe benefits rank next to attractive salaries and good working conditions as motivators of efficiency and maximum production of personnel.
2. Fringe benefits serve a double purpose: (1) they provide needed personal benefits that teachers often would not provide for themselves; and (2) they are provided without increases in the income taxes that would accompany the substitution of the same benefits paid for by the teachers themselves from increased salaries.

TABLE 15.1   A Summary of Fringe Benefits

Program	Frequency	General Provisions
Retirement	In every state	A guaranteed amount (depending on length of service and contributions) on retirement; disability and death benefits; withdrawal required when employment in the state is discontinued, but may be reinstated on return; withdrawal privileges (with interest) of employee contribution for those who leave the system before retirement; some plans provide for investments in stocks and mutual funds that will offset any losses due to inflation.
Social security	Nationwide	Joint contributory: members pay part and the state pays part; available to certified and usually to full-time noncertified employees. Federal program, which supplements state retirement; survivor benefits for on-the-job workers; death benefits; guaranteed monthly income on retirement; employee takes benefits with him as he moves from one state to another.
Sick leave	In nearly all districts	Full salary while employee is ill—up to a stipulated number of days, which are usually cumulative to some established maximum number. Required in some states; some districts pay teachers for unused sick-leave days accumulated; not usually available to noncertified employees.
Personal leaves	In relatively few districts	For emergencies other than illness; usually not more than 1 to 5 days per year; the circumstances of each request are usually considered on their own merits, rather than according to a universal policy; not usually available to noncertified personnel.

TABLE 15.1 *(Continued)*

Program	Frequency	General Provisions
Leaves of absence	In relatively few districts; becoming more widely accepted	Usually provides for extended leaves without salary for study or professional improvement, disability, political activity, travel, or maternity reasons. Some districts provide some compensation for sabbatical or improvement leaves for certified employees; seldom available to noncertified personnel.
Insurance	Becoming widespread; most districts are using it in some form	Employer provides benefits without increasing employee's salary, thereby saving the income tax due; usually provides group insurance: health and accident, hospitalization, and life. Many districts now provide liability insurance for tort action on all school employees.
Workmen's compensation	Nationwide	Provides various options of benefits for injury and disability of all school employees; usually required by the states as protection for the risks of employment; mandatory in some states, optional in some, and not available in one or two others.
Tax-sheltered annuities	Nationwide	Federally granted privilege to public school teachers to invest part of their earnings in an annuity payable at a later time; delays federal income tax on these earnings until the benefits are received; since the retired teacher will probably be in a lower tax bracket, there will be tax savings.
Severance pay	In very few districts	Employee usually gets the value of his unused sick leave and other unused leave pay; a very recent and infrequently used fringe benefit; not available to non-certified personnel.
Income tax deductions	Nationwide	Provides income tax deductions (federal) for certain necessary and approved expenses of public school teachers while studying and otherwise improving their professional training required for retaining their present position of employment, as required by the school district or the state; not available for the purpose of position advancement.

3. Fringe benefits help to increase employee job satisfaction and thus reduce disruptive curricular changes resulting from faculty resignations and consequent replacements.
4. Some of the matching employer costs of retirement, insurance, and other fringe benefits are now being absorbed as state rather than district expenditures, thus making such benefits available to the personnel of financially weak districts as well as all others.

TEACHERS AND SCHOOL FINANCE

It is no secret that in the past teachers as a group have not been particularly concerned or informed about the rudiments of school finance. The manifold stories of teacher naiveté in this field have seldom been exaggerated or magnified. A few teachers received their initiation to the subject when their local or state professional organizations appointed them to teacher-salary committees, but the problem of financing education was of little interest to the rank and file classroom teacher.

The proverbial pendulum is slowly beginning to swing in the opposite direction. Teachers by choice have been insisting and are continuing to insist on a stronger voice in decision making, particularly as it affects reward for service. Increased salaries, more substantial fringe benefits, and better working conditions have accompanied the recently discovered muscle resulting from collective bargaining, professional negotiations, and other techniques now being used by a profession that appears to be surprised and uncertain about the attendant responsibilities accompanying such power.

But salaries and other benefits are not a product of spontaneous generation; they must come from somewhere, and the normal budgets of most school systems are already overburdened. Teachers, who formerly viewed the fiscal affairs of schools as a foreign language to be learned only by administrators and boards of education, now find themselves as colleagues of all those who have an interest in finding additional sources of school revenue and responsibility therefor. Further progress in providing for the still-rising costs of education is virtually impossible without the united efforts and sympathetic understanding of all large sections of American society, including the vast numbers of professional teachers who stand to receive important benefits in future years.

But how will this be accomplished? How does the profession proceed to convince its members that teacher intelligence on school finance is just as necessary as an elementary school child's mastery of the fundamentals of arithmetic? The processes involved are certainly not

367

difficult to comprehend if the learner is interested and motivated. The subject of school finance becomes difficult when pursued to its inner depths, but the argument here is only for the teaching profession to have a knowledge of basic and elementary principles.

Only recently has the average teacher begun to realize the potential results of his lack of understanding and skill in the field of school finance. Only recently, too, have state legislative bodies deemed it necessary to turn to the profession for assistance in finding new sources of revenue for schools. Only informed and interested people can respond successfully to this new challenge.

Brighton referred to the implications of lack of knowledgeable involvement of teachers in school finance problems:

> One factor which has worked against teachers in their struggle to make their voices heard in financial policy determinations is the fact that the school budget to many teachers has been a baffling mystery. Furthermore, there has been a willingness on the part of many to relegate the area of school finance to the budget officer or superintendent of schools. . . . I think that what the NEA and state teachers professional associations are trying to say is that the basic premise should be: Because of its fundamental importance, school finance should be the concern of everyone connected with education. Problems and issues of school finance challenge the best efforts of teachers, administrators, specialists, and all others who have ability to help if adequate support for education is ever to be achieved.[8]

Thus, it seems that present-day personnel administration has reached the point where teachers must develop some acumen in school finance if the teacher rights and participation objective is to be more than a mere platitude. Teachers, teacher organizations, and administrators face the wholly new consideration of providing the means and the motivation necessary to raise the level of teacher knowledge to the point required to help provide valid answers to the provoking problems in financing education.

A number of avenues are open for fulfilling such a need: required courses in the basics of the subject, in-service training projects, workshops, civic study groups, practical assignments to the members of negotiating teams, and many others. But most important of all, teachers must understand that their participation in negotiations and in salary disputes puts the onus on them to understand the implications and the problems involved in obtaining higher salaries and benefits. They are citizens too, and just as it is impossible for school boards to draw addi-

8. Stayner F. Brighton, "Teaching Teachers About School Finance," *A Financial Program for Today's Schools* (Washington, D.C.: National Education Assn. Committee on Educational Finance, 1964), pp. 118–19.

tional dollars out of depleted budgets, so it is impossible for an uninformed group to arrive at consensus on teacher salary demands. A beginning point may very well be established with the teachers themselves, particularly the career-directed ones, in assuming responsibility for learning the ABCs of school finance. The time to start is now, before a defensive school board and general public legislate against the whims as well as the jusifiable requests of an uninformed but demanding organization of teachers.

THE CHANGING ASSIGNMENTS OF TEACHERS

Innovations of various kinds in the schools in the last decade have changed the traditional pattern of teacher assignments. Programmed learning, flexible scheduling, large-group instruction, team teaching, closed circuit television, individualized and continuous-progress instruction, and other similar programs have accelerated the movement toward differentiation of staff assignments. The improved use of qualified teaching personnel, with emphasis on specialization and expertise in instructional techniques, has necessitated greater intensity of training with concomitant increases in salaries. Many of the minutiae, or chores, that have hitherto fallen to the teacher can now be assigned to aides, clerks, or less well-prepared teachers, and the more difficult and technical aspects of education left to the well-trained and experienced professional teacher.

Today's teacher finds much to aid and abet the instructional process, and much of this is expensive in terms of original cost. He also has, in addition to relief from the clerical aspects of the business, mechanical aids and devices to enrich the program and minimize its monotony. Projection machines, teaching machines, educational television, automatic data processing equipment, and the like, are no longer looked on as threats to the security of the teacher. Rather, they are accepted for what they are—potential supplements to upgrade and reinforce the instructional program. Audiovisual materials are no longer considered luxuries to be provided for the most affluent school districts; they are now part and parcel of the ongoing instructional program in every progressive school.

Retention of teaching personnel in public school work has always been a big problem. Large classes, relatively low salaries, lack of socioeconomic status, increasing militance of students, impossible social problems involved in needed programs for integration of the races, and little opportunity for advancement have combined to discourage many teachers and cause them to leave the profession. While school districts have tried to stop this loss with greater rewards for service, employment of aides and teaching assistants, better leave policies, smaller classes and lighter work loads, and other such benefits, high teacher turnover persists. Teachers are among the most mobile of all professional workers. They tend to change positions often, always seeking and seemingly never finding, the kinds of positions that they are willing to call permanent.

What are the ramifications of the problems of assignment and retention of teacher personnel from the financial point of view? What will be the net cost effect of paying higher salaries for the best obtainable professional teachers and lower salaries for various grades of assistants? What will be the fiscal result of teacher utilization of the vast array of mechanical and automatic data processing machines and devices now becoming an integral part of the instructional program? What is the dollar effect of the extensive recruitment and in-service programs necessary to replace the large numbers of dissatisfied and itinerant teachers? The answers to these and other related questions are of great concern in considering the problems of financing the schools of the future.

Generalizations related to the financial implications of widespread adoption of educational technology and the new methods of assigning and utilizing teaching personnel are difficult to make. Harris noted that "no one really knows how much the prospective technological advances of the next 10 years are going to cost. Estimates vary greatly. But these advances will be abortive unless adequate financial resources can be mobilized and there are some major breakthroughs in education."[9] Nygaard and Roelfs also noted the difficulty of estimating the costs of such educational advancements:

> The implications for finance of this new approach to staffing are not clear at this time. Conflicting viewpoints prevail as to whether a reduction in school expenditures can be anticipated by adopting these new utilization procedures. Agreement is general that initially the installation of automatic data processing equipment and the equipment necessary for improving individual learning will result in a large expenditure for capital outlay. More experience with this approach will give further evidence as to the effect on operating costs of such innovations as team teaching, and what is commonly referred to as the Trump Plan of organizing a secondary school instructional program.[10]

9. Seymour E. Harris, "The Economics of Technological Advances in Education," in Edgar L. Morphet and David L. Jesser, eds., *Planning for Effective Utilization Technology in Education* (Denver; Designing Education for the Future, August 1968), pp. 353–54.
10. Nygaard and Roelfs, "Personnel Policies," p. 315.

ADMINISTRATIVE AND SUPERVISORY SALARIES

Much of the information already discussed concerning teacher salaries, schedules, and fringe benefits applies equally well to administrative and supervisory staff members. Professionally, all certified personnel have much the same kinds of problems. Certainly they are all striving for the same goal—the education of boys and girls.

Some differences exist in how rewards for services are determined for administrative and supervisory personnel, however. The main ones are:

1. The salary of the chief administrator, the superintendent of schools, is most often decided on a bargaining basis, ostensibly on the basis of his training and past record; the extent of competition for the position may also have something to do with the salary offered to the successful candidate.

2. Salaries of the administrative and supervisory staff do not fit the teacher salary schedule. Such employees receive higher salaries for several reasons: (1) their certification requirements are higher; (2) their positions require knowledge and skills in more fields; (3) they have responsibilities for the actions of more people; and (4) they serve for a longer period of time each year (eleven or twelve months, compared to nine or ten for teachers).

3. In the minority of school districts in which administrative and supervisory salaries are related directly to teacher salaries, there are two common ways of determining them: (1) on the basis of a stipulated number of dollars above the salary for teachers with the same training and experience; or (2) on the basis of a predetermined ratio involving such salaries.

4. Some districts determine the salaries on the basis of the teacher salary schedule plus additional amounts per teacher or per pupil, or both, enrolled in the school.

5. Administrative and supervisory positions generally lack tenure and do not provide stated annual increments for service. Local school boards, particularly in rural communities, tend to hold such salaries down for at least two reasons: (a) they may not be fully aware of the special training required or the contribution that these staff members make to the educational program, and (b) many board members have never had direct experience of their own with incomes of the size of those of administrative and supervisory employees; they tend to establish salaries having some relation to their own degree of affluence.

NONCERTIFIED PERSONNEL SALARIES

Over the years, school administrators and boards of education have seemed to emphasize the importance of developing attractive salary schedules and providing good working conditions for certified personnel, but they have often neglected similar conditions for noncertified employees. Many reasons can be cited for this, the principal one being that since the purpose of the school is to provide instruction and almost 75 percent of the current expenditures budget goes for instructional and administrative salaries, this is the area where original emphasis should be placed. Then, too, the qualifications of noncertified personnel vary greatly, and their appointment is often board-member- rather than superintendent-oriented. While the superintendent in most districts nominates certified personnel for appointment by the board with little or no objection by the latter, board members, especially in smaller districts, often like to make their own nominations for noncertified personnel. They often know who needs such a job and tend to treat such appointments as patronage positions. They may feel, too, that they are qualified to judge potential candidates for positions of this kind, in contrast to their feeling of inability to evaluate teacher candidates. Often the availability of employees in this area is such that a school board market exists, which tends to keep salaries low and replacements easy to make.

Another important difference is that while all instructional, or certified, personnel serve under contract for one or more years, service that usually results in tenure after a probationary period, no such arrangement exists for most noncertified employees. They tend to serve "at the pleasure of the board," with no written contract and no guarantee of salary increments based on the passage of time only. Resignations and replacements are commonplace, and such do not usually involve serious questions of ethics for either the school board or the employees.

Fortunately, the conditions in this area of personnel administration are improving. Large school districts with their need for many such employees, increased job requirements, the unionization of nearly all of these workers, and the gradual abdication of school boards from nominating power for all school employees are some of the most important reasons for improved conditions for the employment, utilization, and retention of noncertified personnel. These factors, along with inflation and higher taxes, have forced school districts to raise salaries to a much higher level, thereby adding still another large, but necessary, increase to the costs of public education.

PAYROLL POLICIES AND PROCEDURES

The largest single classification of current expenditures involves payment of salaries to employees. All but one or two of the principal expenditure accounts in a school district's accounting system include provisions for the payment of salaries to employees. Administrators, teachers, attendance officers, nurses, bus drivers, custodians, repairmen, food service personnel, and playground directors represent nine of the eleven expenditure accounts. Only Fixed Charges and Student-Body Activities would ordinarily not include salaries for personnel, and under some circumstances, even these two may have salary money chargeable to them. Collectively, more than 80 percent of the current expenditures of a typical school district will usually be for salaries of employees.

The size and importance of a school's payroll dictates that sound principles and procedures of payroll accounting be followed. Most of these would apply to any and all payroll accounting, but there are some differences. Generally accepted policies and procedures to be followed include the following as a minimum:

1. Arrangements should be made and businesslike procedures followed to guarantee payment of salaries at a specified, regular, and acceptable time. There is no rationale that is acceptable to employees when a payroll division is unreliable and uncertain in delivering salary payments. Only emergency factors beyond the control of the business office can be justified as legitimate reasons for delay or inconvenience in paying salaries.

2. Receiving the salary payment should be made as convenient as possible to its recipient. The onus for delivery should rest with the school district's business office, regardless of its size, and not with the individual payee. The days of requiring school employees to go in person to the school board office or the clerk's home to receive a salary check, or just to wait uncertainly for the convenience of the payroll division, are only a dim memory in most districts. Even when the district is temporarily embarrassed for funds, there is provision in the law for short-term borrowing on tax anticipation notes so that a school district may operate on a businesslike basis, just as any other institution is required to do.

3. All school employees should possess written copies of rules and policies concerning payroll procedures. Said rules and policies should have been established by joint suggestion and approval of representatives of the employed personnel of the district working

373

with representatives of the board of education. Among other things, each school employee should have easy access to the following:

a. A current salary schedule, with full explanation of increments and special provisions, if any.

b. A statement of policy related to payroll procedures as they apply to the teacher on sick leave and also on leave for other reasons. The policy should state how the teacher's salary is affected when a substitute is employed and any other conditions that are directly related to leave privileges.

c. A written explanation of how all deductions required by law are calculated—federal withholding taxes, state withholding taxes, social security, and many others. The employee should be able, should he so desire, to determine whether the amounts for such deductions are correct.

d. A statement of policy concerning willingness of the district (and the conditions to be met) to withhold other deductions at the request of a school employee or his professional organization—membership dues in professional organizations, individual or group insurance premiums, and others.

e. An explanation of the options available to school employees as they relate to payroll dates for 9-month, 10-month, or yearly contracts. Clarification of the school's policy concerning options, if any, which teachers on 9-month contracts may have concerning the summer salary payments is particularly important.

f. A statement in writing concerning the procedure to be followed by an employee in the event of salary dispute or misunderstanding.

4. A well-understood procedure should be followed in reporting to the payroll division relevant information on all individual employees before the regular paying period—days of sick leave, other leave, salary changes, and dates of beginning and ending employment in the case of employees not under contract.

Selected Readings

Candoli, I. Carl; Hack, Walter G.; Ray, John R.; and Stollar, Dewey H. *School Business Administration: A Planning Approach.* Boston: Allyn and Bacon, 1973.

Gauerke, Warren E., and Childress, Jack R., eds. *The Theory and Practice of School Finance.* Chicago: Rand McNally & Company, 1967.

Johns, Roe L., and Morphet, Edgar L. *The Economics and Financing of Education,* 3rd ed. Englewood Cliffs, N.J.: Prentice-Hall, 1975.

Knezevich, Stephen J., and Fowlkes, John Guy. *Business Management of Local Systems.* New York: Harper & Row, 1960.

Miller, Van; Madden, George R.; and Kincheloe, James B. *The Public Administration of American School Systems.* New York: The Macmillan Co., 1972.

16

Financing Student Activities

Charging fees for incidental educational materials and experiences is a widespread practice, which appears to increase year after year in some of our schools. In considering this problem, it should be understood that it involves charging instructional and other fees for school services provided for all students. Registration fees, activity fees, locker rentals, field trip fees, and the like, are under question here. No one questions the requiring of students to pay the cost of shop projects or other "take-home" materials, from which they alone are benefited.

The following oft-repeated statements directly or indirectly negate belief in the practice of charging students for curricular services of any kind:

- The *state* should assume responsibility for financing education.
- Schools should be "effectively free" to their clientele. (No assumption is made that they are to be free to taxpayers.)
- Equality of educational opportunity should be provided for all. (This is impossible when fees are charged.)
- Taxation should be based on the ability principle to the exclusion of the outmoded benefit principle.
- The *financial resources of the state* should serve as a support to the educational program.
- The wealth of the state does not belong to a particular district or group of people.
- Education is an investment *by the state* in its citizens.
- The state must expect that high-quality education is expensive.
- Taxing systems must change; fees paid assume special benefits to individuals.

• The public education of a child or youth shall not depend on wealth other than the wealth of the state as a whole; the quality of his education cannot be a function of the wealth of the parents, neighbors, or of the school district.

One of the results of the increased costs of education, which has been accompanied by widespread taxpayer resistance, has been an increase in the amount and number of school charges made to students, especially at the high school level. These fees are assessed for the most part with the rationale that they help finance activities that otherwise would have to be eliminated from the school program. They represent, too, a lack of acceptance of our much quoted, but much violated, philosophy of free education for all eligible students in this country.

As one reads the numerous stories and accounts in the literature of instructional and other educational costs that are being passed back to the parents of school pupils because of inadequate budgets and other reasons, the story of "the battle to make the schools entirely free" in America, as Ellwood P. Cubberley reported it, is recalled.

> The rate bill . . . was an old institution, also brought over from England, as the term "rate" signifies. It was a charge levied upon the parent to supplement the school revenues and prolong the school term, and was assessed in proportion to the number of children sent by each parent to the school. In some States, as for example Massachusetts and Connecticut, its use went back to colonial times; in others it was added as the cost for education increased, and it was seen that the income from permanent funds and authorized taxation was not sufficient to maintain the school the necessary length of time. The deficiency in revenue was charged against the parents sending schildren to school, *pro rata*, and collected as ordinary tax-bills. The charge was small, but it was sufficient to keep many poor children away from the schools.[1]

A school patron today may wonder what difference there is between paying the sometimes high registration and other appended costs so "popular" today and the rate bills so frankly criticized by Cubberley. He may wonder, too, if the so-called "battle for free schools" has really been won or if the advocates of effectively free education have lost this philosophical fight and are now in full retreat.

EFFECTIVELY FREE EDUCATION

No school and no education is free until an individual who does not have money, or whose parents do not have money, can attend that school

1. Ellwood P. Cubberley, *The History of Education* (Boston: Houghton Mifflin Co., 1920), p. 684.

or obtain that education. . . . One of the results of lack of free schooling in the United States is that millions of people are in the lower-paid occupational groups, such as unskilled labor, and in the lower grades of clerical occupations. In a large number of cases such conditions reflect not at all upon the ability of the people involved. They are a reflection upon a society that holds sacred a myth that free education is being provided.[2]

For nearly half a century, Harold F. Clark, John K. Norton, E. K. Fretwell, Harry McKown, and others have pointed out the discrepancy between what we say about providing free education in America and what we actually practice. Although these educators influenced the educational philosophy of many school people, there are relatively few effectively free schools in the land today. The myriad of fees and charges that exist in schools by their nature and their size make it difficult or impossible for some pupils to attend. This is one of the worst examples we provide of inequality of educational opportunity and represents a "luxury" we can ill afford. We have only recently, by inaugurating high-cost programs for physically and mentally handicapped children, rejected the traditional idea that equal amounts of money must be spent for all students. We have also declared that more money must be provided per student in isolated schools. The various states are now in the process of weighting the disadvantaged pupils in metropolitan areas, which suffer from municipal overburden. It is equally necessary that we accept this "equality" philosophy for the low-income pupil by eliminating the discriminating fees now being charged, some of which are assessed even in our elementary schools.

Not a New Idea

Certainly the idea of free education carried to this point is not new. Norton coined the term *effectively free schooling* and wrote about it in strong language nearly half a century ago:

> If the second condition for realizing maximum total income is to be met, occupational mobility must be guaranteed. This requires that education be made "effectively free." Schooling must be free enough so that its cost does not constitute an effective barrier to education. *Effectively free schooling is schooling provided under such conditions that persons who should have the schooling are not debarred from it by financial reasons.* . . .
>
> We now provide free tuition in the elementary and secondary levels of education. This is a wise policy but it does not go far enough. Effec-

2. Harold F. Clark, *An Introduction to Economic Problems* (New York: The Macmillan Co., 1939), pp. 133–34.

tively free schooling requires more than free tuition. It means that food, clothing, medical aid, and shelter will be provided if the lack of such provision will keep one from school.[3]

Extent of Fee Charging

Scores of studies have been made of the extent of fee charging in the public schools. The results are much the same in all such studies: fee charging prevails more in certain parts of the country than in others; there is much more of this type of violation of free school philosophy than most people believe; many teachers and administrators have accepted such a procedure as normal and have known of no other system; and as expected, fee charging is less prevalent in elementary schools than in high schools. While the fee-charging practices of the several states vary considerably, a few of them seem to have led the field in the elimination, or nonuse, of these fees and charges.

The doubtful reader who thinks the procedure of charging student fees is exaggerated and justified on the basis of the benefit the student derives might well (1) review the extensive literature on the subject, and (2) reconsider the arguments that favor paying school costs on the basis of the ability rather than the benefit principle. Why should the state require its citizens to attend school and then charge them for the privilege? Why should the school require the pupils to go on a field trip and then charge them for a part of the cost of doing so? How can the school justify its denial of students to attend a lyceum program or a field trip held on school time under faculty supervision because of their lack of money or lack of desire to pay for the privilege?

Fees Affect School Dropouts

The effect of the cost of education on the dropout rate of high school students was noted by Norton in 1940: "Only a minority of the youth of the nation complete their high school education. At least a third of those who leave school at an early age do so primarily because of financial limitations. Many of those eliminated for this reason possess superior intellectual capacity and other qualities which justify further schooling."[4] Admittedly, fees constitute only a small part of the total cost of a student's education, especially when the indirect costs (loss in wages and salaries) are considered. However, the fee problem is a

3. John K. Norton, *Education and Economic Well-Being in American Democracy* (Washington, D.C.: Educational Policies Commission, 1940), p. 2.
     4. Ibid., p. 2.

considerable one in families that have several children in school at the same time.

There is difference of opinion among educators concerning the effect that charging extraclass activity fees may have upon the drop-out rate of students. While the following report touches on that issue, it should be noted that it applies only to activity fees and says nothing about the sometimes overextended charges for textbooks, supplies, and other expenditures that are not optional with students but are a part of the instructional program of the schools.

The Fairfax County, Va., school board has set aside $66,000 for students who cannot afford to take part in extracurricular activities, but it may not be a problem after all. A survey of 620 high school students in the county, conducted by a special superintendent's committee, found that only 29% of the students felt that the costs of extracurricular activities discouraged participation. When asked why they did not participate, "I don't have enough money" ranked 11th on a list of 16 reasons. . . .[5]

Despite the increasing costs of education each year, there are many educators and other taxpaying citizens who favor extending the age and time limits of free education—not only to decrease the number of school drop-outs but also to increase the number of enrollees of students at the senior high and junior college levels. Note the following example of this point of view:

> The concept which many of you in the NEA have endorsed, and which is attracting great support from many other segments of our society, that the free public school system should be expanded in this century to encompass at least the first two years of collegiate training will, in my judgment, command the necessary support of the majority of the taxpayers of this country within the next decade. California is blazing the trail which was pioneered by the city of New York. The people of Oregon have adopted a very generous program of combined local and state effort through their legislature.[6]

ACTIVITIES ARE CURRICULAR

Activity funds are used in most schools to support activity programs, including athletics, forensics, and many others, because it has been

5. *Education U.S.A.* (Washington, D.C.: National School Public Relations Assn., Jan. 5, 1976), p. 106.
6. Wayne Morse, "Federal Support for Education: Now and in the Future," in *A Financial Program for Today's Schools* (Washington, D.C.: National Education Assn., 1964), p. 19.

assumed that they are not a part of the curriculum. Their collective title "extracurricular" is a misnomer for, by definition, the curriculum includes all educational activities sponsored by the school. Because they are "extra," their financing has not often been considered to be a legal claim against the revenues of the school district. As a result of their "back-door" entry into the curriculum, tradition in many school districts even today dictates that they are to be financed otherwise than by school district revenues. Two or three generations of teachers and administrators in some schools have known no other way of financing these activities.

The thrust of the argument here is not to debate the pros and cons of such methods of financing such activities. It is rather to suggest that since they are a legitimate and generally worthwhile part of the education of children and youth, they should be paid for by the same process and with the same funding as all the other costs of public education. This is an echo of what E. K. Fretwell was teaching so enthusiastically half a century ago. It is a replay of what the National Congress of Parents and Teachers has been saying for a long time. That organization has never conceived its own fund-raising activities as simply a means of securing needed supplies and equipment at the local school level. Rather, it conceives its responsibility to be exerting its leadership, its energy, its influence, and its money to convince state legislatures to pass adequate finance laws providing for *all* the needs of the school, including student activities. There is very little that can be said against their position in this matter.

The foregoing argument of the PTA that school finance laws should provide public funds to pay all the costs of education is sound and defensible. An additional one- or two-mill levy, if necessary, dedicated or earmarked for financing the activity program would remove the discrimination that accompanies fee charging regardless of its amount. The point here is that individually and collectively the fees are big problems or nuisances to many individual students or their families. For example, a family with several children attending school often finds itself unable to pay said fees, with the result that their children fail to receive the experiences they should have, or even worse, are forced to consider themselves second-class citizens with limited rights as citizens of the school.

STUDENT FEES AND PUBLIC RELATIONS

One of the problems connected with unpopular and discriminating fee charging is that it tends to destroy patron and community good will toward the school. It is doubtful that school staff members realize the harmful effect on the school's relations with its patrons of such questionable practices as charging excessive fees, assessing high admission prices to school-sponsored activities, the sponsorship of high-pressure magazine drives to build up depleted student-fund treasuries, or soliciting advertising by merchants in student yearbooks that are never seen by anyone except the students on the last day or two of school.

Operation of School Stores

Some schools, especially the larger high schools, operate school stores that sell to students certain types of supplies and convenience articles. Ostensibly, the purpose of this operation is convenience to the student who can secure his school needs—gym shoes, paper, pencils, and the like—with a minimum of shopping time and effort and often at some financial saving to himself. A secondary purpose for this activity is that of having the studentbody earn a profit to be used in financing certain of the school's activities that are not financed with school district funds. Another purpose of such an activity is that of providing practical business experiences for some students with particular interests or abilities in such functions.

All of the above benefits are positive and laudable under most circumstances. However, they must be weighed in each instance against the possible disadvantages and problems they engender. The question of how far the school can go in competing with local businesses is always pertinent. Do the advantages and the profits together outweigh the potential loss in public relations? Will the profits gained under a school store arrangement be off-set by negative votes and attitudes of disgruntled businessmen whose good-will and support are needed in every school system? These, and other similar questions should be considered by every school administrator and faculty before they decide to operate a school store.

Vending Machines

Another major problem faces those schools that provide easy access to vending machines of various kinds for student convenience. What effect will candy and gum dispensers have on the diet and the health of students? Are they self-defeating in purpose as they compete with the school lunch program? Are they a source of irritation to parents and the operators of nearby businesses? The following example is typical of the kinds of problems raised by this type of school operation:

> The practice of selling candy in student stores on junior high and high school campuses in . . . has caused a bit of a stir in the local press. Some

folks raised their eyebrows after the media pointed out that the student stores sold $1.43 million worth of candy last school year and that some pupils sell their free lunch tickets for 25 cents apiece to buy candy. School officials admit that the situation poses a dilemma. They don't want to contribute to growing tooth decay in young people, but the profits from the candy sales are used to finance the band, drill team, debate teams and other extracurricular activities. School officials say, in essence, that the students will go off campus to buy candy if the schools stop selling it, so the schools might as well continue to sell it and put the profits to good use.[7]

Perhaps many of the problems of operation of school stores and other money-raising activities would never be raised if the profit motive could be eliminated and if all aspects of the student's program were financed by public funds. There is much to be said for such "effectively free" education; there is very little that can be said against it—especially in a country that boasts proudly about its unique system of free public education.

SCHOOL BOARD RESISTANCE

Boards of education have been somewhat reluctant to accept the financial "burden" imposed in financing student activities. As a result, a great many students have been denied the advantages of participation in these activities because of a lack of money. Some schools in their anxiety to make the organizations self-supporting, have exploited both students and the public to an alarming degree. That school boards have been moving in the direction of giving greater financial assistance to student activities is indicated by the trend toward the granting of money to help pay, or to pay completely, expenses of school bands, debate teams, athletic teams, and many other extra-class organizations.[8]

Whether or not the trend indicated in the above statement, which was made in 1955, has continued is open to serious question. Changes in school operations come slowly, and it would require many years of concerted effort to reverse the traditional philosophy of student financing of so-called extracurricular activities. To do so would increase the budget requirements of the school district and add problems to an already overburdened taxing system. But the increase would be slight and the benefits great—decreased dropout rates, improved public relations, and greater equality of educational opportunity for all students.

7. *Education U.S.A.* (Washington, D.C.: National School Public Relations Assn., Jan. 5, 1976), p. 106.
8. Percy Burrup, "Handling the Finances of Student Activities," *Nation's Schools* (November 1955), p. 87.

THE COURTS AND STUDENT FEES

Since the charging of fees to students for activities and incidental instructional supplies is controversial, the courts are often required to settle such issues. Unfortunately, they are not unanimous in their interpretation of what free public education actually means. Consequently, there is no "right" answer to the problems schools face in this matter. The following summaries of cases of this type, however, seem to indicate that the courts are becoming more and more adamant in their ruling that education should be free to the students who attend.

A recent opinion by the Texas attorney general, outlawing student fees, will cost school districts in the state nearly $22 million annually, according to a survey by the Texas Education Agency. The largest single loss, almost $16 million, will come from academic fees (lab charges, workbooks, towel fees, etc.). Loss of driver education charges will add $3.3 million, and the end of extracurricular fees, including band uniform cleaning and rental, will mean another $2.6 million.[9]

> Whether fees may be charged for textbooks was decided by courts of last resort in three states in 1970. No rulings on this specific application of state constitutional guarantees of "free" public education had previously been rendered by appellate courts.
>
> Two courts held that textbooks must be furnished without cost to all students. The leading case was decided by the Supreme Court of Idaho. That court found textbooks to be necessary elements of the school's activity, to represent a fixed expense peculiar to education, and to be outside the choice of the student as to quality or quantity. The test adopted in Idaho for items to be furnished free—"necessary elements of any school's activity"—was adopted a few months later by the Supreme Court of Michigan.
>
> Differing in approach and result, the Supreme Court of Illinois examined the meaning of "free schools" as used at the state constitutional convention of 1869–70. . . . It determined that free books for all were not included in the concept. . . .
>
> In 1972 the Supreme Court of Montana held that fees may be charged only in connection with activities which are not "reasonably related to a recognized academic and educational goal of the particular school system.[10]

9. *Education U.S.A.* (Washington, D.C.: National School Public Relations Assn., Dec. 22, 1975), p. 98.

10. E. Edmund Reutter, Jr. and Robert R. Hamilton, *The Law of Public Education, 1973 Supplement* (Mineola, N.Y.: The Foundation Press, Inc., 1973), pp. 37–38.

PRINCIPLES OF STUDENT ACTIVITY FINANCING

In the event that student activities are financed wholly or in part by revenue produced through the operation of the activity, there are certain fundamental principles that should govern such a program. For the most part, these principles are the same as those that undergird the receiving and spending of tax revenues. Some of the significant principles that would decrease the chances of mismanagement of "student activity funds" include:

1. Student activity funds (often referred to as nontax funds) are under the legal control of the board of education and should be handled as such. They do not belong to the activity or organization that collected them; they may be managed to some degree by students under faculty direction and control, but such accounting practices are subject to the same kind and quality of audits and school board responsibility as the district funds.
2. If student accounting is separate from district accounting, all such funds should be placed in a centralized accounting system with all the standard safeguards and protective features of such a system.[11] The structural and managerial aspects of such a system have appeared in print often; there is no point in repeating them here.
3. While students should be involved in helping determine policies concerning receiving and expending such funds, and while they can learn the practical lessons involved in budgeting, accounting, and auditing of monies, they should never be given complete management responsibilities of these or any other funds, except under close supervision by qualified staff members.
4. School administrators should be educating their boards of education and working with legislative groups to make adequate provisions in school finance laws to eliminate this traditional and outmoded extra fee method of paying for this important and necessary part of the school program. The addition of a very small levy, or state allocation of additional funds for this purpose, would save the administrator, the faculty, and the students a great deal of time and effort that could be more profitably spent elsewhere in the school curriculum.

For those who feel that the student should bear a part of the cost of his education by paying such costs, there are several important points to be considered. (1) The student is already paying a high price for

11. See Everett V. Samuelson et al., *Financial Accounting for School Activities,* Bulletin 1959, no. 21 (Washington, D.C.: U.S. Office of Education, U.S. Dept. of Health, Education, and Welfare, 1957), p. 109.

his education indirectly by the salary or wage earning he is forgoing while attending school; while this will ordinarily be recovered by the additional income he will receive after he completes his schooling, that potentiality brings scarce solace to him while he is in school. (2) The school itself is investing much money in each student's education; why does it stop at a given point and demand from him fees that are high from the latter's point of view, but that collectively amount to a very small part of the operating budget? (3) What is so special about the so-called incidental, or activity, program that it should be paid for by the benefit principle while other costs are paid by school funds based on the ability principle? (4) Most of the incidental fees and charges have been ruled by various courts as illegal; it is doubtful that many of them would be upheld if contested in the courts. (5) Provision in the 1957 handbook, *Financial Accounting for Local and State School Systems,* of an expenditure account for student-body activities (Series 1000) is official recognition that there is a legitimate way to pay for these activities with district tax revenues.

Selected Readings

Fretwell, E. K. *Extra-Curricular Activities in Secondary Schools.* Boston: Houghton Mifflin Co., 1931.

Knezevich, Stephen J., and Fowlkes, John Guy. *Business Management of Local Systems.* New York: Harper & Row, 1960.

McKown, Harry C. *Extracurricular Activities.* New York: The Macmillan Co., 1952.

Miller, Franklin A.; Moyer, James H.,; and Patrick, Robert B. *Planning Student Activities.* Englewood Cliffs, N.J.: Prentice-Hall, 1956.

Norton, John K. *Education and Economic Well-Being in American Democracy.* Washington, D.C.: Educational Policies Commission, 1940.

Samuelson, Everett V.; Tankard, George G.; and Pope, W. Hoyt. *Financial Accounting for School Activities,* Bulletin 1959, no. 21. Washington, D.C.: U.S. Office of Education, U.S. Dept. of Health, Education, and Welfare, 1959.

Unit 6

THE PERMANENT NATURE OF SCHOOL FINANCE REFORM

We can expect that successive reformers will find the changes of our period as insubstantial as we have found earlier reforms.

W. Norton Grubb and
Stephan Michelson,
States and Schools, 1974

17

The Future of School Finance Reform

The basic finance patterns that undergird the public school systems in the several states are largely products of the twentieth century. Although most of the state finance programs were not always consistent with prevailing educational finance theory, progress toward improvement was slow until the court cases in the early 1970s. Obsolete methods of obtaining and allocating funds for education were long on discrimination against the poorer school districts and short on the equitability and the adequacy of the revenues they made available for the education of many students. School finance reforms were long overdue; their progress in the 1970s has been phenomenal, but their extension and continued improvement may be in question as the passage of time dims the memories of people and reduces the pressure of court mandates to effect change.

UNANSWERED QUESTIONS FOR FINANCING EDUCATION

As one anticipates the future of school finance reform in the several states and in the nation, answers to many pertinent questions must be considered. Who should be educated at public expense? To what grade level should free education be provided? What should be the responsibility of each of the three levels of government to provide funds for public education? Should the states continue to increase their share of the revenue mix even if it results in loss of local control of education? Is inadequacy in funding a matter of lack of ability to pay, or is the problem a lack of desire or willingness to pay on the part of taxpayers?

389

If these and numerous other questions could be answered accurately, it would be a relatively easy matter to determine the extent and direction school finance reform should take in the years ahead.

SOME ACCEPTED PRINCIPLES AND ASSUMPTIONS

There are some important elements or characteristics on which all educational structure and plans must find common ground and solutions to the financial problems of the day. Education rests its case on several basic assumptions that receive general but not universal support. Some are more readily accepted than others. Some rest on firm and long-accepted opinion and practice, while others seem destined to undergo periodic mitigation and change. Some of these accepted principles that this text has also accepted include the following:

1. The perpetuation of the American form of government is dependent upon an informed citizenry; that can only be attained by the operation of free public schools.
2. Education is a state function because of interpretation of the Tenth Amendment to the U.S. Constitution; financing it is also a state responsibility for the same reason.
3. State responsibility for education includes the right of the state to provide for compulsory attendance of those it deems wise to educate.
4. Education enhances the economic development of a country, but its chief value lies in the fact that it helps protect individual freedom.
5. Education is no longer regarded as merely a privilege for those who can afford it; it is now recognized as a constitutional right of every citizen.
6. Public funds cannot be used to establish or to help operate non-public schools or to prevent desegregation or integration of minority groups.
7. There is a lack of equity and fairness in school finance programs that provide equal dollars per student; weighted pupil units or weighted classroom units are a fairer measure of need.
8. The education of the people of a state or nation and their efforts to support education are more favorable elements toward social and economic progress than the extent of natural resources found within their boundaries.
9. All except a very few citizens owe a tax for the services of govern-

ment and especially for education; some may miss one or more forms of taxation, but few, if any, should miss all forms.

10. Because education provides externalities, the ability-to-pay principle of taxation is more defensible than the benefit principle in providing funds for education.

11. Education is not really a cost or just a necessary "evil" sponsored and financed by government; it is an investment in human capital.

12. Providing adequate funds for education will give a district or a school the opportunity to produce, but it will not guarantee, a good educational program; providing inadequate funds, however, will guarantee a poor program.

LONG-RANGE SCHOOL FINANCE GOALS

In the years ahead, school finance programs will undoubtedly change, but in what direction? Hopefully, reform will continue in the direction of providing greater equity of revenues to school districts on the basis of real need and greater equity in sharing the costs on the basis of better measures of ability to pay. School finance programs in the future should:

1. Provide free education to those adults who could not or did not take advantage of such in their younger years but who now seek it for cultural, social, or economic reasons. Such a goal presents a real challenge to the states to provide education for approximately 54 million persons of working age (sixteen years old and over) who are not now enrolled in school and who have not yet completed twelve years of school.

2. Extend the years of formal education downward to include nursery school education for three and four year olds—particularly for those who come from homes where these important years of growth and development are wasted or misspent.

3. Motivate the children and youth of minority groups to attend twelve years of schooling to at least the same degree and in the same proportions as white children.

4. Enact school finance laws that provide a maximum degree of equity and equality of educational opportunity for all children and youth.

5. Provide school finance laws that not only recognize the problems and inequities in small schools but also in the large city districts.

6. Support education at high enough levels to provide optimum programs appropriate to the unique and individual needs and personal differences of children and youth.

7. Eliminate the great amount of illiteracy, particularly in minority groups, that continues to exist in this country in spite of our free educational system.

8. Provide greater state financial support of education, at the same time leaving much of its control in the hands of local school boards.

9. Clarify the role of each of the three levels of government in financing education and determine the proportionate share of cost that each should pay.

10. Provide less restrictive limits and procedures for local districts in building and paying for capital improvements. This involves equitable practices in providing funds for capital outlays with less reliance on property taxes for this purpose.

11. Provide fiscal independence from other governmental bodies in those districts that still must operate under this form of handicap.

12. Make major improvements in the assessment and administration of the property tax until better measures of financing education are substituted for this form of tax.

13. Provide the financial support on an equitable basis for extension of the school year well beyond the nine months now in vogue in most school districts.

14. Find and apply defensible and legal answers to the controversial problem of allocating public funds for the operation of nonpublic schools.

15. Solve the problem of teacher-board negotiations in such a way that all additional funds provided by legislative bodies to improve local school district educational programs are not funneled into salaries at the price of other important parts of the school program.

16. Develop a way to educate the one-fifth of our population who are excluded from typical American life by a serious lack of education and vocational skills.

Undoubtedly, any list of unsolved problems in financing education could be extended to almost any length desired, but there is little, if any, value in so doing. The point is that in spite of progress and reform of considerable proportions there is much to be done to improve the financing of education in this country. No reasonable person expects that such will be achieved or that all the problems involved will ever be solved, for the solution of one difficulty often creates others. But educators, legislators, and parents have the responsibility and the challenge to work toward these and other desirable goals. The price may be high, but the rewards are great, for the welfare, the education, and the future of millions of children and youth are at stake.

As one looks optimistically at the future of school finance reform his thinking may be influenced by the following excellent statement concerning the subject:

We end where we began—with a historical perspective on the role of financing in the schools. The first conclusion from a historical view is that finance reforms have repeated themselves over and over—in the "discovery" of inequities, in the arguments for greater equality versus local control (or some variant), and in the structure of state programs designed to correct perceived inequities. We can only expect that this cycle will recur, that the reforms stimulated by the current court cases, the citizens' committees, and the legislative battles will prove to be inadequate—perhaps because of the lack of "recapture" from wealthy districts or of insufficient attention to the pupil and district characteristics . . . or perhaps because wealthy districts manage to evade the intent of equalizing programs. We can expect that successive reformers will find the changes of our period as insubstantial as we have found earlier reforms.[1]

It should not be inferred that the finance reform movement will proceed without opposition or without interruption. The needs of schools change as time passes and the priorities for revenues do not remain fixed. Reforms must therefore be flexible with adequate provisions for adjustment to meet the changing needs of students and the changing inequities and inequalities that are certain to develop regardless of the direction or the extent of the reforms achieved. The President's Commission on School Finance emphasized this point in the following:

> We have offered many recommendations for reform of the educational system, with primary emphasis on its financing. We are not unaware that these reforms, if implemented, will have an effect on virtually all the people of this country, be they taxpayers, parents, students, or government officials. We do not doubt that these reforms will be controversial. They will be challenged and debated. This is as it should be. No single set of recommendations can be applied to all situations and circumstances. But if they can productively contribute to a national dialog on one of the most pressing problems of the day, this Commission will have served its purpose.[2]

REFORM MOVEMENT HAS COURT SUPPORT

The reform movement generated in the early 1970s is unique when compared to that of any other such thrust toward improvement in prior years. For the first time the reformers have the support, indeed—the

---

1. W. Norton Grubb and Stephan Michelson, *States and Schools* (Lexington, Mass.: Lexington Books, D. C. Heath and Company, 1974), p. 197.
2. *Schools, People, and Money* (Washington, D.C.: President's Commission on School Finance, U.S. Government Printing Office, 1972).

threat, of our judicial system to require changes and improvements in school finance. While school finance problems and reform movements have always been concerned with financial adequacy and related problems, this one has as its principal objective the erasing of inequities and the provision of equal protection of all children and youth. Hopefully, with such defensible and overdue goals, school finance reform will continue with great thrust and momentum in a positive direction for many years to come.

Appendix

School Finance Problems

Solving the simplified problems in this section should help the beginning student to understand the language and calculations used in school finance. Although a working knowledge of such principles is usually assumed in most school finance texts, it is felt that a problem-solving review may be of benefit to some practitioners as well as to beginning school finance students.

I. TAX RATES

Some states express their tax rates in mills; others express them in dollars per hundred dollars of assessed valuation. For example, in some states the tax rate for school purposes might be expressed as 50.5 mills; in others it would be expressed as $5.05 per $100 of assessed valuation (AV). It could also be expressed as $50.50 per $1,000 of assessed valuation.

Express the following as indicated:

1. 156.25 mills as dollars   1. $_____
2. $0.375 as mills   2. _____mills
3. $17.51 as mills   3. _____mills
4. 57.3 mills as dollars per $100 (AV)   4. $_____/$100 (AV)
5. $3.60 per $150 (AV) as mills   5. _____mills

6. $0.136 per $1 (AV)   6. $_____/$1,000 (AV)
   as dollars/$1,000 (AV)
7. .78 mills as dollars   7. $_____
8. .78 mills as dollars per $100   8. $_____/$100 (AV)
   (AV)
9. .78 mills as dollars per $1,000   9. $_____/$1,000 (AV)
   (AV)
10. 2,341.5 mills as dollars   10. $_____
11. $5,491.54 as mills   11. _____mills
12. $48.54 per $1,000 (AV) as mills   12. $_____/$1 (AV)
   per $1 (AV)

II. PROPERTY ASSESSMENTS, TAX RATES, REVENUE

For taxation purposes property is usually assessed at a fractional part of its sale (market) value. Revenues are determined by applying tax rates against these assessed values. Since states use different percentages of sale value in calculating assessed values, comparisons between states require the determination of sale values and true tax rates.

$$(\text{assessed value}) \ (\text{tax rate}) = (\text{sale value}) \ (\text{true tax rate})$$
$$(AV) \ (tr) = (SV) \ (ttr)$$

Thus, if property valued at $50,000 and assessed at $20,000 has a tax rate (sometimes called apparent tax rate) of 40 mills, it would have a true tax rate of 16 mills.

Problems

1. If the assessed value of a piece   1. _____percent
   of property is 25 percent of its
   sale value, you know immediately that its true tax rate is
   what percent of its apparent
   tax rate?
2. If a piece of property is assessed   2. $_____
   at $12,675 under a fractional
   practice of 65 percent, what is
   the sale value of the property?
3. If a district requires revenue of   3. $_____/$100 (AV)
   $743,712 and the sale value of
   all taxable property is $50,800,-

000 (to be assessed at 60 percent), what will the tax rate be in dollars per $100 of assessed valuation?

4. In problem 3 above, what is the true tax rate in mills?

4. _____mills

Mr. Smith has a house assessed at $21,000 (60 percent of sale value). His tax is $7.50 per $100 of AV. Mr. Jones has a house assessed at $17,775 (45 percent of sale value). His tax rate is 71.8 mills. From this information, answer the following:

5. Who pays the greater tax?
6. How much greater?
7. Using the tax rate and the assessment practices of Mr. Smith's district, how much tax would Mr. Jones pay?

5. _____
6. $_____
7. $_____

Mr. Brown has a house assessed at $19,530 (62 percent of sale value). His tax rate is $5.65 per $100 of assessed valuation. Mr. Barnes has a house assessed at $15,120 (48 percent of sale value). His tax rate is $64.25 per $1,000 (AV).

8. Who pays the greater tax?
9. How much greater?
10. Using the tax rate and the assessment practices of Mr. Brown's district, how much tax would Mr. Barnes pay?

8. _____
9. $_____
10. $_____

School District A has an assessed valuation of taxable property of $49,-410,000. It has 5,400 public school pupils. School District B has an assessed valuation of taxable property of $86,260,000 and 9,500 public school pupils.

11. Which district has the greater ability to support its schools?

11. _____

12. (In problem 11). How much greater?   12. $_____/pupil

John Doe has a house assessed at $18,000 (45 percent of its sale value). His tax rate is $8.35 per $100 of AV. Tom Gale has a house assessed at $22,000 (50 percent of sale value). His tax rate is 69.5 mills.

13. Who pays the greater tax?   13. _____
14. How much greater?   14. $_____
15. If both houses were taxed on full sale value with a true tax rate of 40.3 mills, who would pay the greater tax?   15. _____
16. How much greater?   16. $_____

III. DISTRICT ABILITY TO SUPPORT EDUCATION

If two school districts appear to have the same number of dollars of taxable property per pupil but the figure for District A was determined by using the average daily attendance of pupils while that for District B was determined by using the enrollment, which district has the greater ability to support its schools?   1. _____

With the following information, answer questions 2, 3, and 4 concerning their relative ability to support education:

District	Students	AV	Percent AV is of SV
A	4,200	$10,605,000	50
B	5,400	14,175,000	60
C	1,200	2,400,000	40

2. Which district has the greatest ability to support education?   2. _____
3. Which district has the least ability to support education?   3. _____
4. If all three districts were to be assessed at 100 percent of their sale value, which would have the greatest ability to support education?   4. _____

Compare the ability of the following three districts
to finance education:

	District A	District B	District C
Assessed Valuation	$20,200,000	$30,300,000	$40,400,000
Percent AV is of SV	50	60	40
Students in ADA	1,600	2,200	3,000
Tax Levy	16 mills	$1.55/$100	$14/$1,000

5. Which district can raise the largest amount of money per pupil?   5. _____

6. How much?   6. $_____

7. Considering potential ability (using AV = SV) and using the same tax rates as indicated for each district, which district could raise the greatest amount of money per pupil?   7. _____

8. How much?   8. $_____

IV. USING CENSUS, ADM, ADA IN ALLOCATING STATE FUNDS

Assuming a certain state has a fixed dollar amount of money to allocate to the following three districts on a proportionate share basis, which district would probably prefer to have the state use each of the three methods of allocation?

	District A	District B	District C
Pupils on Census List	2,000	2,500	3,000
Pupils in A. D. M.	1,860	2,140	2,000
Pupils in A. D. A.	1,548	2,052	1,820

1. (Census)—District_____

1. (A. D. M.)—District_____

3. (A. D. M.)—District_____

4. What is the advantage of using ADA in allocating state money to local school districts? _____

5. What is the advantage of using ADM in allocating state money to local school districts? _____

6. What would be the advantage of using aggregate days attendance in allocating state money to local school districts? _____

V. STATE ALLOCATION PLANS
(*Flat Grants*)

With the following information answer the questions concerning the effect of flat grants upon the two districts.

District	Assessed Valuation	Paid By State	Budget Needs	Mill Levy	Number of Students
A	$6,000,000	nil	$240,000	____(1)	360
B	5,000,000	nil	100,000	____(2)	150

Effort Ratio ____ : ____ (3)
Would a grant of $24,000 by the State to each district be equalizing in its effect upon the two districts? Yes____ No____ (4)
The new Effort Ratio would be ____ : ____ (5)
Would a state grant of $100 per student be equalizing in its effect upon the two districts? Yes____ No____ (6)
The new Effort Ratio would ____ : ____ (7)

District	Assessed Valuation	Paid By State	Budget Needs	Mill Levy	Number of Teachers
C	$8,000,000	nil	$400,000	____(8)	50
D	10,000,000	nil	300,000	____(9)	40

Would a grant of $40,000 be equalizing in its effect upon the two districts? Yes____ No____ (10)
The new Effort Ratio would be ____ : ____ (11)
Would a state grant of $500 per teacher be equalizing in its effect upon the two districts? Yes____ No____ (12)
New Effort Ratio would be ____ : ____ (13)

(*Foundation Programs*)

Determine the state funds that would be paid in the following equalization program.

District A has an assessed valuation of $10,580,000. Its budget needs for this part of the program are $495,000. The required local levy is $1.56 per $100 of assessed valuation. Under an equalized program, the state would pay the district $_____ (14)

What are the three parts of any state foundation program?
(15)_____
(16)_____
(17)_____

Using the following information about two school districts, solve the indicated problems.

District	Assessed Valuation	Weighted Pupil Units
A	$40,000,000	2,000
B	15,000,000	900

	Foundation Program	Board Leeway	Voted Leeway
State Guarantee	$600/WPU ($30/WPU/Mill)	$350/WPU ($25/WPU/Mill)	$200/WPU ($20/WPU/Mill)
Required Levy	20 mills	$1.40/$100 AV	$10/$1,000 AV

18. What is the best measure of local ability to support education?

		District A	District B
FOUNDATION PROGRAM	1. Need (in $)	$_____(19)	$_____(20)
	2. Local Effort	_____(21)	_____(22)
	3. State Allocation	_____(23)	_____(24)
BOARD LEEWAY	1. Need (in $)	_____(25)	_____(26)
	2. Local Effort	_____(27)	_____(28)
	3. State Allocation	_____(29)	_____(30)
VOTED LEEWAY	1. Need (in $)	_____(31)	_____(32)
	2. Local Effort	_____(33)	_____(34)
	3. State Allocation	_____(35)	_____(36)
All Three Programs	Total Local Funds	_____(37)	_____(38)
	Total State Funds	_____(39)	_____(40)
	Total Funds	_____(41)	_____(42)

(*Power Equalization*)

From the previous problem, calculate the following:

Ratio of state revenue
to local revenue   (43)_____ : _____   (44)_____ : _____
(Foundation Program)

Under the Power Equalization principle, how much money would the state provide for each of these districts using all three programs?

District A — $_____state money   (45)
District B — $_____state money   (46)

Total amount of
money/WPU — District A — $_____   (47)
District B — $_____   (48)

Comparing the old program with Power Equalization compare the total amounts of money available/WPU for each of the two districts if **A** levied a total of 36 mills and B a total of 38 mills.

	Old Program	Power Equalization Program
District A	(49) $_____/WPU	(50) $_____/WPU
District B	(51) $_____/WPU	(52) $_____/WPU

Repeat the problem with A levying 38 mills and B levying 36 mills.

	Old Program	Power Equalization Program
District A	(53) $_____/WPU	(54) $_____/WPU
District B	(55) $_____/WPU	(56) $_____/WPU

Answers to Problems

I. Tax Rates
1. $0.15625
2. 375 mills
3. 17,510 mills
4. $5.73/$100 AV
5. 24 mills
6. $136/$1,000
7. $0.00078
8. $0.078/$100 AV
9. $0.78/$1,000 AV
10. $2.3415
11. 5,491,540 mills
12. $0.04854/$1 AV

II. Property Assessments, Tax Rates, Revenue
1. 25 percent
2. $19,500
3. $2.44/$100 AV
4. 14.64 mills
5. Smith
6. $298.75
7. $1,777.50
8. Brown
9. $131.99
10. $1,103.45
11. A
12. $70 AV/pupil
13. Gale
14. $26
15. Gale
16. $161.20

III. District Ability to Support Education
1. B
2. B
3. C
4. A
5. B
6. $213.48
7. C
8. $471.33

IV. Using Census, ADM, ADA in Allocating State Funds
1. C
2. A
3. B
4. Encourages school attendance
5. No penalty for student absence
6. Encourages holding more days of school

V. State Allocation Plans

1. 40 mills
2. 20 mills
3. 2:1
4. No
5. 2.37:1
6. No
7. 2:1
8. 50 mills
9. 30 mills
10. No
11. 1.73:1
12. No
13. 1.67:1
14. $329,952
15. Determine foundation program in dollars
16. Calculate revenue from required local levy
17. Calculate state allocation (step 1 minus Step 2)
18. AV/W.P.U.
19. $1,200,000
20. $540,000
21. $800,000
22. $300,000
23. $400,000
24. $240,000
25. $700,000

26. $315,000
27. $560,000
28. $210,000
29. $140,000
30. $105,000
31. $400,000
32. $180,000
33. $400,000
34. $150,000
35. Nil
36. $30,000
37. $1,760,000
38. $660,000
39. $540,000
40. $375,000
41. $2,300,000
42. $1,035,000
43. 1:2
44. 1:1.25
45. $880,000
46. $528,000
47. $1,320
48. $1,320
49. $990
50. $1,080
51. $1,030
52. $1,140
53. $1,030
54. $1,140
55. $990
56. $1,080

Annotated Bibliography

A Time for Priorities: Financing the Schools for the 70s. Washington,
D.C.: National Education Assn. Committee on Educational Finance,
1970.
Papers presented by scholars and practitioners in school finance on
problems, research findings, and trends in financing American education. Discusses the changes and improvements that might be made
in the 1970s.

Alexander, Kern, and Jordan, K. Forbis, eds. *Constitutional Reform of
School Finance.* Lexington, Mass.: Lexington Books, D.C. Heath
and Co., 1973.
A compilation of papers that discuss equity in financing public
schools and the constitutionality of aid to parochial schools. A
resource book that provides guidance for school fiscal planners as
they develop state school support programs.

Aliota, Robert F., and Jungherr, J. A. *Operational PPBS for Education.*
New York: Harper & Row, 1971.
Clarifies what PPBS is and specifies how this process has been applied successfully to local school systems; provides a comprehensive
example of how to collect, analyze, and display the necessary information for a viable PPB system.

Bailey, Stephen K.; Frost, Richard T.; Marsh, Paul E.; and Wood, Robert
C. *Schoolmen and Politics.* Syracuse, N.Y.: Syracuse University
Press, 1962.
A study of state aid to education in some of the Northeastern states;
reviews the problems involved in that development. Emphasizes the
fact that the amount of money state governments provide for aid
to public schools is determined politically.

404

Barr, W. Monfort, and Wilkerson, William R. *Innovative Financing of Public* School Facilities. Danville, Ill.: Interstate Printers and Publishers, Inc., 1973.

Reviews changing practices in school facility financing throughout the nation; concentrates on emerging innovative practices and reviews recent research which indicates logical directions for future changes in financing facilities.

Benson, Charles S.; Goldfinger, Paul M.; Hoachlander, E. Gareth; and Pers, Jessica S. *Planning for Educational Reform—Financial and Social Alternatives.* New York: Dodd, Mead & Co., 1974.

Explores the deeper issues of school finance reforms; speculates on what directions structural revision might take. The issues illuminated are among the most strategic and important in shaping new and viable school finance programs.

Berke, Joel S. *Answers to Inequity: An Analysis of the New School Finance.* Berkeley, Calif.: McCutchan Publishing Corp., 1974.

Discusses the growing mismatches between school district tax effort and yield on the one hand and between educational needs and resources on the other. Refers to suggested laws adopted to reform existing school finance systems.

————; Campbell, Alan K.; and Goettel, Robert J. *Financing Equal Educational Opportunity.* Berkeley, Calif.: McCutchan Publishing Corp., 1972.

Analyzes the interrelationships of finance and equality of educational opportunity across the nation; focuses on New York State, analyzes its problems, and suggests provisions and possible changes to solve its problems.

————, and Kirst, Michael W. *Federal Aid to Education: Who Benefits? Who Governs?* Lexington, Mass.: Lexington Books, D. C. Heath and Co., 1972.

Reports research that charts the patterns of allocation of federal aid to education. Studies the decision making that determined those patterns of distribution, and recommends needed changes in distribution formulas and administrative practices.

Callahan, John J., and Wilken, William H., eds. *School Finance Reform: A Legislators' Handbook.* Washington, D.C.: National Conference of State Legislatures, 1976.

Describes the accomplishments and deficiencies of several of the major state school finance reforms enacted since 1971. Indicates that the record of school finance reform needs improvement if equality of educational opportunity is to be achieved.

Candoli, I. Carl; Hack, Walter G.; Ray, John R.; and Stollar, Dewey H. *School Business Administration.* Boston: Allyn and Bacon, Inc., 1973.

Although the technical skills of the school business administrator are not depreciated, this book emphasizes the point of view that the way he works and relates to pupils, teachers, and others is a major determinant of the success he will enjoy.

Cohen, Michael A.; Levin, Betsy; and Beaver, Richard. *The Political Limits to School Finance Reform.* Washington, D.C.: The Urban Institute, 1973.
Focuses on the political feasibility of alternative ways of financing schools in California, Colorado, Georgia, Maryland, Michigan, New Hampshire, Oklahoma, and Oregon. Discusses the implications of the recent school finance court cases.

Cohn, Elchanan, and Millman, Stephen D. *Economics of State Aid to Education.* Lexington, Mass.: Lexington Books, D. C. Heath and Co., 1974.
Focuses attention on the relationship between state aid and incentives for the efficient allocation of available resources. Discusses the origin and development of state aid formulas and the theory and practice of equalization.

Coombs, Philip H., and Hallak, Jacques. *Managing Educational Costs.* New York: Oxford University Press, 1972.
Explains why cost analysis has become imperative, how educational costs behave, how various educational systems and institutions have actually used cost analysis and how decision makers can profit from cost-analysis studies and practices.

Coons, John E.; Clune, William H. III; and Sugarman, Stephen D. *Private Wealth and Public Education.* Cambridge, Mass.: Belknap Press of Harvard University Press, 1970.
Examines the financial structure in a number of states and shows that the various state aid formulas fail to eliminate the financial inequities caused by differences in taxable wealth per child in different localities.

Education and Economic Well-Being in American Democracy. Washington, D.C.: National Education Assn. Educational Policies Commission, 1940.
Discusses the problem of financing the kind and amount of education that will maintain a high technology in a democratic and industrial society; appraises the contributions that education makes to productivity and general economic well-being.

Education Is Good Business. Washington, D.C.: American Assn. of School Administrators, 1966.
Describes various ways in which good schools strengthen society; looks at some facts about American education to see how econom-

ically it is being conducted; and considers the influence of local school boards on cities and people.

Federal Policy and the Public Schools. Washington, D.C.: American Assn. of School Administrators, 1967.

A series of nine essays focusing on questions and issues around which federal policy toward the schools evolves; provides a basis for understanding the problems and issues inherent in the changing levels of government.

Financial Status of the Public Schools, 1975. Washington, D.C.: National Education Assn., 1975.

Presents social and economic trend data that document efforts of the educational profession to secure adequate and continuing funding for public education; reports on school finance reforms to provide greater equality of educational opportunity.

Financing Education: Who Benefits? Who Pays? Washington, D.C.: National Education Assn. Committee on Educational Finance, 1972.

A series of scholarly papers prepared by authorities in the fields of school finance and economics providing evidence of the fact that although many children have enjoyed the benefits of a well-financed education, many others have not.

Financing the Public Schools—A Search for Equality. Bloomington, Ind.: Phi Delta Kappa, 1973.

Considers the philosophical bases of the public schools, directions provided by the courts, current financing programs, educational programs and services, revenue sources, and provides an analysis of alternative school finance programs.

Friedman, Burton D., and Dunbar, Laird J. *Grants Management in Education: Federal Impact on State Agencies.* Chicago: Public Administration Service, 1971.

Examines the impact of grants management on state education from several perspectives—from that of public administration, public finance, governmental accounting and auditing, and intergovernmental relations.

Friedman, Milton. *Capitalism and Freedom.* Chicago: The University of Chicago Press, 1968. Discusses the relation between economic freedom and political freedom, the role of government in a free society, the control of money, the role of government in education, the distribution of income, and other topics in the field of economics.

Future Directions for School Financing. Gainesville, Fla.: National Educational Finance Project, 1971.

Discusses in plain language such topics as equal education, taxes, variations in fiscal capacity and effort, factors affecting educational needs and costs, state and federal roles in education, and blueprints for state educational equality.

Gauerke, Warren E., and Childress, Jack R., eds. *The Theory and Practice of School Finance.* Chicago: Rand McNally & Co., 1967.
A comprehensive synthesis of research and writing in the field of school finance. Identifies education as an economic good; projects public school finance into the total economic fabric of society; and emphasizes change and research in school finance.

Grubb, W. Norton, and Michelson, Stephan. *States and Schools.* Lexington, Mass.: Lexington Books, D.C. Heath and Co., 1974.
Stresses the existence and origin of school finance inequality, school finance patterns, existing mechanisms for distributing funds to local school districts, alternative state aid plans and formulas, and related school finance problems.

Hartley, Harry J. *Educational Planning, Programming, Budgeting.* Englewood Cliffs, N.J.: Prentice-Hall, Inc., 1968.
Portrays program budgeting as a means of accelerating improvements in state and local educational systems. Describes the planning-programing-budgeting system (PPBS) as a revolutionary and effective approach to administrative planning.

Hirsch, W. Z. *Financing Public First-Level and Second-Level Education in the U.S.A.* Paris: International Institute for Educational Planning (UNESCO), 1973.
Points out the difficulties encountered in a modern democracy by an educational system with highly decentralized sources of finance; analyzes the steps taken to remedy such problems and discusses the nature of available resources for education.

Johns, Roe L., and Alexander, Kern. *Alternative Programs for Financing Education.* Gainesville, Fla.: National Educational Finance Project, 1971.
Presents and evaluates alternative models for state school finance plans; presents alternative models for federal aid and makes recommendations on school fiscal policy; summarizes the findings of NEFP study reported in volumes 1-4.

————; Alexander, Kern; and Jordan K. Forbis. *Financing Education—Fiscal and Legal Alternatives.* Columbus, Ohio: Charles E. Merrill Publishing Co., 1972.
Contains a comprehensive summary of the basic findings and recommendations of the National Educational Finance Project; discusses the legality of various state school support alternatives in light of the recent court decisions.

————; Alexander, Kern; and Stollar, Dewey H., eds. *Status and Impact of Educational Finance Programs* (vol. 4 of NEFP study). Gainesville, Fla.: National Educational Finance Project, 1971.

Provides suggestions based on sound theory and empirical research for improving the equity and equality of state and federal school finance programs; classifies and evaluates the school finance programs of the several states.

————; Goffman, Irving J.; Alexander, Kern; and Stollar, Dewey H. *Economic Factors Affecting the Financing of Education* (vol. 2 of the NEFP study). Gainesville, Fla.: National Educational Finance Project, 1970.
Explores in some depth the economic factors involved in the financing of education; presents unedited chapters submitted by economists with different points of view. Presents some generalizations and potential solutions to school finance problems.

————, and Morphet, Edgar L. *The Economics and Financing of Education*, 3rd ed. Englewood Cliffs, N.J.: Prentice-Hall, Inc., 1975.
Analyzes the significance of *Serrano* and other similar court decisions and their influence on future policies of school financing; presents new insights and some unresolved problems and issues dealing with the financing of education.

Journal of Education Finance. Gainesville, Fla.: Institute for Educational Finance and the American Education Finance Assn., published quarterly since Summer 1975. An organ for the publication of articles, research reports, and reviews of information concerning the broad field of school finance. Oriented to the new school finance programs resulting from the recent court decisions in school finance.

LaNoue, George R., ed. *Educational Vouchers: Concepts and Controversies.* New York: Teachers College Press, 1972.
Discusses the role of government in education, the pros and cons of educational vouchers, the economics of the voucher system, some legal questions involved, and a debate in the House of Representatives on the use of vouchers in education.

Levin, Betsy, ed. *Future Directions for School Finance Reform.* Lexington, Mass.: Lexington Books, D.C. Heath and Co., 1974.
Reviews the major court cases concerning school finance programs and sumarizes the reforms that have been made in a number of states as a result of those decisions. Next steps needed to provide equal educational opportunity are discussed.

————; Cohen, Michael A.; Muller, Thomas; and Scanlon, William J. *Paying for Public Schools—Issues of School Finance in California.* Washington, D.C.: The Urban Institute, 1972.
Offers California citizens a brief analysis of the difficult problems which the state faces in financing its public schools equitably; makes

a brief presentation of general alternatives and takes a look at legislative measures being considered.

————; Muller, Thomas; and Sandoval, Corazon. *The High Cost of Education in Cities.* Washington, D.C.: The Urban Institute, 1973. Discusses the higher costs for equivalent educational services in central cities and of certain justifications for unequal levels of service; provides an understanding of some of the elements that account for educational cost differentials.

Lindman, Erick L. *Dilemmas of School Finance.* Arlington, Va.: Educational Research Service, Inc., 1975. The first in a series of ERS Monographs designed to bring school administrators and others the experience, views, and thinking of noted authorities on current issues, problems, and practices in school administration, with emphasis on finance.

Managing Public School Dollars. New York: American Institute of Certified Public Accountants, 1972. Stresses the way in which a board of education can utilize existing management tools and data to meet its responsibilities. Discusses some of the newer tools available, including PPBS, program budgeting, program cost accounting, and others.

Mecklenburger, James A., and Hostrop, Richard W., eds. *Education Vouchers: From Theory to Alum Rock.* Homewood, Ill.: ETC Publication, 1972. Traces the history of the current interest in vouchers, introduces its advocates and major critics; contains the essential portions of the Alum Rock Feasibility Study of 1971; contains strong views on Alum Rock and subsequent proposals.

Meltsner, Arnold J.; Kast, Gregory W.; Kramer, John F.; and Nakamura, Robert T. *Political Feasibility of Reform in School Financing; The Case of California.* New York: Praeger Publishers, 1973. Examines the attitudes and recent behavior of various political forces in California—citizens, lawmakers, the governor's staff, school superintendents—and their concerns about equality, fiscal responsibility, and school management quality.

Morphet, Edgar L., and Jesser, David L., eds., *Emerging Designs for Education: Programs, Organization, Operation and Finance.* Denver: Designing Education for the Future, 1968. Discusses some important improvements that need to be made in almost every aspect of education in the years ahead; identifies some emerging practices and trends and points to some feasible alternative courses of action.

Murphy, Jerome T. *State Education Agencies and Discretionary Funds.* Lexington, Mass.: Lexington Books, D.C. Heath and Co., 1974.

Discusses the impact of unrestricted financial assistance on complex organizations. Points out reasons why Title V of the Elementary and Secondary Education Act of 1965 did not live up to its proponents' hope to stimulate reforms.

O'Connor, James R. *The Fiscal Crisis of the State.* New York: St. Martin's Press, 1973.
Develops a theory of economic growth that is rooted in the basic economic and political facts of late capitalist society; discusses the relationship between the private and state sectors and between private and state spending.

Ovsiew, Leon, and Castetter, William B. *Budgeting for Better Schools.* Englewood Cliffs, N.J.: Prentice-Hall, Inc., 1960.
Conceives the budget and the process by which it is produced as useful means for gaining a number of administrative goals beyond the mere listing of income and expenditures; emphasizes the need for and value of educational planning.

Owen, John D. *School Inequality and the Welfare State.* Baltimore: Johns Hopkins University Press, 1974.
Discusses the principles underlying inequality in the distribution of educational resources in this country; considers the obstacles to change and assesses the prospects for improvement and reform in school finance programs.

Pincus, John A., ed. *School Finance in Transition.* Cambridge, Mass.: Ballinger Publishing Co., 1974.
A report of the Rand Educational Policy Study commissioned by the Ford Foundation in 1971 to study the impact of school finance reforms resulting from *Serrano* and other related court decisions affecting state school finance programs.

Reischauer, Robert D., and Hartman, Robert W. *Reforming School Finance.* Washington, D.C.: The Brookings Institution, 1973.
Considers three major school finance issues: (1) the aggregate fiscal position of the public issues; (2) the disparities in expenditures and tax burdens under current systems of school finance; and (3) nonpublic school problems.

Rogers, Daniel C., and Ruchlin, Hirsch S. *Economics and Education.* New York: The Free Press, 1971.
Focuses attention on the economic tools and concepts that are necessary for analyzing educational problems; reproduces a number of basic studies illustrating the applicability to education of certain economic concepts and problems.

School Finance in Transition. Washington, D.C.: National Education Assn. National Conference on School Finance, 1973.
Discusses state school finance proposals in the light of the *Serrano*

case and the U.S. Supreme Court's reversal of *Rodriguez.* Presents several different points of view and a good understanding of the problems involved in finance reform.

Schools, People, and Money. Washington, D.C.: President's Commission on School Finance, U.S. Government Printing Office, 1972.
The report of a two-year study of the Commission concerning the responsibilities of each level of government for financing education; notes the financial plight of nonpublic schools and considers the problem of state financial assistance to them.

Shannon, Thomas A. *Has the Fourteenth Done It Again?* Washington, D.C.: American Assn. of School Administrators, 1972.
With the background of recent school finance court decisions (beginning with *Serrano* v. *Priest*) in mind, the author considers ten questions and issues with which school finance people will have to concern themselves.

Sokol, John, and Lohman, Maurice A. *Computational Exercises in School Finance.* New York: Teachers College Press, 1966.
Contains exercises and problems designed to help the student to develop a familiarity with the more basic problems encountered in school finance; concerned mostly with property assessments, tax levies, and school district revenues.

The Realities of School Finance. Washington, D.C.: American Assn. of School Administrators, 1971.
Presents graphs and a brief discussion emphasizing the need for additional funds for education; points out the disparities found in local tax bases, and the actual and proposed relation of local, state, and federal governments to school finance.

Tidwell, Sam B. *Public School Fund Accounting.* New York: Harper & Row, 1960.
Sets forth accounting principles and procedures which, if followed by school business officials, would provide school board members, school administrators, and the public with complete financial information about the school district.

Understanding Education's Financial Dilemma (report no. 24). Denver: Education Commission of the States, 1972.
A basic description of the issues and implications of the *Serrano*-type court cases concerning school finance programs and their impact upon educational finance systems in the various states; suggests possible improvements.

Index